SHATTERED

SHATTERED

INSIDE
HILLARY CLINTON'S
DOOMED CAMPAIGN

JONATHAN ALLEN

and AMIE PARNES

CROWN
NEW YORK

All rights reserved.
Published in the United States by Crown, an imprint of the Crown Publishing Group,
a division of Penguin Random House LLC, New York.
crownpublishing.com

CROWN and colophon is a registered trademark of Penguin Random House LLC.

Library of Congress Cataloging-in-Publication Data is available upon request.

ISBN 978-0-553-44708-8
Ebook ISBN 978-0-553-44709-5

Printed in the United States of America

Jacket design by Christopher Brand
Jacket photograph: Kyodo News/Getty Images

10 9 8 7 6 5 4 3 2 1

First Edition

For the lights of my life—Stephanie, Asher, and Emma
—JA

For Remy—who has redefined love and hope
—AP

Contents

Contents

INTRODUCTION

WHEN WE FIRST BEGAN REPORTING FOR THIS BOOK IN late 2014, Hillary Clinton was the candidate to beat for the presidency. Her résumé—first lady, senator, and secretary of state—was unassailable. At her peak in the last job, two-thirds of Americans had approved of her performance. More important, she had spent a great deal of time and energy trying to correct the flaws of her 2008 Democratic primary loss to Barack Obama. And most political analysts believed that Democrats, coming off his consecutive victories, had two powerful advantages in presidential elections: a mortal lock on states that provided 242 of the 270 electoral votes needed to win the White House and a superior handle on the mechanics of turning out voters.

Hillary and her husband, former president Bill Clinton, had been preparing for this bid for six years. They had rewarded friends and punished disloyal Democrats after the 2008 race. Bill had raised money for Obama and delivered a rousing endorsement of the sitting president at the 2012 Democratic National Convention, a move that helped seal the Obama-Clinton bond. He had campaigned in Democratic primaries against candidates who the Clintons felt had betrayed Hillary in 2008. Once she was out of government, Hillary herself had hit the hustings for Democratic Senate candidates in the 2014 midterm elections. And, in 2013 and 2014, a super PAC run and funded by her allies had raised millions of dollars and collected hundreds of thousands of names of potential supporters. They were Ready for Hillary.

Having written the 2014 book *HRC: State Secrets and the Rebirth of Hillary Clinton,* we were convinced that she was indeed running and that no other Democrat could defeat her in the primary—the same conclusion that kept most serious Democrats from running against her. Moreover, as party political figures told us, the fear of reprisal meant that there was a cost for Democrats who didn't jump on her bandwagon. Some, like Missouri senator Claire McCaskill, endorsed her long before she committed to a run. In short, Hillary had every imaginable institutional advantage in winning the Democratic nomination. As David Plouffe, the mastermind behind Obama's 2008 victory, put it in a private conversation in September 2014, "She's bulletproof."

Of course, there were reasons to think that she wouldn't just waltz into the White House. It's hard for a party to win three consecutive presidential elections. The rise of the Tea Party and other anti-institutional forces in both parties had wreaked havoc on the establishment since Obama's first election. And Hillary had always been a polarizing figure in American politics—particularly when she was a candidate.

But, heading into our reporting, we thought there was a pretty good chance that we would be writing the inside story of Hillary shattering what she had called the "highest, hardest glass ceiling."

We were surprised, then, when Clintonworld sources started telling us in 2015 that Hillary was still struggling to articulate her motivation for seeking the presidency. And we were taken aback by how much infighting was going on below the surface of her campaign at a time when, unlike 2008, very little of it had spilled into the press. In so many ways, and as some of our sources acknowledged, Hillary was fighting the last war. She did that with varying degrees of success. But the variable she couldn't change was the candidate.

Over the course of a year and a half, in interviews with more than one hundred sources, we started to piece together a picture that was starkly at odds with the narrative the campaign and the media were portraying publicly. Hillary's campaign was so spirit-crushing that her aides eventually shorthanded the feeling of impending doom with a simple mantra: *We're not allowed to have nice things.*

Every time it looked like she had hit her stride in the race, a new obstacle appeared in her path. And yet, there were few moments between her kickoff rally and the closing of the first polls on Election Day when she wasn't the favorite. So it wasn't until the results came in that all of our reporting finally made sense—that the foreboding signs along the way had been pointing in the right direction even when they were at odds with the available data.

We made one decision early on in our process that proved crucial in allowing us access to key players even at times when most of the media were walled off from Hillary and her senior staff. We agreed to conduct all of our interviews on background, which provided anonymity to our sources. That gave them an extra sense of security on the off chance that we broke a vow that we observed throughout our reporting: none of the material would appear before the election. We spoke to nearly everyone we asked to interview, up and down the ranks of the campaign, and many of them talked to us during pivotal periods of the race.

Without these guarantees, which protected our sources inside and outside the campaign from the possible reprisal of the next president, many of them would not have talked with us at all. Others would have been much less candid. The trade-offs enabled us to get an extraordinary look at the last, tumultuous chapter of the Clinton era.

In that final hurrah, Hillary broke one glass ceiling—becoming the first female nominee of a major political party—and forever put to rest the question of whether a woman could be seen as commander in chief. She collected nearly 65.9 million votes—more than any Republican nominee in American history, just 64,822 fewer than Barack Obama in 2012, and almost 3 million more than Donald Trump. And she did that while facing a set of trials and tribulations unlike any other in American campaign history: a partisan congressional investigation; a primary opponent who attacked her character; a rogue FBI director; the rank misogyny of her Republican rival; a media that scrutinized her every move while failing to get that Republican rival to turn over his tax returns; and even a Kremlin-based campaign to defeat her.

In the end, though, this was a winnable race for Hillary. Her own missteps—from setting up a controversial private e-mail server and giving speeches to Goldman Sachs to failing to convince voters that she was with them and turning her eyes away from working-class whites—gave Donald Trump the opportunity he needed to win.

This is the story of how it all unraveled again for Hillary. We expect that it will generate a feeling of righteousness, and perhaps a touch of sympathy, in those of you who don't like her. For many of Hillary's millions of supporters, we know that it will leave you feeling shattered all over again.

SHATTERED

Chapter 1

"OR I WOULDN'T HAVE RUN"

ILLARY CLINTON HAD A NEW RENDEZVOUS WITH DESTINY on her mind. Her motorcade sped toward Roosevelt Island on the morning of June 13, 2015. In a little more than an hour, she would officially kick off what she hoped would be a trailblazing, glass-ceiling-shattering campaign for the presidency. For most of the previous forty-eight hours, she had been trying to give a feel of historic importance to her first major address. It just wasn't there yet.

She picked up the phone and called her chief speechwriter, Dan Schwerin. After two days of trading drafts with Hillary, after waiting through the delay of a power outage at her Chappaqua, New York, home, the bearded thirty-two-year-old with a signature chestnut pompadour was just about to board the tram connecting Manhattan to the East River island. He had stayed up all night, pulling together tweaks to the 3:30 a.m. version of the speech, and he looked hungover. Now, battling exhaustion and the sweltering heat, Schwerin pulled out his laptop one more time and sat down on the platform so that Hillary could dictate her final edits.

The key passage of the speech was an explanation of why she was running for president: "to make our economy work for you and for every American." In the middle of that run—about how she would do it and who she would fight for—Hillary wanted to connect herself and her campaign to Franklin Roosevelt, the president who defined the aspirations of the Democratic Party and much of the nation for generations.

"Here on Roosevelt Island," she said to Schwerin, "I believe we have a continuing rendezvous with destiny."

He tapped the echo of FDR's 1936 Democratic convention speech into his computer at 11 a.m. and took the next cable car to the island. Few would notice the last-minute change. The cluttered speech had become a testament to the aimlessness and passive-aggressive infighting that plagued the early stages of Hillary's campaign. Hillary had tried to put together a team this time that would feature far less internal drama than her failed 2008 bid. Back then, big personalities had clashed openly, aired dirty laundry and strategy details in the press, and sometimes pursued their own goals at the expense of hers. In the intervening years, she'd assigned a lot of the blame for her loss to the warring inside her campaign. But that was hardly the only ailment from 2008 that she hoped to remedy. She hadn't sold a vision for the country. She'd run away from being a woman instead of leaning into the unique aspect of her political story. To manage her campaign, she'd tapped a friend rather than the top pro. She'd let her husband run wild on the trail. And she had failed to take advantage of the latest technology to build a movement of grassroots supporters and donors.

From a strategic standpoint, she'd dumped millions of dollars into Iowa, the first-in-the-nation caucus, even though that only elevated the importance of her devastating third-place finish there. She'd gone on the attack against a better-liked rival whose platform more closely mirrored the values of the party's base, creating a boomerang effect on her personal standing. Perhaps worst of all, she'd obsessed over winning the popular vote in big states rather than targeting the all-important delegates and superdelegates whose votes at the Democratic convention determined the party's nominee.

But the idea burned into her mind as much as anything else was that she had lost because she'd hired people who put their own interests above getting her elected. The absence of palace intrigue on her opponent's side—the "no drama Obama" campaign—was the kind of purpose-driven loyalty she pined for.

Over the next seven years, Hillary would rebuild her political organization while working at the State Department and the Clinton Foundation, punish those who had been disloyal to her, and prepare herself to mount a second bid for the most powerful job on the planet. When she conceded to Obama in 2008, she'd thanked voters for putting "18 million cracks" in the glass ceiling of the presidency. By the time she finished the 2016 campaign, she believed, that glass ceiling would lay shattered beneath her feet. And yet what Hillary couldn't quite see is that no matter how she recast the supporting roles in this production, or emphasized different parts of the script, the main character hadn't changed.

HUDDLED AROUND A white table in the conference room of the Clintons' midtown Manhattan personal office in the early spring of 2015, months before she would go to Roosevelt Island to deliver her first major address, the first hires of Hillary's worst-kept-secret campaign outlined a plan to fly her to Iowa. They had pegged the Hawkeye State, where caucus-goers had doomed her first bid for the Oval Office, as the best spot for her kickoff speech. But Hillary didn't like what she was hearing. She didn't want to go big, at least not yet. And she didn't want the first major address of what could be a history-making campaign to be set against a minimalistic backdrop like some farmer's back porch.

To the chagrin of campaign manager Robby Mook, who would have to build a billion-dollar apparatus, Hillary had been dragging her feet about making things official. She understood that her team needed to start raising funds, hire more staff, and begin recruiting volunteers. But she also knew she had to be fully prepared for this battle. And she just wasn't ready.

Mook, clean-cut with close-cropped brown hair and lively hazel eyes, was antsy. At one point, there was even discussion of his starring in a campaign-launching video announcing the formation of an "exploratory" committee. But Hillary was wary of repeating some of the major mistakes of her 2008 bid. She had rushed into her announcement that year to compete with Obama, and she had made it all about her: "I'm in it to win," she'd said in her campaign-opening video. This time, she wanted to show she was listening to voters—talking with them one-on-one or in small groups and in informal settings (all with the knowledge that everything she did would be dutifully reported by a press corps hungry for nuggets from the trail).

"We've come so far under President Obama, but we have so many problems," she told her advisers. "I want to make sure I'm the right person." Given that everyone in the room had ostensibly been hired to run her campaign, and that some of them had been in on earlier discussions about the timing and logistics of her launch, no one believed she was really so ambivalent. But, sitting by a bank of three windows, twenty-seven floors above the bustle of Seventh Avenue, Hillary rendered a clear verdict on the Iowa kickoff plan: "No."

She would go to Iowa in April, she said, but not to deliver a launch speech—and not in a private jet. She would drive, in a van, and try to find people along the way who weren't expecting to run into her. After a quarter of a century locked inside the political bubble of the New York–to–Washington stretch of the Acela corridor, Hillary was eager to find out what people thought about the state of the country—and about her. She didn't want to officially kick off the campaign until she'd had a chance to repeat what she'd done when she first ran for a New York Senate seat: gather information from voters. "She wanted to do that before giving a big speech and having a big event and saying 'I have all this figured out,'" said one aide. "We didn't have it all figured out." Her big opening address would come at a location with more historic consequence, but for now, a "soft" launch could go forward—an upbeat video followed by the road trip.

The time would come for her to speak into the winds of history, but, as much as she knew Iowa wasn't the place, she also knew that her moment hadn't yet come. She'd been off the political battlefield for seven years. As secretary of state, she'd worked to win concessions in diplomatic back rooms across the world, but she didn't have to worry about securing millions of votes. Barack Obama had been elected president and the Tea Party had risen in the time since she'd last been on the campaign trail as a candidate. The nation's political bearings had shifted. And, if her 2014 book tour had taught her anything, it was that she was rusty as hell. Talking to voters, she hoped, would help her sharpen her political skills and develop her vision for the country's future.

Obama had been relentlessly superb at telling voters why he was running for president and giving them a window into how he would govern. He was confident, cocky even, about his vision. Hillary, a modest, midwestern Methodist with a love of minutiae, was unshakably focused on the trees rather than the forest. This campaign would test the A student's ability to adapt—to subordinate her nature to her need to win.

In preparing to campaign again, she studied Obama's February 2007 launch speech in Springfield, the one he delivered on the steps of the Old State Capitol—the one that connected him with fellow Illinois state legislator Abraham Lincoln, who had freed the slaves in an act that set the first stone on Obama's improbable path to the presidency. "She kept harkening back to Obama in Springfield," said one of Hillary's top advisers. "She had gone back to read that speech and how important it was for people as a marker of what he would do in the presidency. She viewed it as an important kind of road map for her governing principles and her actual plans to be president."

In her mind, the first landmark address of what she hoped and believed would be a historic campaign couldn't be about the politics of the moment, about tipping a few Iowa caucus-goers in her direction. It had to be about how she could reshape the nation from the Oval Office. For Hillary, a wonk in the best and worst senses of the word, that meant devising her policy agenda before she ever stepped to the podium. Most politicians understand that voters are looking for big, bold principles—easy-to-grasp concepts—and that the details can be filled in to fit them. For Hillary, policy is vision, and she would try to build a platform, program by program, into a blueprint for the country.

This prospect was actually a relief. It was more comfortable for her to sit in four-hour meetings at the conference table with her policy chief—the reedy, whip-smart Jake Sullivan—than to define herself by a small set of guiding principles and shape her policy ideas to fit them.

Hillary adored the thirty-eight-year-old Sullivan, enough to joke publicly about her confidence that he would someday be president of the United States. He had served Hillary as deputy chief of staff at State, a position from which he gradually vacuumed up all or parts of the jobs of several senior colleagues. Hillary appreciated both his competence and his ambition. His instincts on policy and politics matched hers. So she turned to him to run what she thought was the most important part of the campaign: the substance. That's what bonded Hillary to her young protégé—they geeked out over policy—and it's what she wanted at the heart of her first address to the voting public.

"This is her deeply held thing: elections should be about policy," said one senior Hillary adviser. "There's a textbook quality to her articulation of things." That would make every step of narrative building its own form of excruciating drudgery. But it would soon seem like a minor nuisance for a campaign that was miserable even before it started.

IN EARLY MARCH, just as she was planning to reintroduce herself to a nation that felt it knew her all too well with a video announcement of her campaign, the *New York Times* reported that Hillary had used an e-mail address tied to a personal server at her family home in Chappaqua to conduct official State Department business. The e-mail story would bedevil her straight through Election Day, robbing her of the ability to create a positive narrative for her candidacy and, as one top adviser put it, returning to her like a cold sore. "You never know when it's going to pop up," this adviser said. "You think you're over it and then [it pops] up again."

At the time, it was impossible to know how long the e-mail story would last and just how badly it would damage the campaign.

"Did you have any idea of the depth of this story?" campaign chairman John Podesta asked Mook when it broke.

"Nope," Mook replied. "We brought up the existence of emails in research this summer but were told that everything was taken care of."

"That's reassuring," Podesta shot back. "Yikes."

"Yeah," Mook responded. "This is going to be an interesting campaign. I'm in this zen place now where I'm focusing on the website and telling myself this is all background noise!"

For those who couldn't bury their heads, praying for divine intervention was an attractive alternative. "I'm lighting candles in church all the time," pollster John Anzalone told Mook.

When the e-mail story first hit, Hillary's aides were still trying to get a feel for one another. The crisis acted as a catalyst for infighting. Publicly, she was running a no-drama campaign. But behind the scenes, Hillary's brain trust broke into tribes:

- The Mook Mafia, led by Mook; Marlon Marshall, his top lieutenant; Elan Kriegel, the data analytics chief; and Oren Shur, the paid media director
- The State Crew, led on the inside by Huma Abedin, the vice chairwoman; Jake Sullivan; Nick Merrill, the traveling press secretary; and Dan Schwerin, the chief speechwriter; with longtime Clinton advisers Cheryl Mills and Philippe Reines invisibly guiding Hillary behind the scenes
- The Consultants, led by Joel Benenson, the chief strategist; Jim Margolis, the ad-maker; and Mandy Grunwald, the longtime Clinton message maven
- The Communications Shop, led by Jennifer Palmieri, the communications director; Kristina Schake, her deputy; and

Christina Reynolds, the research director, who had worked with Palmieri on the John Edwards campaign

At the start, Podesta was seen as a high-level troubleshooter. Short, wiry, and in his midsixties, the marathon-running former top aide to Presidents Bill Clinton and Barack Obama had deep ties to every power center in the Democratic Party. He was supposed to play an adult-in-the-room role on the campaign, coordinating with Bill's office, the White House, Democratic interest groups, and major donors. In theory, Podesta would provide air cover in Clintonworld, lessening the burden on Mook and allowing the campaign manager to focus on executing.

But even as Podesta provided guidance to Mook, the two clashed stylistically from the outset. "John is very intuitive and from the gut," explained one senior Hillary aide, "and Robby requires a lot of information." As Podesta would come to learn, Mook guarded that information jealously to maintain his own power.

Podesta was also wary of at least one member of Hillary's State Crew. When the e-mail scandal first burst into the open, Philippe Reines, who had a rare direct line to the boss after running her media operations at the State Department and in the Senate, went to war with Jennifer Palmieri, the new communications director for the campaign, over how to respond. Reines, highly obsessive, ultraloyal to Hillary, and possessed of an acid tongue, pointed his finger at Palmieri when Hillary complained that deliberations about the timing of her first public remarks on the e-mail server were leaking to the media.

"This is creating trust problems on her end," Reines wrote to the campaign's top officials, establishing for everyone that he had a closer relationship with Hillary than her new communications chief. Palmieri fired back to the group, insisting that she wasn't the source of leaks.

"I am telling you right now that if there is any hint of trust issues with me, I am not taking this job," she wrote.

Podesta replied just to her. "Chill," he wrote, before taking a shot at Reines. "Remember the source of the email got us in this hot mess."

He told another friend that Reines was "the only person about whom you're torn between patting him on the back and trying to get him committed to Bellevue."

It all came to a head as the campaign debated plans to hold a news conference and give a one-on-one interview to NBC's Andrea Mitchell. On the night of March 8, 2015, Reines spoke to Hillary, who wasn't yet sold on her team's pitch. The next day, aides' bickering continued over a leak that Mitchell would get an interview and that there might be an impending press conference.

"This has gone too far," Reines wrote to Podesta, who opened the thread up to Mills and Hillary.

"Philippe, You got to stop this," Podesta wrote. "If we are going to be at each others throats before we start, we are going nowhere."

Reines took umbrage and wrote a long and sharp series of e-mails in which he offered to step away completely from the campaign. He'd never really be too far from Hillary, he knew, because she trusted him more than her new communications team.

"She has a very tough job to do tomorrow," Podesta admonished his colleague, referring to the first news conference on the State Department e-mails. "Do you really think it helps get her in the right head space to tell her she can't trust anyone she just brought on board? Why are you fanning this with her?"

In addition to the dissonant chorus within the as-yet-unlaunched campaign, Hillary maintained a network of donors, friends, allies, and advisers who could circumvent the official channels and plant ideas, good and bad, in her head. Often they went through Abedin, but some had a direct line to Hillary. One set had formed a semi-official "senior advisers" panel years earlier to help plan her post–State Department career. Podesta, Mills, and Sullivan were part of that group of straight shooters, which also included Hillary's White House chief of staff Maggie Williams, Bill's White House political director Minyon Moore, News Corp executive Jim Kennedy, Hillary's State Department protocol chief Capricia Marshall, and

Roy Spence, the branding genius who had marketed the famous "Don't Mess with Texas" antilitter campaign in the Lone Star State. Originally, they had advised her on the logistics of undertaking projects—like working at the Clinton Foundation and giving paid speeches—that they thought would suit her and leave open the option of running for president. The basic mandate was "proceed with ideas that would work either way," said one of the senior advisers. The approval of speeches to Wall Street banks and her work at the foundation would later prove to be missteps.

There was a certain duality to Hillary's vast political empire: while it was true that most of the voices inside and outside the campaign had something valuable to contribute, when taken together, they were cacophonous. Rarely did everyone agree on a particular course of action, and often the counsel Hillary got came with the baggage of the adviser's agenda in maintaining good relations with the candidate or trying to make a rival look bad.

Both Palmieri, a Podesta protégée, and Benenson were hired in part because Hillary knew she had to signal to donors, Democratic officials, and the party's voters that she'd learned to open up her tightly knit circle to new perspectives and replicate the no-drama approach that had served Obama's campaign so well in 2008. And yet, the whole structure of the campaign, with chieftains but no clear leader, was a recipe for the kind of creative—and sometimes explosive—tension that had characterized Bill Clinton's second term in the White House and Hillary Clinton's 2008 campaign.

In addition, the people close to Clinton didn't know politics, and the political pros she'd hired didn't know her very well. That compelled her most trusted aides to try to prove themselves in the political arena and the campaign-trail veterans to jockey to get closer to her. Everyone was throwing elbows. And it was happening before she'd even made the campaign official.

Schwerin, the chief speechwriter, found himself at the center of all that distress as he tried to fashion her first big address, which would take place not in Iowa but on Roosevelt Island, a narrow strip of land in the East River named after FDR. She would speak from

Four Freedoms Park, a monument to his legendary 1941 speech to Congress. The venue was Hillary's preferred location for kicking off the campaign, and she hoped to deliver a speech there that would echo through history like Roosevelt's. If she won the presidency, her remarks would be seen as an important historical marker.

It's hard to turn the numbingly mundane details of state-craft into winning politics. But that's the charge Hillary handed Schwerin, who had been a press assistant in her Senate office, a speechwriter in her State Department, and the ghostwriter of her post-State memoir. He was a well-liked fixture within the small but influential State Department clique that transitioned into top jobs on her presidential campaign.

With neatly kept facial hair that made him look just a few years more mature than his actual age, Schwerin struggled from the start to write anything that could pass muster with Benenson and Palmieri. After years at Hillary's side, he was accustomed to working directly with her. But in the new campaign's power structure, he had to go through the consultants and the communications director to get to her. Schwerin's personal relationships with Hillary, Abedin, and Sullivan protected him, but some of the others on the campaign thought that he was in over his head. About a month before Hillary's big launch, he asked colleagues on the campaign to recruit a star wordsmith for help.

Benenson and Margolis reached out to Jon Favreau, the vaunted speechwriter for Barack Obama, to help draft the kind of visionary message that had eluded Hillary in her first campaign for the presidency. Favreau, then thirty-three, had seen a lot in his short life as a political operative. He had helped navigate Obama through the famous "race" speech in Philadelphia in 2008, the first inaugural address ever given by a person of color, and several reports to Congress on the state of the union. By putting words in the mouth of a politician with a unique gift for giving wings to oratory, Favreau had ascended to an elite rung of political speechwriters by the time he arrived at the White House in 2009.

His natural writing skills were bolstered by a meticulous work ethic and years of serving an exciting boss with oratorical flair. After speaking to Obama about speeches on a more philosophical level and then boiling the prose down to story form, he would hole up in his basement-level White House office for weeks at a time before major addresses. Then he would sit beside the president on one of the biscuit-colored couches in the Oval Office as his boss used a red pen to perfect his work. Favreau once told the *New York Times* that writing for the word-conscious Obama was like serving as "Ted Williams's batting coach." Now, he was being asked to perform a similar feat for a candidate who lacked the splendid splinter's vision.

Ultimately, the recruitment of Favreau would serve as the harbinger of a bizarre and bazaar-like speechwriting process. It would have been enough of a challenge for him to channel Hillary after working so closely with Obama for so many years. But there was a wrinkle: Favreau wasn't being asked to write the speech himself. He would just be assisting Schwerin, the campaign's primary speechwriter, who was also collecting ideas from an array of former Clinton advisers and new bandwagon-hoppers. Even the ringer had to work through a committee.

Once Favreau came on board, he was paired with longtime Clinton speechwriter Lissa Muscatine to put some extra punch into the speech, by then scheduled for June 13. They both knew how to put words in someone else's mouth. They understood the essence and curves of great oratory, how to connect the memorable one-liners with the true substance of an argument, how to twine the speaker with her narrative, and how to talk into history. It was Muscatine who had written Clinton's landmark speech to a Beijing women's conference in 1995, with its signature line—"human rights are women's rights and women's rights are human rights." Muscatine knew Hillary's voice as well as Hillary did.

These two high-end scriveners, of different ages and different perspectives but similar talent, actually found that they really liked working with each other. Muscatine was impressed with Favreau's skill and his deference. After all, the guy had all the reason in the world to be an arrogant prick. His words had already helped elect a president—twice. But if he saw himself as above writing for Hillary, he never let on. And Favreau was fascinated with Muscatine's feel for Clinton's leanings and rhythms, her personal history and the history she hoped to make. Plus, he wanted Hillary to win. Like Margolis and Benenson, with whom he'd worked on Obama's campaigns, Favreau saw her as the best chance to cement and extend Obama's legacy.

On the surface, the writing pair was a microcosm of a campaign operation that sought to join the Clinton and Obama wings of the Democratic Party, mix baby boomers with millennials, and open up the famously insular Hillaryland to fresh voices and ideas. It was clear, even then, that she could distance herself only so far from Obama—and that there were elements of his presidency she would want to exalt. But Hillary still struggled with the question of whether she was running for Bill Clinton's third term, Obama's third term, or her own first term. "How do you take credit for eight years of Democratic progress but also get that things haven't gone far enough?" said one aide who wrestled with the conundrum. "She hired all of us to help her figure this out, and I think at the beginning we struggled to do that."

That confusion was reflected in the conclusion that Favreau and Muscatine both reached early on: The campaign was an unholy mess, fraught with tangled lines of authority, petty jealousies, distorted priorities, and no sense of greater purpose. No one was in charge, and no one had figured out how to make the campaign about something bigger than Hillary. Muscatine felt that the speech said nothing because it tried to say too much.

Favreau thought Clinton's campaign was reminiscent of John Kerry's, where he had gotten his start in 2004—a bunch of operatives who were smart and accomplished in their own right but weren't united by any common purpose larger than pushing a less-than-thrilling candidate into the White House. Hillary didn't have a vision to articulate. And no one else could give one to her. In fact, the more people she assigned to the task of setting the tone for her campaign, the more muddled her message became. The list of writers on the first address included, but was not limited to, Schwerin, Muscatine, Favreau, Benenson, Mook, Palmieri, Podesta, Grunwald, Sullivan, and Schake, who was Michelle Obama's image maven before joining the Clinton campaign.

On one eye-rollingly mundane conference call with her speechwriting team early in the process, Hillary talked about what she wanted from the exercise. Though she was speaking with a small group made up mostly of intimates, she sounded like she was addressing a roomful of supporters—inhibited by the concern that whatever she said might be leaked to the press. Her marching orders were to find a slogan and a message. The absence of any talk about her actual vision for the country or the reasons voters should choose her stunned some of the participants. "There was never any question, and no adviser prompted discussion of 'why you, why now?'" one of them recalled.

From the earliest planning stages of the campaign, Hillary's advisers had debated the extent to which she should correct for her 2008 loss by more overtly running as a woman. "I think running on her gender would be the SAME mistake as 2008, i.e. having a message at odds with what voters ultimately want," Mook had written to Mills. "[L]ots of people are going to say it would be neat for a woman to be president but that doesn't mean that's actually WHY they will vote for her. . . . It's also risky because injecting gender makes her candidacy about HER and not the voters and making their lives better." That sensitivity would factor into her decision not to overemphasize Eleanor Roosevelt, a fellow first lady, in her speech. But other advisers, and ultimately Hillary, felt that gender was an important facet of her narrative. A favored approach was to place her in a lineage of women in her family, starting with her late mother, Dorothy Rodham, and running through to her granddaughter, Charlotte. As the day of the speech drew closer, Dorothy's story of personal hardship took on a more prominent role because of a desire "to better illuminate Hillary's motivation," Schwerin explained to colleagues. And yet as the drafts rolled in, Favreau and

Muscatine realized that while there were a lot of shoutouts to particular constituencies, there was little in the way of an overarching definition of the candidate. Schwerin struggled to take all the input and wrangle it into a Hillary narrative. Meanwhile, Favreau and Muscatine decided to draft their own version, which, according to one source, "ran into the buzz saw of internal dynamics"—the same bureaucracy that hampered Schwerin. The speechwriting process was "the first time when everyone was pulling it out on the table and measuring up," said one Hillary adviser. Right out of the gate, there was nothing quite like the aimlessness and dysfunction of Hillary Clinton's second campaign for the presidency—except maybe those of her first bid for the White House. From this process, nothing could emerge alive.

In early June, Palmieri told Podesta and Margolis she'd make sure the speech turned out right. "I'm taking the reins," she said. But she couldn't just swipe Schwerin's pen. If she undercut him and outsourced his job, she risked making an enemy out of a protected citizen of Hillaryland. Though some of Hillary's aides were both competent and loyal, the candidate favored the latter over the former, which is one major reason the campaign's gears often got stuck. "There's one goal here: to win the fucking election for president," said one source familiar with the speechwriting process. "It's like do you want to win the goddamn thing or are we in junior high school again?"

Palmieri's dilemma crystallized the way the convoluted power structure encouraged the denizens of Hillaryland to care more about their standing with her, or their future job opportunities, than getting her elected. For all of her autopsies, Hillary's management style hadn't really changed since the 2008 campaign.

"Dan Schwerin isn't the issue," said one of Hillary's top aides. "It's the candidate herself."

FRUSTRATED WITH THE process and the product, Favreau dropped out about a week before Clinton stepped to the podium.

As a parting shot, he delivered to Benenson and Palmieri a frank assessment of the shortcomings of the operation and the speech. It was coming in way too long, lacked a central rationale for why Hillary was running for president, and sounded enough like standard Democratic pablum that, with the exception of the biographical details, it could have been delivered by anyone in the party. Beyond that, it was the product of a write-by-committee paradigm that never would have passed muster in either of the Obama campaigns. There was no strong leader running the show.

Around that time, Hillary decided to give Schwerin a direct line to her, without interference from his internal and external critics. "Dan and I are going to finish this speech," she told her team. "Back off." During the last forty-eight hours before the speech, she and Bill went through draft after draft, shipping edits to Schwerin. She didn't like the text yet, and neither did Bill, who tried his best to add some poetry—the buzzy Bill Clintonisms that frame an idea. Said one adviser: "It changed from the last time our eyes were on it and when she's up there, and that only means one thing: WJC, baby." But the basic frailty remained what Favreau had pointed out: the failure of the speech to connect Hillary to a cause larger than herself. And no one could change that, not even Bill Clinton.

IN THE WEE hours of the morning, on the day of the kickoff rally, Hillary was still looking at a Frankenstein's monster of a speech. It wouldn't get much better for the changes Schwerin tapped out from the tramway platform before closing his laptop and riding to Roosevelt Island. And so, under a blistering sun on a hot Saturday in mid-June, with a glare so bright she struggled to see the speech on the teleprompter in front of her, Hillary Clinton whimpered her way into the election. Reporters immediately noticed that an overflow area set up with massive TV screens was empty. While Hillary surrounded herself with supporters in images broadcast across the nation, the crowd was remarkably small given that the event was held in a city of more than eight million people in a state she had represented in the Senate.

The speech started as an acknowledgment of political icons—Roosevelt, Obama, and Bill Clinton—and mixed in applause lines for constituencies Hillary wanted to court, including African Americans, Hispanics, the LGBT community, and women of all races and sexual orientations. She sprinkled in bromides about economic opportunity and how "prosperity can't just be for CEOs." But there was no overarching narrative explaining her candidacy, no framing of Hillary as the point of an underdog spear, no emotive power. "America can't succeed unless you succeed," she offered in a trite tautology. "That is why I am running for president of the United States."

Even those in her camp who defended the speech acknowledged that there were too many cooks in the kitchen, that the text was too watered down to serve as a call to action, and that Hillary was less than inspiring. And these were the kinder criticisms. "That speech had a simple mission, which was a requirement," said one source close to Hillary. "This was the chance to make a credible persuasive case for why she wants to be president. She had to answer the why question. It's not because of her mother. Her mother's an inspiration, but that is not why. It has to sort of feel like kind of a call to action, a galvanizing, 'I'm bringing us together around this larger-than-all-of-us' idea or cause, and I don't think it did that. I don't think it did either of those."

Some of Hillary's aides longed for her to find her own David Axelrod, someone who could really help her articulate a vision and stay on message. From the earliest days of the campaign, many of Hillary's closest friends discussed how to push Mook out or down to make room for someone with a better understanding of the candidate and a better ear for the more populist mood of the electorate. Mook appeared to be running a less dramatic version of Hillary's 2008 campaign, but that was in large part because he preferred to avoid airing problems internally and because Hillary had made clear that leaking would not be tolerated. She had built a team almost designed to feud, and she personally went around her own aides to task outsiders with assignments. To the extent that lines of authority existed, they were blurred. That first speech "reflected a lot of what would come afterward," said one person involved in the process. The infighting still raged as it had seven years before. But acts of aggression were executed passively, and the disputes didn't make it into cable news broadcasts. All of the jockeying might have been all right, but for a root problem that confounded everyone on the campaign and outside it. Hillary had been running for president for almost a decade and still didn't really have a rationale.

"I would have had a reason for running," one of her top aides said, "or I wouldn't have run."

Chapter 2

THE MERCENARIES AND THE MISSIONARIES

THE SUREST SIGN THAT THE YOUNG MAN HILLARY CLINton tapped to run her 2016 campaign was a power player savvy beyond his years came in late 2010. Robby Mook was a boyish thirty then, a rising star among Democratic operatives. He'd been beckoned from Las Vegas for a dinner with New York representative Steve Israel, the incoming chairman of the committee charged with electing House Democrats, in the wake of a historic midterm loss of congressional seats.

Israel wanted Mook to run the day-to-day operations of the Democratic Congressional Campaign Committee, and he pressed the young man on what they should do first to set up for the 2012 elections in two years. Unflinching, Mook responded with the words of a professional political assassin.

"Clean house," he said.

It was a classic high-end Washington power move. Fire everyone. Force people to reapply for their jobs. Those who remain know to whom they owe their allegiance. And use the new openings to bring in loyalists. That Mook wanted to burn down the DCCC and rebuild it in his image wasn't a unique instinct. That he was playing Beltway power games this astutely so soon in life marked him as a much higher-level operative than the vast majority of his contemporaries—and most party elders, for that matter.

By early 2014, when Hillary was beginning to think seriously about how she would put together a campaign for 2016, Mook was perfectly positioned to run the preliminary process. He'd just come off managing the campaign of one of Hillary's closest allies, long-time Clinton moneyman Terry McAuliffe, for the governorship of Virginia in November 2013. Mook won acclaim within Democratic circles for getting McAuliffe across the finish line, even though the margin of victory ended up being much smaller than Democrats had expected heading into Election Day. He was a free agent and a hot commodity at a time when most operatives, including Guy Cecil, the political director of Hillary's 2008 campaign and a frequent mention for campaign manager during the run-up to her 2016 bid, were ensconced in guiding midterm House and Senate election efforts.

On the first day of April in 2014, long before Hillary would publicly acknowledge that she was gearing up to run, Mook e-mailed Podesta and Hillary consigliere, Cheryl Mills, who were expected to take on the roles of campaign cochairs, to present a series of options for how Hillary could get the ball rolling. "I was frankly surprised yesterday by her openness to starting a PAC, etc.," Mook wrote. "For that reason, my recommendation here is to open an exploratory committee—it has advantages over a PAC and I think they're the same in the eyes of the media." Importantly, he added, "I assumed for all scenarios that nothing happens before the midterms." Mills quickly agreed with his plan for a post-midterm exploratory committee.

Mook was already operating inside a framework first developed for Hillary by David Plouffe, President Barack Obama's longtime strategist, who had put together a preliminary memo for Hillary in December 2013. As Obama's campaign manager in 2008, Plouffe had despised Clinton; that he was now advising her was an important signal of just how completely she would co-opt the Democratic establishment even before she began running. Plouffe had no love for Hillary, but he was a loyal Democrat and had determined early on that he wanted to build on Obama's legacy. He was also an influential advocate for Mook.

By sending the memo, Plouffe was trying to "force some action" on Clinton's part, said a source who spoke with him at the time. "He was concerned they were squandering the advantage they had in terms of prep time." With the assistance of two others, he wrote "a blueprint for how you might launch a campaign," the source said.

In a private exchange with Podesta that winter, Plouffe emphasized that it was important to have the right culture and mission, to manage Bill Clinton, and to effectively target Latino voters. On the first point, Mook fit the right mold for a campaign manager—or at least he seemed to. He had a reputation for running loyal operations with little drama and even fewer unauthorized leaks to the press. Mook also displayed some characteristics that, for better and worse, aligned with Hillary's own traits. He wanted all of the available data at his fingertips before he made a decision and tended strongly toward the option with the most hard evidence behind it. "He's just extremely rigorous," said one Mook ally on the campaign staff. "Testing and retesting and digging in on everything. It drives people crazy in a healthy way and forces them to think through every angle of something." Mook's attention to data and evidence allowed him to justify his decision making to Hillary in a language she respected; it was the way in which he was most like her.

Mook wasn't the only candidate for the campaign manager's job—five Democratic operatives were seriously considered—but he used his advantage as the first person in the door to get closer to Hillary and prove his utility to her. Over the course of 2014, even as he supplied Hillary with the names of other possibilities to run the campaign or assume high-ranking roles, Mook emerged as the natural choice to take the job. By the time Hillary drew up a short list of finalists late that year, he was already the prohibitive favorite.

Yet for all Mook's advantages—including having the support of Plouffe and the überinfluential McAuliffe—his newness to a senior role in Clintonworld would create tremendous hurdles for him as he tried to wrangle what was sure to be a sprawling campaign. He had worked for her in 2008 as a state director, but he would never be close to Hillary like Abedin, who had been at her elbow for nearly two decades, or Sullivan, who had traveled with her to more than one hundred countries during their years together at State. The Clinton orbit included so many longtime friends and advisers—so many planet-size satellites—that a newcomer like Mook could never be fully in control of it. "Robby had a structural issue that he just had to deal with and there were certain areas that weren't really going to be his," one Hillary ally explained before listing some of the topics outside Mook's authority: "e-mails, the foundation, speeches, candidate time, policy."

After the 2014 midterms, when Democrats got walloped across the country and Republicans took control of the Senate, Mook grew anxious to move Hillary forward into the race. In the hours after the defeat, he dashed off an e-mail to Podesta and Mills. The party was about to descend into chaos, he worried. "The circular firing squads will unleash tomorrow and there will be a smorgasbord of over-interpretations," he wrote. "I'm already hearing the modeling people say that TV doesn't work and the TV people saying analytics doesn't work. And I'm sure someone tomorrow will say campaigning on women's issues doesn't work. It all still works and the dynamics of 16 will be completely different . . . I would be way more prospective than retrospective."

Mook worried that an anti-Hillary candidate would gain traction while voters wondered about the fire in her belly. *If she's slow to get in,* he thought, *people will think she doesn't want it enough, that she's not hungry enough.* Plus, there was a golden opportunity for Hillary to take control of the party and put her stamp on it at a time when Obama's brand had been scraped by the shoals of a low-turnout election. She could be a rescuer, a savior, of the Democratic Party.

Hillary was in much less of a rush. She'd been amassing a fortune giving paid speeches to private companies, including Wall Street banks, and she didn't see the need to prolong what would be a grueling campaign. She even told friends and advisers that she was reluctant about jumping in at all. "She didn't want to run for president," one person she spoke to at the time said. "She did not want to do it. She just concluded that no one else could win." This may have sounded like the idea of running was thrust upon her by circumstance, but in truth, she had spent the years since her 2008 primary defeat building herself and her operation in anticipation of a possible second bid. The real question wasn't whether she would begin campaigning but whether she would stop.

The process for making a final decision would run for more than a year, with Hillary trying to understand all of the angles. She needed to get a better feel for fund-raising in an Internet age, how Supreme Court rulings on campaign finance would affect her, where a party apparatus long neglected by Obama stood, and how voter targeting, analytics, and social media would factor into a winning candidate's plans. In a way, her process was the logical extension of the conversation she'd been having with her closest confidants since 2008.

Hillary was still absorbing information as Mook pressed her to start giving more definitive indications that she was running and begin spending money on building the actual campaign. He presented her with three options for how to transition from a non-candidate to a candidate-in-waiting. The first alternative, which included the formation of an exploratory committee and an earliest-possible launch date, was the one he favored. Even as he pointed Hillary toward a campaign, some of her closest and longest-tenured allies—most notably Mills—advised against it. But by late 2014, Mook was given the green light to begin convening meetings with potential staff and advisers. He held them in a nondescript Washington law office with the Democratic Party's new guard of elections experts, including Obama campaign veterans Mitch Stewart and Jen O'Malley Dillon.

Hillary met with O'Malley Dillon too. Even though she had given Mook an inside track, Hillary didn't want to eliminate good options. Like EMILY's List president Stephanie Schriock, who had been in the mix earlier, O'Malley Dillon came with a track record that no candidate could afford to ignore in trying to pick the right campaign manager. Strawberry blond and bespectacled, she had served as the deputy campaign manager for operations on Obama's reelection team and as his battleground states director in 2008. Mook had a reputation for being a field organizer; O'Malley Dillon had much more real-world experience in that realm. She'd worked to turn out voters at every level from state legislative races to several prior presidential campaigns, and Hillary wanted to get to know her better. Their meeting took place on a busy December day for Hillary, who also had Senator Elizabeth Warren, a progressive favorite, on her schedule. But she cleared about ninety minutes to assess O'Malley Dillon.

As they sat down in the living room of the Clintons' brick Colonial on Whitehaven Street, amid pictures of family members and a pantheon of international celebrities, Hillary kicked her feet up onto the coffee table. The two women had never spoken to each other before, but the gesture put O'Malley Dillon at ease as Hillary began probing to find out what kind of campaign manager her interviewee would be.

How would you build the infrastructure of the campaign? What would your organizational chart look like? How would you shape the message? Where would data and digital operations fit into your plan?

O'Malley Dillon explained how the Obama campaigns had operated, how state organizations could be built, where elected officials could be counted on to deliver their own constituents to the polls, and where Hillary would have to create infrastructure to turn out voters.

Hillary began to home in on one line of inquiry.

Do I have to build a big national footprint or can I rely on the Democratic National Committee, state parties, and outside groups to shoulder some of the burden? She wanted to get a sense of whether O'Malley Dillon was a big spender.

Mook knew that Hillary viewed almost every early decision through a 2008 lens: she thought almost everything her own campaign had done was flawed and almost everything Obama's had done was pristine. Hillary felt that profligate spending was one major cause of her undoing. *The money needs to be tightly managed,* Mook thought. And, having spoken to her over the course of months, he'd acquired a sense of the direction she wanted to go in. Hillary thought she needed a more professional staff and cleaner lines of authority than she'd had in 2008. That, in theory, would reduce the infighting that had plagued her first bid.

There were a lot of differences between the two finalists for the job, but two stuck out. First, O'Malley Dillon preferred a big formal staff with a strong leadership structure like what she'd helped build for Obama, but Mook thought those campaigns were too top-heavy. Having worked with Hillary in 2008 and Obama after that, his favored structure—with power streamlined toward him—was something of a hybrid. Second, Mook was a data analytics disciple who decided where to hire staff, send the candidate, and pay for ads based on the information number crunchers gave him about voters. He saw the modern tools as effective and cost-effective. It was a lot less expensive for data experts to collect and analyze information provided by voters than it was for pollsters to conduct extensive opinion research. If the models were built right, and the inputs were accurate, data analytics could also save money by more efficiently targeting voters who were likely to show up and support the campaign's candidate. Best of all, he could cite the data reports as evidence to back up his decisions.

O'Malley Dillon, on the other hand, saw data analytics as an important tool but not the only one. Ultimately, Mook's approach better suited both Hillary's belief in evidence and, after having spent millions on her campaign in 2008, her desire to keep costs down.

Hillary liked O'Malley Dillon and wanted her in the fold. But she'd already gone a long way with Mook, and she decided to stick with him. "At that point, it would have meant taking away someone who had been building things," said one source familiar with Hillary's vetting who said she made the right choice.

Mook's 2010 instinct, to clean house at the DCCC, had only been sharpened. Behind the scenes, according to people familiar with his moves, he worked to neutralize potential power rivals in a variety of ways. For example, knowing that Hillary wanted O'Malley Dillon involved with the campaign, he put her on retainer and brought her in to work on a series of projects, including early planning for the general election. But she would never have an official role, and talk of her taking over as the top executive at the Democratic National Committee never materialized. "Robby boxed her out," said one campaign official.

Mook liked to be the only one with a full view of the campaign's arms, from budgeting to polling, data analytics, and field organizing. "I didn't work with counterparts in some departments," said one campaign official. "The way that Robby operated was—and this is not a criticism—a real hub-and-spokes kind of manager." But that structure, in which Mook had the only full view, would become a persistent point of contention for some veterans of Hillaryland and senior officials on the campaign.

Mook's obsession with control served him well, but colleagues saw his self-interest coming at the cost of the candidate. He had already begun to develop a reputation for caring as much about his own brand, and promoting his own people, as he did about getting Hillary elected. In the media, his allies had made sure his job in McAuliffe's campaign was portrayed as a dress rehearsal for managing Hillary's 2016 operation. His organizing ability, aspirational nature, and understanding of how to build loyalty helped him nurture a cultlike power base within a campaign and in certain Democratic circles. In the words of one Democratic insider who knows Mook well, he had "a desire to maintain the kingdom rather than win the war." For the most part, he favored people he'd worked with—the Mook Mafia—to fill the upper ranks of the campaign team. The set of allies he hired from past campaigns he'd worked on included Marlon Marshall, Elan Kriegel, and Michael Halle, as well as Oren Shur, who had bought ads for the Democratic Governors Association the year McAuliffe won in Virginia.

Mook had tried to set himself up to hold all the keys to Hillary's operation. Yet right from the start, a threat to his vision of total control already existed in the form of a scrappy grassroots super PAC called Ready for Hillary. And not even the expressed wishes of Bill and Hillary Clinton could keep Mook from crushing it.

FOR OVER TWO years, inside a fifth-floor suite on North Kent Street in the dress-shirt-and-slacks Washington suburb of Rosslyn, Virginia, the thirty staffers of the Ready for Hillary super PAC had worked to lure Hillary into the presidential race. They built a list they boasted had three million Hillary supporters, identified nearly two hundred thousand donors, and raised $15 million to lay a foundation for the Clinton campaign and give Hillary a much-needed head start.

Derided by some Clinton insiders and the media as a bunch of self-seeking amateurs—particularly in the beginning, when one Clintonite joked with another that they should start a rival super PAC called "Geeked Up for Hillary"—the small staff of Ready for Hillary actually had strong ties to the Clintons' inner circle. The ringleader of the group, Adam Parkhomenko, a shaved-bald, part-time reserve Washington cop, stood out for his slavish devotion to Hillary and a raw energy notable even in the adrenaline-junkie world of American campaign politics. Parkhomenko had worked for Clinton's first 2008 campaign manager, Patti Solis Doyle, and later in the office of Capricia Marshall, who handled politically sensitive tasks like fighting for delegates after it was clear Obama would win the primary. When the first campaign was over, he organized a dead-end effort to pressure Obama to put Clinton on the ticket. By the time he was thirty, he had spent more than a decade obsessed by the singular goal of pushing Hillary Clinton back into the White House.

Whatever strange brew led Parkhomenko to focus his entire life on Hillary's ascent, it was intoxicating enough to her inner circle that his RFH effort, coheadlined by career activist Allida Black, won more than a tacit blessing from the highest ranks of the Clinton machine as he began ramping it up in 2013. While many Clintonites were initially skeptical of the super PAC, Parkhomenko eventually won most of them over by proving that he wasn't just tapping into small-dollar donors but was also securing big-league names like financier and philanthropist Warren Buffett. Knowing that Buffett was big on seeing a return on his investments, Parkhomenko and his staff wrote an old-fashioned letter to the investor and discussed their own success with digital and online advertising. They told him that while he wouldn't get a financial return on his investment, he would reap rewards for his candidate. Six days later, Buffett sent a response, along with a $25,000 check and an admonition to verify that the donation was legal by Federal Election Commission standards. He was all in for Clinton, he said, adding that Ready for Hillary was the first outside group he was going to support. "As long as you can promise I'm not doing anything illegal under the FEC limits, you may cash this $25,000 check," he wrote in ink on the typed letter.

Because of Clinton's abiding loyalty, and because Ready for Hillary had made significant donor and volunteer contacts, the assumption among Hillary-watchers was that the super PAC would be absorbed into the official presidential campaign when it launched. But, as Mook began to quietly construct the apparatus for 2016, he took a dim view of RFH's future in his operation. In his view, shared by other professionals on the campaign, Ready for Hillary had grossly overexaggerated the group's lists. After accounting for bad e-mail addresses, one official later groused, "It wasn't half a million names."

Slowly, a tension began to build about how—or even whether—to incorporate Parkhomenko's staff, his legions of grassroots supporters around the country, and the small-donor base he'd built from nothing. That friction, known only to a small set of Clinton's most trusted advisers, was bubbling beneath the surface when Hillary convened a preholiday planning meeting in 2014—four months before she would release the video announcing her campaign. And she was concerned enough about the resolution of the Ready for Hillary question that she made sure her top aides could all hear, loud and clear, what she wanted done about it.

"How many staff are there?" she asked. "How many work for Ready for Hillary?"

"About thirty," one of her aides replied.

"Every single one of them gets a job on my campaign," Hillary decreed.

There was good reason for Hillary to be concerned about keeping Parkhomenko and his team involved. From its start in 2013, Ready for Hillary seemed to inspire and harness a certain spark and spunk Clinton lacked during her first presidential run. It wasn't quite the excitement generated by Barack Obama's hope-and-change tour, but Ready for Hillary built grassroots enthusiasm for a candidate whose natural cautiousness militated against inciting the masses. More than anything, it gave Clinton a network across the states.

At its core, the battle over Ready for Hillary was a war between the mercenaries and the missionaries. In one corner stood Mook, a professional political assassin—regarded as an expert in organizing and managing a campaign—who could earn his place on the list of great political operatives by electing Hillary president.

Parkhomenko, an alpha male in his own way, was the missionary—an amateur organizer and professional activist—who would have thrown himself from a rooftop if he thought it would secure the presidency for Hillary. Both archetypes were familiar in Clintonworld: the cold-eyed, self-serving strategists who build up themselves by building up one Clinton or both and the sycophants who prove their loyalty to a Clinton by devoting their entire lives to the family. Hillary wanted them to coexist. But Mook did not.

In the early days of the campaign, and for months before the launch, Mook seldom missed an opportunity to rip Parkhomenko and his squad. Throughout 2014, he griped to Mills that RFH would unnecessarily complicate the campaign's work and create legal headaches; Mills was unimpressed and questioned whether Mook's objections were valid. When Mook found out that RFH was reaching out to Obama's Iowa precinct captains to secure their support for Hillary in January 2015, he fumed to Podesta in an e-mail:

"This goes in my category of things that should really be left to the campaign. This could damage politics." In the end, RFH's staff continued to organize for Hillary in the early states, and the precinct captains they signed up in Iowa would prove a crucial force in the caucuses there.

Knowing Hillary wanted to bring in the RFH crew, Podesta assigned Parkhomenko and Craig Smith, a former aide to Bill Clinton and senior adviser to the super PAC, to produce a memo listing the set of Ready for Hillary staffers, their titles, which positions on the campaign they wanted, and the posts for which they would actually be qualified. Parkhomenko drew up the memo, and it was delivered to Podesta.

Ready for Hillary aides were ecstatic about the new jobs they were going to get on the Clinton campaign. Not only had Hillary declared her desire to hire them, but Podesta also gave verbal assurances to Smith and Parkhomenko that the RFH staff would be brought on board. "There will be no gaps in your paychecks," Podesta said. The RFH upstarts began looking at apartments in Brooklyn. Parkhomenko told his team members that they would each get a call from a hiring authority on the campaign—it might not be for the job at the top of their wish list, but they would be taken care of.

But for many, their phones never rang. They obsessively refreshed their e-mail in-boxes and found nothing from top campaign staffers. There were no texts from Hillary for America. The Parkhomenko-Smith memo found its way into the circular file at the Clinton campaign headquarters. That's not to say no one from Ready for Hillary got a job on the campaign. Months later, when reporters started asking questions about Ready for Hillary staffers who hadn't been hired, Hillary again asked about them at a meeting with Mook and Marlon Marshall. They assured her the RFH crew was being taken care of. Then, on April 1, 2015, the campaign hastily announced that Parkhomenko and several others had been added to the payroll. He was given the title of director of grassroots engagement, but in his new job on the inside, he had a very small team and virtually no budget. Mook had neutralized him.

Smith e-mailed Podesta on April 10 to complain about the situation: "Just so you know, as of today, 6 of our people have been given jobs," Smith wrote. "Today I have to lay off 17 people."

Podesta tried to placate him: "Doubt that is a permanent condition, but let me know details of the people left out." It was hardly a promise to take up arms in defense of RFH.

It seemed like a no-brainer for Clinton's campaign to tap into the state-by-state network that Parkhomenko had built to serve it. The group's lists had value, and lawyers for Ready for Hillary and the Clinton campaign would spend weeks planning how they could legally transfer all the data from the super PAC to the campaign. In addition to Hillary, there was one other force in Clintonworld that had a soft spot for Parkhomenko and his crack unit of organizers: Bill Clinton.

"Whose bright idea was it to shut down Ready for Hillary?" he repeatedly asked Smith, knowing full well that it was Mook's. But Mook, never a fan of Ready for Hillary and certainly in no mood to empower another organizer in his own campaign headquarters, sent a clear signal that RFH wasn't really welcome in Brooklyn or anywhere else the campaign operated. Knowing Hillary's concern for RFH, Mook would later acknowledge that the lists compiled by the group were helpful. But he viewed the personnel as a nuisance at best and a threat at worst. There was no room in his kingdom for the princes of the defunct super PAC. Once he'd extracted the group's lists, which he thought had limited value, they were done.

As one Democratic insider familiar with Mook's thinking put it, "When you're done with a condom, you throw it out."

Parkhomenko proved easy enough for Mook to topple, but there were more perilous fault lines running through the campaign and the larger Clintonworld maw. It was nearly impossible, if not impossible, to grab hold of all the various independent actors who had access to Hillary. Podesta, Abedin, Palmieri, Sullivan, and others within the campaign had direct lines to her. So did any number of advisers, donors, and friends. On matters pertaining to her private-server issue, she had a team of lawyers whose need to protect her did not necessarily line up with the best political strategies for the campaign. And, of course, Bill Clinton and Chelsea Clinton influenced the candidate. The map of Clintonworld looked like a traffic jam on a Venn diagram, with so many interlocking and concentric circles that it was next to impossible to determine who was in Hillary's ear. Try as he did, Mook would never be able to exert full control. In fact, early tangles demonstrated the limits of his domain. Mook, who thought Podesta wasn't present enough, would sometimes make decisions without consulting him. That infuriated Podesta. In theory, they were supposed to work in tandem, with Podesta keeping in touch with Democratic elites, guiding messaging and troubleshooting, while Mook tended to the mechanics of the campaign. But their lines of authority were never that clear, and Hillary's intimates could influence her on any particular issue at any moment. She had set up rival power centers everywhere. And no one had enough authority to make the others play nice. Nor was anyone empowered to both enforce Hillary's will and tell her when she was wrong without fear of reprisal.

Several Clinton insiders said at the time that it was unclear who was really running the campaign. To the extent anyone was truly in charge, it was Hillary. But aides and advisers often pointed to Abedin as the staff member who influenced Hillary the most—despite her inexperience as a campaign operative. As she had at State, Abedin concerned herself with elements of the operation for which she had no credentials. But she had a corner on the most valuable commodity of any presidential campaign: the candidate's time. Abedin was with Hillary around the clock. She had the final say on where Hillary went and who had access to her. Rather than just being a gatekeeper, Abedin took on the role of channeling Hillary for the rest of the campaign. That created internal resentment, as it had at the State Department.

Besides, Clinton aides groused, Abedin was a walking political time bomb. Her husband, former congressman Anthony Weiner, had quit the House after sending sexually explicit tweets to women and then lost a mayoral bid after revealing he hadn't stopped sexting women he'd met online. And that was just the screaming tabloid headline aspect of Abedin's potential for inflicting damage on the campaign.

She had e-mailed the former secretary of state as much as anyone through the private server. Some of the messages contained information that was later deemed to be classified. Abedin was a subject of interest for the House Benghazi Committee, and, separately, for Iowa senator Chuck Grassley. He was investigating the work she'd done for Teneo, an international consulting firm founded by Bill Clinton's longtime consigliere, Doug Band, when she was on the State Department payroll. Grassley thought that was a major conflict of interest, and even some of Hillary's advisers privately agreed. Having Abedin serve as Hillary's traveling aide was one thing, but giving her the title of vice chair and allowing her to expand her portfolio into major campaign decisions made little sense.

But Abedin's defenders, and they were legion, often said she got a bad rap for closing Hillary off. In a campaign in which no strategist could really translate the candidate, no one had a better feel for Hillary or could act as the all-important go-between on the ground for the sprawling Clintonworld. That made her indispensable to both the candidate and the rest of the team, her supporters pointed out. But many feared speaking their minds around her. She couldn't be counted on to relay constructive criticism to Hillary without pointing a finger at the critic. If Hillary was a candidate often isolated from her formal campaign—and she was—Abedin was the croc-filled moat encircling her. The Royal Huma Guard made it harder for Hillary's senior- and midlevel aides to get time with the candidate, and that made it impossible to really know the woman they were selling.

"She's incredibly protective to a fault," said one Clinton ally. "If I was running for president, I would want my staff to be able to reach me. If you can't reach her, then Hillary becomes cardboard Hillary. You've never spent time with her. She never really knows what you do."

Mook tried and failed to limit Abedin's power in January 2015, just as the wheels of the campaign had begun to turn. Abedin was lining up a role in which she would have the title of vice chair, proximity to Hillary, and control over the candidate's schedule. In a memo to Podesta, Mook asked for input on "how much we'd want her to still participate in scheduling if she does the HQ job." Abedin, he said, would be valuable in providing institutional memory on phone calls and in meetings, but "I don't want people confused about who is in charge (i.e., the scheduler needs to be in command of that process)."

When Podesta didn't respond for four days, Mook re-sent the message. Abedin would get everything she wanted. And there should have been no confusion on Mook's part: neither he nor anyone else could put Abedin in a corner. *Okay,* Mook thought after failing to gain traction, *that's done.* He would remain wary enough of Abedin that when he disagreed with her and told Hillary about it, he would then call Abedin to let her know, so that she didn't think he was going behind her back.

Mook also clashed with Palmieri, a Podesta protégée, in the early months of the campaign. In one briefing for campaign surrogates in Washington in the summer of 2015, Palmieri led off with a review of the messaging strategy. When she was done, she turned to Mook. Robby can give an update on the organizing strategy, she said, because that's his domain. People in the room were taken aback. *In theory, wasn't everything in the campaign manager's domain?*

But Palmieri had tremendous autonomy as the chief communications officer. And, as a former White House communications director, she had reason to believe her acumen was far superior to Mook's when it came to the strategy and tactics of talking to the media. But, in a relatively public fashion, she had asserted herself as his equal and appeared to demean him in the process.

Another wing of the sprawling apparatus was centered at the Clinton Foundation. Hillary paid Bill's top aides when they worked on campaign matters. The former president himself represented one of the trickiest political thickets for Hillary. He was her closest adviser, and yet his off-the-cuff remarks on the campaign trail had inflicted serious damage in 2008. After that year's primary, Bill had given just as much support as was required to help unify the party. In 2012, he had reemerged as a force for Obama's reelection bid. But the Bill question always was more fraught for Hillary. He could be her strongest validator and at the same time overshadow her on the campaign trail, or, as a result of his personal emotional investment in her success, go off half-cocked and dominate a news cycle with negative headlines.

As the campaign staff would soon find out, it was virtually impossible to keep Bill out of the news, especially when Democrats started publicly second-guessing his legacy on topics ranging from criminal justice to gay rights. His desire to help Hillary win and his defense of his own legacy would be in constant conflict throughout the campaign. And the specter of his extramarital sexual activity, and Hillary's response to it, would become a major theme of the Republican strategy to defeat her.

Inside the campaign, a bonfire of the vanities raged. Each division had its own silo: Mook in charge of the budget and operations, Palmieri at the helm of a sprawling and warring communications staff, Abedin in charge of Hillary, Sullivan guiding policy, and Elan Kriegel running the powerful analytics team. There was also a holy trinity of consultants who competed with Mook for influence: chief strategist Benenson, adman Margolis, and longtime Clinton message guru Grunwald. Podesta floated outside the structure. Some of Hillary's advisers thought she'd aligned her roster the wrong way. "She has too many people in jobs who should not be doing the jobs they're doing," one of them said.

Much of this infighting might have been avoided had someone been given the authority to have the final say on matters large and small. But Hillary distributed power so broadly that none of her aides or advisers had control of the whole apparatus.

Chapter 3

FEELING THE BERN

IN APRIL 2014, BERNIE SANDERS CALLED LIBERAL RADIO talk show host Bill Press to his Senate office for lunch. Both men, like many white liberals, had started with great hopes for Obama's presidency but had grown disappointed. After watching the president come up short of implementing a full progressive agenda, Bernie couldn't stand the idea of Hillary pulling the country back into the Clinton White House years. She was centrist and transactional—exactly the wrong direction, he thought. "His feelings about her, which were less than positive, revolved around policy differences and revolved around her allegiance to an old form of campaigning relying on big money and the people who raise it for you," said one Sanders confidant who spoke to him around the same time. "This kind of campaigning, of going to rich people and asking them for money and modulating your policies in a way that didn't inspire people, that was a losing formula. In terms of him not liking stuff about her, that's what he disliked the most." He wanted someone to run at her from the left, either to beat her or force her into taking more liberal positions. But no one had stepped up yet, not even the lion of the new left, Massachusetts senator Elizabeth Warren. *If there's nobody else,* Bernie kept thinking, *maybe it ought to be me.* Press had heard Sanders was considering a bid, and, as they sat down to eat, he asked whether it was true.

"Yeah, I've been thinking," Bernie replied. "I want to make sure that the progressive issues are front and center in the 2016 campaign. Hillary's not going to raise them on her own. Somebody's got to do it." Bernie never said as much, but the unspoken condition of his candidacy was the absence of Warren. If she ran, Press knew, Bernie wouldn't. Still, the thought of a true progressive running in 2016 was as exhilarating as the idea of a Clinton coronation was uninspiring.

But Press had one major concern. He didn't think Hillary was just like the Republicans. He wanted a Democrat to win the presidency, and he worried that Bernie might run as a third-party candidate, siphon votes from the Democratic nominee, and hand the White House to the GOP.

"You know, you're an independent," Press said. "To me, that's a problem because if you run as an independent . . ."

No, no, no, Sanders assured him. "I would never be a Ralph Nader. I would never do anything to hurt a Democrat's chances of winning the White House." Where Sanders drew that particular line, and whether he would actually help the eventual Democratic nominee, were questions that would, much later, create knuckle-whitening angst within the party.

Press was intrigued and offered a measure of encouragement to Bernie. "You know, if you are really seriously thinking about that, you should get people together who have been involved in presidential campaigns and just get their reaction," Press counseled. "Tell them what you're thinking of, and people who've done this might tell you if it's even doable."

"That's a good idea," said Bernie, who was one step ahead of Press. "Would you organize that for me?"

IT WOULD HAVE been tough to dream up a caricature of a candidate so unlikely to catch fire in a presidential race. For starters, Bernie was already seventy-two years old, nearly three years beyond the age Ronald Reagan was when he became the oldest president inaugurated for the first time in 1981. Though he had been elected to the

Senate twice, and the House eight times before that, he had always run as an independent—as a man without a party in a capital city in which only Republicans and Democrats wielded real power. He openly identified with socialism, an ideology to which few Americans subscribed. And he was disheveled enough, in a beat-up blue blazer with wild strands of white hair encircling his balding pate, that he could easily be mistaken in the Capitol for a lost scientist.

Inside the Washington bubble, Bernie had long been looked at as a revolutionary without much of a following. He'd had some success in writing amendments that brought the left and right wings of the two parties together, and the Senate had proved a much better venue for his brand of politics than the House had. But his list of real legislative accomplishments was short and relatively undistinguished. He didn't slap backs or cut deals. Over the years, he'd railed against presidents of both parties, which had a tendency to limit his influence. And yet, as perhaps the most reliably liberal voice in Congress, he had built a following among progressives who caught clips of him on C-SPAN. The uncompromising and incorruptible style that made him a failure at the inside game of Washington was precisely the reason he was poised to take advantage of a populist renaissance in the electorate.

That populist renaissance had begun on the Republican side, with the rise of the Tea Party in 2009. Those anti-Washington shock troops had disrupted the town hall meetings of Democratic lawmakers pushing Obamacare, nominated small-government Republicans in primaries in 2010, and provided the boost for the GOP to take control of the House in that year's midterm elections. They were mirrored on the Democratic side by the Occupy Wall Street movement, which had failed to achieve its goals not because of a lack of passion but because of organizational weaknesses and because the left had less appetite for destruction with a Democratic president in office.

The public's anger with Washington had built steadily over the intervening years, but it was divided: Conservatives believed the government had grown too powerful and redistributed too much money from taxpayers. On the left, voters often viewed the existing government as an impediment to greater redistribution of wealth and more benefits for the middle and lower classes. However, these two sets of populists did overlap in a few essential areas. They were mad about corporate subsidies, trade agreements, and American military intervention overseas. They scapegoated different segments of society—immigrants on the right and bankers on the left, for example—but agreed that the Washington establishment, in which Hillary and many of the seventeen Republican presidential candidates were major players, wasn't serving the country well. Bernie felt that way too. So while no one in Washington was paying attention to Sanders in April 2014, the tinder for an anti-Hillary outsider was spread across the country, just waiting to be lit.

After leaving Bernie's office, Press got to work immediately. He planned a dinner at his Capitol Hill home, an elegant townhouse an easy walk away from the cramped, 900-square-foot, two-floor row house Sanders had bought for nearly half a million dollars after winning his first six-year Senate term in 2006. As Press called around, he found that it was difficult to assemble a crew to even meet with Sanders. He asked Democrats whether they would come to an off-the-record gathering just to hear Sanders's ideas. No commitment necessary or expected, he said. But few heeded his call.

"There were still people who would not come because they were already supporting Hillary, and there were people who would not come because they were afraid Hillary would find out," said a source familiar with the effort.

In the end, it was a very small circle that gathered at Press's house on April 9, 2014, a full year before Hillary announced her campaign: Sanders and Press; their wives, Jane and Carol; Sanders press aide Michael Briggs; Democratic strategist Peter Fenn; Susan McCue, former chief of staff to Senator Harry Reid; and Democratic campaign operatives Tad Devine and Mark Longabaugh. Brad Woodhouse, who would go on to run a super PAC supporting Clinton, was also in attendance.

The group was large enough that Carol Press served beef stew in the living room rather than around the dining room table, and Sanders made a pitch very similar to the one he had given Bill Press at their lunch meeting a few weeks earlier. Then he polled the room, seeking input on the various aspects of a campaign and whether he should run—and how he should do it if he did.

McCue, who ran a super PAC, asked if Bernie might create one. Devine thought that was a terrible idea because it was so off-brand for a political reformer. No one told Sanders he shouldn't run, but there was a consensus in the room: he'd have to run in the Democratic Party. That wasn't an easy pill for Sanders to swallow. He had studiously avoided association with the party, caucusing with House and Senate Democrats to secure seats on committees in Congress but never calling himself a Democrat or doing all but the most perfunctory of fund-raising for the party. Sanders wasn't sold on the idea of becoming a Democrat yet. It would mean sacrificing a major piece of his identity.

SIX MONTHS LATER, in mid-October, a former two-time summer intern in Sanders's House office was on her way to speak at family weekend at the University of Vermont in Burlington when she ran into the man who had hired her, Sanders's state director Phil Fiermonte. This former intern now sat on the board of UVM Honors College, but she was better known as a longtime fund-raiser, scheduler, and troubleshooter for President Barack Obama.

Over the course of two decades, Alyssa Mastromonaco, a petite brunette so obsessively organized that she set calendar reminders to take her vitamins, had risen through the ranks from intern for the fringe socialist congressman to deputy chief of staff at the White House. When people wanted to see Obama in the Oval Office, they had to talk to her first. Mastromonaco, an operative on John Kerry's 2004 campaign and Obama's 2008 bid, was one of Sanders's few connections to the big leagues of presidential politics, and he wanted to get her counsel.

"Bernie is going to be here tomorrow," Fiermonte told Mastromonaco. "He'd like to see you." And that's how one of Obama's most trusted aides found herself in a ninety-minute meeting with the man trying to foment a national political revolution from tiny Burlington. Seated in the senator's office the next day, Mastromonaco listened to her former boss talk about the prospect of running.

"I'm not sure about this," Sanders confided. "A lot of people have told me I should run."

"You should only do it if your heart is in it," she replied. "And you shouldn't do it as an issue candidate."

Sanders was worried about whether there was a lane for him to run in. After all, Clinton had already sucked up a lot of the political oxygen in Democratic circles.

"Do you think there's a place for me?" he asked.

"I think there's a place for everybody," she said. "I don't think it's good for Democrats if there's no challenge during the primaries."

While Mastromonaco saw Sanders as a primary challenger to Clinton, Sanders told her he still wasn't sure that was the route he wanted to take. He had been elected time and again as an independent, and he'd been critical of both parties on the campaign trail and in Congress. Becoming a Democrat was no small matter for him.

"I don't see how you could do it any other way," she counseled. She knew he'd get no traction running outside the two-party system. "If you want to be a real outsider, where's the stage?" she asked.

What she meant was that Sanders wouldn't get coverage from the media and wouldn't be invited to participate in presidential debates. If he ran as an independent, she knew, no one would hear him.

Sanders also wanted to know about the rigors of the campaign trail and what had made the difference between the losing 2004 Kerry campaign and the winning Obama bid in 2008. It was interesting, Mastromonaco thought, that Sanders really didn't know what it was like to be on a presidential campaign. Most candidates have some familiarity because they've run before, been vetted for vice president, or even served as a high-level surrogate. Not Sanders. This was all new to him.

The most valuable insight Mastromonaco shared with Sanders was the difference between the party-regular candidacy of Kerry and the fresh-outsider campaign of Barack Obama. Kerry's status as a Democratic insider both helped and hurt: It brought him institutional support, but it also meant there were a lot of people in his ear about how he should run his campaign. He was always convinced that he was missing one key staffer who could solve all of his problems. If someone told Kerry something he didn't want to hear, he would find someone else who would rubber-stamp his opinion. Obama, with the help of advisers David Plouffe and David Axelrod, built a cohesive team that was neither beholden to, nor heavily influenced by, Democratic Party insiders. They would rise and fall together, unfearful of missing out on the advice of party stalwarts.

Whenever Hillary Clinton got an endorsement in 2007, Mastromonaco told Sanders, Plouffe's invariable response was "We don't give a fuck. Stay focused. It doesn't matter." The lesson for Sanders in 2016 was clear: For every Democratic politician who endorsed Hillary and for every major donor who wrote her checks, there was a debt to be paid. Bernie could run without that baggage. Beholden only to his supporters, he could be more agile and more pure than Hillary. He could be like Obama.

Bernie took it all in. Then he asked Mastromonaco the most dangerous question in all of left-wing politics: Will you come to the next meeting?

WHEN SANDERS'S TINY band of rebels reconvened at Press's townhouse a few weeks later—on November 19, 2014—it had grown a little bit. Mastromonaco, who was starting a job as chief operating officer of Vice Media, came to give counsel. So did Representatives Keith Ellison of Minnesota and Barbara Lee of California, leaders of the Congressional Progressive Caucus that Sanders had founded in his first term in the House.

Sanders's Senate chief of staff Michaeleen Crowell, who had a legendary distaste for Hillary, scribbled notes on a pad. For several others, including Devine and McCue, it was a return engagement. This time, Carol Press made chicken cacciatore, and C-SPAN played in the background as Sanders's kitchen cabinet grew more serious about plotting an insurgent campaign for the presidency.

Devine, who had counted delegates for Jimmy Carter in 1980 and worked on presidential campaigns for a long string of Democratic candidates not named Clinton, delivered a presentation on the race. He believed that if Bernie could design a dream primary system suited to his strengths, he couldn't do much better than starting with Iowa and New Hampshire—the first two states on the calendar. Bernie knew agricultural and environmental issues, which mattered to Iowa and New Hampshire voters, as well as anyone. The demographics—nearly all white and not very wealthy—fit him too. Moreover, Iowa Democrats were dovish, and New Hampshire voters had shown an affinity for presidential candidates from neighboring states.

"Senator," Longabaugh piped in, "I actually think you can win the New Hampshire primary."

Not knowing at that point how many candidates would enter the race, Devine emphasized the importance of the first two states in winnowing the primary field and in creating momentum for the eventual winner. To compete against Hillary, though, Bernie would have to raise $40 million to $50 million before he got to New Hampshire, Devine said. This sounded like quite a lot of money to the penurious Sanders. He didn't understand why he'd need to hire press secretaries in each of the states instead of just one for the whole campaign.

Devine laid out more of the challenges that Bernie would have to overcome. Hillary would have advantages at every turn, including her monster fund-raising network, her existing relationships with superdelegates who would have votes at the convention, and the institutional power of a Democratic Party to which Bernie did not yet belong.

If the first meeting was a toe in the water for Sanders, he was now up to his hips in the chilling and soon-to-be-turbulent tides of a presidential campaign. Sitting next to McCue, a cold-eyed, warmhearted political mercenary, Mastromonaco spoke up to warn Sanders about the rigors of hitting up donors for money.

"Fund-raising is so hard," she said. Mastromonaco knew what she was talking about. She'd worked on Hope Fund, the revolutionary Obama political action committee that had laid the groundwork for his buck-raking by helping other Senate candidates collect cash and then raiding their donor lists. Altogether, Mastromonaco told Sanders, Hope Fund had built a list of fifteen thousand to twenty thousand donors in a set of states where there had been competitive Senate races. That wouldn't be enough this time around, she argued. But it would turn out that Mastromonaco had vastly underestimated her former boss.

After listening to everyone, Sanders spoke up. He emphasized that his goal would be to seize enough attention and support to set the agenda for the Democratic primary. Still, he said, I haven't made up my mind.

That could be a fatal error, Press thought. It would be a mistake, he warned Bernie, to let Clinton jump into the race first. And, as Democratic insiders knew in those days right after the midterm debacle, she was being advised to get out of the blocks early. Sanders risked a failure to launch if he waited too long.

"Bernie, you've got three weeks," Press told him. Get in now, before the calendar turned to 2015.

Sanders wasn't ready. But he wanted to know which of his allies were committed. "If I decide to go, are you with me?" he asked. Then he went around the room. Yes, yes, yes, yes, came the replies. Everyone was with him.

OVER THE HOLIDAYS, Sanders became more certain about his run, and on January 26, 2015, Guy Cecil, who had lost out to Mook in the Clinton campaign manager sweepstakes, sent a flash message to Brooklyn: "Just an FYI that Sanders is calling around to interview campaign managers."

Bernie's small crew may have been loyal, but he didn't have a rainmaker. Not many professional political operatives had an appetite for getting in a fight with Hillary Clinton. So Sanders hired a longtime loyalist, Jeff Weaver, who was running a comic book–and–video game shop in the Washington suburbs. Weaver, bald with a clean-cropped white beard and square, black-rimmed glasses, was a student-activist type now nearing fifty. He had graduated from driving Sanders in the 1986 gubernatorial campaign to managing his 2006 Senate bid, and he'd served as Sanders's chief of staff on Capitol Hill. While political operatives had climbed all over one another to run Hillary's campaign, Sanders was left with the most willing choice.

By late April 2015, Bernie Sanders was almost ready to launch. Hillary had just jumped into the race with a weekend video release, and he could no longer afford to wait if he hoped to stop her coronation.

Sanders had been planning this moment for more than a year, and perhaps, in his midnight confessions, for a lifetime. But he wasn't really prepared for a presidential run in the traditional sense. He had heart and a vision for America that, like Donald Trump's, couldn't be realized without stoking revolutionary sentiment in the electorate. Few thought that popular frustration with Washington meant that voters would turn to a candidate with virtually no experience making deals in the nation's capital. Most of Hillary's consultants and advisers didn't take Bernie as a serious threat. He had no money. He had no organization. He had virtually no support inside the political establishment. He didn't even have a place to make an announcement. Mook was overheard at one meeting saying he wasn't sure whether he'd rather have Bernie in the race—which could give Hillary a workout before the general election—or not.

But Hillary recognized early on that he could catch fire and cause her heartburn. "He's going to be a bigger problem than Martin O'Malley"—the former Maryland governor and presidential hopeful—she told an aide that spring as she filmed a video at her home in Washington.

Bernie was still trying to get his head around the meaning of a presidential campaign both for his career and for his personal life. In mid-April, he summoned Devine to Burlington for a weekend. At his home, and in local restaurants, he peppered the strategist with questions about the rigors of running.

"You're going to lose your privacy," Devine said. "Things you wrote thirty or forty years ago are going to be brought up." With a little success, Bernie would eventually get a Secret Service detail, which would further impinge on his personal liberty. And, as if Devine had to remind him, the chances of beating Hillary weren't that great.

For Bernie, winning wasn't the only thing. I'm a backbencher in Congress, he told Devine. I want to come out of this in a better position to push the issues I care about. He wanted a higher profile in the Senate if he ran and lost. "A presidential campaign, if done well, can accomplish that," Devine replied.

On Wednesday, April 29, Sanders's aide Michael Briggs called over to the Democratic National Committee to ask whether he could use a room in the janky old headquarters building a few blocks southeast of the Capitol. Sanders wanted to launch his campaign, and he'd been told that Senate rules precluded him from doing that inside the Capitol. He was in a jam, and he was hoping the DNC would help out. Mo Elleithee, then the communications director for the DNC, fielded the call and took the request to the chairwoman, Debbie Wasserman Schultz, a Florida lawmaker who pledged neutrality in the primary but was widely viewed as a Clinton ally. DNC officials believed that it wasn't appropriate to give Sanders the imprimatur of the party, or at least that was a good enough reason to turn him down. Wasserman Schultz made the decision: no. It was the first of many instances in which Wasserman Schultz's actions convinced Sanders's team that she was putting her thumb on the scale for Clinton.

Anxious to get in, Sanders called a press conference for the next day on a grassy plain a few dozen yards from the Capitol. At a time when the nation's hatred for all things Washington—and particularly congressional—had neared its zenith, it would have been inconceivable for any other candidate to announce his or her campaign for the presidency from the shadow of the Capitol on a patch of grass known as "the Senate Swamp." For Bernie, it was the only place available on short notice.

It would be inaccurate to say that he announced with little fanfare. At the time, the hundred or so reporters, camera operators, aides, and gawkers in attendance amounted to a huge crowd for a septuagenarian whose sixties-radical speaking style and socialist worldview seemed miscast for the national political stage.

Bernie seemed surprised not only by the turnout but by the sound his own voice made when he spoke into the microphones on a wood-colored podium in front of him. As he started speaking, he recoiled.

"Whoa!" he exclaimed.

Before he moved into the guts of what he was going to say, Sanders noted that he had to "get back" to the Senate for work. "We don't have an endless amount of time," he said. Then he laid out the core principle of his campaign.

From his earliest days as an activist, Sanders had been angry about injustice—racial and economic. He believed the American economic system was a game rigged for the wealthy, and now, he could sense, so did many Americans in both parties and outside the political process. He wasn't altering his core philosophy to match up with the frustrations of voters; they were coming around to his way of thinking.

"The major issue is, how do we create an economy that works for all of our people rather than a small number of billionaires," he said. He connected that goal to the outsize influence he believed wealthy donors have on the political process, calling for campaign finance reform and a reversal of a set of Supreme Court decisions that opened up the floodgates of soft money contributions. He mentioned climate change and student debt. And, before closing, he turned to the question of how he would run his campaign.

"I hate and detest these 30-second ugly negative ads," he said.

"I believe that in a democracy what elections are about are serious debates over serious issues—not political gossip, not making campaigns into soap [operas]. This is not the Red Sox versus the Yankees," he said.

Within five minutes, he was done, save for taking a few questions from the press. They wanted to know about the Red Sox and the Yankees.

Would he go after Clinton hard on their differences—on trade and the Iraq War?

"We don't know what Hillary's stances are on all the issues," he gently chided, referring to her fence-sitting on the Keystone XL Pipeline and the Trans-Pacific Partnership trade agreement that Sanders opposed. And what about the use of military force?

"I voted against the war in Iraq," he said, distancing himself from Clinton's 2002 vote to give President George W. Bush the authority to invade. And, asked whether he was in the race to push his ideas forward, he responded simply that he was in the race to win it.

But the most portentous answer came after he stepped away from the podium, as Lynn Sweet of the *Chicago Sun-Times* caught up with him. After all the years of running outside the party construct, was Sanders now a Democrat?

"No," he said. "I'm an independent."

DONALD TRUMP'S ENTRY into the campaign, from the imposing Trump Tower, could hardly have been more different.

Former Texas agricultural commissioner Jim Hightower once said of George H. W. Bush that he was born on third base and thought he hit a triple. Well, by that measure, Trump was born on third base and clearly thought he'd stopped there, ever so briefly, to drink in the roar of the crowd as he trotted home in celebration of a grand slam. The larger-than-life billionaire came to money the old-fashioned way—he inherited it—but he earned his fame with a rare mastery of showmanship. And, like any great showman, he knew how to make a memorable entrance.

With his former model wife, Melania, at his side, Trump cascaded down an escalator into the lobby of the skyscraper bearing his name on June 16, 2015. The day before, the putative Republican front-runner, Jeb Bush, had launched his campaign. Trump was determined to draw an immediate contrast with the former Florida governor, who had spoken Spanish in a video accompanying his announcement.

About a minute into his own speech, Trump delivered a broadside against immigrants. "When Mexico sends its people, they're not sending their best," he thundered. "They're sending people that have lots of problems, and they're bringing those problems with us. They're bringing drugs. They're bringing crime. They're rapists."

He rambled and railed for forty-five minutes about bad trade deals, expensive wars, and an Obamacare law that he described as the "big lie." Trump's rhetoric was blustery, but his message was direct: Americans are falling behind, victims of insiders who give preference to outsiders. It was nativist and xenophobic, and it struck an emotional chord with downtrodden working-class white men.

The candidate who understood the id of Republican primary voters best was the man initially judged least likely to capture the GOP nomination. A real-estate mogul turned reality TV star who had three marriages and a pro-wrestling appearance to his credit truly understood the Fox News audience. Trump had been itching to get into the presidential race since the early part of 2015. He placed several calls to Bill Clinton in the spring, hoping to get the former president—and onetime golfing partner—to offer an assessment of the race. That he wanted to win the Republican nomination and beat Bill's wife for the presidency didn't matter to either man. That he could get ahold of Bill Clinton—even though it took repeated tries—was but one indication that he was exactly the insider he would claim, throughout the election, that he was not.

Bill finally called Trump back in late May, just a few weeks before the golden-coiffed celebrity-feud impresario jumped into the race.

Trump asked Bill what to expect from a presidential campaign.

It's a big challenge, the former president confided. Your life will be laid bare. But Bill stopped short of advising Trump on whether or not to run. By that point—a call to the former president—the decision had surely been made. Trump had spent years laying the groundwork—he'd aborted potential campaigns in 2000 and 2012, helped lead the "birther" effort to delegitimize Obama, and spent countless hours courting high-profile media types in the run-up to his launch.

Aside from the occasional golf outing, contributions Trump had made to the Clinton Foundation and Hillary's Senate campaign coffers, and the Clintons' attendance at his third wedding, Trump and Bill weren't particularly close. Their daughters, Chelsea and Ivanka, had developed a relationship over the years of running in the same Manhattan circles, but there was no reason for Trump to call Bill, except to hear what the sage of the Democratic Party had to say. Bill was in the habit of dispensing political analysis to anyone who asked.

At that moment, Bill Clinton didn't see Trump as a threat to win the Republican nomination or the presidency, much as he hadn't anticipated the rise of Bernie Sanders. But who would have expected a billionaire who lived at the top of a tower he'd named after himself to ride a populist wave past the Republican field? Only Trump.

And yet, just five weeks after his announcement, Trump surpassed Bush in the RealClearPolitics average of polls for the first time, a lead he would relinquish just once—when Ben Carson briefly edged past him in November 2015—on his way to the Republican nomination.

Trump's ascendance fascinated the media, frustrated the other sixteen Republican candidates, and dominated public and private political conversation across the country. In a way, it was a gift to Hillary. Though he took his shots at her, Trump obscured the early failings of her campaign. But it was even more of a present to Sanders, who was able to build his insurgent campaign while the full scrutiny of the national media was diverted elsewhere. Moreover,

Trump's daily denunciations of international trade deals and American foreign policy echoed Sanders's message. The American electorate was angry with the political class. The recovery from the recession had been quicker for Wall Street and big corporations than for ordinary citizens. They both railed against a Washington establishment that seemed to reward political and financial insiders no matter which party was in power.

Trump took advantage of the increasing power of the Tea Party by appealing to the mistrust of government ingrained in lower-income, less-educated voters. He ran on nostalgia, adopting a campaign slogan—"Make America Great Again"—ripped off from Ronald Reagan, and traced the decline of the country to the mid-1960s. Though he didn't mention the Johnson era's Civil Rights Act, Voting Rights Act, or public subsidies for housing and health care, Trump's dog whistle was just the right pitch to attract the support of white supremacists and nearly all-white crowds of thousands at his campaign rallies.

A similar dynamic was taking hold among liberals, who no longer found the "socialist" label affixed to Sanders to be so off-putting. In early August, he drew a reported 27,500 supporters to a rally in Los Angeles, where the comedian Sarah Silverman elicited cheers with her observation that "Bernie always seems to be on the right side of history." As a member of Congress, his most noteworthy positions were in opposition to legislation: the Iraq War authorization, the Patriot Act, the 2008 Wall Street bailout, and a variety of trade deals.

For both sides, Hillary was the perfect symbol of everything wrong with America. At times, Trump and Sanders would act as the right and left speakers on a stereo blaring a chorus on repeat: Hillary's a corrupt insider who has helped rig the political and economic systems in favor of the powerful.

Chapter 4

THE SUMMER OF THE SERVER

IN THE SUMMER OF 2008, YEARS BEFORE HER PRIVATE e-mail server became a campaign issue, Hillary learned about the power of digital snooping. At the time, she was conducting an autopsy of her failed bid against Barack Obama, and she wanted an honest accounting of what had gone wrong. So she instructed a trusted aide to access the campaign's server and download the messages sent and received by top staffers.

She believed her campaign had failed her—not the other way around—and she wanted "to see who was talking to who, who was leaking to who," said a source familiar with the operation. Her political director, Guy Cecil, had talked with members of the media from his campaign account. Her chief strategist, Mark Penn, was a tyrant. And far too many of her minions had fought for turf and status rather than votes.

Prizing loyalty most among human traits, Hillary was unsettled by these acts of betrayal. So as she dragged staffers into meetings in Washington to assess what had gone wrong, disloyalty and dysfunction were seldom far from her mind. The men and women she met with, apparently unaware that she had access to their e-mails, were amazed that a woman who had been traveling the country in pursuit of the presidency had such a detailed grasp of the machinations at the campaign's command center in the Washington suburbs.

"I was struck by how good of a sense she had before I walked in there of the problems that were going on," said one aide. "She had a mosaic pieced together that if you read a transcript of it, you would have thought it was someone who had sat at headquarters every day, and it was remarkably accurate. She just had it pegged."

The e-mail review was just one piece of an extensive post-mortem project Hillary conducted that summer so that she could address what she and top aide Cheryl Mills called "deficiencies" in her political operation. Neither Penn nor Cecil would be brought back for the no-drama-mantra 2016 campaign. Cecil, long perceived to be a leading candidate for the campaign manager job, was taken off the list weeks before the final decision was made.

After years of watching adversaries comb through her public records for any hint of a scandal, and after accessing her own aides' e-mails, Hillary well understood the danger of exposing her own private thoughts to scrutiny. And that was reason enough to want them shielded from political enemies, journalists, and the public.

WHILE HILLARY SPENT a lot of time calculating risks, she was often a terrible judge of how her actions could backfire and turn into full-blown scandals. When news of her private e-mail server first surfaced in the *New York Times* on March 2, 2015, she looked at it as the campaign's first wave of "choppy waters" rather than the tsunami that it would become.

It's not that she failed to understand that more negative press was on its way, or that she might have a legal problem on her hands. But her response, and that of her team, reflected an epic underestimation of an existential threat to her candidacy. At times, under the stress of an unrelenting feeding frenzy of reporters, Republican lawmakers, and federal investigators, Hillary and her advisers would lose faith in one another's judgment and competence. The candidate would blame her staff for failing to contain the damage, and, privately, they would fault her for failing to take the steps necessary to do that.

The seeds of the scandal were sown in two places: on Capitol

Hill and in federal court. In 2014 the House Benghazi Committee asked the State Department for e-mails related to the attacks that killed four Americans in Libya in September 2012. But State discovered it didn't have the secretary's records—because she hadn't used an official government e-mail account. Hillary's allies pushed for the department to ask all of the former secretaries of state for any official correspondence from private e-mail accounts, giving her the thin cover that she wasn't the only official to use a nonpublic address. Then, in late 2014, Hillary's lawyers handed over fifty-five thousand pages of messages that they deemed to have been connected to her official duties. Hillary's aides separated out and attempted to destroy another trove of tens of thousands of e-mails judged to be of a purely personal nature.

Outside of government channels, news agencies were running into the same problem that the Benghazi Committee originally faced. In January 2015—several weeks after he first filed a Freedom of Information Act request for Hillary's records and several weeks before the *Times'* report on her private server—Vice News' Jason Leopold sued the State Department for rejecting his FOIA application.

Once the news of the server broke, the anti-Clinton nonprofit Judicial Watch filed a lawsuit in federal court seeking Clinton's records. The Associated Press also filed suit around the same time. This series of actions would lead federal judges to order the State Department to release Clinton's work-related e-mails to the public.

At first, her aides tried to laugh it off. The day after the *Times* story popped online, Palmieri and Schwerin floated the idea of inserting a joke about the e-mails into an upcoming speech to the abortion rights group EMILY's List. It was neither the first nor the last time that her team's instincts ran toward making light of the situation. Time and again, consultant Mandy Grunwald, one of the few veterans of Clinton scandals on the campaign team, shot down the idea by arguing that humor opened Hillary up to unforeseeable consequences if the story turned out to be more damaging than it appeared at first blush. As one of only a handful of seasoned elders in the room, Grunwald could sometimes be out of step with the rest of the campaign's aides. But her analysis was often on point.

Over the course of several days in early March, Hillary joined conference calls with her lawyers and top campaign aides to discuss an initial statement in response to the story, whether to hold a press conference, what she should say in her on-camera remarks, and how to word a question-and-answer document that would be released to allies and the press. The back-and-forth led to a power struggle between Philippe Reines and Palmieri and, ultimately, the testy set of exchanges between Reines and John Podesta. Several lines of tension were evident in an e-mail Podesta sent to his colleagues late on the night of March 8, noting that Hillary wanted to push off a planned press conference for one more day.

"Change 99. We want to execute this plan, but want to do Tuesday rather than Monday," he wrote. "Can we keep our yaps shut and execute on that program?"

Podesta had initially wanted to release all of Hillary's State Department correspondence, writing to Clinton consigliere Cheryl Mills shortly after the story broke on March 2 that "we are going to have to dump all those emails so better to do so sooner than later." But that would have had disastrous consequences. Whether she knew it or not, her e-mail held classified material. If she published the messages, she would expose herself to possible prosecution. The debate over how to react was just one reason why Hillary was slow to get out in front of the story.

She also didn't want it to interfere with a Clinton Global Initiative event with Melinda Gates—a reminder of her blindness to the massive conflicts of interest created by the intersection of her presidential campaign, her government service, her philanthropic work, her pursuit of personal enrichment, and her husband's various and sundry public and private activities. The main reason that it took her so long to go on camera to discuss the metastasizing e-mail story, though, was that she could provide no good answers. There was little she could say that was politically advisable, legally airtight, and true. But pressure was mounting on her to say something—anything—that explained her thinking.

Fellow Democrats were paralyzed by the inaction of Hillary's operation, unable, and in some cases less than willing, to defend her publicly when she hadn't really done so herself. Moreover, they couldn't go on television or radio to discuss other issues without getting asked about Clinton's e-mail. President Obama demonstrated the perils of flying blind when he said in an interview that he'd found out she used a private e-mail address at State when he saw it in the news. Mills dashed off an urgent missive to Podesta. "We need to clean this up," she wrote. "He has emails from her—they do not say state.gov."

The president of the United States, and all the Democratic officials below him, were now embroiled in the kind of scandal that reminded them of exactly what they didn't like about the Clintons: the secrecy and the willingness to jeopardize everyone else's interests in service of their own. Democrats fumed privately about Hillary's recklessness—and yet, many of them also thought it was an overblown story.

Early on the morning of March 9, the day before she would finally address the situation in a back-and-forth with the media, Hillary spoke privately to California senator Dianne Feinstein, an ally who urged her to start talking publicly. Feinstein said she would take up Hillary's cause whether or not Hillary had spoken for herself yet, but she and other Democrats would need talking points in hand to defend her. There was no more time to dither and dally.

It was easy for Democrats on Capitol Hill to see the danger to Hillary; the House Select Committee on Benghazi was busy fanning the flames of the story, and its chairman was vowing to use his gavel to get to the bottom of it: "You do not need a law degree to have an understanding of how troubling this is," said Trey Gowdy, a South Carolina Republican who had worked as a prosecutor before being elected to the House. And yet Hillary, a Yale-educated lawyer surrounded by some of the nation's best attorneys, was having great difficulty seeing the storm on the horizon.

Hillary finally spoke to the press on March 10. Despite, or perhaps because of, the intense legal vetting of her remarks, she said things that turned out to be patently false—most notably that she never sent or received classified information through the e-mail address attached to her private server. Ironically, Hillary told her aides after the press conference that she thought she had nailed it.

Hillary wouldn't launch her campaign for more than a month, and already she was neck-deep in a scandal that would overshadow almost everything she said and did for the next twenty months. For Republicans, the e-mails were a godsend because they revived a moribund Benghazi Committee that had the power to investigate, subpoena, and ultimately drag her into a hearing room. Benghazi was supposed to be the big scandal, but it was her exclusive use of private e-mail accounts, rather than the official State Department system, that would put her in the crosshairs of a Republican Congress and the Federal Bureau of Investigation.

Ultimately, journalists and investigators in the administration would cause her far more problems than the Benghazi Committee, but the panel played its role in keeping the story alive during the early months of the campaign and making it impossible for Hillary to communicate a positive message. At the time of her March press conference, Hillary and some of her closest confidants thought she had begun to put the e-mail issue to rest—and that any tie to Benghazi would benefit her.

"They will go after the server but that takes us back to Benghazi which is good for us," Podesta wrote in an e-mail to Neera Tanden, a former Hillary Senate and campaign aide who succeeded him as president of the liberal think tank Center for American Progress. Forty-four-year-old Tanden, possessed of a tiny frame, a warm, toothy smile, and a high-pitched voice that belie her penetrating intellect and epic snark, would emerge as the outside ally with the clearest view of the strengths and weaknesses of Hillary and her team. But, at the time of the first e-mail press conference, she too had yet to fully appreciate the threat.

"I don't know how the story advances," she told Podesta. "So that's good."

Reflecting the relatively unperturbed mood of the campaign at the time, Podesta joked with Hillary, when one of his messages didn't reach her, that she had a "funky server." And Hillary thought she'd handled herself well. She gave her team high marks for helping her navigate through what she treated as a relatively minor distraction on her journey to the presidency.

"Thanks for helping steer the ship thru our first choppy waters," she wrote to Podesta.

Inside the Clinton bubble, John Anzalone gave Hillary and her team even more reason to hope the worst was behind them. The wiry pollster, a son of two Michigan Teamsters, ran one of the nation's top public opinion firms out of Montgomery, Alabama. He had a little swagger, the kind that came with having helped reelect Barack Obama, and a tuft of curly black chest hair was always peeking out from an open collar.

On the day Hillary addressed the press, "Anzo," as he was universally known, had something else in his back pocket: fresh polling data on what concerned voters about her. He'd asked folks to volunteer what bothered them most. Only 7 percent said the e-mails. A couple of days later, he added a little meat to the bone.

The same proportion, 7 percent, said they might reconsider their vote because of the e-mail story, while 10 percent responded that they were still trying to figure out what to make of it all. Anzalone saw the combination as a substantial share of the electorate—17 percent fit into one of the two categories, and the questions were asked in a way designed to control for simply partisan reactions. But he wasn't alarmed, arguing that Hillary should keep an eye on the 10 percent who were still unsure of their feelings.

"Winning over those 10% becomes our challenge," he wrote to Hillary's other top advisers. "If there is no new twist to the story naturally we probably win them over on other issues."

But, of course, there would be new twists, seemingly on the hour. For the remainder of the spring and summer, a mudslide of e-mail stories buried Hillary's chances of running a clean, straight-forward campaign on the issues that mattered to voters' sense of security and opportunity.

Between the Benghazi Committee, which would take depositions from Cheryl Mills, Huma Abedin, and Jake Sullivan among other Hillary aides, the drip-drip nature of evolving federal lawsuits, and judicial orders for the State Department to release Hillary's e-mails on a rolling basis, the early months of the campaign became a private and public hell. It was only a matter of time before voters would know that Hillary had not told the truth about not sending or receiving classified information. As the State Department vetted her e-mails through the federal government's intelligence agencies, those agencies flagged material in the correspondence that was, or should have been, classified. They went through this process to ensure that classified or sensitive portions of her e-mails were redacted before being released to the public.

In May, as Bernie was starting to campaign in earnest and it was becoming clear that the press wouldn't let the e-mail story go, Hillary's aides began planning her first national television interview of the campaign, a chance to strike back at the widely held perception that she was hiding from the press. Palmieri asked Abedin to find out which newscaster Hillary would prefer, and the answer that came back was "Brianna." That meant CNN's Brianna Keilar, and Palmieri worked to set up a live interview on CNN. Only it turned out that Hillary had said "Bianna"—as in Bianna Golodryga of Yahoo! News, the wife of former Clinton administration economic aide Peter Orszag. By the time the mistake was realized, it was too late to pull back.

Hillary went through with the interview on July 7, and it was a disaster. "People should and do trust me," she insisted under a barrage of questions from Keilar. One aide described Hillary as "staring daggers" at her questioner through the exchange. If the interview was meant to show Hillary at ease with the press and confident that her e-mail scandal wouldn't hurt her, it failed. But things were about to get worse.

Later that month, the State Department's inspector general reported that a handful of Hillary's e-mails contained information that was classified at the time the messages were sent. While it's not possible to send e-mails directly from the government's classified systems to outside accounts, there are a few ways in which classified material can end up in outside e-mail—for example, information that should have been classified was not categorized that way by the sender, or someone unwittingly included secret or sensitive passages in a message sent outside the classified systems. Hillary and her aides argued that she was being railroaded by agencies retroactively classifying information in some cases, and, in others, citing material that was not marked classified when it passed into and out of her in-box.

Ultimately, what they were saying was that Hillary clearly didn't intend to transmit classified information—a legal distinction that would become important when federal investigators considered whether to charge her with a crime. In addition, the vast majority of the e-mails that included classified material were traded with people who had security clearances consistent with the levels at which the information in question was classified. That is, Hillary wasn't giving out secrets to people who shouldn't have had them; she was just e-mailing the right people on the wrong system. But from a public relations perspective, the technicalities didn't matter. Hillary had told the nation that she didn't traffic in classified information, and government investigators put the lie to that assertion day after day. In many cases, the twists and turns—the discovery of more highly classified material—played out first in stories leaked to the media for maximum impact.

For months, Hillary tried every approach but confession and contrition. That was killing her politically. When she was asked at a press conference in August whether she'd wiped her server clean of the e-mails she hadn't turned over to State in 2014, she turned flippant. "What, like with a cloth or something?" she asked, miming housework with her hand before ending the session with reporters.

Even as she joked publicly about the imbroglio, Hillary was boiling over inside. She didn't think she'd done anything wrong. In her mind, there was no legal prohibition against her exclusive use of a private server—even though it ran starkly counter to the spirit of regulations designed to preserve government officials' correspondence. She was being treated like a common criminal—or, worse, a traitor to the nation she'd faithfully served as first lady, senator, and secretary of state.

Her antagonists were the same set who had come after her time and again during her husband's presidency: Republicans in Congress, big-money conservatives at the heart of what she had once called a "vast right-wing conspiracy," and a complicit, if sometimes unwitting, media. She wasn't contrite; she was indignant.

Of course, Hillary should have been angry with herself. She'd taken actions that could have prevented her records from becoming public during a presidential run, and the maneuver had backfired badly. But Hillary instead turned her fury on her consultants and campaign aides, blaming them for a failure to focus the media on her platform. In her ear the whole time, spurring her on to cast blame on others and never admit to anything, was her husband. Neither Clinton could accept the simple fact that Hillary had hamstrung her own campaign and dealt the most serious blow to her own presidential aspirations.

That state of denial would become more obvious than ever to her top aides and consultants during a mid-August conference call. Benenson, Grunwald, Margolis, Anzalone, Podesta, Mook, Abedin, and Schwerin were among the small coterie who huddled in Abedin's mostly bare corner office overlooking the East River at the campaign's Brooklyn headquarters. Hillary and Bill, who rarely visited, joined them by phone.

Hillary's severe, controlled voice crackled through the line first. It carried the sound of a disappointed teacher or mother delivering a lecture before a whipping. That back end was left to Bill, who lashed out with abandon. Eyes cast downward, stomachs turning—both from the scare tactics and from their own revulsion at being chastised for Hillary's failures—Hillary's talented and accomplished team of professionals and loyalists simply took it. There was no arguing with Bill Clinton.

You haven't buried this thing, the ruddy-cheeked former president rasped. You haven't figured out how to get Hillary's core message to the voters. This has been dragging on for months, he thundered, and nothing you've done has made a damn bit of difference. Voters want to hear about Hillary's plans for the economy, and you're not making that happen. Now, do your damn jobs.

"We got an ass-chewing," one of the participants recalled months later.

Hillary came back on the line to close the lecture. It was hard to tell what was worse—getting hollered at by Bill or getting scolded by the stern and self-righteous Hillary. Neither was pleasant. You heard him, she admonished. "Get it straight."

It was an astonishing moment—and one that would stick in the minds of Hillary's aides for the rest of the campaign—for two reasons. First, Hillary was already inaccessible to most of her own staff, preferring to communicate through Abedin. So, a phone call featuring both Hillary and Bill was a real rarity. But more important, the scapegoating tone and tenor revealed that the Clintons were either living on another planet or at least having emotional and intellectual difficulty coming to terms with the reality that only Hillary was culpable and only Hillary could turn things around.

Hillary's aides didn't need to wonder why her economic message wasn't breaking through. It wasn't rocket science. She hadn't told the truth to the public about her e-mails, and she was under federal investigation.

On the ground in Iowa, the e-mail scandal was hurting her ability to build a volunteer organization. "We're asking someone to give a bunch of their time. All they're hearing is how untrustworthy she is," said one campaign official. And it was death among actual caucus-goers. "We saw it in all the research. It was a slow burn. The caucus electorate, any primary electorate, is disproportionately watching cable news. And it was every day for six months."

Beyond giving caucus-goers pause and hampering her volunteer-recruitment efforts, the scandal appeared to tamp down the willingness of Hillary supporters across the country to lobby friends on Facebook and followers on Twitter. "There's a social cost to supporting Hillary," one of her aides said. The e-mail issue "made it weird and costly for people to be for her."

After the lecture, and knowing they were running into powerful headwinds, Hillary's team in Brooklyn resolved to come up with a new plan for focusing the press and the public on the substance of her agenda. The immediate result was a relatively well-received speech she gave at the Iowa Wing Ding Dinner on August 15. "Every time she had a chance to shine, she got some relief," said one aide who was closely watching the ups and downs of Hillary's standing with voters. The brief shining moment hardly knocked the e-mail story out of the news, but it calmed the former first couple—at least temporarily—and campaign aides continued to waver between patting themselves on the back for a job well done and tiptoeing around the gut feeling that nothing would change unless Hillary could be convinced to come out of her bunker.

Back in mid-March, right after the story broke, 50 percent of Americans saw Hillary as honest and trustworthy, according to a CNN/ORC poll. By May, a clear majority of 57 percent thought she was *not* honest and trustworthy. That number wouldn't drop through the summer, as Democratic primary voters continued to question her honesty in significant numbers.

"The press covered Donald Trump to the complete exclusion of the other twenty-seven dwarves in that stupid clown bus the Republicans have," one longtime Hillary pal said. "Her coverage was just as much, but it was only about one thing—the e-mails."

That dynamic played right into the hands of Sanders, who held himself out as an honest change agent and tweaked Hillary here and there on her lack of transparency—a theme that hinted at the e-mail scandal, questions about the Clinton Foundation, and her refusal to release transcripts of the private paid speeches she'd given to Wall Street banks before the campaign. When Hillary had been advised by some allies not to speak to banks before the campaign, one confidant said, her response had been "They'll hit us on something."

The e-mail story and the Wall Street speeches illustrated the contrast Bernie was trying to draw with Hillary—he was honest and she was corrupt—and they were giving ever more oxygen to a once-quixotic Sanders campaign.

Donors and allies furiously e-mailed and called everyone they could on the campaign to urge Hillary to apologize—with real, earnest contrition—to get control of a campaign spinning wildly off the rails. But Hillary thought that was a losing strategy because it wouldn't end the saga. "I'll apologize," she said to her staff, "and then it'll keep going."

On August 22, Tanden reached out to Podesta with some advice and sharp insight into the electorate's double standards in dealing with Hillary. "Her inability to just do a national interview and communicate genuine feelings of remorse and regret is now, I fear, becoming a character problem (more so than honesty)," Tanden wrote. "People hate her arrogant, like her down. It's a sexist context, but I think it's the truth. I see no downside in her actually just saying, look, I'm sorry. I think it will take so much air out of this."

Tanden added a note on Hillary's obstinacy. "She always sees herself bending to 'their' will when she hands over information, etc. But the way she has to bend here is in the remorse. . . . A real feeling of—this decision I made created a mess and I'm sorry I did that."

As Hillary and her aides would soon find out, not even that kind of measured apology would do the trick. In the meantime, Podesta responded to Tanden, telling her that he and Palmieri were working on Hillary, trying to get her to move in the direction of an apology. Tanden suggested that Chelsea Clinton might be able to influence her mother. But in a series of conversations, it was clear that no one wanted to be the heavy, and there was no one person, alone, who could change her course. Bill was her most powerful adviser, and he didn't like the idea of an apology any more than she did.

THE DEATH MARCH of the server summer took a deep toll on the denizens of Hillaryland. By late August, more than four months into the campaign, the Brooklyn stronghold felt more like the Tower of London than a presidential campaign office.

Eleven stories above Brooklyn Heights in a 659,000-square-foot building that also housed Morgan Stanley and the United States Attorney's Office for the Eastern District of New York, Hillary's top aides were as miserable as midlevel bureaucrats in an agency with no clear plans for how to attain its mission. They were disconcerted by Hillary's detachment from them and from the reality of her situation. Joel Benenson, a veteran of Obama's campaigns, was the most vocal malcontent, and, accordingly, the Clintons were growing ever more annoyed with the chief strategist. He shouldered most of their blame for the campaign's inability to crack through the e-mail story with her economic message. He also had failed to anticipate Sanders's rise, and his instincts on how to deal with the Vermont senator—ignore him—were at odds with the Clintonian urge to eliminate any threat, no matter how small.

For his part, Benenson acted as though everyone else, including the Clintons, had something to prove to him, not the other way around. He was "condescending, dismissive, nasty" to everyone, including the Clintons, one colleague said. "He doesn't mean to be an asshole." Only a few years younger than the Clintons, his aggressive self-confidence and the gray patches in his beard betrayed his otherness on a campaign full of ambitious aides who carefully cultivated their positions in Clintonworld. His frustrations were legion and he seldom held them back. In a permanently paranoid state, Bill and Hillary became convinced that he was a source of leaks to the press, and whether there was a direct line of communication or just coincidental thinking, his criticism of his boss was echoed by David

Axelrod's public commentary on Hillary and her campaign. This was exactly the kind of behavior that they perceived as perniciously disloyal, and it infuriated them.

The most important hallmark of a winning campaign—unity forged by success—was absent. There had been little to cheer about during a summer dominated by the e-mail scandal. The week in April that Hillary announced, a CNN/ORC poll showed her with a 69 percent to 5 percent lead over Bernie Sanders. In a survey taken from September 4 to September 8, that lead had narrowed to 37 percent for Hillary to 27 percent for Bernie. Other pollsters pegged her lead at closer to twenty percentage points, but she was perilously below the 50 percent threshold in every test of Democratic opinion.

Hillary's slide in Iowa and New Hampshire matched the ground she'd lost at the national level. Sanders took his first lead in Iowa in early September—by a single point in one poll and by ten points in another—at which time he'd already vaulted ahead of her in New Hampshire. Hillary needed a fundamental course correction, and nothing her team had tried by the Labor Day weekend had worked.

When voters were asked to describe her with a single word, "liar" was the one most frequently used. A lot of that came from Republicans, but it had a psychic effect on Democrats who had looked at her as the party's likely nominee.

Over the course of the summer, the confidence of party insiders had been replaced by a degree of paranoia that nearly matched Hillary's own outsize phobia. She was convinced that leaks of information had helped doom her 2008 campaign. In reality, the leaking and disloyalty were symptoms, not the cause, of the dysfunction in her first run for the White House. As long as she was seen as the prohibitive favorite to win the primary and the election, Democrats would fear being branded traitors or leakers. But if she wasn't going to be in a position to reward or punish them, they had no reason to worry about whether they were rated as ones or sevens on her loyalty scale. After the 2008 campaign, two of her aides, Kris Balderston and Adrienne Elrod, had toiled to assign loyalty scores to members of Congress, ranging from one for the most loyal to seven for those who had committed the most egregious acts of treachery. Bill Clinton had campaigned against some of the sevens in subsequent primary elections, helping to knock them out of office. The fear of retribution was not lost on the remaining sevens, some of whom rushed to endorse Hillary early in the 2016 cycle.

This time, nothing was coming easy: her campaign was under fire every minute of every day. Worst of all, it was the candidate herself who was responsible for the initial e-mail blunder, and she and her husband were still intractable on the question of when she would apologize, if ever.

While all of Hillary's top advisers thought she should go out and apologize, whether she'd done anything wrong or not, Bill had a much different take. If she were to say anything, he thought that it should be to explain her thinking—to "turn in" to the story. She should explain to people why she did it, he told allies, and why she didn't see anything wrong with it. If everything went right, that would give her the benefit of coming out of hiding on the subject and at the same time expose her to no more legal jeopardy than she was already in.

For months, Hillary said privately what she argued publicly: she was allowed to structure her e-mail the way that she did. Whatever advice her campaign aides gave her, it was clear to them that she was getting conflicting counsel from the lawyers assigned to make sure that she didn't create problems for herself while the FBI was investigating whether any crimes had been committed with regard to the handling of classified information. But now the political problem was more acute than the legal quandary. Besides, as the *New York Times* would later report, she started getting pressure from her friends on a vacation in the Hamptons in late August.

Meanwhile, her aides continued to work feverishly on a communications plan that would address Hillary and Bill's concerns about pivoting to her agenda without forcing her to say "I'm sorry."

On August 26, during a visit to Iowa, Hillary went further than she had before in placing the blame on her own shoulders.

"It clearly wasn't the best choice. I should've used two emails—one personal, one for work," she said. "I take responsibility for that decision, and I want to be as transparent as possible, which is why I turned over 55,000 pages, why I've turned over my server, why I've agreed to—in fact, been asking to and have finally gotten a date to—testify before a congressional committee in October."

It was an incremental move in the right direction, but Hillary was still far from a place of real contrition. Podesta worked on both Clintons, and one source close to Bill said he was influential in moving the former president from the no camp to the yes camp. Without Bill reinforcing Hillary's instincts, she was isolated and began to relent. Finally, in late August or early September, she told her staff what they'd been waiting to hear all summer.

"Okay," she said. "I'll think about it."

That meant she'd do it—if in her own way. She tried in an interview with NBC's Andrea Mitchell on September 4 and fell a little short of the mark. Hillary said she was "sorry" for the confusion over her e-mail but didn't actually apologize for the decision to exclusively use a private account connected to a private server. Her aides exulted in having won the concession from her, but the press was unimpressed. Tanden observed that it was a good performance, particularly if a more full apology was in the offing.

"Apologies are like her Achilles heel," Tanden noted. "But she didn't seem like a bitch in the interview. And she said the word sorry. She will get to a full apology in a few interviews."

Four days later, in an interview with ABC's David Muir, Hillary gave her team, the Democratic Party, and the press what they desperately wanted—full contrition for the decision she'd made in the first place. That having done so at the beginning might have saved her five months of political free fall didn't seem to register.

"I should've used two accounts," she told Muir. "That was a mistake. I'm sorry about that. I take responsibility."

Hillary had been prescient about external threats to her campaign. She'd courted Democratic influencers and donors assiduously, turned President Barack Obama into an unflinching ally, and hired the top available talent to run her campaign at all levels. She'd even seen Sanders and Biden as legitimate rivals for the nomination. But when it came to her own behavior—to the threat she posed to herself—she'd been incapable of gauging its gravity and reluctant to avail herself of the only option for fixing it. Too little, too late, she'd now tried to address it.

The reaction inside her campaign and across the Democratic universe was the same: *finally*. Hillary's apology, though, was anything but the final word on her e-mail.

Chapter 5

THE BIDEN THREAT

JOE BIDEN WAS SICKENED BY WHAT HE SAW AND HEARD: images of his career and the sound of his voice narrating the story of the 1972 car crash that killed his first wife and their daughter, and from which his two sons barely escaped with their lives. The early October ad, slickly produced by allies trying to draft him into the race, appeared to be designed to elicit the kind of public sympathy that eluded Hillary.

It created a different feeling in Biden. Though he sometimes cited his personal history in preaching perseverance to others, he was disgusted by his supporters' attempt to use it as a political ploy.

Biden found it "jarring and distasteful," said one longtime ally. "For the family, it was both a political wake-up call, as well as a personal wake-up call." Political in that Biden concluded the spot was so tone-deaf, so blatantly manipulative, that he couldn't trust there was top-notch talent available to guide him through a presidential run. Personal because he and his family couldn't stomach spending months—perhaps more than a year—surrounded by that fatal crash and the brain cancer that had killed his son Beau at the end of May.

"That's not what defines us," Biden told his kitchen cabinet of advisers. "We're not going to run a campaign about tragedy."

For months, years really, Biden wrestled with the question of whether he should, as some vice presidents had, seek to succeed his boss in the Oval Office. He was annoyed that the media focused so much attention on Hillary and her second bid for the presidency when he was sitting in plain sight in the White House. He was also being overlooked by the president whom he had faithfully served for eight years, a painful if silent rebuke. Obama and his aides refused to take sides publicly, and some still had no appetite to help Hillary. But few thought Biden, who would turn seventy-four the month of the 2016 election, was the right person to represent Democrats in the campaign.

Biden knew that if he wanted to run, he couldn't drop out of the national political discussion. Even if he didn't end up in the race, backing out early would diminish his relevance at the White House and in politics. As months ripped off the calendar, he remained unsure.

Inside the Clinton camp, though, the threat of a Biden campaign was a mounting concern. "We became pretty well persuaded in August, maybe in late July, but certainly in August heading into September that this was within contemplation," one of Clinton's top aides said. "And that he was coming closer and closer to doing it."

Clinton and her aides worried that Biden would occupy the same lane—building on Obama—and that their substantive policy differences would be so small that their battle would turn on personality, which could be excruciating for both of them. Biden was well liked and Clinton was mired in disapproval of her character, which would only be exacerbated by a nasty personal fight. That could damage her chances in the general election, even if she was able to defeat the vice president in the primary. Biden's penchant for saying impolitic things would be an area ripe for exploitation for the Clinton team. He, and his legacy, would suffer. While they fought over who had the better style, Sanders would float above the mudslinging by continuing to focus on issues. "It's ticky-tack shit that would just not be good and then they would grate on each other and then it would be a downward spiral," the Clinton aide said.

From the outset, the vice president saw immense challenges to mounting a campaign against Clinton. His concerns, expressed to a relatively small circle of longtime advisers, centered on a few basic constraints.

First, he would have trouble collecting cash, not just because so many top Democrats had already committed to Hillary but because fund-raising had always been a problem for him. Second, it would be hard for him to recruit talent against the front-running Clinton because she had locked up most of the party's top-flight political operatives. Tony Blinken, Biden's longtime aide on Capitol Hill and in the White House, and his wife, Evan Ryan, a State Department official under Hillary, had donated to Clinton over the summer. When Politico published a story on August 14, 2015, outlining how the Biden strategy was taking shape, it noted that Ron Klain, who had served for a time as the vice president's chief of staff, was already hard at work preparing Hillary for her first debates with Sanders and former Maryland governor Martin O'Malley. Podesta, who clearly thought Klain was talking, was furious. He shot Klain an e-mail demanding a chat the next morning.

The story "has people really buzzed up," complained Podesta, who had told others on the campaign that Klain could be trusted. "I must say I feel a little like the Al Pacino character in Donnie Brasco."

Klain didn't like having his loyalty impeached—nor his ability to keep his work for Hillary confidential—especially while he was working around the clock to help her. He replied in pointed fashion to Podesta.

"If you want to fire me now before I do my fourth all nighter this week on HRC's debate book I'm happy to be ousted now," Klain wrote.

Podesta forwarded the chain to Palmieri, asking if he'd been too harsh and noting that he felt burned for having vouched for Klain internally.

"Yes," Palmieri replied, it was harsh. "But we are not f'ing around."

The obsession over loyalty signaled just how much pressure Hillary's team was under at a time when she should have been cruising toward an easy nomination. Sanders was gaining ground; Biden, who could steal from her bases of moderate white Democrats and African Americans, was looking at getting in; and she couldn't buy a day free from her suffocating e-mail scandal.

Biden referred to Klain and others who were siding with Hillary as folks who "used to be" with him but were "not on the team" anymore. Klain would later tell Podesta that it was hard for him to "play such a role in the Biden demise" and that he was "definitely dead to them."

In addition to the trouble he had keeping his own camp together, Biden wasn't positioned to inherit the president's political operation. Two of Obama's top aides, Podesta and Palmieri, had joined up with Clinton out of the gate. Many former Obama campaign and White House staffers had fanned out across the country, determined to stay out of politics as much as possible for a while, although some of them advised Hillary's team informally. At best, Biden could hope to summon parts of a splintered Obama circle. And many of the president's donors had already signed up with Hillary.

To top it all off, Biden hadn't run a competitive race since 1972, when he unseated Cale Boggs, the Republican senator, winning 50 percent to 49 percent. Having run unsuccessfully for president twice before, Biden wasn't dissuaded by the thought of defeat—at least that's what he told his advisers and friends. "I'm not afraid of losing," Biden would say to anyone who would listen. "I'm comfortable with losing. I'm not comfortable with getting blown out." The fear was that he would embarrass himself and tarnish the legacy he'd built over thirty-six years in the Senate and two terms as Obama's vice president. And, like Hillary, Biden worried about "what he would have to do to her and what she would have done to him," one of his advisers remarked.

Still, there were a few compelling reasons for Biden to run, including one very personal cause, and they pulled him toward the race as much as the prospect of humiliation repelled him. For some time, the Biden clan had been focused on the future of Biden's eldest son—first his political career and then his mortality. Beau Biden was in his first term as attorney general of Delaware when he suffered a medical episode described as a "mild stroke" in 2010. Three years later, he was admitted to a hospital in Texas and diagnosed with brain cancer. If Beau had not fallen ill, Joe would not have contemplated running for president in 2016, said those close to him.

"The whole family was organized around Beau," said one person close to the vice president. "That was the future."

The elder Biden didn't want to interfere with his son's political ascent and worried that his own presidential bid would make it harder for Beau to win statewide office in Delaware (they would have been on the ballot at the same time if Joe ran for president and Beau ran for governor in 2016).

It was reported that just before he died, with his face partially paralyzed and his mind often unable to find the right words, Beau pushed his dad to make one final run for the Oval Office. The episode renewed Biden's focus on the question of whether he would run.

Biden gave himself about a two-month window, from Labor Day until the end of October, to assess his chances and his desire to run. In early September he invited Robert Wolf, a familiar face on business news channels and a heavy-hitting early Obama donor, to the White House for a one-on-one meeting. The vice president explained that he saw himself as the right person to secure Obama's achievements on health care, Wall Street regulation, and protecting the children of undocumented immigrants from deportation. He also wanted to know whether Wolf, a bellwether for Obama donors and Democratic Wall Street financiers, was open to backing him if he ran against Hillary. But Wolf, from his own conversations with the president, knew Obama supported Hillary for the job. Wolf said he planned to back her. Biden asked him to reconsider—or at least keep his powder dry. Wolf left the meeting thinking Biden's head was in the race, but his heart was not yet there.

The meeting set off alarm bells in Brooklyn. Podesta had heard Wolf was "cranky" and went to see the Wall Street titan. It turned out that Wolf wanted to be included in the campaign—not just as a donor but as a resource on policy. He longed for a personal relationship with Hillary and worried that, as an original Obama supporter, he'd be overshadowed by finance industry players who had been with Hillary longer. Podesta thought a Wolf endorsement of Biden would be taken by the political class as a sign of the president's allegiance to the vice president. And, as Podesta told Hillary, "Biden is courting him hard."

In late September, after Wolf canceled a meeting with Hillary because he was moving apartments, Hillary asked Podesta if the situation was urgent enough for her to make a point of calling Wolf before their rescheduled meeting. "I am pretty sure he wouldn't jump but taking a minute to say [you] look fo[r]ward to seeing him would be a nice touch," Podesta replied. Wolf, he said, was "solid, but not rock solid" and a direct line of communication to Hillary "would lock him down."

She met with Wolf after a fund-raiser at Jay-Z's 40/40 Club in New York on October 1. Hillary listened to his thoughts on financial regulatory reform and infrastructure spending. Then she told him he should contact her or her top staff at any time. That's what he'd been hoping to hear. Wolf was now securely in her column and happy to announce his support for her publicly. The timing, she thought, couldn't have been better.

For Biden, as for other Democrats who had considered running in 2016, Hillary's ability to co-opt the major institutions, political leaders, operatives, and financiers of the Democratic Party was deeply frustrating.

AS THE CALENDAR turned from September to October, anti-Clinton Democrats knew time was running out for the vice president to muscle his way into the race. While the summer of e-mail and Bernie's insurgency had given Democratic voters reasons to consider an alternative to Hillary, the establishment view was that Sanders would get destroyed in a general election. It might already be too late, Biden supporters worried. If he waited too long to make a decision, that, in and of itself, would be the decision.

Publicly, Hillary tried to project a lack of concern about Biden's deliberations. When journalists posed questions about it, she would repeat some version of the mantra that the vice president should "have the space and opportunity to decide what he wants to do."

But privately, her longtime friends and allies expressed the fear and angst over facing Biden that she had kept bottled up in public. "People tell me he's getting in. They're convinced. I don't know how he gets in without looking like he knocked over the only girl that's been viable in our entire lives," one trusted Hillary friend and confidant said at the time. "That's a big, bad thing to do, especially when they occupy the same space on the spectrum."

Hillary had always seen Biden as a serious threat to run. From the moment Barack Obama won reelection in 2012, the news media focused on her, and Biden was, at best, an afterthought. This disinterest allowed him to operate under the radar and without the pressure of being a candidate-in-waiting. But Hillary knew that Biden still harbored presidential ambitions. After all, he had run twice before and certainly saw himself as the person with the most logical claim to Obama's mantle.

For years, she'd pursued a strategy of previewing the contrasts she'd draw against him in hopes of dissuading him from entering the race. Her clear, dead aim was to box Biden out by locking up donors, endorsements, and advisers, and by showing him how difficult it would be for him to run to her left on domestic policy or to her right on foreign policy.

As early as 2013, Clinton criticized a Biden-driven budget deal that had permanently locked in Bush-era tax cuts for all but the wealthiest Americans. That agreement so angered Senate Democrats that Majority Leader Harry Reid told Obama that Biden wasn't allowed to be part of future budget negotiations. Hillary never mentioned Biden by name when she spoke about it, but it was clear she would try to wrap that deal around his neck, as a sign that he wasn't truly progressive on domestic policy, if he ever ran. And speaking to a private group in Atlanta that same year, Clinton made a point of distinguishing her support for the raid that killed Osama bin

Laden from Biden's opposition, according to the *Atlanta Journal-Constitution,* which had sources in the room.

"I know she's running for president now, because, toward the end, she was asked about the Osama bin Laden raid. She took twenty-five minutes to answer," Georgia state representative Tom Taylor, a Republican from Dunwoody, told the newspaper. "Without turning the knife too deeply, she put it to Biden."

She had even tried to turn a negative story line about her ties to the financial services industry into a liability for Biden. In 2001 Clinton voted for an industry-friendly overhaul of the nation's bankruptcy laws, and liberals, including Elizabeth Warren and Bernie Sanders, had made hay of it. Confronted about that vote on the campaign trail, Clinton passed it off on Biden. "When I got to the Senate, I wanted to see some changes so that alimony and child support would be protected, and so I negotiated those changes and then the people who had been handling the bill said, 'Well, if we take your changes, you have to support it,'" Clinton said. "That's the way the Senate works.

"And so I said, 'It's really important to me that we don't hurt women and children, so I will support it even though there are other things I don't like in it,'" Clinton continued. "And it was Vice President Biden, who was the senator from Delaware, and the Republican co-sponsor that I was talking with, so I said I'd support it even though I'd opposed it before."

The comment enraged Biden almost more than anything else Clinton had said during the time he was mulling whether or not to oppose her, according to one Biden source familiar with his thinking. "She's playing ugly," Biden told confidants. "If she thinks she's going to force me out of the race like this, she has another thing coming to her."

More than ever, after those comments in particular, Biden believed he was being muscled into a corner. He felt, with good reason, that he had earned the space to make a decision without being shit on by Clinton.

Running like an incumbent from the outset, Hillary had geared her whole campaign toward depriving any other Democrat of the institutional support necessary to mount a challenge, from donors to superdelegates. She wanted other Democrats to be afraid to run against her, or to support any would-be rivals. It had worked with most of the Democratic Party, but Biden wasn't going to be easily intimidated. The presidency he had been seeking for three decades was within his grasp, and he wanted to keep his options open as long as possible.

As the vice president's deliberations took on a more public role that summer and fall, a Clinton team that had been sleepwalking through the pre-primary season—preoccupied with the e-mail scandal rather than Sanders or Biden—snapped awake and kicked into anti-Biden overdrive. The vice president represented a DEF-CON 1 threat to Hillary's candidacy in a way that Sanders alone did not. The greatest danger Biden posed was his potential to strip away black Democrats in southern states and Latinos in the West from the strongholds Hillary was counting on. With Sanders firing up wild-eyed white liberals, independents, and millennials, Clinton couldn't afford to cede delegates in the Deep South or the West. And Biden, as Obama's vice president, might be able to make a credible case to African American and Latino voters that he was the true and rightful heir to Obama's legacy. Plus, Biden was relatively popular with working- and middle-class whites who had backed Clinton over Obama in 2008 but were now flocking to Sanders—and to Trump on the Republican side of the race.

Podesta's frustration grew steadily toward the end of the summer. In August he wasn't convinced Biden wouldn't run. By September 1, he told friends that he was hearing Biden had told labor leaders he would get in the race. By mid-September he and the rest of Hillary's senior team were having meetings about how the campaign would respond to a Biden bid, replete with discussion of the political ammunition Hillary would use to attack the vice president.

As the Clinton camp's assessment of Biden moved from guy-keeping-his-options-open to serious-threat-to-enter-and-shake-up-the-race, Mook and his lieutenants scrambled to set up operations in states that would vote after South Carolina's primary at the end of February. Prior to that, Mook had focused primarily on the first four contests on the calendar—Iowa, New Hampshire, Nevada, and South Carolina—and, within that set, heavily on Iowa. But a Biden candidacy would increase the likelihood of an extended fight for the nomination, and Mook suddenly needed to show a presence in states that Hillary had largely ignored. "The moment the campaign actually started doing stuff outside the first four states was when there was a serious possibility that Joe Biden was going to get into the race," one campaign aide acknowledged.

Biden might be able to win a three-way race. Even if he didn't, he was strong enough, along with Sanders, to possibly deny Hillary the delegates needed to win the nomination on the first ballot at the Democratic National Convention. At that point, anything could happen.

Chapter 6

MRS. OCTOBER

ONE EVENING IN EARLY SEPTEMBER 2015, ROBBY MOOK stopped in at a private home in the coastal paradise of Bolinas, California, for what promised to be a relaxing break from the frenetic pace of running a campaign operation a continent away in Brooklyn. Instead, he ran into a buzz saw in the form of Susie Tompkins Buell, a heavy-hitting donor and close friend of Hillary. As the fog of summer was still clearing, when few people paid close attention to politics, the *New York Times* had just published a story about a coming Clinton campaign strategy shift. Hillary would "show more humor and heart," the headline declared.

In the piece, Clinton's top aides—including Mook and Palmieri—admitted that there had been significant blunders made by the campaign, notably the months-long denial that there was a problem with her use of a private e-mail server. And that the American public perceived her as too robotic and aloof. But, they promised, the *real* Hillary would emerge following Labor Day weekend.

That Hillary, they claimed, was relatable to nearly anyone, downright funny, and didn't take herself too seriously. More than anything, they said, she was authentic. The image makeover was timed to preview Clinton's appearances on *The Ellen DeGeneres Show*, *The Tonight Show Starring Jimmy Fallon*, and countless other lighthearted programs where Clinton would dance the Nae Nae, reveal that she kept up with the Kardashians and *Homeland,* and ask hosts to playfully tug on her hair.

Buell was displeased. By announcing a *strategy* to make Hillary seem more real, her team had actually achieved the opposite effect. Clinton supporters across the country read it the same way. It was a pure what-the-fuck moment—a major unforced error that buttressed qualms about Hillary's honesty and trustworthiness at a terrible time. Buell, channeling the collective outrage of the pro-Clinton forces, scolded Mook.

"Why would you say something like that?" Buell demanded. "There's nothing more disingenuous than having the campaign quoted within the article."

Mook didn't have a good explanation because there was no good explanation. Instead, he defended himself by assuring her that the campaign's data looked strong. To Buell, the precocious campaign manager was frustratingly left-brained. *You get so lost chasing the numbers,* she thought. *They're like your gauge. You're distracted from your emotions. You just get driven to increase numbers.* The campaign's inability to reveal Hillary's authenticity—and its ham-fisted effort to manufacture a false version of it—was infuriating. The Hillary Buell knew, foulmouthed and fun, didn't need a bunch of political operatives inventing a more genuine persona for her. She needed them to help her drop the armor built up over decades that shielded her most human traits.

Trying to placate Buell, Mook offered up Palmieri as a sacrifice. The large, domineering communications team was pretty much a separate shop within the operation, he campaign-splained. Palmieri and her staff had leaned too far over their skis because they were trying to rush away from the ugly summer of e-mail and focus the media on the entertainment-show tour they'd planned for Hillary. It was clear that in telegraphing the Hillary charm offensive, they had patted themselves on the back at the expense of the candidate's already damaged credibility. The campaign looked hapless.

"That's what worried people," said one Clinton backer familiar with Hillary's contributor network. "That pissed more donors off."

Buell was hardly alone in questioning the competence of the campaign. Calls, text messages, and e-mails from a number of Hillary allies bombarded the staff in the wake of the article.

"An inauthentic strategy to make her look authentic is absurd," fumed longtime Clinton ally Brent Budowsky.

One prominent Obama donor decried a campaign "being run by amateurs," and couldn't believe it would help manufacture a story about its efforts to alter the candidate's persona to make her seem more authentic. "It was a joke."

The campaign needed to contain the fallout from the story—and fast. Mook and Podesta tried to assuage angry donors across the country, and it was soon evident to staffers that they had hurt Hillary not just with her adversaries but with her most faithful supporters. They would later say they had participated in the story only after a reporter had caught wind of a shift in communications strategy.

Still, her campaign looked like the gang that couldn't shoot straight. Under the gun to stall Sanders's momentum and convince Biden that there was no path for him to win the nomination, Hillary was instead reinforcing the idea that her rivals were more genuine characters.

The e-mail scandal had buried her already-weak message and convinced the majority of Americans that she was a liar who couldn't be trusted. She had known from the start that her reentry into the political space would cost her the stratospheric approval she'd enjoyed as secretary of state. But like frogs who don't notice the water around them coming to a boil, Hillary and Bill took too long to appreciate just how much the e-mail scandal—and the candidate's refusal to simply apologize up front—was poaching her image.

Her long evolution to a more comprehensive "sorry," punctuated in the interview with David Muir in September, helped stop the bleeding. But she needed to do more than just cauterize the wound, because the threat to her seemingly inevitable nomination was rising. Sanders was starting to catch fire in Iowa and with the liberal white millennials who had replaced the intelligentsia as influencers in the virtual world. Biden was also looming.

But in the seeds of the campaign's most recent screwup lay the answer to her temporary salvation. Despite the tactical malpractice of rolling out the effort to humanize Hillary in such a clumsy fashion in the *New York Times,* the strategy of putting her on camera in more whimsical and humorous settings was a sound one. In early October, it provided her high beams and a GPS with which to find the road back to a position of strength.

As she would time and again throughout the campaign, Hillary found her way by going home to New York. Her appearance on the season premiere of *Saturday Night Live* on October 3 had been discussed at a very low level for months. It all came together in a whirl just when Hillary most needed a moment of levity to free herself from the drudgery of a campaign that had been weighted down by e-mails.

Luck, in this case, was the residue of design. The show's producers had one big question that week as they wrote Clinton into the script: "Is there anything she won't do?"

"No," Kristina Schake, Hillary's deputy communications director, replied.

Hillary told her aides that she was open to the writers' vision for a skit. The idea was to show how she could roll with the punches; a tightly controlled segment wouldn't serve that end. Let's see what they come up with, she said to Schake. "They're the comic geniuses."

The day before Clinton was set to appear on the show, she campaigned in South Florida and filled her coffers with a trio of fund-raisers there. At the same time, she and Schake reviewed the concept the *Saturday Night Live* writers had sketched out.

"So, you'll play a waitress," Schake told Clinton, a woman whose every need had been catered to over the past quarter of a century. Clinton liked the idea. "That sounds really funny," she said.

Twenty-four hours before she would appear on the show, Clinton showed up at a Marc Anthony concert in downtown Miami, trying to make inroads with young Latino voters. Around 1 a.m. she flew back to Washington in time to appear at a Human Rights Campaign breakfast on Saturday morning. Some comedy prep was necessary to ensure she wouldn't bomb, but the HRC breakfast wasn't something Clinton could put on the back burner. The most recognizable LGBT rights advocacy organization in the nation had the potential to be an important part of Clinton's coalition or a bulwark against her. She had implemented new policies at the State Department, in accordance with the White House's wishes, that extended same-sex-partner benefits to bureaucrats overseas and had spoken eloquently on LGBT rights as human rights during her tenure in the Obama cabinet. But her late "evolution" to supporting gay marriage was a sticking point with younger members of the rank and file. It was a contrast point with Sanders and Biden.

The Human Rights Campaign had wanted her to be the featured speaker at its annual dinner that night, but she'd declined so that she could appear on *SNL*. Her stand-in at the dinner? None other than Joe Biden, who had stepped out in front of Obama during the 2012 campaign cycle to announce on *Meet the Press* that he favored same-sex marriage. Hillary was on a political edge, in danger of ceding part of her coalition to the vice president.

It wasn't until later that evening, standing in the show's greenroom on the eighth floor of the famed 30 Rock building, that Hillary finally practiced her role with a series of cue cards. Even as she read from the cards, the *SNL* writers were busy tweaking the lines. She had to practice several times, according to one person in the room, because her instinct was to interact with Kate McKinnon, the comedian who portrayed her, instead of robotically reading from the cue cards. For a candidate who was constantly being told she had to connect better with voters, the idea of glancing away from McKinnon to read her lines seemed to be a cheat.

She shook off the awkwardness, and, in the legendary Studio 8H, Hillary transformed from an overserved political animal to a steady-handed bartender, from someone struggling at all times to be heard, to someone who earns her keep by listening. McKinnon as Hillary, and Hillary as "Val" the bartender, joked about Hillary's late arrival on a variety of positions, including her opposition to the Keystone XL pipeline and support of gay marriage. The net result: viewers heard Clinton's current positions on the two issues and saw her poking fun at herself.

At one point, McKinnon's Clinton lamented the rise of Trump.

"Ah, Val, I'm just so darned bummed. All anyone wants to talk about is Donald Trump," she says.

The real Hillary played confused. But it was a moment she was prepared for. She'd been developing an impression of Trump since well before the *SNL* skit dropped in her lap, according to people close to her. And that portrayal was written in accordingly.

"Donald Trump? Isn't he the one that's like 'uh, you're all LOOOSUHS'?" the real Hillary intoned.

It's easy to assign too much meaning to a single *Saturday Night Live* performance. But Clinton's appearance garnered positive media attention, and it was the first rung in her ascent out of the depths of a six-month campaign funk. It got the media talking about something other than the stultifying e-mails. It also provided a psychic boost for Hillary, who had felt the crushing weight of the e-mail debacle, the threat of a Biden candidacy, the looming Benghazi hearing, Sanders's unexpectedly strong challenge, and the public judgment that she was dishonest. In that way, *Saturday Night Live* was the launch point for an October that proved to be the high point of 2015 for her.

Chatter about a Biden candidacy heated up the week after the Human Rights Campaign dinner and Clinton's *SNL* appearance, and anti-Biden opposition research began surfacing in the media. Almost every policy knock against Clinton was a knock against Biden too—and on some topics, he'd fare worse. Like Hillary, Biden was for the Iraq War before he was against it. And he was the Senate sponsor of the Clinton White House anticrime law that had led to the mass incarceration of young black men. In addition, he'd ushered Clarence Thomas onto the Supreme Court, spent the early part of his career in the Senate trying to end school busing, and represented perhaps the most business-friendly tax haven in the nation, Delaware, for thirty-six years. As a lawmaker and as an Obama administration negotiator in the Senate, he never seemed terribly uncomfortable giving up items on the liberal wish list to get deals done. That didn't make him a bad guy—the bargaining had enacted a wide range of Democratic-leaning policies—but it left him vulnerable to lines of attack that would dredge up closed chapters of his past and introduce them to new audiences.

Hillary, who had been reluctant to take a position on the controversial Trans-Pacific Partnership trade agreement, moved to box Biden in. Liberals hated Obama's proposed pact with Pacific Rim countries because they believed it would result in jobs being shipped overseas, the lowering of labor standards in the United States, or both. Bernie was dead-set against it and talked about his position frequently on the campaign trail. As secretary of state, Hillary had helped negotiate the deal, and that meant coming out against it would be complicated politics. But Biden was in an even tougher spot. The central theme of his prospective candidacy would be defending Obama's legacy. Could the sitting vice president campaign against such a major piece of the president's second-term agenda, even if it was unpopular with the Democratic base? Probably not, her aides thought. But Sullivan wanted her to embrace TPP on a national security basis—specifically that it would create powerful alliances between the United States and a number of countries in China's sphere of influence—and he thought she could avoid a flip-flop label by doing that.

Though Hillary was portrayed by opponents as an unrestrained free trader, her thinking was actually more nuanced than that. She heard Sullivan's view, understood it, and could even make the case he proposed without missing a beat. But she was concerned about the economic impacts on American workers. "She just felt like there weren't enough winners," explained one adviser who spoke to her about the decision. She also understood the political imperative to be on the right side of big labor.

On October 7, she announced that she opposed the deal in typical Hillary fashion—with caveats and a lot of wiggle room. "As of today, I am not in favor of what I have learned about it," she told Judy Woodruff of PBS. "I don't believe it's going to meet the high bar I have set." She was conflicted enough about it that she didn't come out so forcefully as to convince union leaders or voters that she would kill it. Instead, she looked like she was pandering to them—and not well. Still, she was staking out important ground in advance of a possible Biden entry into the race.

By the second week of October, the net Hillary had thrown around Biden had started to tighten uncomfortably. He stopped consulting with a larger circle of advisers and cut down to just a small handful of his most trusted confidants, including his son Hunter. It was becoming increasingly difficult to find Democratic operatives or donors who could be counted on not to intentionally or unintentionally relay information about Biden's plans to Clintonworld. The truth confronting Biden and his advisers was that, between Hillary's strategy for boxing out other Democrats and Biden's indecision, they simply hadn't built a strong enough foundation to mount a successful run—and now it was virtually impossible to construct a battleworthy campaign machine. Biden had asked some national money bundlers and political allies in early states to be at the ready, but he hadn't put together anything close to the scale of the political operation Clinton had already built. He would have to pry Democratic donors, staff, and superdelegates away from a Clinton campaign that could credibly argue at the time that it would be political suicide to leave her for Biden. As much as the Clinton team worried about Biden, Biden rightly worried that he could go down in flames. It was the kind of thing that only the voters could sort out, and the risks of having to relive the tragic losses of his first wife and two of his children and of tarnishing his own legacy were big obstacles to overcome.

Still, as two of the most portentous moments of 2015 drew

close on the calendar—the first Democratic debate and Clinton's testimony before the House Select Committee on Benghazi—Biden hadn't made a final decision. It appeared that he was waiting to see how Clinton performed in the spotlight.

AS BIDEN PLAYED Hamlet in the VP's office, Hillary rehearsed for her first big political performance of the season—the opening Democratic debate. Unlike Hillary, Bernie had no experience debating at the presidential level. But he did have positions that more neatly fit the activist-heavy Democratic primary electorate. Bernie would portray her as out of touch with progressive values. Hillary thought he was out of touch with the realities of governance. It frustrated her no end that Bernie would promise the moon without offering a plan to get there.

Raising the minimum wage and college-tuition assistance were prime examples of Sanders's digging in at an outpost on the left and making Hillary look cautious, conservative, and very much a creature of the establishment. Every time she said she wanted to increase the federal minimum wage to $12 an hour—the main proposal from Senate Democrats—Bernie said he'd settle for no less than "fifteen bucks." When she said she wanted students to emerge from college without debt, Bernie reminded voters that his plan would let them attend for free. Hillary's advisers thought it was reminiscent of the scene from *There's Something About Mary* in which a crazed hitchhiker tells Ben Stiller's character that he can make a fortune by turning "eight-minute abs" into "seven-minute abs."

"She's seven-minute abs," said one of her advisers. "This guy's fucking four-minute abs."

The other issue that weighed heavily on Clinton's mind before the debate was that she couldn't go negative on Bernie. He could bore into her on the debate stage, but she couldn't risk fighting back too hard against the well-liked underdog. Sanders had a patina of purity and, from the Clinton campaign's perspective, was getting an even easier ride from the media than Obama had in 2008. Bernie could leverage that purity to attack her more aggressively. Sanders knew there was a risk to his brand, but he was ever more willing to take it as he climbed in the polls and saw a chance to win the nomination. Where Obama had made subtle character contrasts with Clinton, Sanders was leaning even harder into the public's belief that she was dishonest, implying that she was bought and paid for by donors on Wall Street and in the fossil fuel industry. The combination of an edge on pure liberalism and driving at character issues had helped Sanders surge. In national polling he had cut a fifty-point Clinton lead to about twenty points. In a couple of polls conducted in Iowa in late August and early September, he actually passed her before she managed to rebound.

As Hillary went round and round with her debate-prep partners at the Doral Arrowwood Hotel in Westchester, New York, she and her team sought to answer the question of how she could beat him on policy. The simple solution would have been to move to his left, but Hillary couldn't afford to flip-flop all over the debate stage, and she didn't want to trap herself into liberal positions that would be hard to defend in the general election. Instead, she went back to a tactic familiar to anyone who followed the 2008 Democratic primary. She would try to blunt Sanders's attacks by saying they were both progressives—and then pivot by asserting that she could actually enact her plans.

She had tried unsuccessfully to do this to Obama. The calculation now was that it would work better against Sanders, who was plainly more liberal than the president. She hoped the framework would appeal to voters who weren't quite sure Sanders could effect the changes he promised on the campaign trail.

Then, a few days before the debate, Sanders handed Hillary a gift. During an appearance on NBC's *Meet the Press,* Sanders was asked whether he was a capitalist.

"No," Sanders replied. "I'm a Democratic socialist."

Checkmate. Bernie had just anchored himself to a position so far to the left on such an elemental question of political philosophy that she wouldn't have to do much heavy lifting to portray him as too far on the fringe. Hillary believed the Democratic Party—the one she knew—would never nominate someone who publicly rejected capitalism and embraced socialism. In her establishment-aligned mind, capitalism was the force that drove entrepreneurs and small businesses, a sector of the economy that many Democrats could identify with much more easily than the financial services industry that Sanders tied her to with great effect. She knew instantly that it would be a topic of conversation in the debate, and she believed she could score points on it. Fortune was turning in her direction, if ever so slightly.

But there was one line of attack that former Maryland governor and long-shot candidate Martin O'Malley had pursued that had the Clinton team worried, particularly with the prospect of both of her legitimate rivals pounding her on it (former Virginia senator Jim Webb and former Rhode Island governor Lincoln Chafee would also be on stage for the debate but would not factor into the race). O'Malley had been hitting Clinton hard on her e-mail scandal, not on the substance of it but rather on how enduring it had become. The basic case he made, again and again, was that it was such a distraction that it prevented Democrats from making a positive case about their agenda for the American people. It had certainly sidetracked Hillary, and the other candidates were having trouble breaking through too. It was a powerful attack because it was true.

Hillary drew two conclusions: she would be asked about the e-mails first and O'Malley would go harshly negative on the scandal. Her fear was that Sanders would be able to slide in between and talk about the real issues confronting the American public, rising above a petty fight between O'Malley and Clinton. He could win the exchange that way.

Her aides believed she needed to take control of the issue quickly by making the argument that there were more important issues than the e-mails. "We wanted to get her there first," one aide said. "Her getting there first neutralizes the whole deal."

In her final prep session, on the day of the debate, Clinton was reflective. Hillary could sense that her tuner was off, and that

gnawed at her. "I'm really trying to put my finger on what the electorate, the Democratic primary electorate, the broader electorate is
thinking and feeling right now," she told an adviser. "What is the
appeal of a Sanders and what are their concerns about me?"

She wanted to know how she should calibrate in terms of the
Obama legacy, whether Democrats wanted to build on it or make
more dramatic changes. Sanders's success was evidence that some
preferred the latter, but how many? It wasn't clear, but she and her
team believed that most Democrats thought Obama was on the
right track. Here she was, six months into her campaign, having
traveled the country, and she still didn't quite grasp the underlying
sentiments of the electorate. Sanders had tapped into feelings that
she couldn't access.

WHEN CLINTON SEQUESTERED herself with a small retinue of
staff in a trailer outside the Wynn Las Vegas before that first debate
on October 13, 2015, she was in a somber mood. She said nothing as she walked into the arena, flanked by a Praetorian Guard of
Podesta, Sullivan, debate coaches Ron Klain and Karen Dunn, Secret Service officers, and television producers. The silence was unsettling. Bernie was coming on strong, and this would be his first
chance to prove that he was a real contender for the nomination.
It was time for her to fight for her political life—for her values and
her ambitions—and she didn't seem like she was in the right frame
of mind for a scrap.

She's going to be too subdued, Sullivan thought.

Bernie, the underdog with the wind at his back and a rare gift
for electrifying the party base, would bring his energy and charisma
into the arena. But would Hillary muster the acuity to execute her
game plan?

Sullivan needn't have worried. Her outward calm, at a time
when pulses raced on both sides of the Clinton-Sanders divide,
betrayed nothing of the powerful, low-humming debate machine
that was being brought to a purr inside. In the opening minutes,

she turned the question of her level of commitment to progressive values into a weapon. "I'm a progressive," she said, pausing for a beat to set up an implicit criticism of Sanders. "But I'm a progressive who likes to get things done." Sanders walked right into a trap when he was asked about his embrace of socialism, bringing up the c-word—capitalism—that Hillary was waiting to hear.

"Well, we're gonna win because first, we're gonna explain what democratic socialism is," he said. "Do I consider myself part of the casino capitalist process by which so few have so much and so many have so little by which Wall Street's greed and recklessness wrecked this economy? No, I don't. I believe in a society where all people do well, not just a handful of billionaires." Bernie was offering a window into his desire to sell a brand-new system of governance unlike the American experience.

"I love Denmark," Hillary mocked lightly. "We are the United States of America." Rein in capitalist excesses, she said, but it would be a "grave mistake to turn our backs on what built the greatest middle class" in the world. She had hugged America and turned Bernie into an exotic European elitist. Good for the primary, better for the general.

Not only would he fail to recover, but he quickly wandered into a bigger trap set by a combination of Clinton's student-like preparation and a generous helping of his own bad luck. As she had hoped, Hillary got the first crack at a question about her e-mails— President Obama had just called it a "legitimate issue," Anderson Cooper reminded—and she mentally plucked the right page from her playbook.

"Tonight, I want to talk not about my e-mails, but about what the American people want from the next president of the United States," she said, stealing what she thought would be Sanders's approach.

"Let me say—let me say something that may not be great politics," he said. "But I think the secretary is right, and that is that the American people are sick and tired of hearing about your damn e-mails."

Hillary didn't give him a chance to finish his thought. She moved toward him, clasped his hand, and, barely containing her glee, said: "Thank you! Me, too. Me, too." The audience roared its approval.

While his advisers had pushed him to seize on the e-mail controversy in the lead-up to the debate and the practice sessions at his hotel in Henderson, Nevada, Sanders told them he would not. "I'm not going to attack her," he told them. "I'm going to talk about the issues. It's not an issue as far as I'm concerned." And when Clinton tried to close the door on the scandal as a primary campaign issue, Sanders put a lock on it. While his senior aides were at odds with the candidate on the approach, it satisfied them. "We had the sound bite, he won," one of the advisers said. "It wasn't the greatest argument in the world but at least it was an argument."

It would also be the most potent moment of the debate for Hillary, one the cable networks played repeatedly in the highlights of the matchup. She had been struggling to get the electorate to look past the e-mail issue and move on. But with her opponent's help, it seemed like she might finally get the oxygen she needed to talk about policy, the only thing she ever felt comfortable discussing in elections.

Bernie would later note that there was still an ongoing investigation, but, as Clinton and her team had hoped, the anchor weighing down her campaign had been lifted, at least for a little while, within the confines of the Democratic primary.

Afterward, Clinton was, as usual, unsure of her own performance. How had she handled the big moments? What did it look like to viewers? Had she made her points effectively?

"What do you guys think?" she asked as she caught up with her top aides backstage. "How did I do?"

They knew she had cleaned Bernie's clock. "You killed it," one of them responded.

"Really?" she asked.

Really, she was assured.

But if Hillary was the candidate who won the debate, Bernie wasn't the one who lost it. That was Joe Biden. The reviews coming out of Clinton's debate debut were strong enough to make Biden's lane look much narrower than it had just a few hours earlier. That put Biden in a precarious position, caught with a very short moment in which to make an announcement and a resurgent rival. Hillary hadn't stumbled. She'd looked capable. Fewer Democrats were questioning whether she was a potential zombie candidate—one who was unstoppable in the primary but unelectable in the general. Bernie had even absolved her of the e-mail scandal. The day after the debate, in an interview with Andrea Mitchell on MSNBC, Podesta squeezed Biden further. "If Vice President Biden wants to enter and compete for the presidency," Podesta said, "then it is time he make that decision."

The window for Biden was closing, not opening. If he waited until after her upcoming Benghazi hearings, said one source with ties to both the Biden and Clinton worlds, it was "going to look like Benghazi was what caused him to get in." For a politician who would stake his candidacy on his authenticity, and who had delayed making a decision so his family could grieve his son's death, jumping into the race after Clinton was hauled before a partisan committee might smack of opportunism and undermine his narrative.

And the optics of waiting around for Clinton to fall, of perhaps pressuring her into a misstep, didn't sit well with many Democrats. Whatever they thought of Clinton's handling of the e-mail situation, Democrats were uniformly behind her on the larger question of whether she was to blame for the September 2012 attacks that killed four Americans, including Ambassador Chris Stevens, in Benghazi, Libya. Their support had been solidified a few weeks earlier, when House majority leader Kevin McCarthy made the inexplicably poor political decision to tie the Benghazi Committee's existence to Clinton's falling poll numbers.

"Everybody thought Hillary Clinton was unbeatable, right? But we put together a Benghazi special committee, a select committee. What are her numbers today? Her numbers are dropping," McCarthy had said in late September.

The remark was such an incredible gaffe—an outright affirmation that an entire congressional committee had spent millions of dollars politicizing the deaths of Americans to hurt her presidential hopes—that it factored heavily in the GOP's deciding not to elevate McCarthy to Speaker of the House after John Boehner retired.

"Between Kevin McCarthy and Bernie Sanders they bookended her on that, and may have just made it to where it would be really difficult to do anything," one Clinton ally said after the debate. "I think that may have shaken Biden."

Whatever effect it had, the die was cast. On October 21, the day before the Benghazi hearing, Biden went to the Rose Garden, with Obama and Second Lady Jill Biden at his side, to announce that he wouldn't seek the presidency. The collective sigh of relief from Clinton's Brooklyn headquarters was almost audible on the White House lawn.

At Rural Society, an Argentine restaurant across the street from the *Washington Post,* Jeff Weaver and Tad Devine from Sanders's team sat down at the bar to watch Biden speak. They had always believed it was better for them if Biden ran, because it would be easier to defeat Hillary in a three-way race than a head-to-head competition. And, they thought, Biden was more likely to take votes from Hillary than from Bernie. This had all the makings of a downer.

But halfway through the vice president's remarks, they realized the subtext of Biden's message. He was calling for free college for kids, railing against big-money donors, and promising to actively defend Obama's legacy against any candidate who challenged it, as Hillary had done at times.

Weaver and Devine were gleeful. Biden was validating Bernie's message as he bowed out, and, better yet, he wasn't going to run on it himself. It was also hard to miss the contrast with Hillary. Devine excitedly turned to Weaver. "That's our speech!" he exclaimed.

It was an amazingly partisan and anti-Clinton sentiment to express from the pulpit of American government, but it was Biden's political swan song for the 2016 election cycle. Hillary was grateful for that, if more than a little distracted by her impending rendez-vous with House Republicans.

TWO DAYS EARLIER, Hillary had summoned aides to Whitehaven for "murder boards"—the D.C. slang for prep sessions before a contentious congressional hearing. Philippe Reines, Brian Fallon, and a newcomer, former Obama White House aide Phil Schiliro, were among those who sat down with her around a dining room table that had become Hillary's Washington nerve center for major deliberations. They wanted her to watch her p's and q's from the witness table, but Hillary was in fighting mode after three years of investigations into her role in the Benghazi attacks.

I'm sick and tired of this, she thought from her seat at the head of the table. *This has been probed eight times. I'm going to stand up to these guys once and for all.*

"She clearly wanted to be one degree more than feisty," said one adviser who was in the room.

Her staff quickly realized that if they didn't talk her down, she might erupt on camera. They wanted her to think about rising above the committee. "It was the first and last piece of advice that everyone gave," said an aide who was there.

Over the course of three days of mock hearings, Hillary's aides and advisers peppered her with questions they thought the Republicans on the Benghazi Committee would ask. And they did it in ways intended to get under Hillary's skin. Reines, foreshadowing a later role on the campaign, played what he thought of as an amalgam of the "idiot contingent" on the committee. That included Georgia Republican Lynn Westmoreland, who liked to imply that the Benghazi deaths were the result of Hillary being asleep at the switch.

Bill Clinton, who had sided with Hillary's aides about the importance of her demeanor, wandered in and out during the prep sessions, laughing at Reines's version of a hillbilly congressman. Cheryl Mills and Jake Sullivan knew the committee's lines of inquiry well, as each of them had already testified before it. Hillary had started the murder boards with a strong grasp of US policy in Libya and the details of the terrorist attack there, but she still couldn't understand what one aide called "the pathologies" underlying the case that her handling of Benghazi should disqualify her from the presidency. For hours at a time, only pausing for lunch, they walked her through all the Republican narratives that had taken hold to date as well as "the fever dreams and the conspiracy stuff" that moved well beyond security issues at the Benghazi compound, the aide said. By the end of three days of drills and coaching, she'd lost her desire to punch back and just wanted to get through this trial by fire. Her team had succeeded in tempering her instinct to fight.

On the morning of the hearing, October 22, 2015, Hillary and nearly a dozen of her lawyers, advisers, and aides filed into a conference room in the suite controlled by the committee's Republicans to await the start of the proceedings. Amid bookshelves and a small kitchenette, both sides acknowledged the awkwardness of Hillary and her team discussing the investigation in the offices of a GOP committee that had spent the better part of two years probing her private communications. Republican Chairman Trey Gowdy's aides even offered to sweep the room for listening devices—an olive branch that was declined in exactly the self-consciously polite manner in which it was extended. The moment was more than awkward, though; it was drenched in tension.

For any presidential candidate, a campaign presents a series of high-stakes challenges. But testifying before a congressional panel for the better part of a day was unusual, to say the least. A Republican tribunal would have hours on end to try to take down the likely Democratic presidential nominee in a taxpayer-funded forum broadcast across the nation. Hillary would sit alone at the witness table, facing inquisitors on a dais, knowing that anything she said could and would be used against her in a political ad.

As the minutes before her testimony ticked away, Hillary's aides began to think their murder boards might have overdone the intensity with which the Republican members of the committee would come after her. That was the goal, to be so aggressive in the murder boards that the hearing seemed like a breeze for Hillary. But once the hearing began, they realized they had erred too much on the side of civility.

In his opening statement, Gowdy self-righteously beat his chest, telling the national audience that the investigation was about finding "the truth"—about the mission in Libya, requests for more personnel, and "why our military was positioned as it was on the anniversary of 9/11." Not that Hillary was responsible for the posture of the Defense Department as secretary of state. Then he addressed Hillary directly.

"Madam Secretary, I understand there are people—frankly in both parties—who have suggested that this investigation is about you. Let me assure you it is not. And let me assure you why it is not," he said, wrapping himself in the flag. "This investigation is about four people who were killed representing our country on foreign soil." He delivered with such dramatic intonation that he might as well have been Tom Cruise in the film *A Few Good Men* grilling Jack Nicholson about whether he'd ordered the "code red."

Gowdy and his colleagues truly seemed to believe they could produce a smoking gun that showed Hillary had demonstrated poor judgment, ineptitude, neglect, or malice. However, they clearly underestimated the possibility that *she* would be the one who would stay cool, stick to the facts, and make *them* look ridiculously partisan. And that was exactly what happened.

Long before lunchtime, the political press, the conservative intelligentsia, and the entirety of the Democratic universe had decided that Hillary was pulverizing her Republican interlocutors. Savvy Republicans tweeted that it was hard to watch their representatives in Congress failing to score points on Hillary, and Democrats delighted in pointing out just how crazy some of the lines of questioning were.

As Hillary concentrated more intently on ensuring that viewers could hear her side of the story, Republican lawmakers lost their focus. The more even Hillary's keel, the more they pushed to capsize her. Several of them insinuated that she cared more about her reputation than the lives of the four men who died. Alabama Republican Martha Roby may have taken the cake by demanding to know whether Hillary had spent the wee hours of the morning *alone* at home after she left the State Department on the night of the Benghazi attacks.

In the final hour of the nearly eleven-hour marathon hearing, just after 8:30 in the evening, Hillary broke into a coughing fit. She sipped a glass of water, but continued to cough. Gowdy asked if she'd like a sixty-second break to catch her breath. But in a scene made for Hollywood, Clinton said no. "Let me just grab," she said, clearing her throat, "a lozenge." After reaching for the cough drop and popping it in her mouth, she continued, powering through with a bit more rasp in her voice. Through it all, Hillary maintained her composure.

Even before the hearing had concluded, the media had drawn its conclusion: she'd whipped Gowdy and his crew of amateur interrogators. When Kansas representative Mike Pompeo had gotten into it with Clinton, the conservative writer John Podhoretz tweeted, "Why doesn't Pompeo just go over and swear her in for president now—if he goes on like this he'll practically get her elected."

The candidate herself felt like a championship boxer who had weathered a long but never-close bout against an inferior challenger. After walking back into the conference room in the GOP's committee headquarters, Hillary pantomimed her exhaustion. She slumped her shoulders and made the front of her body concave, drawing laughter from advisers who could also finally relax.

She hugged Sullivan, Mills, and Fallon. She dispatched Nick Merrill, the erstwhile traveling press secretary, to find out what Gowdy was telling reporters. Merrill reported back quickly: Gowdy had said he'd learned nothing new from the hearing. Republicans had inadvertently staged an eleven-hour infomercial testament to her competence, soundness of mind, compassion for the victims of the Benghazi attack, and serenity in a crisis. It was worse than a waste of time for congressional Republicans; it was the high-water mark of Hillary's campaign so far. She looked presidential in comparison to her adversaries.

And yet her best performance had come under the umbrella of a Benghazi investigation that naturally portrayed her as the defendant. Survival was a victory, but no other candidate had to endure the horrible optics of being hauled before a congressional committee to testify about the deaths of four Americans. Regardless of whether she outmaneuvered the Republicans on the committee, they had nothing to lose—and many voters were either incensed about her handling of Benghazi or exhausted by the cloud of scandal that seemed to follow her. It might be unfair, but the GOP could score points against her just by reminding voters that she was often under investigation.

After Merrill's report, the team huddled to discuss whether she should respond to what Gowdy had said. There was nothing more Hillary could gain. "You know what," Palmieri said, announcing a reprieve, "just go home."

With the Benghazi hearing behind her, Biden out of the race, and Bernie breathing down her neck, she'd need her reserves for the three-month sprint to the Iowa caucuses.

Chapter 7

"I WAS CERTAIN WE WERE GOING TO LOSE"

ILL CLINTON WAS PISSED OFF. HE HOLLERED AT JOHN
Podesta loud enough to be heard through the walls of the little
anteroom he'd laid claim to on the tenth floor of the historic
Savery Hotel in downtown Des Moines, Iowa. It was the goddamn pundits he was watching on TV. They were getting it all
wrong again as the results of the Iowa caucuses trickled in. Hillary
was leading, but it was going to be tight—"OH-EM-GEE!" Wolf
Blitzer said on CNN. "It doesn't get a whole lot closer than that."

That assessment invited parallels to Hillary's 2008 loss to
Barack Obama. It was, in Bill's view, an absurd comparison. After
all, that had been a three-way race, and she was still likely to come
out the winner on this night, not the third-place finisher. But journalists saw an upstart challenger competing with her in Iowa—and
déjà vu was a hard story line to resist. "This outcome tonight en-
sures that this race is going to go on for months and months on the
Democratic side," Blitzer's colleague Jeff Zeleny reported that night
from Sanders's headquarters.

The perception all along had been that Hillary was such a prohibitive front-runner heading into the Democratic nomination
fight that she should have cleaned up easily. Bill had a much different perspective: Iowa had never been Clinton country, and Hillary
had increased her share of the caucus return from under 30 percent

in 2008 to 50 percent—give or take a little—in 2016. Plus, unlike Obama, Bernie was tailor-made for Iowa. The state is overwhelmingly white, littered with colleges, and decidedly working class in its cities. Even if Bernie managed to eke out a victory, this was Hillary showing strength, not weakness. Why couldn't they see the difference?

On one level, it was just another of Bill's routine fits about television personalities—he'd cursed Tim Russert's name after the *Meet the Press* host had declared Obama the winner of the 2008 primary in May of that year. But it was also another sign of his inability to tamp down his emotions at pivotal moments in his wife's political career. At the start of the day, he'd gone for a walk with his aides to try to release some of the building stress, and, at one point, he played "Oh hell"—a combination of the card games Spades and Bullshit—with them. He was a protective husband and a concerned Democrat, and now he was shouting eight years of pent-up frustrations at his longtime friend and adviser.

When Bill had spent himself, Podesta calmly walked into an adjoining space that was part of the Clinton suite for caucus night. There, amid Hillary's phalanx of anxiety-ridden consultants, he found the man he was looking for, Iowa state director Matt Paul. Balding, bespectacled, and in his midforties, Paul had left his job as communications director for agriculture secretary and former Iowa governor Tom Vilsack to run Hillary's Iowa operation. He had been with her at stops across the state for the better part of a year. Having served on Howard Dean's presidential campaign in Iowa, and as a former aide to Vilsack and Senator Tom Harkin, Paul knew the state's electorate as well as anyone.

Podesta beckoned Paul with a quick but pointed nod: *You go in there and deal with him.* Paul gathered himself and walked in to find the former president sitting in a leather chair. Bill was wearing a suit and a pair of leather gloves; his arms were crossed. Even if the yelling hadn't been audible through the walls of the boutique hotel, it would have been clear that he was in a foul mood. His eyes were fixed on Paul.

If there's ever a time to make sure I know my shit, the staffer thought, *this is it.*

Bill fired questions at him. What's still outstanding in Polk County? What about Johnson County? And how about Cedar Rapids?

Paul walked Bill through the state, and where caucus results still hadn't been reported, county by county. Slowly, the president's anger subsided, even if his anxiety didn't. Hillary had gotten out to a lead consistent with where her team thought she would be heading into caucus night: She was up a handful of points. But Sanders was steadily closing in on her.

After Paul briefed Bill, the two men repeated their conversation in the nearby room where the rest of Hillary's team was nervously assessing the situation. Even in front of the others, Bill bore down on Paul. One source in the room noted a marked shift in Bill's personality. "Usually when you're with him, he's a storyteller," the source said. On this night, "he was just an information-gatherer." He wanted to know what the staff didn't know and why they didn't know it. It's much harder to figure out who is winning in a caucus state—and particularly in Iowa—because the results aren't measured in votes cast. Instead, they are reported as the number of "state delegate equivalents" based on the proportion of the vote that each candidate gets from his or her performance at caucus locations. The numbers can come in as very small fractions.

Over and over, Paul gave updates to the former president—or, more often, reports that there weren't meaningful updates—but remained upbeat, if not rosy, about Hillary's chances of pulling it out. Paul concluded that what really mattered was which caucus sites in Polk County remained unreported. If they were in the core of Des Moines, Hillary was screwed. If they were outside the city, she would win. Pollster John Anzalone, who also knew the state like the roads around his Alabama home, looked at the same numbers and got a bad feeling. He back-channeled to Podesta while Paul was reporting to Bill. "This is not getting better," he told Podesta. "This is going to keep going down. He could potentially overtake us."

▼

AT THE OUTSET of the campaign, there were two schools of thought on the proper expectations for Hillary's performance in Iowa. On the one hand, it was never supposed to be this close. Hillary had done everything she could to clear the Democratic primary field. She'd lined up money, key endorsements, and the top available talent. When Hillary first set foot in Iowa in April 2015, on her soft-launch road trip in a black Chevrolet Express 1500 dubbed the "Scooby Van," she was determined not to repeat the mistakes that had doomed her to a third-place in 2008. Few remembered that her Iowa bronze medal had netted her fourteen delegates, just one fewer than first-place finisher Barack Obama. For all the importance of delegate math in winning a Democratic presidential nomination, Iowa was always about the narrative. Taking the caucuses—no matter the margin—had outsize influence in the way a candidate was regarded by the national media, donors, and voters in other states. The Iowa effect had propelled Obama to the nomination in 2008.

The second school of thought recognized that there was preexisting hostility to Hillary and her worldview in the state and that it was never going to be an easy win if there was another legitimate Democratic candidate. In three previous campaigns in Iowa, a Clinton campaign had won just once—in 1996, when Bill, the sitting president, was running for renomination unopposed. Iowa Democrats, a progressive and overwhelmingly white set, had reasons to seek an alternative to Hillary: many of them didn't like her hawkishness or her close ties to the financial services industry, which had plied her with campaign contributions and given her astronomical personal speaking fees. "Iowa for them is this kind of thing that's fucked them over and over and over again," said one aide of the Clintons. "They were nervous about it from the start."

But her expectations and those of the professional political class were at odds: she and Bill thought it was a tough state; everyone else thought anything short of a clear victory would be a failure.

Paul, her Iowa state director, started gearing up for the campaign in March 2015, the month before Hillary announced that she was running. He pursued a pretty straightforward organizing strategy: lock down the Democratic machinery, precinct by precinct, and make sure that every Clinton-leaning Democrat in the state felt that he or she was in constant contact with the campaign.

Throughout the early months of the campaign, even as Hillary was struggling to get her message across and as Sanders began to gain steam, Clinton's team on the ground in Iowa was busy at work with the blocking and tackling of organizing supporters. She had failed to do that in 2008—back then her aides had assured her she was fine when she was not—and she would be a stickler in 2016 for details on how many people attended each of her events, how many pledges of support had been signed by caucus-goers, and how many times she had met with each county party chairman. Of course, Hillary had the support of big-name Iowa Democrats like Harkin and Vilsack, a former two-term governor, but the approach was to permeate the lower levels of Democratic elected officials and liberal interest groups. That was the way to deny rivals the institutional support that could help them organize their campaigns as Hillary built hers.

Sanders, by contrast, was building without the infrastructure a candidate typically needs to compete in the Iowa caucuses. Like his online fund-raising, his base of support in Iowa grew organically. By the summer of 2015, he was riding a wave—the media called it "the Sanders surge"—and it would grow and grow.

Still, with three previous Iowa campaigns between them, Hillary and Bill were convinced that it was next to impossible for a candidate to win the caucuses without traditional organizing. "I knew it always stuck in the back of her mind, always stuck in the back of [Bill's] mind," one Clinton adviser recalled of the former first couple's take on Sanders's momentum. "Can you do this purely on energy in the state? How do you have to harness it? How much do you have to organize? Even with all of that, you've got to organize it."

In the lead-up to her campaign announcement, advisers had urged Hillary to compete hard in Iowa, hyperlocalize the issues in the state, and "get to know" Iowans, something she couldn't do on a rope line. Where her husband could charm at a rally or one-on-one, Hillary was most impressive and most comfortable in small groups. She could listen to a dozen voters and their stories at a table, then go back around it and repeat everyone's name and concerns before offering her take. In doing so, she demonstrated that she had been listening to them more than most politicians. Iowa voters expect a chance to meet with presidential candidates in person, to get to know them and take stock of them. In that way, the state's caucuses are the closest most presidential candidates get to old-school retail campaigning. Some front-runners prefer large rallies—Sanders and Trump would do a lot of that—but Hillary wanted to campaign like an underdog, which would both give her face time with Iowans and, she hoped, present her as something other than the anointed candidate.

An aide involved in the Iowa strategy said the roundtable model also allowed the campaign to start off at a sustainable pace and gave Hillary grist for future meetings with like-minded Iowans. "She is a person that is driven by what people tell her and that is like ammunition for her to talk about the things she wants to talk about," the aide said.

Hillary also bypassed the national media to communicate with Iowans through local outlets, as much because it signaled that she cared about Iowa as for any influence the hometown papers and broadcast stations might have with their readers, listeners, and viewers. "The strategy from our perspective was that you're dealing with an electorate that is highly plugged into whatever the outlet is," said one aide. "So while the national media does drive a fair amount of the narrative conversation, it was really important that people be seeing her talk to the local affiliate in Des Moines, talk to the *Des Moines Register* for an hour."

The summer months of 2015 were as punishing for Hillary in Iowa as they were nationwide. Sanders kept building a force for what he called a "political revolution," and Hillary kept trying every possible route to get out from under the weight of her e-mail scandal—every route except apologizing. By August Bernie was catching up to her, and her team decided without much dissent to begin airing two positive ads. There was an inherent long-term cost to that. Once she started running expensive spots, she couldn't stop until caucus night, or it would be pointed to as a sign that she was pulling up stakes. But she had to do something to arrest Sanders's surge.

Both ads featured her late mother, Dorothy Rodham, and framed Hillary's candidacy around fighting for children and families. At the time, Hillary's aides believed she needed to fill in a vacuum for voters. They hadn't yet heard her motivation for running. "There wasn't a real clear sense of why she was in it. Minus that, people want to assign their own motivations—at the very best, a politician who thinks it's her turn," one campaign staffer said. "It was true and earnest, but it was also received well. We were talking to Democrats, who largely didn't think she was evil." The ads were perceived mostly on the level of Hillary embracing her gender through her mother, but there was an underlying theme that played well in focus groups and pointed to an area where Hillary might be able to persuade voters with positive messages about herself. One of the ads went deep into Dorothy's background as a child sent away by her parents to live with grandparents who didn't want her— and the role models who helped turn her life around with lessons of compassion and love. Dorothy was a fighter, and so, the ad said, was Hillary. At the end of the spot, Hillary says she is running for all of the "Dorothys" out there who need a champion. Voters liked her "strength, resilience, [and] take no shit attitude," said a person familiar with focus group data.

Hillary's decision to go up on the air forced Bernie to reconsider his own strategy. In Washington, Devine showed the two new Hillary ads to Bernie and Weaver. They were good, all agreed.

"What do you think we should do?" Bernie asked.

"I don't think we can play their game," Devine replied. First of all, it would play into Hillary's hands for Bernie to start draining his treasury to keep up with her. Second, because Bernie was averse to conducting opinion research, his campaign wasn't really ready to put together a high-end political spot. They chose to stay the course. "We didn't freak out and join them and waste money doing stuff that we weren't ready to do," one Bernie ally said, adding that it "worked for us."

But Hillary's ads helped stabilize her in polling. "That ultimately was a key decision because it gave us a reset moment after what was a brutal summer," said one top Clinton adviser. All the while, her Iowa operatives, led by Paul, focused on wrapping up the support of every possible institutional player in the state. The idea was to prevent Sanders from putting together the ground troops and political infrastructure to match the energy pumped into his campaign from activists and students. Rather than just court the typical high-level endorsers and surrogates, they went deeper into the roster of elected officials. In particular, they targeted young women who had been elected to office, like North Liberty mayor Amy Nielsen, who went on to win a state House seat in 2016. Having a younger cohort among her retinue of older elected officials would show Iowans that her campaign wasn't just for the Medicare-eligible set that tilted heavily in her direction.

On the ground, things began to look up toward the end of the summer, and Hillary seized control of the Iowa race again in that magical October on the strength of her performance in the first debate and the Benghazi hearings. With Joe Biden no longer a factor, and Martin O'Malley unable to find traction, Hillary seemed to have a powerful upper hand through November and early December.

But everything went sideways in mid-December. Thinking Iowans would be tuned out of the political race during the holidays, Hillary eased up on the gas. At the same time, Sanders finally blitzed the airwaves with television and radio spots. "We made a calculation that people would be sort of checked out over Christmas and come back over the New Year," a member of her team confided. "That was a mistake to give him that room."

Hillary's internal analytics survey numbers showed a nearly 10-point swing toward Bernie in December. Improbably, Sanders, the iconoclastic old socialist with the wild hair, windmill arms, and willful disregard for convention, had surpassed her in New Hampshire and was starting to pull away there. Hillary's advantage in Iowa, which bounced as high as thirty-two points at the end of October, had fallen into single-digit territory—and in some of the public polls, Sanders was the one ahead by a few points. Her national lead, which had also reexpanded in October and November, would soon wither again. "Our numbers tightened," said a source involved in Hillary's Iowa operation. "We knew New Hampshire was a buzz saw. So, we knew the pressure that was on us."

It was inexplicable to Hillary's team, except to say that Bernie had tapped into the mood of the electorate and Iowans finally started to make serious assessments about the candidates between Thanksgiving and Christmas.

If Hillary had relaxed a bit when Biden chose not to run—and she had—now she was very much on edge. She didn't like what she was seeing or what she was reading in the newspaper, and she had run short on patience with her campaign manager. Over the holidays, as her numbers slid, Hillary lit up Mook's phone. She wanted to know what the hell was happening and what he was going to do to fix it. The overall picture had slipped from optimistic to worrisome to alarming. The campaign manager tried to reassure her. We don't need Iowa to win the nomination, he said, reminding her that his original, conservative projections had her losing the caucuses. It would be great to win, especially to take the state by a big margin, he said, but everything will be fine if Bernie manages to prevail.

From a purely mathematical standpoint, that was true. Bernie wouldn't net a lot of delegates, no matter the outcome. But Iowa was the first state in the race, and it could act as a springboard for him. Secondarily, pride was on the line for Hillary in a state that had rejected her before. The decision to compete there, and thus to keep Iowa in the spotlight, had long since been made. Mook had put a lot of the campaign's eggs in the Iowa basket, knowing that it took a long time and a lot of resources to run a months-long race there. Now that Hillary was in danger of losing, that decision would either turn out to show prescience in shoring her up or foolhardiness in wasting resources. Bernie's big lead in New Hampshire magnified the hero-or-goat nature of the Iowa outcome for Mook. And back-to-back Bernie wins in the first two states on the calendar had the potential to give Bernie unstoppable momentum. Bill Clinton was the only candidate in either party in the previous four decades to lose both states and come back to win a nomination.

Still, Iowa was way too close for comfort. In addition, both Clintons had been hearing a lot of grumbling from within the party—and within the campaign—about Mook's neglect of the rest of the state contests. If Hillary lost Iowa, a double hit could be coming because Mook hadn't deployed enough resources to be certain Hillary could hold off Sanders after New Hampshire. "The calendar was teed up for him to do some serious damage to us early," said one longtime Clinton hand.

Mook called an early January meeting with the rest of the campaign's top brass to talk about Iowa: Podesta, Paul, Palmieri, Marlon Marshall, Michael Halle, and a few others. Some of them dialed in to what was a decidedly sober meeting at the campaign headquarters in Brooklyn. Channeling Hillary, from their earlier discussions, Mook wanted to see if there was anything the campaign needed to do in terms of advertising, field organizing, and targeting caucusgoers. "It was like, 'OK, this is getting tight,'" one participant in the meeting said. "Are we doing everything we can right now? Or what else do we need to do, from getting more surrogates in the state, looking at our targeting, expanding the universe of people we're talking to."

With Hillary's operation running at full steam again, Bernie hit a plateau. He leveled out in Hillary's internal numbers, leaving the two candidates roughly even with just a few weeks until caucus day. "The month of December was brutal," recalled one aide involved in trying to ensure Hillary's ground game would carry her past Bernie.

Because the caucuses would be a referendum on the front-runner, and because Bernie had all the energy, the trick wasn't to convert Sanders people into Clinton backers. Already, Hillary's aides believed it was hard to change attitudes toward her. Trying to do so would take too much expensive persuasion and would likely fall short anyway. Instead, the challenge for Hillary's team was turning out the targeted number of people who would caucus for her, not just statewide but in each precinct. Throughout the campaign, Mook would give short shrift to persuasion efforts—a bias that either reflected a savvy understanding of the electorate or a costly miscalculation of Hillary's capacity for building a broader coalition.

In Iowa, the only focus was on winning delegates to the *state* Democratic convention, a math exercise that didn't necessarily require Hillary to win more total votes but to take a majority in the right set of caucus sites. In all, that meant having nearly two thousand precinct chairs hitting their targets, which could come either from already-identified Clinton backers or, potentially, from finding new people who were inclined to support her. Outwardly, Mook wasn't in a state of panic. But he was serious, and he knew Iowa was much more fertile ground for corn than it was for Clintons.

MOOK AND MARLON MARSHALL, the states director, stayed in close contact with the campaign's Iowa field team for the final three weeks, trying to figure out how to best allocate resources to win at caucus sites across the state. Mook's equanimity was one of the reasons he was chosen to run the campaign, but everyone in the operation was a little rattled, including the Clintons. Hillary's communications shop wanted to more aggressively attack Sanders to drive his numbers down—an instinct in line with the Clinton way of handling foes—while senior strategists knowingly advised that she would hurt herself by going after a popular figure who hadn't been negative enough to warrant return volleys.

It was the latest round in a running debate over how to handle the rise of Sanders. Bill and Hillary had wanted to put him down like a junkyard dog early on. She'd let him get too far without a punch already, she thought. Instinctively, the Clintons wanted to pound on rivals—whether campaign opponents, congressional Republicans, prosecutors, or women who had accused Bill of sexual misconduct. But it hadn't always proved to be the most effective strategy. Hillary had hammered away at Obama in 2008, and it had boomeranged.

The paradigm was similar with Bernie. Her negatives were high, and he was well liked. On the advice of her campaign counselors, Hillary largely restrained herself. The problem, her close confidants knew, was that if they gave her an inch to attack Sanders, she'd take a mile.

So on January 12, a day after Joe Biden had praised Sanders's "authenticity" on the issue of income inequality and said it was "relatively new for Hillary" to talk about it, Chelsea Clinton lit into Sanders as she stumped for her mother in New Hampshire. It was odd for the candidate's daughter to become the vehicle for an attack, but the Clintons were spoiling for a fight. It was better that a charge come from someone other than the candidate, so that Chelsea's words could be embraced or rejected by Hillary depending on how they played.

"Senator Sanders wants to dismantle Obamacare, dismantle the CHIP program, dismantle Medicare, and dismantle private insurance," Chelsea said of Sanders's Medicare-for-all health care plan. "I don't want to empower Republican governors to take away Medicaid, to take away health insurance for low-income and middle-income working Americans. And I think very much that's what Senator Sanders' plan would do."

Across the Democratic universe, and particularly in Sanders's camp, the dusting off of the Clintons' scorched-earth playbook was taken as a sign of desperation. And accurately so. "I was surprised and thought it was out of character," Arizona congressman Raúl Grijalva told *The Hill* newspaper. "It seems the Clinton campaign is going into full destruction mode very early in this process."

The fact-checking website PolitiFact instantly rated Chelsea's claim as "mostly false." The attack previewed an angle Hillary would take—that Sanders was so liberal he rejected Obama's legacy—but it gave Sanders and his allies a perfect opening to stab Hillary back.

When he was asked about it, Sanders smiled and replied, "As much as I admire Chelsea, she didn't read the plan."

The episode reinforced the idea that Clinton was running scared. It reminded Democrats that Hillary would go negative and do it dishonestly, and she had turned to her daughter to defend her. The Clinton campaign insisted that it was an unplanned moment. But when Bill Clinton did the same thing a week later, also in New Hampshire, it was pretty clear that the Clinton family still didn't believe that the risk of a low-approval candidate attacking a well-liked one outweighed the prospective gain of drawing blood.

The candidate herself remained a little more precise in her messaging. She delivered rebukes to Sanders over health care in a January 17 debate in Charleston, South Carolina, that were part of a much more powerful message than portraying Sanders as naive. While some analysts rated the debate a victory for Sanders, Clinton reinforced the architecture of her southern firewall by tying herself to Obama and charging that Sanders would undo the good work of the president's administration—echoing what Chelsea and Bill had said on the trail. "We have the Affordable Care Act. That is one of the greatest accomplishments of President Obama, the Democratic Party and of our country," Clinton said. "To tear it up and start over again, pushing our country back into that kind of a contentious debate, I think is the wrong direction." Her approach was a gentle but clear contrast rather than a gut punch.

No fewer than five public polls began testing Clinton and Sanders in Iowa the day after the debate. Clinton led by nine points in two of them and by six points in one of them, but she *trailed* by four points in a fourth and a single point in the fifth. Taken together, they showed that Bernie was in striking distance. Inside the Clinton campaign, the trend line looked ghastly. For months, Bernie had slowly built his surge. Now, with caucus day quickly approaching, his movement was gathering strength and velocity. It was viral and exciting—palpable on the ground and in the polls. He'd blitzed Hillary in December, taking her team by surprise, and now he was positioned to sack her. As Iowans took their last measure of the two candidates, what stood out was Bernie's energy and Hillary's dishonesty. Everything was breaking Bernie's way, and the question was whether Hillary's superior operation could withstand the crush of support for him.

"Where we saw a big dip was about ten days out," one Clinton aide said of the campaign's internal polling. "In one instance we lost seven points in the matter of a week. We knew this was going to be close. We knew that his positives were going up and our negatives were going up. And just based on what we were hearing—based on the numbers we were getting back—we knew, if you will, that the struggle was very real."

Some of Mook's internal critics began rattling their sabers, setting the expectation that if Hillary lost Iowa, his job—or at least his influence—would evaporate. He hadn't predicted a win in Iowa in his early projections, and he had poured resources into the state anyway. There had been little choice: Hillary couldn't afford not to compete there at all, and, once she started campaigning there, a loss would be taken by the media, her donors and supporters, and Sanders's donors and supporters as a major blow to her campaign. Hillary knew from experience that money would dry up if she started losing, and that it could be hard to stop a moving progressive train as it gathered steam. Moreover, because she was getting clobbered in New Hampshire, and because Nevada was close, a defeat in Iowa could quickly turn into a three-state slide.

And then, in quick succession, Hillary received two blessings from the *Des Moines Register*. The first was the paper's endorsement. It was hardly an assurance of victory, but the editorial was firm in its conclusion that Sanders's platform was pie in the sky. "A successful Sanders presidency would hinge on his ability to remake Washington in his own image," the *Register* wrote. "It's almost inconceivable that such a transformation could take place, even with Democrats controlling both chambers of Congress."

Five days later—and two days before the caucuses—she got the second blessing: the final in a series of *Register* polls conducted in conjunction with Bloomberg Politics showed her with a three-point lead. That tracked very closely to the campaign's analytics-driven expectations, which gave her a four-point edge, 47 percent to 43 percent. In theory, she would take the caucuses with a close but comfortable margin.

FOR ALL THE obstacles Hillary faced in Iowa—her e-mail scandal, the antiwar and anti–Wall Street tilt of the caucus electorate, Sanders's surge in popularity, and the Clintons' poor track record in the state—she went into caucus day expecting to win. Coming in first mattered for two reasons: a victory might break the Sanders fever in the Democratic Party and it would reassure her own panicky donors and supporters. By this point, she knew she was in deep trouble in New Hampshire, which magnified the importance of getting that first tally on the board.

"There was some sense it was going to be close, but not that it was going to be asshole-puckering close," said one of her senior advisers.

On caucus day, the Clinton high command was split between two locations: the Savery Hotel downtown, where Bill's voice rattled the walls, and the campaign's Iowa headquarters nearby. The latter spot was dubbed the "boiler room" by its denizens, a nod to the pressure-cooker nature of running numbers on an election night. Hillary's team had estimated that there would be a lot of new registrants—people who signed up on the day of the caucuses—and that they would break for Bernie 75 percent to 25 percent or as much as 80 percent to 20 percent.

All night, they fielded reports from precinct captains across the state. They had designed a special app to collect the results, and the data came in a bit faster than the tallies viewers could see on the television screens in their homes. As Hillary's lead on Sanders narrowed—a function of the closeness of the race overall and the order in which caucus sites reported—dread gnawed away the optimism that had marked the start of the day.

"It was very tense," said one source in the boiler room.

As the numbers came in, it became clear that, whoever won, the margin was going to be almost nothing. For all intents and purposes, it would be a draw. But both campaigns and the national media knew that someone would be declared the winner. If Hillary lost, she'd have to fight stories of an epic failure. If she won, she would have survived the Sanders surge. The boiler room kept in touch with the crew at the Savery Hotel, though the communication was interrupted because Paul had forgotten his phone charger. He had to borrow one from veteran Clinton media consultant Mandy Grunwald to keep the lines open.

Reading the data in the boiler room, members of the analytics team were surprised by the reports on new registrants. The overall number was a little more than they had expected. But they had also underestimated the margins for Bernie. The first-timers were breaking 90 percent to 10 percent in his favor. Running the data through their models, they could see why the race was so tight. "That was what plugged into a fraction of a point versus one and a half, two points," said one of Hillary's top Iowa specialists. But it still wasn't enough, they calculated, for Bernie to eclipse Hillary's lead.

The race was too close for the Associated Press or the broadcast networks to make a call, but the analytics and field operatives reported to Mook that the slowly evaporating lead wouldn't disappear altogether. "We were confident that we had it," the aide said.

Hillary's get-out-the-vote team on the ground, bolstered by a handful of talented veteran organizers, had been built with the expectation that Bernie wouldn't do as well as he did. They overperformed, and their work had bailed out the analytics squad. That was good news in that Hillary had eluded defeat, but the outcome served to obscure flaws in Elan Kriegel's modeling—namely, that it hadn't correctly accounted for the number of new registrants or the degree to which they would break for Hillary—and Mook's corresponding allocation of resources for in-person contact with caucus-goers. "The seeds of what we see across the campaign were present there," said one person familiar with the campaign's strategy and tactics.

"It was a warning sign that they just barely scraped by, and I don't think they took that seriously."

THE QUESTION AS numbers continued to trickle in on caucus night was whether Hillary could, or should, declare herself the winner if there was even a sliver of a chance of the overall outcome flipping. Not only would it have been an embarrassment to be wrong, but it would have reinforced the narrative that Hillary's word couldn't be trusted. At the same time, she couldn't afford to let Sanders call himself the winner to a national television audience first.

Soon after Anzalone warned that the numbers might not hold, Hillary appeared in the doorway and leaned against the jamb. It was her second trip down the hall from her room to the strategists' bull pen. The first time, she'd been cheerful and optimistic. Now she was anxious inside with an all-business exterior. The change in demeanor was palpable, and it brought everyone to attention.

With her fate in Iowa hanging in the balance, she asked for guidance. Should she go out and claim victory—and, if so, when? Or should she give a more anodyne statement because the results were still trickling in? It wasn't just a question of whether she would win, but how she should spin this split decision from Iowa caucus-goers. Hillary had a preference, but she wanted to get everyone on board before making the call. "All right, guys, now this is serious. What are we doing?" she asked, obviously impatient and leading her witnesses. "Am I going to give this speech or am I going to wait?"

Palmieri argued that whatever the content, it was essential that Hillary speak before Sanders. Hillary should get on the road to her rally at Drake University as soon as possible.

Bill Clinton thought Hillary should tell Iowans and the nation that she would be declared the winner, and he said as much. Mook, who had arrived from the campaign's boiler room, told Hillary that the final result would fall somewhere between losing by two-tenths of a percentage point and winning by two-tenths of a percentage point. But, he said, she was likely to be the victor. He advocated that her aides call her the winner without the words passing her own lips. It was that close. Hillary went with Mook's recommendation, a vote of confidence for her embattled campaign manager.

"Give us five minutes," Podesta said of the need to fashion a speech that hinted at victory without declaring it. "We'll figure it out and split the baby."

A winter storm was quickly approaching Des Moines, and Hillary needed to get on a plane to be in New Hampshire for a weeklong sprint through the first primary state. The next morning would be too late: flights out of Des Moines, packed full of national reporters, campaign operatives, and senators who had come to stump for various Democratic and Republican candidates, would be delayed or canceled.

"Let's go," Hillary prodded. "Get in the cars."

During those same hours, Bernie and his team lived through a mirror-image scenario. Weaver and Devine were at the campaign's Iowa headquarters when the team's data analysts saw an improvement in Bernie's chances of winning. The first exit polls had shown him down nearly ten points, but actual returns were coming in better. He was gaining on Hillary. And the number crunchers started projecting that the outcome would be very close. Weaver and Devine hightailed it to Bernie's hotel room to watch the returns come in and to strategize with their candidate.

The numbers kept getting better and better as they watched television with Bernie and his family. It was becoming clear that it would be hard for the media to declare a winner anytime soon. But, like Clinton, Bernie had to get out of town before the coming storm. He motioned to Devine to join him in the bedroom. Bernie lay down as his strategist paced the room. What, if anything, should he say before he took off for New Hampshire?

Devine laid out the challenge.

"Say 'Thank you, Iowa,'" he said, explaining, "if we declare victory while she's a little ahead, we're going to look like jerks. Let them declare victory so they can look like jerks."

As Bernie scribbled the words onto a yellow legal pad, Devine explained how they could work to excite his base without putting him in the position of falsely calling himself the winner if he ended up losing. "'Thank you, Iowa.' That's what you say when you win," Devine said. "But you're not really declaring victory." Bernie got it. He kept writing as Devine dictated the next line.

"It looks like tonight we have a tie in Iowa—" Devine started.

"No," Bernie interjected, taking his pen from the page. "A *virtual* tie!"

When they'd written a single paragraph, Devine told Bernie that was enough new material. Go into your stump speech, he said, and then "let's get the hell out of town."

DAN SCHWERIN REWROTE Hillary's speech as she and her team piled into a motorcade and made what felt like an hour-long trip to the Drake University campus five minutes away. As he tapped out edits to her remarks, he strained to hear above the deafening sirens from Clinton's police escorts.

In the end, she didn't use his words. She scrapped the prepared text and spoke extemporaneously. Wearing a dramatic red that matched the shade of the forward-pointing arrow in her campaign logo, she expressed a sentiment that would come to define not only the result in Iowa but her long slog to the nomination. While the campaign had war-gamed various possible scenarios in regard to that evening's outcome, they never predicted this roller-coaster ending. On stage that night, Hillary was, she said, "breathing a big sigh of relief."

Matt Paul, who rode in the motorcade to Drake, believed he'd done everything he could have for Hillary. The caucuses were a test of Sanders's message and momentum against Hillary's superior organization. He had spoken to Hillary and Bill countless times about that question. Could Sanders win purely on energy and enthusiasm? In the final several weeks, Sanders's campaign began to build the infrastructure to match the sentiment that had captured the hearts of liberal, young, and politically unaffiliated Iowans. To counter Sanders, the Clinton team focused on making sure that every ally heard from a top campaign official five or six times over the course of the caucus season—and on training precinct captains to master the intricacies of the complex caucus process. "Had we not had every single organizer that we had, had we not reached out to every possible group or every newly elected person or every advocacy community, we would have lost," said one Clinton adviser. "The current was that strong against us. At the end, it was all that muscle." Mook's field operation had been *just* strong enough to withstand Bernie, but not by the margin his analytics team had predicted and not by enough to quiet his critics. He was flying very close to the sun.

As Hillary spoke, Paul huddled backstage with her national campaign team to say his good-byes. He heard some of the speech, but not all of it. Like everyone else, he was disappointed by the numbers on the scoreboard. And when she appeared backstage with Bill on her way out of town, Paul told her as much.

"I wish it would have been more," he told the couple.

"Don't let anybody ever tell you that she didn't win," Bill said.

"In August, I was certain we were going to lose," Hillary said.

Chapter 8

THE PRIZE AND THE PAIN

LESS THAN A YEAR BEFORE THE IOWA CAUCUSES, IN APRIL 2015, Hillary had flown to New Hampshire to meet with two dozen old friends at former state senate president Sylvia Larsen's home in Concord. As a steady rain came down outside, Hillary, sitting in an easy chair in an art-filled living room with a grand piano, listened to the longtime residents share what was on their minds and how they thought she might carry the primary there. She was focused on substance and policy, but Terry Shumaker, an old Clinton friend who had served as ambassador to Trinidad during Bill's administration, thought there was something missing from the conversation—the personal piece. "Everybody knows who you are but nobody knows who you are," Shumaker told her. He loved her, and he thought others would feel the same if they knew her the way that he did. Her friends found her generous, thoughtful, and funny in person, but that seldom translated in front of strangers or at campaign events. It was a problem that had dogged her throughout her public life, and it would bedevil her again if she didn't open up more. "People don't know what makes you tick," Shumaker said.

It was ironic that a woman who had been on the national stage for a quarter of a century, who had lived the triumphs of victory and the tragedies of defeat and humiliation in public, could still seem inaccessible to so many Americans—even to her supporters. But Shumaker, who had plenty of Republican friends and knew a lot of

Democrats who weren't Hillary fans, understood that one reason people thought she lacked honesty is that they had watched her for so long and felt like they had seen so little of her. She'd been stung before, though, when she spoke from the heart. She was ridiculed during the 1992 campaign for saying she wouldn't stay home and bake cookies, for separating herself from women who would stand by their man no matter what, and later for arguing that she and her husband were the victims of a "vast right-wing conspiracy." She'd suffered the backlash of talking about her values openly over the years. That had hardened the thick shell of someone who was intensely private by nature.

Shumaker believed the trait that best defined Hillary was her indomitability, and he thought others would appreciate hearing more about that. Back in 1999, he met with her in the White House and inquired about the rumors that she might run for the Senate.

"Yeah, I'm thinking about it," she said coyly.

"Come on," he chided. "It's me."

"Yeah, I'm going to do it," Hillary confided.

"Are you sure the prize is worth the pain?" Shumaker asked.

Hillary smiled as she turned her palms upward. "What else can they do to me?" she asked.

Shumaker knew where Hillary had acquired this attitude: from her mother, Dorothy Rodham. As New Hampshire chairman of Bill Clinton's two presidential campaigns, he had gotten to know Dorothy and her story. Shumaker had always wanted Hillary to explain to voters how her mother's resilience had formed her own character.

But he usually found his friend to be surprisingly resistant to talking about Dorothy. It was hard for him to understand. Candidates often opened up about their parents' influence as a way of putting context around their values. That was harder for Hillary, who struggled with the fear of leveraging her mother's tough upbringing for political gain. Hillary had written about her mother's perseverance in the 1996 book *It Takes a Village,* but she wasn't on the campaign trail then. Dorothy Rodham died in November 2011, and, with her passing and the passage of time, Hillary felt less reluctance to make her part of this campaign's story. When Shumaker attended an early campaign event at an Exeter bookstore and heard Hillary detailing her mother's hardships, he thought she should do more of it.

"That was wonderful," Shumaker told her as they browsed the bookshelves after the event. "You can't talk too much about your mother. . . . Nobody knows this stuff."

"I never wanted to talk about her while she was alive. I thought it was exploitative," she said. "It's still difficult for me to do."

But it was part and parcel of her strategy for 2016, all the same. On Mother's Day in 2014, an early excerpt of her book *Hard Choices* appeared in *Vogue*. The section, which had little to do with the rest of the book's focus on Hillary's work as a diplomat, presaged how the campaign would use her late mother to explain, in human terms, why Hillary was almost inhumanly tough internally and externally. And in August 2015, Hillary's first two ads of the campaign featured Dorothy. That piece of Hillary's narrative dovetailed with her frequent talk of her daughter and granddaughter on the campaign trail. Eight years after she'd tried so hard not to talk about her gender, the references to the women in her family were a low-risk way of reminding voters about it in this election.

But as the months wore on, it didn't seem to matter much how Hillary packaged herself to New Hampshire voters. When Sanders began to catch up to Hillary in Iowa in the late fall and early winter, he also surged way ahead in New Hampshire. The scary thing for Clinton's team, which was led on the ground by Mike Vlacich, a Queens, New York–born, New Hampshire–educated campaign rat, was that she was getting pummeled even though her favorable ratings among Democrats were in the high seventies and low eighties. After he started putting a little bit of money into the state, Sanders's favorability rating reached into the midnineties in the Clinton campaign's polling, something none of her operatives had ever seen before. Everyone in New Hampshire was feeling the Bern, even those who planned to vote for Hillary. Sanders's negative ratings were about the size of the margin of error.

Vlacich, who had a prominent cleft in his chin and was topped by a crop of thick black hair, could sense an earthquake within the local electorate that would wipe out the basic rules of campaign politics. Even if the internal polls had shown Hillary leading by a few points, he argued to his colleagues, the trends were going in the wrong direction and fast. He could feel the cold earth shifting beneath his feet. Sanders was running away with it, and no one could stop him. At one point before the Iowa caucuses, Benenson had shown a positive clip of Martin O'Malley to a focus group in Londonderry, New Hampshire, and the response to it was negative.

Bernie's surge led to some testy moments for the Clinton team. Vlacich got peppered with questions about what could be done to reverse the trend. The obvious answer: go negative on Sanders. But the consensus, as in Iowa, was that it wouldn't work.

Vlacich did want more money to help Hillary. He believed the campaign had to compete hard to prevent a complete wipeout. He had a series of what one source described as "heart-to-hearts" with Mook over the budget. It was Vlacich's role to ask for more, and it was Mook's place to say no. There wouldn't be extra money for a state where Hillary had virtually zero chance of winning. In successive polls released before the Iowa caucuses, Sanders expanded his lead in New Hampshire to between twenty points and thirty-one points. Hillary was headed for a shellacking, and there was a reasonable argument that she shouldn't invest much time, energy, or money in New Hampshire.

ABOARD THE JET in the wee hours of Tuesday, February 2, 2016, the Iowa caucus result didn't feel like a victory at all. Sullivan, one of several aides huddled around Hillary, encapsulated the agony for his colleagues. "Literally, only the Clinton campaign can win—get the Iowa monkey off its back—and it's like it sucks," he said. "That is our lot in life." That lot was about to get a lot worse.

Hillary was already past it, poring over the New Hampshire polling and the composition of the electorate. None of what she was seeing or hearing from her aides was pretty. She was in a deep hole, and Mook didn't think she could climb out of it. He wanted her to spend as little time and money as possible in New Hampshire.

"Ditch it," he said. "Go twice and focus on Nevada."

Hillary pushed back. "I don't like giving up on states, and I don't think it's the right thing to do," she told her aides as the small plane flew east through the night sky. There was another, more important reason to go all out on the hustings in the Granite State. "We cannot write off New Hampshire," she said. "This is a state that we need in the general," she reminded.

So Hillary braced herself to campaign in this last week like she had a shot at winning. She knew she was much more likely to lose than win, but she hadn't completely ruled out a miracle. She'd pulled one out in 2008 in New Hampshire, and the state had revitalized Bill in 1992. He didn't want her to skip it, either. "There was a belief that they could come back," said one senior aide who talked to both Clintons. "Talk about data driven versus gut driven. There was just sort of a mystical thing around New Hampshire." New Hampshire may have been mystical, but the campaign was decidedly earthbound.

BY THE TIME she touched down in New Hampshire after the Iowa caucuses, the rumor mill was fast at work about a massive campaign shake-up, the kind of desperate move that would rattle the confidence of supporters and donors and telegraph to the media that Clinton's campaign was in real trouble. From Hillary's point of view, they were failing her. They hadn't anticipated the rise of Bernie, they hadn't been able to create a message to break through the e-mail scandal, and they had just barely, by the skin of their teeth, run Iowa well enough to win. She was going to make changes—big changes—but they would have to wait.

Mook had the most reason to be nervous about his job. Long-time Clinton confidants outside the campaign had been agitating for months for Hillary to get rid of him. She had heard from allies across the states that Mook wasn't building the campaign's ground game enough for an all-out war against Sanders. He'd focused too much on the first four states, and even the operatives there felt underresourced. His penny-pinching was becoming a real issue across the country. In addition, veteran Democratic hands found him to be secretive, a problem that was flagged by Podesta and other power brokers in the Brooklyn headquarters, Clinton allies in Washington, and top political operatives in the states. He'd created an insular and loyal staff below him, but he'd been predictably unable to control the crosscutting circles of Clintonworld.

Mook tried not to let the gossip distract him. *If I think about this, I'm going to go crazy and jump out a window,* he thought. But it was impossible to ignore.

While some of her allies wanted her to get rid of Mook, Hillary was fed up with her consultants. Their direct contact with Hillary and Bill had slowly moved from frequent meetings to infrequent conference calls to almost nothing at all.

With their own necks on the line, aides talked about what it would take to get Hillary closer in New Hampshire. The bigger the blowout, the more likely it was that heads would roll. They knew they needed divine intervention to win, but perhaps they could narrow the gap on their own. "It was always considered a miracle to win," one of her advisers said. "The conversations were more about what we could do to get ourselves in striking range."

Still, she trudged around the small state to meet face-to-face with voters, tried to rally women to her cause, and generally pretended that she wasn't going to get her head handed to her. She was greeted with a paradox of sorts on the trail: she was getting traction with voters at her events, her campaign headquarters was bustling, the volunteer organization across the state was strong, and yet each night's polling data showed that none of it was making a whit of difference.

"I can't believe that these numbers are real," she said in one private moment, struggling to understand how she was trailing by so much despite a feeling of energy at her events. "I don't know what more we could do here." The answer was nothing.

Her aides, as they would do in state after state, set expectations low for the media. In contrast to 2008, they poor-mouthed her chances consistently so that losses wouldn't look so bad and victories would seem much bigger. It was smart communications strategy generally speaking, but it also framed Hillary in the role in which she was best liked: underdog. Her team tried to demonstrate that Hillary was pulling out all the stops to win every vote she could. A flood of her surrogates traveled to New Hampshire to make the case for her: Bill Clinton, Chelsea Clinton, writer and actress Lena Dunham, soccer legend Abby Wambach, and former secretary of state Madeleine Albright, several political luminaries from Sanders's home state of Vermont, more than a dozen members of Congress, and a variety of other marquee names.

For Hillary, there was a certain catharsis in campaigning hard. If she was working, she wasn't wallowing. It was a trait that defined her for her loyalists for decades: the ability to grind it out every day, even when the odds were stacked high against her. To those around her, Hillary seemed happiest at off-the-record events with small groups. Compared with the big speeches and the crush of media attention, she liked the retail aspect of campaigning.

Whatever the size of the event, Mook wanted to keep Hillary from visiting far-flung parts of the state. He and his team were trying to keep the margin closer by turning out supporters in vote-rich areas, which often meant having to talk Hillary and Bill out of traveling away from the population centers to convert Bernie fans.

These decisions were guided by data analytics, which evaluated the likelihood that each voter would show up and back Hillary, and Mook's dogmatic belief that it was better to focus on turning out supporters than persuading a rival's voters to switch candidates. The smaller the town either Clinton appeared in, the farther they ventured into enemy territory, he thought, and the more it would be a waste of time and energy.

This strategy would become a point of contention, with Bill in particular, who pushed to talk to rural voters. He had a better feel for people in hardscrabble parts of the country than Hillary or Obama or really anyone else in the Democratic Party. He knew, intuitively, that Hillary had work to do outside the cities and suburbs in swing states. He had come from nothing—the man from "Hope"—and had connected with working-class whites in 1992. Competing against Obama, Hillary had run up the score with that set. But now, with a choice between Bernie and Hillary, they were rejecting her. Bill wanted to get out of the bubble and shake hands. He'd been champing at the bit for quite a while. For most of 2015, he was Hillary's silent partner. He'd sit in on strategy meetings, pore over numbers, and offer his advice. But, very intentionally and at the behest of Hillary's strategists, he held back from a public role at his wife's side.

On one level, as a person familiar with his thinking said, Bill had "overlearned the lessons of 2008." He felt he had been scapegoated for her primary loss back then because he had said impolitic— and racially charged—things on the campaign trail and because he'd been overbearing at times with campaign aides. This time, he wanted to be more measured. He would offer his opinions, press for information and justifications for campaign decisions, and share his thoughts with Hillary about what was being done well and what wasn't. Over time, he would become more repetitive and forceful with Mook. But in the early phases of the campaign, he minded his p's and q's as best he could.

Bill thought the campaign manager was a capable operative but worried that the next-gen Mook was too invested in data to the exclusion of politics. Neither a traditional poll nor Mook's preferred analytics—voter-behavior models based on surveys and demographic data—were as finely tuned as his own sense of political winds, Bill thought. They were an important part of a modern campaign but not the only part. "You couldn't place all of your eggs in the data/polling basket," one of Bill's confidants said of his thinking. "He had the ability to sort of figure out what's going on around him, to sort of take everyone's feedback and synthesize it and measure [it] along with his experience and then report back."

Bill had done this thing twice. His handle on politics was as natural as Jimi Hendrix's feel for the guitar. Hillary couldn't grasp the sentiment of the electorate, the resentfulness white working- and middle-class Americans felt watching the wealthy rebound quickly from the 2008 economic crisis while their families struggled through a slow recovery. Her team didn't really get it, either.

Beyond his own fear of being turned into a villain if Hillary lost, he knew she had to send the message to voters that she was doing this on her own merit, not as the anointed wife of a former president. The optics, her team thought, were crucial to avoiding the coronation narrative that had hurt her in the last campaign. But during the e-mail summer, when Hillary was struggling to articulate a positive message, fellow Democrats were as eager for Bill to hit the trail as he was to emerge from the shadows of the campaign. "He should have been a visible presence all along," columnist Brent Budowsky wrote in an alarmed e-mail to Podesta in September 2015. "He is the great validator in American politics, the Babe Ruth of national politics when almost all other politicians, including Hillary, are widely distrusted."

For the final three months of the year, Bill started to shake off cobwebs by raising money for the campaign. At those stops, he heard complaints about Hillary's staffing decisions, worries about Bernie's surge, and concerns about the e-mail imbroglio. This litany of dissatisfaction reminded Bill of the 2008 campaign. Back then, his role was unclear, and he hadn't been utilized well. But now, he and his team were fully integrated into the strategy and tactics. Bill could get in touch with Brooklyn whenever he wanted to, but as he spent more time talking to donors—and eventually voters—around the country, his confidence in the campaign's management team dwindled. He wasn't impressed with the consultants who had failed to get his wife's economic message out of the gate, and he wasn't sold on Mook's capacity to run the operation after a nearly debilitating, whisker-thin win in Iowa.

As he started campaigning for Hillary in New Hampshire in January 2016, Bill came to realize two things. First, he, Bill Clinton, of the silver tongue and golden touch, was a little rusty. He was too good not to know it himself. And second, he couldn't stand Bernie Sanders.

You hear Bernie Sanders talk, he thought, *and you'd never have thought George Bush ran this country for eight years. To him, everything that's wrong with America, especially our social problems, are a direct result of whatever bad policy I set in motion.* Bill understood that he'd be attacked in the campaign—and he was getting it from both sides—but that didn't mean he liked it. A week before he hit the trail, Donald Trump tweeted, "Hillary Clinton has announced that she is letting her husband out to campaign but HE'S DEMONSTRATED A PENCHANT FOR SEXISM, so inappropriate!" Trump argued that Hillary's tolerance of Bill, after his affair with Monica Lewinsky and allegations of sexual misconduct against several other women, made her the candidate who was worse for women. Like Trump, Bill sometimes talked about women in less-than-respectful terms—but he tended to do so in private settings. In June 2014, as Bill was getting ready to speak at a Jefferson-Jackson dinner in Fort Lauderdale, Florida, his chief of staff, Tina Flournoy, mentioned to him and a small group of his aides that she was going to see the Rolling Stones in Europe.

"Mick Jagger used to give my mother-in-law wet dreams," Bill offered.

Trump was on his third marriage and had flaunted his own philandering, but there was no reason for Bill, a former president, to get in a fight with a Republican primary contestant. Bernie, on the other hand, was a different beast entirely. Because Hillary's opponent was targeting the party's progressive base, Bill had to suppress his instinct to hit back to avoid sparking a pro-Bernie backlash among ultrasensitive modern Democrats. It was frustrating.

He was also learning that the laws of political thermodynamics had changed since he'd last campaigned for Hillary. Maybe it was an anomalous year, or maybe he just hadn't kept up with the times, but

Bill was surprised by how little voters wanted to hear a politician's response to attack lines. In the old days, he'd get a chance to make his case. He understood that millennials blamed his 1994 crime bill for the mass incarceration that Hillary said she would put an end to, but he struggled to accept younger voters' reluctance to learn about the history of the law. It was in the cold New Hampshire winter that Bill started to come to terms with the degree to which the 2016 electorate was angry.

Bill's time on the ground only encouraged his skepticism of Mook's reluctance to send him outside population centers. Having grown up in Arkansas, Bill understood that a major political player—a senator, a governor, or a former president—could bridge ideological divides by just showing up in small towns that never got much attention from elected leaders. He liked to go to small towns in northern New Hampshire, Appalachia, and rural Florida because he believed, from experience, that going to them and acknowledging he knew how they lived their lives, and the way they made decisions, put points on the board. Mook wanted Bill in places where the most Hillary-inclined voters would see him. That meant talking to white liberals and minorities in cities and their close-in suburbs.

That was one fault line of a massive generational divide between Bill and Mook that separated old-time political hustling from modern data-driven vote collecting. Bill was like the old manager putting in a pinch hitter he believed would come through in the clutch while the eggheaded general manager in the owner's box furiously dialed the dugout phone to let him know there was an 82 percent chance that the batter would make an out this time. It's not that Bill resisted data—he loved poring over political numbers—but he thought of it as both necessary and insufficient for understanding electoral politics. One longtime Bill confidant put the difference this way: Robby was an expert in GOTV (get out the vote) data, and Bill came from a time when GOTV meant "go on television"—not to get interviewed but to get free media exposure that amplified his appearance in a small town and ensured everyone there knew he'd been by to check in. Trump's mastery of turning social media posts into twenty-four-hour reporting on his campaign echoed Bill's instincts for getting free press.

There was another aspect to Bill's desire to go into small towns. He believed—as did Hillary's top advisers—that it didn't make much sense for him to do national television interviews. There, he could be sandbagged by questions about whatever topic was Washington's obsession of the day and get sidetracked from the message he wanted to deliver. But Bill thought it was important to get earned— free—media exposure in smaller places. He'd rather go to a small town in a state and get the local newspaper to cover his speech and the questions he frequently took in rope line interactions with voters and reporters. The model, which seemed to work well and which allowed him to pick and choose what he'd respond to, added to his confidence in his own old-school formula for politicking.

Bill's frustration with Mook had grown during the lead-up to the Iowa caucuses and in the aftermath, when it was clear that the campaign manager's pet analytics models had overstated Hillary's margins. Even more, the close race had forced Bill to stare into the abyss of the possibility that Hillary would lose the first two states and never regain her footing. In New Hampshire, he pushed and pushed to get out of the southern population centers—Manchester and Nashua—and didn't get to do as much of that as he would have liked.

"Honestly, I would love to have you go there but I feel we've got to have you where the votes are," Mook told the former president.

After having campaigned in New Hampshire throughout January, Bill knew just as well as Hillary did that she was going to lose the state. But he believed there was a chance to keep the margin under ten points, which would provide a moral victory. Meanwhile, the numbers were moving in the opposite direction.

Bill may have thought he or Hillary could persuade voters, but she would have needed a stronger vision to make the case. She had plans for every imaginable corner of public policy, but they were loosely strung together. There was no simple vision unifying them—no central, defining promise of a Hillary presidency. Bernie, on the other hand, presented a very clear idea of where he wanted to take the country. He told voters he would break up a system that favored the privileged over the masses. What he lacked in breadth and depth, he made up for with a bright, tight thunderbolt of a message that benefited from the echo effect of Trump's populism in the Republican primary. His platform of breaking up big banks, providing universal single-payer health care, and subsidizing free college tuition for students suffocated her among the white economic liberals who dominate the Democratic electorates in Iowa, New Hampshire, and many other states. But this was not the only set of voters she found in the primaries, and the calendar after New Hampshire would allow Hillary another chance to fashion a message that would get her campaign on track.

A few days before the election, Hillary tapped Sullivan and Schwerin to turn her message toward the voters of color she would need to win in upcoming contests. Unlike her 2008 campaign, Hillary's 2016 sequel was obsessed with the critical goal of winning as many delegates to the Democratic convention as possible. By the time in 2008 that she realized Obama had a better strategy for racking up delegates by dominating her in low-turnout caucus states and among African American voters, it was way too late for her to reverse the cold mathematical reality of her defeat.

In that year, African Americans had voted as a bloc in southern primaries, delivering massive delegate hauls to Obama. Based on polling, reports from allies in various states, and Hillary's longstanding relationships in the black community, she and her team believed she had a substantial advantage with African American voters in 2016. But through Iowa and New Hampshire, two of the whitest states in America, it was an untested question. To kindle her own southern firewall in South Carolina on February 27 and in several Super Tuesday states on March 1, Hillary had to press her edge with black voters.

At a meta level, that meant breaking out of the box Sanders had trapped her in by talking only about economic issues and taking positions so liberal that they would be unsustainable in a general election. He could out-socialist her every day of the week and twice on election Tuesdays, and he did. If she had said she thought bankers should be taxed at 90 percent, he would have said 95 percent. These economic issues, Sanders believed, would endear him to voters of color. After all, African American and Hispanic workers would benefit from minimum wage increases, a Medicare-for-all health care system, and more redistributive tax policies—and, on many of his programs, disproportionately so.

But Hillary thought there was more at stake than just pure economics for these voters. Internal campaign data culled just before the New Hampshire primary showed that Hillary's "criminal justice" message played well with African American voters. The groundwork for appealing to the African American community was already there. In the early days of the campaign, she had given a speech calling for the end of the "era of mass incarceration," piggybacking on bipartisan criminal justice reform efforts in the Senate, and rejecting the results of major portions of the 1994 crime law her husband had supported and signed. The best-scoring attack lines against Bernie with both races were on his scrapping Obamacare for a single-payer national health care system and his votes on gun issues. Sanders's singular focus on economic equality gave Hillary the opening to portray him as inattentive to other issues of importance to African American voters.

For some time, African American elected officials, friends, and advisers had been telling Hillary how she and Sanders were perceived in the black community. The key difference—which could turn out to be a strength or a liability—was that black voters knew Clinton and didn't know Sanders. That gave him an opportunity to define himself and gain ground on her. But if she could get there first—while he was celebrating his victory in New Hampshire and in the debate a couple of days later—she would have the chance to define him in negative terms.

So while Sullivan and Schwerin holed up to draft her speech on New Castle, an exclusive island off the coast of New Hampshire, Hillary flew to Flint, Michigan, a majority-black city where a water-poisoning crisis had left residents feeling that their government had failed them. Leaving New Hampshire two days before the primary might have raised eyebrows, but knowing how badly she was going to lose—and how much she needed to differentiate herself with black voters—no one on her team raised an objection. In any case, by the next day, it would be hard for her aides to focus fully on the world outside her campaign, or even beyond their own jobs.

On the afternoon before primary day, several of Hillary's senior staffers were working in an unfinished conference room attached to the Radisson Hotel in Manchester when a bruising Politico story surfaced. It foretold a campaign staff shake-up. Benenson and digital director Teddy Goff were called out as weak links.

The aides sat in mortified silence as they thumbed the faces of their phones and the scroll bars of their laptops, looking for their own names and those of both friends and rivals. The truth was, Clinton's senior staff—including Podesta, Mook, Benenson, Palmieri, Sullivan, Schwerin, Schake, and Grunwald—had hardly said a word to one another all week in the drab and dour conference room, preferring to quietly bide their time until Tuesday's political execution by the New Hampshire electorate. But now the silence turned oppressive. "We didn't really know," said one source who was in the room.

Goff was stunned. He thought he had a good relationship with Hillary, and that her inability to catch fire online—his mission—had more to do with the social stigma of being with her and against Bernie than it did with any failure of strategy or tactics. She just couldn't go viral for anything positive. But no one was surprised by the idea that Benenson was on the hot seat.

Mook, who knew he was on shaky ground despite the public acclaim he'd gotten for pulling out Iowa and having dodged the brunt of the Politico story, advised his colleagues to focus on their work, not the media surrounding it.

"Put your head down," he told them.

In the hours that followed, some aides received personal reassurances about their standing. Abedin pulled Goff aside and told him that Clinton had e-mailed to say "she loves you." But it was a moment of crisis for most of the team, and no one wanted to be in New Hampshire any longer than they had to.

MOOK HEEDED HIS own advice. Not two hours later, he instructed his team to prepare for a major strategy shift after the loss, one that aligned with the turn Hillary took in going to Flint. It would be important, he said, to sell the idea that Bernie was the favorite in Nevada on the 20th and Hillary would be dominant in South Carolina on the 27th. In theory, that would help temper the barrage of coming stories about Bernie's resurgence. Second, he said, the new message had to "root her candidacy in a moral mission and shore up trust issues." And third, he announced a major change in the campaign's tack against Bernie. "We are re-aligning our surrogate team to hit Bernie much harder, with a disciplined focus on (1) his plans don't add up and he won't deliver and (2) he is not ready to be commander in chief." Surrogates would be trained to go after Sanders much more aggressively in on-the-record remarks to the media, one that reflected Hillary's desire to get tougher with him.

By this point, Sullivan and Schwerin had been working on Hillary's New Hampshire concession remarks for several days. The basic idea was a Trojan horse. On the outside, her speech would appear to be a basic acknowledgment of her loss. But it would carry a new message designed to show that she was the candidate for voters of color and women, and that Bernie was not. The two men fashioned a tagline—"Breaking Barriers"—and presented the speech to Hillary on the morning of the February 9 primary.

You guys missed the point, a frustrated Hillary thought. *This doesn't draw a real contrast with Bernie.* It wasn't enough for her to vow to deliver for voters when he was promising more. She had to show that his plans were pie in the sky and that she could bring results that would improve their daily lives. She wanted to go at Bernie much harder, to drive the point home with no ambiguity. Earlier that week, during a debate, she'd accused him of executing an "artful smear" by suggesting—but not outright saying—that she was corrupt. He was an inferior candidate, she thought, and he was mopping up the floor with her in New Hampshire. It was time to hit back. She told Sullivan and Schwerin their branding was too aspirational and that it didn't work as a contrast against Bernie. She was also upset that they had written her a full speech—the kind she might give on the heels of a victory—rather than quick remarks that could let her slip away from a bad performance quickly. "We weren't expecting a long formal speech tonight and then discovered there was one," Abedin told Podesta. "And she wasn't happy." Hillary beckoned Schwerin and Sullivan to iron it out. She ultimately accepted the "Breaking Barriers" slogan, reluctantly, and they shaved her speech down to about 10 minutes.

Hillary was at her wit's end when it came to her messaging—dismayed by the campaign's lack of inspiration. Here she was, a year into her campaign and about to get trampled by a socialist, and "Breaking Barriers" was the best her staff could come up with. She wasn't panicked, but she was coming to grips with the idea that, even with years to think about it, the campaign team she'd built was no better than its 2008 predecessor at helping her find an articulable vision for the country.

In late January, as Hillary's campaign began to think about "evolving the core message," Ron Klain chimed in with a succinct analysis of what was missing. "We need to invest more time in describing what HRC wants to do for America, if she becomes President," he wrote to her top campaign brass. "What is it that she wants to do as President? How would America be different? What should people be excited about? . . . What we need to deliver is a more compelling message on America under HRC."

Schwerin replied with a telling insight into Hillary that everyone in her orbit understood but couldn't, or wouldn't, impress upon her. "I think Ron's right, but the irony here is that HRC talks about hardly anything else," the frustrated speechwriter asserted. "Her stump has always been a long recitation of what she wants to do as President. We've rolled out a million detailed policies. Our problem is missing the forest for the trees. We've never found a good way (or at least a way she embraces) that sums up her vision for how America would be different."

It was a vision Hillary herself couldn't articulate for them. But the one aspect of her campaign that she was most confident about was that none of the tribes, separately or in collaboration, had any idea how to construct a winning message for her. In her view, it was up to the people she paid to find the right message for her—a construction deeply at odds with the way Sanders and Trump built their campaigns around their own gut feelings about where to lead the country.

AS THEY WOULD on other election nights, the Clintons retreated to a warren of rooms at their hotel to await the results. In New Hampshire, it was the Radisson—a sprawling facility that could accommodate 2,500 people. Outside, there was snow on the ground, and the roads were icy throughout New England. Any comfort Hillary Clinton could find that night would be cold.

The drubbing was so bad that the networks didn't wait ten minutes, or even five, to call it. They declared Bernie Sanders the winner within a minute or so of the polls closing. At the end of an ugly week, with some of their jobs reportedly on the line, that struck Hillary's brain trust as funny. Her aides chuckled like condemned prisoners awaiting the gallows.

As her top aides shuffled onto an elevator to head to the "victory" rally, Hillary made sure to join them for the quick ride down. She was determined that they not lose their sense of purpose, and she wanted them to know she appreciated that they had worked hard even in defeat. It was an especially important moment because she knew they had all read the story about a staff shake-up. She'd been asked about it on Rachel Maddow's show on MSNBC the night before and, while brushing off the specifics, essentially acknowledged that she was constantly assessing the state of her campaign. In the face of all of that, Hillary sensed a need to be gracious and to let her aides know she—and they—would be back to fight another day.

"Thank you," she said softly.

When Hillary found Vlacich backstage before she delivered her concession speech, he was heartbroken. For all his experience running statewide campaigns in New Hampshire, he hadn't been able to crack the code for Hillary.

"I'm really sorry about this," he said. "But we're going to get them in November."

"I can't think of what more we could have done," she said, hugging the bear of a man as he struggled to hold back tears. "You did a great job."

Bill shook his hand.

Hillary went out to give her speech before the final votes from Sanders's heart-stopping twenty-two-point win had been reported. She struck upbeat notes as she began to pivot toward a new emphasis on social injustice that she hoped would help her lock down the votes of black and Hispanic Democrats. Sanders gave her an opening to do so because of his singular attention to income inequality. Hillary knew, by contrast, that many Democratic voters believed that racism, for example, couldn't be solved simply by closing income gaps.

"When people anywhere in America are held back by injustice, that demands action. That is why I believe so strongly that we have to keep up with every fiber of our being the argument for, the campaign for human rights. Human rights as women's rights, human rights as gay rights, human rights as worker rights, human rights as voting rights, human rights across the board for every single American. Now, that is who I am. That is what I've always done," she said to applause.

At one of the bleakest moments of the campaign, with Bernie rising and Clinton's high command worried about getting fired, Bill and Hillary offered a small gesture of consolation to their team as they departed New Hampshire. Hillary ordered up a larger plane for the flight to New York and offered a ride home to the Brooklyn staff who had come to the Granite State at her insistence. As they boarded, the Clintons hugged their aides and tried to buck them up for the long road that would follow the short flight. On the hop from Manchester to New York, she and Bill settled into adjoining seats at the front of the jet. They fell asleep, her head on his shoulder and his head propped against hers.

Hillary had hidden her emotions as the drubbing unfolded. But she was demoralized and angry. She thought she'd built a campaign capable of zooming through the primaries. Even after everything she'd done to correct for her 2008 campaign, she now faced another brutal slog. She'd defied her own instincts by not taking shots at Bernie. Now he was the comeback kid, and she looked beatable. She was going to have to fight, both internally and state by state, for this nomination.

"Now, it's going to go to July and it's going to be bloody," she confided to an aide in an unguarded moment before she left the state. "We should have figured out a way to deal with Bernie earlier."

Chapter 9

BASE POLITICS

ECRETARY CLINTON, YOU'RE NOT IN THE WHITE HOUSE yet." It was February 11, in Milwaukee, Wisconsin, the site of the sixth Democratic presidential debate, one that came at a critical moment for both candidates. With his victory in New Hampshire, Sanders actually held a lead in pledged delegates. He was bringing in money faster than he could count it, and the question was whether he could build a wave strong enough to sweep over Clinton. This meeting with Sanders, who was getting much more adroit in debates and who now had the wind at his back, held tremendous risk for Hillary. And she was getting hammered.

When Hillary talked about what she'd do as president, Sanders snapped back with the line about her measuring the Oval Office drapes. When she defended her original formulation that Latin American refugees should be turned away, Sanders suggested she lacked compassion. "Who are you sending a message to?" he asked rhetorically. "These are children who are leaving countries and neighborhoods where their lives are at stake." And when Hillary noted she talked foreign policy with Henry Kissinger—whom many liberals consider a war criminal—Sanders was ready with a sharp rejoinder: "I happen to believe that Henry Kissinger was one of the most destructive secretaries of state in the modern history of this country. I am proud to say that Henry Kissinger is not my friend. I will not take advice from Henry Kissinger."

Internal and external polling still showed her leading among African American and Hispanic voters, communities that had enough voting power to bail her out. But her margin in Nevada, the next state to vote, was closing fast, and Sanders flooded the state with ground troops to try to pull off an upset. Hillary could put on a brave face for the cameras and even with most of her aides, but the arduous schedule and the punishing rejection of New Hampshire voters were taking a psychic toll. It showed in the debate.

Time and again, Sanders punched and counterpunched effectively. He might have been a little too aggressive at times, but Sanders was at his best in a big moment. He didn't seem ready, however, for what would turn out to be the biggest exchange of the night. In fact, no one but the Clinton camp was expecting it. Polling data and anecdotal evidence from allies strongly suggested that black voters would be turned off by Sanders's criticism of Obama over the years. "We knew that particularly African Americans, but not only African Americans, found it distasteful that people would be attacking the president, and in particular Bernie's call for him to have a primary opponent in 2012, which didn't sit well," said one Hillary adviser who was involved in the prep for the Milwaukee debate.

It was an act of disloyalty that few Democrats knew about, but it's one she would make damn sure every black voter had heard about by the time he or she went to the polls. It was the key to defining Sanders for black voters before the primary turned to the Deep South. Hillary had lined up to take this shot at Bernie a few days earlier in her New Hampshire concession speech.

"Today Senator Sanders said that President Obama failed the presidential leadership test," Hillary declared. "And this is not the first time that he has criticized President Obama. In the past he has called him weak. He has called him a disappointment. He wrote a foreword for a book that basically argued voters should have buyers' remorse when it comes to President Obama's leadership and legacy. . . . You know, from my perspective, maybe because I understand what President Obama inherited, not only the worst financial crisis but the antipathy of the Republicans in Congress, I don't think he gets the credit he deserves for being a president . . . who got us out of that." Hillary had been interrupted by applause.

Sanders was taken aback at the new line of attack. He wasn't used to being called out as insufficiently supportive of Obama. In his liberal circles, it was de rigueur to criticize Obama for failing to take a harder line. But he didn't see himself as an opponent of the president or his agenda. He called the attack a "low blow," noted that he had supported much of Obama's work from the Senate, and referred to himself as a friend of the president. He seemed satisfied with his response.

Then Hillary moved in for the kill.

"Calling the president weak, calling him a disappointment, calling several times that he should have a primary opponent when he ran for reelection in 2012, you know, I think that goes further than saying 'we have our disagreements.' "

Sanders landed a quick zinger—"Well, one of us ran against Barack Obama; I was not that candidate"—that won most of the attention from the press that night. But what he didn't appreciate was the extent to which African American voters had not only forgiven Hillary for running against Obama but had respected her for agreeing to go work for him. Hillary had done her homework. She and her husband were still held in high regard by most black voters—who had seen them work on issues of importance to communities of color for many years—and didn't like the outsider Sanders attacking the president or her. Hillary knew all of that intuitively, she knew it from the feedback she got from friends and political allies, and she knew in her bones that she was simply and clearly more at home in the black community than Sanders ever would be. In one exchange, she had successfully put daylight between Sanders and Obama and drawn herself even closer to the African American community. She had placed Bernie outside a coalition that included her, Obama, and most black voters. It was a strikingly deft maneuver from a candidate often criticized for her lack of political skill.

Pinning Bernie into a white base and refocusing her attention on minority voters would have important implications for both the nomination fight and the general election. While no community is monolithic—and Bernie was able to peel off some support from younger minority voters—Hillary's massive advantage among African Americans and Latinos was the key to her strategy for accumulating delegates to the Democratic convention.

The 4,765 Democratic delegates were split into two types: a set of 700-plus party leaders, called "superdelegates," who could vote for whomever they chose, and more than 4,000 "pledged" delegates who were bound to vote for a candidate based on the outcome in their home district or state. Each candidate would win a percentage of the statewide pledged delegates based on the percentage of the vote he or she won, and each would take a share of the pledged delegates available in each of the state's congressional districts based on his or her percentage of the vote there. Importantly, states with more population have a larger number of available delegates, and the delegates aren't spread evenly throughout a state's congressional districts. The total number of delegates available in a district is pegged to the district's performance for Democratic candidates in previous elections. It's all very complicated, but it boils down to this: A candidate who does best in the most Democratic parts of a state can rack up a lot of delegates fast. In many states, the delegate-rich districts are majority-minority. Hillary and her delegate-crunching team knew that running up the score among black and Hispanic voters would net her an outsize share of the delegates in populous states with more delegates available. Bernie had won New Hampshire by 22 points, but that netted him just a 15-to-9 delegate haul. Hillary could more than erase that with a good showing in a single black-majority district in Mississippi.

From that Milwaukee debate through the end of the campaign, Hillary would never stray from the African American base that provided her sustenance in key primary states and numbers in November battlegrounds. But there was a trade-off. "Our failure to reach out to white voters, like literally from the New Hampshire primary on, it never changed," said one campaign official.

▼

NO ONE IN Clintonworld was more in tune with Hillary's state of mind than Huma Abedin, the ever-present body woman, scheduler, and personal adviser. During the 2008 campaign, Hillary had surrounded herself with friends and aides who had been with her for nearly two decades. On this campaign, most of her advisers were professionals who had been brought in for their expertise rather than their understanding of the candidate. It was an issue that wouldn't ever go away: Hillary was being advised by people who thought they knew her—she'd been in the public eye for most or all of their adult lives—but really didn't have a feel for who she was at her core.

While Hillary had long since grown weary of the high-paid consultants, even most of the campaign aides she liked and trusted weren't personally close to her. Many of them were a generation or more younger, and the cohort that had gained power internally was almost entirely male. Even before the devastating loss in New Hampshire, Abedin knew Hillary needed a little tender loving care.

So Abedin reached out to Minyon Moore, a Chicago-born alum of Jesse Jackson's presidential campaigns who had worked in the Clinton White House, handled delicate political tasks for Hillary, and exchanged daily devotional quotations with her.

Minyon, Huma said, come quick.

Moore abandoned her schedule in Washington to spend five or six days on the campaign trail, crisscrossing the country—Minnesota, Nevada, Colorado, South Carolina, and New York—in Hillary's small jet and, like an amateur psychologist, listening to her friend. Moore was worried that no matter how much Hillary tried to tune out attacks from Sanders and from the half-dozen Republicans who remained in the race for the GOP nomination, some of it was getting to her. Her friend was anxious about the state of the campaign and about the mood of the electorate.

On one of the flights, Hillary unburdened herself to Moore. "I don't understand what's happening with the country. I can't get my arms around it," Hillary confided. Moore just listened. "How do I get answers to this?" Hillary asked.

It was a quandary that would plague her throughout the campaign. After nearly a year on the campaign trail, and hundreds of stops at diners, coffee shops, and high school gymnasiums and just as many roundtables with young professionals and millworkers, Hillary still couldn't figure out why Americans were so angry or how she could bring the country together. She had tried to learn the lessons of 2008 and had built a campaign that was different, if too similar in some respects, this time around. But fundamental changes in the electorate eluded her grasp. She couldn't find ways to connect with portions of the primary electorate that were driven to Sanders because he represented an all-out assault on the establishment thinking at the core of her being.

When she peeked at the Republican primary, she saw campaigns running into a similar problem. Jeb Bush—the favorite going into the race—was being pummeled by Trump. Like Sanders, the freewheeling billionaire businessman turned political force was taking advantage of the populist fury that had swept the nation. From her perspective, these guys weren't offering plausible solutions. But they were good at channeling anger.

Meanwhile, she was running into the same trap as 2008. She was becoming the inevitable candidate of the status quo, the one she tried so desperately to avoid this time around by offering a raft of new policy proposals. Her message wasn't getting through— even in the moments that weren't dominated by the e-mail scandal. The one thing Hillary could put her finger on was that her 2016 team wasn't doing any better of a job of figuring out how to connect her to the national sentiment. She was in a bubble, and so were the people around her. Together, they had a feel for national politics from the 2008 and 2012 campaigns, when the public was less dissatisfied with the Democratic establishment's inability to solve their problems.

John Podesta and Neera Tanden, who were closer to the progressive movement because of their ties to the liberal think tank

Center for American Progress, had warned that Sanders was positioned to tap into liberal angst. But Hillary didn't fully believe it—
until it happened—and she was backed up by sycophants and those
on her campaign who weren't as attuned to the left. And though
Bill's instinct to talk with voters outside of cities seemed right, he
was, in other ways, practicing what some Clintonworld denizens
viewed as the politics of the past. Like Hillary, he still thought he
could win the argument over whether the existing government could
solve people's problems. "Bill Clinton does not really get where the
country is. He has this perception of politics which is very much
like the 1990s," one of Hillary's advisers said in the midst of the
primaries. "The fact the government hasn't worked in a couple of
years is really altering both parties."

A FRUSTRATED, CONTEMPLATIVE, and subdued Hillary Clinton landed in Las Vegas on February 13, 2016, one week before the
state's caucuses. Bernie's legions flooded the state, and the news
media fixated on the possibility that Sanders could send her reel-
ing by knocking out a second straight victory. She couldn't help but
be reminded of the intense battle she'd fought with Barack Obama
in Nevada in 2008, the contest that had forged the reputations of
Mook and Marshall.

That had been a traditional fight between two campaigns using
similar tried-and-true organizing tactics. But there was something very different about the paradigm in 2016. This time, Sanders continued to show he didn't have to slog through months of
door knocking, flesh pressing, and phone banking to build a force
on the ground. The Bernie phenomenon was particularly scary to
Hillary's team in Nevada for two reasons: caucuses are traditionally low-turnout affairs, and Nevadans are particularly politically
disengaged.

Hillary's top aide in the state, Emmy Ruiz, had arrived in Nevada almost a year earlier, before the official launch of the campaign, at the direction of Marshall. With a small team and limited

resources—Mook had already focused the lion's share of the campaign's money and attention on Iowa—the Texas-bred daughter of Mexican immigrants spent most of 2015 and early 2016 creating a field operation for Hillary. Ruiz and her lieutenants traveled across the state on a lower-key version of one of Hillary's hallmark listening tours, gathering information about the electorate and starting to spread the word about Hillary's priorities. Through the fall and winter, they formed relationships with a budding Hillary contingent in the state, including a group of so-called DREAMers—nonvoting immigrants who were brought to the United States as children by their parents.

They basically followed the playbook for a state-level campaign. But by the time Hillary arrived a week before the caucuses, it was clear to Ruiz that they were fighting an asymmetrical force in Sanders. His campaign could post something on Reddit or Facebook and thousands of followers would show up for a rally in a state where politics was seldom at the forefront of anyone's mind.

Hillary sat down with Ruiz in her hotel room atop the Art Deco–style Four Seasons in Las Vegas that Saturday. Huma was there, and so was Rory Reid, the son of Senate minority leader Harry Reid. Downstairs, at the world-famous Mandalay Bay Casino, amid flashing lights and ringing bells, thrilled weekend wagers downed cocktails, pumped coins into slot machines, and threw dice onto craps tables. Upstairs, inside the stale quiet of Hillary's room, a heaviness filled the air. Hillary felt like the entire world was against her. Sanders had landed a few blows at the debate in Milwaukee, and she couldn't buy a break in the press. She stared into the abyss of a second failed attempt to win the Democratic nomination. If she lost Nevada, she might rebound in the southern states that followed, but she might not. Either way, it would pierce the narrative that Sanders couldn't win in states with significant minority populations and increase the likelihood of a brutal battle for the nomination.

To make matters worse, Hillary felt miserable physically. She wasn't just sick and tired of the attacks on her, she was literally tired and sick. A sinus infection gnawed on the insides of her skull. The moment itself became a test of her capacity to do what she told voters she would do for them—fight through barriers. She struggled with this one, battling illness and despondence.

"What's the plan?" she asked, her voice loaded with fatigue. "What are we doing?"

Though the questions were specific to Nevada, they also represented the larger existential issues Hillary wrestled with through the early months of 2016. This wasn't the Hillary who usually showed up for briefings. That Hillary peppered her aides with questions designed to elicit detailed information. This one was going through the motions. She was off.

Like Abedin, who had called in Moore as a reinforcement for this campaign swing, and Moore herself, Ruiz saw before her a candidate who needed an emotional lift, an injection of optimism and energy. Ruiz, who had worked on the 2008 campaign but really came to appreciate Hillary when the former secretary of state spoke at a mutual friend's low-profile funeral in 2014, took it upon herself to buck up her boss. Throughout the campaign, Hillary's aides felt the need to lift her spirits. Publicly, they portrayed her as undeterred by defeat—Podesta would later tell a reporter that "after New Hampshire she didn't just take the loss or get all down"—but the drubbing had vexed and deflated her. The campaign, which she'd resisted jumping into, was proving to be joyless. Ruiz hoped to change that with a plan of action that would play to Hillary's favorite way of campaigning. But first, she had to deliver the bad news.

"What we're doing is not working," the usually high-strung Texan explained in an even tone. Bernie was closing—and fast. "We're changing course," Ruiz told Hillary. She proposed a gamble in a much higher-stakes contest than the games of blackjack and roulette playing out on Mandalay Bay tables below them. Bernie was going big—huge rallies and a 30,000-foot message about unrigging the American economy. Hillary, she said, should go small in the final week. She had to go to Nevadans, where they lived, ate, and worked. And she had to do it around the clock. She should prove she could outwork anyone—a value highly regarded by the very union and working-class people of color she needed to spend hours with at caucus sites—Ruiz said. And she would loosen up a bit, get off script, by interacting openly with voters in sessions that weren't open to reporters.

Part of the plan was specific to Nevada and its fast-approaching caucus. But part of it was a gambit to pull Hillary out of her funk. She could move out of the campaign bubble, feed off the energy of the people she hoped to represent in the White House, and drink in a little love at a time when she was feeling down. That part was unspoken, but central to Ruiz's thinking.

While contemplative in her decision-making process and prone to taking only calculated risks, Hillary harbors a deep bias for acting over standing pat. It was that trait that drove her to support the raid that killed Osama bin Laden in 2011 at a time when Obama's advisers were badly divided over the risks of a covert strike. And so, high above Las Vegas that Saturday, in a hotel connected to a renowned casino, the cautious candidate came to understand that she would have to gamble on an unorthodox new strategy if she hoped to hold off Sanders and turn her campaign around. At the risk that ceding the public stage to Sanders would fuel his surge, Hillary committed to working the kitchens, high school band rooms, and soccer fields of Las Vegas.

She nodded her approval.

The next day, Hillary met with a group of DREAMers at one of her campaign offices in Las Vegas. Her campaign moved the press out after her opening remarks, and Hillary asked if anyone wanted to ask her a question. At first, the room was silent. Then, a few of the children posed questions. One young girl, fighting back tears, told Hillary she was afraid her parents, who had entered the country illegally, would be deported.

"Come here," Hillary said.

The girl got up and walked across the room to where Hillary sat, as the adults in the room applauded her. Hillary, still seated, wrapped her arm around the girl.

"I'm going to do everything I can so you don't have to be scared and you don't have to worry about what happens to your mom or your dad or somebody else in your family," Hillary said. "I feel really, really strongly, but you're being brave, and you have to be brave for them too, because they want you to be happy, they want you to be successful, they don't want you to worry too much. Let me do the worrying. I'll do all the worrying. Is that a deal? I'll do the worry. I'll do everything I can to help, OK?"

Then the girl hugged Hillary.

Ruiz and her team watched video of the moment over and over again, some of them crying. Back in Brooklyn, Oren Shur's video team stayed up into the wee hours of the night cutting the raw footage into a television spot. They called it "Brave."

The ad struck a nerve in Hillaryland because it showed compassion; her concern for children, families, and minorities; a young girl reaching out to hug her; and a genuineness that Hillary had trouble evincing in larger settings. In just sixty seconds, the ad tore away layers of Hillary, accessing what her aides and allies called the real Hillary. She had gone small—to a private meeting with DREAMers—and come away with a means of translating her intimacy to the masses.

Until that moment, her ads hadn't been as strong as Sanders's. A little less than two weeks before the Iowa caucuses, Bernie had released a spot called "America" that mixed images of Americans at work and play with those of him shaking hands with voters and those of his big campaign rallies. Playing to the backdrop of the Simon and Garfunkel song of the same name, it contained no words. But it was widely praised for placing the candidate within an American community.

Now, Hillary could show, in a fashion that wasn't prepackaged, that she was running to be a champion for someone else. She would do the worrying and the fighting for the underdogs in society, like the ten-year-old Latina so frightened about the possibility of her parents being sent away. It was the message Hillary wanted to convey in her campaign, but the near-miss in Iowa and crushing loss in New Hampshire had given her plenty of reason to doubt that she could persuade voters of its authenticity. The moment with the little girl finally tapped directly into her motive for running, allies said.

AT HER LOWEST point on the campaign trail, faced with Sanders's rising popularity, anxiety among her allies, and her own self-doubt, Hillary moved into safe spaces. She was going home in ways abstract and concrete. Moore created that on her plane, giving her a friend—not an aide, a consultant, a donor, or a well-wisher—to open up with. Going small in Nevada meant she would have a comfort zone at campaign events. And on the Tuesday before the state's caucuses, Hillary literally went home to New York—to Harlem—to reset her message in a way that she hoped would appeal both to minority voters she needed to win in Nevada, South Carolina, and the Super Tuesday primaries on March 1 and, hopefully, to the white voters with whom she continued to struggle.

Her theme, rolled out in part in her New Hampshire concession speech and built upon in the Milwaukee debate, revolved around the "Breaking Barriers" concept that Schwerin and Sullivan had spun. Long before Hillary began campaigning for president, many of her closest friends had come to the conclusion that she had to find a way to connect her personal narrative to the hardships of working- and middle-class Americans and position herself as a worthy champion for their causes. Intellectually, Hillary could grasp the benefits of the construct: it cast her—the former first lady, senator, and secretary of state—as a hero; it was genuinely true that she had blazed trails in politics and policy; and it tipped the balance of emphasis a little further away from her and toward the people she hoped would elect her president.

But for nearly a year on the campaign trail, she hadn't been able to connect all the dots. She spoke about "I" and "you," but almost never "we." When supporters declared their allegiance to her online, they did it with #I'mWithHer. For whatever reason—she chalked it up to midwestern modesty—she felt uncomfortable presenting herself as the heroine. And yet critics saw her reluctance to use "we"—like Bernie Sanders and Donald Trump and so many other candidates did—as evidence that her campaign was all about her. It was one of the subtle but unmistakable ways in which every action of Hillary's—every uttered pronoun, even—became a political Rorschach test.

There was nothing particularly catchy about "Breaking Barriers" as a slogan or a mission statement. But it served its purposes well enough: making her personal story part of the narrative of the campaign—not only did she promise to break down barriers for voters, but she had the credibility of being a barrier-breaker herself, appealing to minority voters who worried about both economic and social constraints on their opportunities and outcomes and reaching out to white voters who cared about social justice.

Hillary had begun teasing the "Breaking Barriers" mantra in New Hampshire and Wisconsin, but she really hammered it home in Harlem. "Hold me accountable. Hold every candidate accountable," Hillary told a mostly black audience in a speech defined by its concentration on racial justice. "You deserve leaders who will do whatever it takes to tear down all the barriers holding you back and then replace them with those ladders of opportunity that every American deserves."

In spirit this was the campaign she wanted to run, even though she didn't love the catchphrase. In her mind, her whole life had been about public service, from helping poor families through the Children's Defense Fund to high-level government jobs. It was ridiculous, she thought, that anyone could portray her as purely motivated by self-interest. What the hell had Bernie Sanders ever accomplished to improve the quality of anyone else's life? He could talk until he was blue in the face about economic justice, but she'd fought for decades to even playing fields at the micro and macro levels. What did Bernie think Hillarycare was about? And the Children's Health

Insurance Program? And how could anyone pretend that racial injustice wasn't a key barrier to the economic advancement of people of color? She had fought for the most forgotten people in American society, the poor women and children—often black and Hispanic—throughout her adult life. More than that, she had scars from those brawls, from being demonized for elevating the invisible people in American society, even at the expense of the haves. She cared about opportunity *and* outcome, about incentives *and* assistance. The Harlem speech just felt right to her. For the first time in weeks, maybe months, she was at home on the campaign trail.

"I am so comfortable speaking about this stuff," she told Moore on the plane back to Washington for a fund-raiser in Northern Virginia. "I feel like these are things I need to be talking about." But Hillary still didn't love the "Breaking Barriers" slogan; it was a temporary salve. She still wasn't articulating a vision that could turn her from a candidate inexorably linked with the past into an avatar of the future.

Tactically, she was doing what needed to be done to win delegates, the all-important if unsexy measure of success in presidential nominating contests. She was all science, no art. This time, though, she had built herself a victory lab: the best delegate strategists and a top analytics team. She also had the hard-earned experience to believe only one goal mattered—the 2,383 delegates needed to secure the nomination. The route to that number ran through the heavily black Democratic primary electorates of the Deep South states and the heavily Hispanic congressional districts west of the Mississippi. Hillary staked her strategy on the premise that she could run up the score with minority voters and build an insurmountable delegate lead on the strength of their support. Now, having survived Iowa and New Hampshire, it was time to execute.

But the execution had to come against the backdrop of tension inside the campaign headquarters and anxiety among the Clinton faithful around the country. The blowout in New Hampshire had rattled the Democratic firmament, and now the pressure was coming from everywhere. "It was a very hard ten days" between the New Hampshire primary and the Nevada caucuses, said one campaign aide. "It was brutal."

As they tried to right the ship, Clinton and her top aides fielded a stream of calls, e-mails, and text messages demanding to know what the hell had happened and what they were going to do to fix the campaign. It was a frustrating and lonely moment for Hillary. Her husband had started to bear down on Mook. He wanted to know everything about the playbook for Nevada. "We have a strategy," Mook told Bill, according to one ally. "Nothing has changed in Nevada. We are sticking to it."

The margin might narrow, he reassured both Clintons, but Hillary was positioned to win. Hillary chose to stick to her guns. "She had faith in Robby," the ally said.

Hillary may have felt assured, but she couldn't convince her supporters to look past sensational headlines, an ugly defeat in New Hampshire, or a waiting-for-the-other-shoe-to-drop fear of her e-mail scandal. She was starting to feel better, but they were not. "We had a full-on office plan to really go after our people and say, 'This is why this happened this way. . . . Stay with the plan,'" one top Clinton lieutenant recalled. It didn't really work. Donors, members of Congress, and assorted Democratic chatterers couldn't—or wouldn't—relax.

Representative Marcia Fudge, the dominant political presence in Cleveland, lobbied Marshall hard for answers. She and other members of the Congressional Black Caucus wanted to make sure Hillary was focused on South Carolina. Marshall was a point of contact in part because the CBC didn't trust Mook from his time as the cutthroat top executive at the Democratic Congressional Campaign Committee, when his boss, Steve Israel, had gone to war with black lawmakers over members' dues to the party and the party's policy of neutrality in primaries.

Similarly, Hispanic lawmakers told Clinton and her aides they should be focused on Nevada and its Latino population. Women senators burned up phone lines too, and they had more direct means of getting in her ear. Several of them had traveled to New Hampshire for Hillary only to see her get crushed.

Former New Mexico governor Bill Richardson, annoyed by the campaign's failure to utilize him, sent Podesta a snarky note about an unreturned e-mail from January. "Maybe you guys don't need any extra help given recent results," Richardson wrote in the days after the New Hampshire primary. "You don't need to respond if you're too busy. Just have someone send me the talking points."

Calls came in from the Castro brothers, Texas representative Joaquin and housing and urban development secretary and vice presidential hopeful Julián. Former interior secretary Ken Salazar—who served with Clinton in the Senate—wondered how he could help ahead of Nevada, when things seemed the most grim. Former HUD secretary Henry Cisneros and Representatives Ben Ray Luján of New Mexico and Xavier Becerra of California were concerned about the Hispanic vote and picking up where the campaign left off in 2008. Representative Sheila Jackson Lee of Texas, a longtime Clinton supporter who sat behind her during much of her Benghazi testimony, and other members of the CBC dialed up top campaign aides to tell them black voters wouldn't turn out like they did for Obama without a full push by the campaign. Lee was a gadfly in Congress whom most people just wrote off as crazy. But some of the other callers were taken more seriously.

Hillary would have to fight hard to secure votes, they said. "Listen, this isn't going to be easy," Fudge reminded Marshall. Senators Debbie Stabenow of Michigan and Barbara Boxer of California, whose daughter was once married to Tony Rodham, Hillary's brother, checked in with Clinton's political director, Amanda Renteria, on a regular basis—though largely to relay the concerns of others and advise when Hillary needed to do a little hand-holding on Capitol Hill.

The questions came fast and furious: Why did Hillary's campaign spend time and money in New Hampshire if they were going to get beaten that badly? And if they could have made it closer, why didn't they spend more and earlier? Was there a fundamental flaw in the campaign's strategy?

"Give it time," Renteria counseled over and over. "Trust us."

But the younger operators of the Clinton machine—including Mook, Renteria, and Marshall—hadn't yet earned the trust of the party establishment. If anything, Democratic leaders, particularly older members, were worried that Hillary had built another iceberg-seeking campaign ship.

The younger generation of Democratic officials, one Hillary adviser explained, mostly wanted to help. But the older Democrats, the alumni of Congress and the Clinton administration, pressured campaign officials about their strategy, tactics, and competence. Campaign contributors, those with a monetary stake in the game, fretted even more than the party leaders. "They're the ones that get more persnickety," a senior campaign official said.

These bed wetters consumed more and more of the campaign's time just as Hillary needed to turn the corner and sprint through late February and early March. It wasn't just that they didn't trust her team—they didn't trust Hillary. For the first time in her career, she held the hopes of the Democratic Party in her hands, and that made the party pooh-bahs nervous. After all, she'd done the crazy thing with her e-mails, given speeches for money at a time when it could clearly come back to bite her, and run a disaster of a campaign operation in 2008. Was New Hampshire a bump in the road or a rockslide that would knock her and the Democratic Party off the cliff? And with Donald Trump starting to emerge as the favorite in the Republican primary field, might they go into battle against him with a self-styled socialist? They scrambled to make sure both of her hands were on the wheel, at ten and two.

IF BEATEN DOWN a bit, Hillary remained confident that the turn toward Nevada, South Carolina, and a Super Tuesday slate of states dominated by voters of color would bring victories and a sense of stability. But the Sanders surge—his near-win in Iowa and stomping of Clinton in New Hampshire—left doubts in the backs of the minds of her Brooklyn brain trust. Now the margins mattered a lot. Could Sanders use that momentum and his economic message to break through with black and Hispanic voters? If so, how much?

"With Senator Sanders, he quite frankly is a senator from Vermont," said one Hillary aide discussing his challenge in South Carolina. "There's no history there with the African American community, versus someone who's been known to have fought for the African American community for twenty-five years. So I knew we were going to win. I did not know the margin, and I knew we had to earn it too."

Meanwhile, Bernie was pouring resources into Nevada. There was an opportunity for him to win a second straight contest, pick up momentum, and then test the Clinton theory that South Carolina and the black vote were a true firewall. The Silver State was kind of a forgotten state in the Democratic primary process. Iowa, New Hampshire, and South Carolina topped the national news pages and broadcasts. But suddenly, Nevada became another opportunity for Sanders to gain ground and for Clinton to fall behind.

She could hear his footsteps. Elan Kriegel, Hillary's thirty-four-year-old analytics guru, shared updates on the state of the race with her and a small set of top campaign aides and advisers every two or three days. He was regarded as something of an oracle in the Brooklyn headquarters, deriving his power from a combination of the mystique surrounding his unique numbers and the belief that both Mook and Hillary had in the power of data. While he would share the results his algorithms spit out, he kept his methods close to his vest.

On Valentine's Day, his horse-race analytics surveys had Hillary up seven points. Three days later, and three days before the caucus, it was down to five points. Kriegel sounded optimistic but cautioned that an enthusiasm and education gap—Bernie voters were more likely to know how the caucuses worked—could alter the landscape. The campaign would devote attention to teaching participants about the process, he reported. By the day before the caucus, the analytics team's surveys showed a four-point Hillary margin, 48 percent to 44 percent. Kriegel added a worrisome footnote to his report that day: "We are concerned about some data that suggests people of color are less excited to caucus than white voters," he wrote to colleagues in a message that foreshadowed trouble for Hillary down the line. "If this manifests itself, it could impact the margin negatively." The trend was going in the wrong direction. Like Iowa, Nevada would test whether Mook's no-more-than-necessary field operation—an exacting deployment of resources based on analytics projections— could withstand the energy of Bernie's masses.

One longtime ally who was on the ground in Nevada called in to Brooklyn the night before the caucuses. "What's going to happen?" the ally asked a top member of Hillary's brain trust.

"We're going to lose," the campaign aide replied, explaining that Hillary's internal polls showed a slight-but-too-small lead for her. Sanders had overperformed in public and internal polling in both Iowa and New Hampshire. He had the momentum. "He wins," the aide predicted.

That foreboding feeling permeated Brooklyn. Two of Hillary's top communications aides, Brian Fallon and Christina Reynolds, prepared a set of talking points that would paper over a loss in Nevada, pressing the media to focus on the upcoming contests in South Carolina and on Super Tuesday. The tone of the talking points was described as "defensive" by a person who saw them.

But on the ground in the Silver State, Hillary's aides were getting a different feeling. On Friday night, as Hillary spoke at a big rally in Las Vegas, Ruiz noticed that many of the DREAMers who had been familiar faces at Clinton events for months weren't present. It gave her pause. She asked a member of her staff why they weren't there. It was because they were in the office making last-minute phone calls to shore up votes. The dedication reassured her.

That night, Ruiz, who had fielded questions all week from reporters asking what happens if Clinton loses Nevada, made adjustments to Hillary's schedule for caucus day. In addition to stops designed to put her in front of small groups of service workers—the kitchen staff at casinos—Ruiz decided to send Hillary to Henderson, outside of Las Vegas. It was a sign of confidence that she would hit her targets in her stronghold and reflective of a desire to go on offense in a part of the metropolitan area where Sanders was the favorite.

"If we're going to war, we're going to war," said one person familiar with the plan.

ON SATURDAY, FEBRUARY 20, Hillary's aides gathered in a boiler room at Caesars Palace to monitor results as they came in from caucus sites across the state. The first data—reported by the news media—sent shivers down their spines. The results of an entrance poll—taken as people went into caucus rooms—suggested a significant edge for Sanders. Bernie's team, in another boiler room, was looking at the same information coming in, and Jeff Weaver and Tad Devine exulted in their chances. Bernie called and summoned the two aides to his hotel.

While they were in the car, thinking about how Nevada could really turn the race on its head, Devine's phone rang. It was Podesta. The Clinton campaign chairman was upset. The day before, Bernie's brother, Larry, had wondered aloud to a reporter whether Bill was "really such a terrible rapist" or "a nice rapist."

President Clinton doesn't like being called a sexual predator, Podesta told Devine, especially not by a Democratic candidate. *What kind of bullshit strategy is that?* Devine tried to calm Podesta, whom he'd known since the 1988 Michael Dukakis presidential campaign. "Did you see what I said?" Devine said of a television appearance he'd made the previous day. "Larry is eighty years old. He lives in England. He gave this interview, and he's not going to talk to the press anymore. This is not a strategy." Podesta was not assuaged.

As Podesta blew off the steam of a tense day, Clinton aides were concluding that the entrance poll was off. That didn't necessarily mean Hillary would win, just that Sanders wasn't going to coast to victory. Then Fox News called the caucus for Clinton early. Counterintuitively, that was bad for her. "We needed people to finish caucusing," said one of Hillary's aides. They made more rounds of phone calls to ensure that Hillary supporters weren't leaving caucuses early. They also checked the results, because they weren't sure that Fox was right.

Finally, after confirming the numbers, Mook directed Ruiz to give Hillary the good news. They went upstairs together to the Clinton suite. Hillary, wearing a sateen lipstick-red suit, was reviewing her remarks with Bill when Ruiz and Mook arrived. She knew she had won, and she hugged Ruiz. Ruiz was overcome with emotion. She cried.

The Saturday caucus had been a second major test of Sanders's momentum versus Hillary's machine (Iowa being the other), and, after the New Hampshire blowout, it mattered a lot more for the media story line, the fund-raising efforts, and the blood-pressure level of her allies that she win this state with relatively few delegates to the Democratic convention. Nevada's position on the calendar— third—gave it outsize significance in shaping the narrative of the campaign.

For months, Hillary's team had pointed to South Carolina as her fail-safe. She could withstand losses in any of the opening states—or all three—and come back with victories in the Deep South that would give her a lead in pledged delegates. That was what the strategy memos said. But campaigns aren't fought on paper. In the end, Hillary outmuscled Sanders on the ground in Nevada, using plans drawn up by Mook, Marshall, and Ruiz.

While Sanders rapidly closed the gap in the final weeks—and many in her camp believed she would lose—Hillary posted a respectable margin. The final score: 53 percent to 47 percent. In terms of the overall trajectory of the campaign, she was winning by not losing. Still, Nevada provided the kind of emotional lift Hillary really needed. She'd won despite being sick, tired, and confused about the mood of the electorate. She'd broken Bernie's momentum and reset the media narrative.

"If Nevada had gone south, this is a much different problem. He's a much different problem," one of Hillary's top lieutenants said midway through the primary calendar. "Everyone wants to say that South Carolina was the wall. But at the end of the day, Nevada really was key in turning this race around. It wound up being the wall."

In a side room at Caesars, Mook gathered Hillary's organizers into a circle with Bill Clinton and told them to drench themselves in the moment. "You are literally going to remember this day for the rest of your life," he said. "So soak it up." Then, calling on the former president, the man who'd been on his back relentlessly for ten days, to join in, they burst into a cheer: "H-R-C, twenty-sixteen," they chanted over and over again, sounding like a high school swim team getting amped up for a big meet, as they jumped up and down and clapped in rhythm.

It was a big victory for Mook, but he was hardly off the hot seat. The following day, he and Podesta began casting their eyes toward a shake-up of another arm of the Hillary apparatus. "We have to blow up the consultant team," Podesta told Mook in a conspiratorial note. "I have an idea," the campaign manager replied. Benenson, the top consultant, was in their sights. But Mook's power was in jeopardy too.

Chapter 10

TURNING THE CORNER

BILL CLINTON DIDN'T LIKE WHAT HE SAW—OR RATHER what he didn't see—on a trip to South Carolina in mid-February, right after the debacle in New Hampshire and before the Nevada victory. Bernie's organizers were everywhere, and Hillary hardly seemed to have a presence at all. He sent word to Brooklyn to add ground forces. "He wants to know what he can do to get more resources here," Bill's chief of staff, Tina Flournoy, told Mook.

Bill had almost as much on the line as Hillary in the February 27 primary. Eight years earlier, he'd embarrassed himself and hurt her when he had denigrated Barack Obama's victory there by comparing it with Jesse Jackson's wins in 1984 and 1988, implying that it was no great accomplishment for a black candidate to win in a state where the Democratic electorate was so heavily African American. Now he had an opportunity for redemption, and he was anxious about scoring big in South Carolina both for securing Hillary's standing in the race and restoring his reputation.

Bill was in Mook's ear a lot, from twenty minutes to ninety minutes by phone most days throughout the campaign, but the close call in Iowa and the brutal defeat in New Hampshire had focused his attention more squarely on the campaign manager. Mook thought the former president was overly concerned. He told Flournoy that he was hiring a few more people, but that Hillary was in good shape with a twenty- to thirty-point lead. If Bernie cut into her advantage by more than a few points, he advised, it would be "because of bigger forces" than her field operation. Flournoy gently reminded him that Bill was now focused on the ground game and would continue to press for more organizers in upcoming states with similar demographic profiles.

Mook left nothing to chance, recruiting more volunteer help and adding paid staff recommended by politicians in the state. He dispatched Marlon Marshall, his top lieutenant, to make sure that the field organizers there worked their asses off. More than anything, Hillary had to win big to earn a real lead in delegates and set the table for the March 1 Super Tuesday primaries a few days later. And either way, with an already-annoyed Bill breathing down their necks, Mook and Marshall couldn't afford to show anything less than full attention to the South Carolina ground game. Their challenge was rooted half in the reality of needing to capture delegates and half in cementing the perception in the minds of Bill and his friends in the state that they were hustling.

Already, a change had taken place at headquarters. Mook brought Marshall into more strategy meetings and huddled with his longtime pal more often and more obviously in the office. Mook and Marshall were plotting strategy and tactics for the raft of states that would vote on Super Tuesday and a smaller, but still important set of contests on March 15. Colleagues thought Mook was also making a show of fixing the problems with the campaign's field operations—and, at the same time, demonstrating that it was Marshall who owned that account. "Robby was in trouble, and then it was Robby and Marlon because of the field piece," one campaign aide said. For months, they had talked about South Carolina as the first real Hillary stronghold, the state where she would haul in a pile of delegates and either start to pull away or, if she'd struggled in the first three contests, get on track. Now Hillary had to put up the votes.

Hillary had been laying the groundwork to run up the score with

African American voters for years. Before Barack Obama won Iowa in 2008, some forget, he trailed Hillary in South Carolina primary polling. She was the candidate of African American voters until he proved himself capable of winning the primary. In a fit of pique that year, Bill had insulted black voters—including the powerful veteran congressman Jim Clyburn—with his offhanded comments comparing Obama to Jackson.

The healing process for Hillary and the black community, particularly South Carolina's African American voters, began when she endorsed Obama for president. The wounds were almost fully closed when she accepted his offer to become secretary of state. After leaving State, she spent time at black churches, including a Christmastime service run by former State official Suzan Johnson Cook at the Apollo Theater in Harlem. By the time of her second go-round for the presidency, the scar was a sign of the strength and longevity of the relationship, according to black political operatives in the state and around the country.

Hillary had set up only a bare-bones campaign operation in Columbia, the legacy of Mook's early call to focus the lion's share of primary resources on winning Iowa.

But her first hire in South Carolina, Clay Middleton as state director, turned out to be her masterstroke. Getting him on board was reflective of an essential truth about the campaign: she positioned herself to defeat all comers by meticulously co-opting the party's best operatives, wealthiest donors, most prominent politicians, and sharpest policy minds.

Middleton had been Obama's political director in the state in 2008 and was, along with South Carolina Democratic Party chairman Jaime Harrison, one of the two most promising Clyburn protégés in the state. His presence on the campaign team created continuity between the Obama and Clinton worlds and provided an important nexus to Clyburn, the state's preeminent Democratic power broker. Shortly after acquiring Middleton's services in May 2015, Hillary made her first visit to South Carolina since the 2008 primary. She was in the state the next month too, one day before a gunman murdered nine people in a church in Charleston. Hillary jumped on the gun issue with little hesitation. "How many innocent people in our country—from little children to church members to movie theater attendees—how many people do we need to see cut down before we act?" she said in a speech to Latino political leaders in Nevada the day after the massacre.

She subsequently released a plan that not only called for legislation to reduce access to guns but also promised to take executive action to close the so-called gun-show loophole. Guns became one of her most potent issues in the Democratic primary, as she hammered Sanders for voting against the Brady Bill, a 1990s law that created the background-check system for gun purchases, and for voting to protect gun manufacturers from liability lawsuits. She couldn't believe that Sanders would vote against funding American troops overseas—giving guns to soldiers—but objected to limitations on weapons of war at home. And there was no place in the country where the gun debate was more poignant than in South Carolina. Even in October, long before she started using the issue, Hillary knew that it was a contrast she could draw with Sanders that wouldn't create a backlash because it was one of the few topics on which she was closer to the heart of the Democratic Party's liberal primary base.

HILLARY KNEW SHE needed to win black voters overwhelmingly to get the party's nomination. She wouldn't fare well with liberal whites or in small-turnout caucus states where bad losses meant bleeding delegates. But if she could run up the score and net large delegate hauls in states with large minority populations, her poorer performance with white progressives wouldn't stop her from advancing to the general election. In South Carolina, African Americans were likely to constitute a majority of the primary electorate. She expected to win there. The only question was the margin, and that mattered because it would be a bellwether for other African

American population centers, particularly in the South. She wanted to crush Bernie and signal to black voters in other states that she was the black community's preferred candidate.

For a campaign desperately in need of a big victory to boost its own morale and reassure donors and Democratic officials that Sanders wasn't in a position to defeat her, South Carolina loomed as an oasis. Hillary needed that comfort too. Several of her longtime aides and girlfriends—Cheryl Mills, Capricia Marshall, Kiki McLean, and Minyon Moore among them—traveled the state to campaign for her and help her revel in success. Moore was on Hillary's mind a lot in February. Hillary had been trying to get her to work on the campaign from the very beginning to no avail. But after the blowout in New Hampshire, Hillary pushed harder. Brooklyn needed a shake-up. The constant infighting between Mook and Podesta had left much of the headquarters staff wondering who was in charge, and some aides felt like they couldn't raise issues with Mook for fear of reprisal. His detractors had a tendency to find themselves sidelined. Hillary thought the no-nonsense Moore could improve the environment in Brooklyn by melting the ice at the top of the campaign leadership. Cajole, guide, lead, whatever you have to do, Hillary told her friend. Moore relented, agreeing to move to Brooklyn.

Inside Hillary's suite on primary night, the television set was off as the polls closed. That was unsettling to Moore, who was anxious to see what was happening. Hillary was in the mood for chitchat, though. She asked McLean about her job. There was so much riding on this night, Moore thought, and Hillary acted like she didn't give a damn about the results. "She didn't seem to have a care in the world," one of the women recalled.

The state director, Middleton, was in the room next door with the full complement of Clinton aides, ready to break down the results as they poured in. In their room, the television was on and it was tuned to CNN. When the polls closed at 7 p.m., they had to wait a moment or two for the cable network's analysts to offer their own punditry before the first update on the results. But at about 7:01 p.m. CNN called it for Clinton based on exit polling. Middleton walked into Hillary's room with the other aides to tell her the good news. As she hugged him, Moore slipped past the entourage to go into the staff room and get numbers.

While Hillary delivered her victory speech that night, her aides were glued to their smartphones. "We started to see the margins," said one adviser. "I thought it was going to start off big and then slowly kind of stabilize. And it just kept growing." When she reassembled her aides after the speech, they gave her news she wasn't expecting.

"You're up by almost fifty points," one of them said.

Hillary's face froze momentarily in a look of shock. Stunned, she said nothing. It was more than a decisive victory. She'd cleaned Sanders's clock not just in the popular vote but in the all-important delegate count, racking up thirty-nine to his fourteen. In the vote-rich black-majority Sixth District, represented by Clyburn in Congress, she won seven delegates to Sanders's one—equivalent to the number of delegates he had netted in winning New Hampshire. More people voted for her in that district than cast ballots in any of the state's other six districts.

She "knew that we were going to be going into a good Tuesday, at least in the South, after that," said the adviser. Hillary and her team boarded a plane to Memphis. She was absolutely elated. And she wanted a drink. Once in the air, she and her team toasted the victory with champagne.

Bill wasn't there to bask in his return to grace, though. He was campaigning for Hillary in Oklahoma after getting into a verbal fight the previous day with a veteran at a rally in Bluffton, South Carolina. Bill's temper, never far from the surface, would emerge time and again in the 2016 campaign.

"I'm not your commander in chief anymore," he lectured the veteran turned protester. "But if I were, I'd tell you to be more polite."

AS FEBRUARY CAME to a close, Hillary was three for four in the early states—better than Mook's original projections. Her campaign had focused intently on them and spent heavily to build infrastructure and air expensive television ads, particularly in Iowa and New Hampshire. But Hillary was generally stingy this time around. Too stingy, in the eyes of many of her aides.

She headed into Super Tuesday—the March 1 cluster of contests in Alabama, Arkansas, Colorado, Georgia, Massachusetts, Minnesota, Oklahoma, Tennessee, Texas, Vermont, Virginia, and American Samoa—having put together state-by-state campaign operations on the fly. Where her campaign had spent months preparing for Iowa, and to a lesser degree New Hampshire, Nevada, and South Carolina, she blitzed the Super Tuesday states in a matter of weeks.

In most of the states, there was little formal operation at all. Hillary's original playbook, devised by Mook, hadn't really contemplated the possibility of a 2008-like march through fifty states. The campaign gave lip service to that idea, but didn't back it up. Plan A had been to win in Iowa and New Hampshire and never look back. Plan B was to clean up in late February and early March without much of a ground presence. There was no real plan C. Hillary's organizers, volunteers, and donors in the states were livid about the lack of attention in their own backyards. They directed their frustration at Amanda Renteria, Hillary's national political director, and their complaints grew in number and intensity as March 1 drew closer. Moving from state to state, Renteria heard the same demanding question over and over: "Where the heck are the resources?"

No money. No paid staff. No advertising. No literature. No bumper stickers. No yard signs. Indeed, there were few signs at all that Hillary Clinton was running for president in these states until the very last moment. They couldn't understand why a campaign that had raised so much money was holding back on the basics of vote building. Mook thought he was doing exactly enough through the air campaign, and on the ground, to maximize efficiency. Where others worried about winning states, he was focused first on piling up delegates.

Mook was the perfect man for that job, penurious and cocksure about his plan for winning the nomination. In a different year,

Hillary might have fired him after the close shave in Iowa, and there had been rumblings from friends about getting rid of him long before that. Instead, she was in the process of quietly reshuffling the power structure of her campaign. Within a couple of weeks Benenson would essentially be demoted from chief strategist, and Renteria would be stripped of her staff. Mook would remain the campaign manager and keep control of the budget and the operations side of the campaign, but his power would be diminished by the ascendance of other players, including veteran Hillary-whisperers Jake Sullivan and Moore, in Brooklyn.

Hillary would keep the changes under the radar by increasing and decreasing the influence of certain staffers rather than by hiring and firing them. At the outset of the campaign, she told close friends that she didn't want a repeat of 2008, when fired former staffers ground their axes and then drove them into her back. It was much better, she thought, to keep control of aides who had lost power, to let them remain in the tent and committed to her victory, than to free them up to stand outside the tent and piss in. But there was no question as she headed into Super Tuesday that Benenson and Mook had been imperfect hires for their jobs. Benenson couldn't channel her, and Mook had made the near-fatal mistakes of underestimating Sanders and investing almost nothing early in the back end of the primary calendar.

Sullivan's rising influence could be seen in his work with Dan Schwerin on her post–New Hampshire speech, his role in her debate prep, and his inclusion in virtually every aspect of her campaign strategy. He detested the idea that he had learned to mimic her, but the truth was that no one on the official campaign staff understood Hillary's thought process, particularly regarding policy but also in terms of politics and communications, as well as Sullivan. Like Hillary, he leaned toward substance and policy over politics, making him an even better match for her personality. But hers weren't always the right instincts.

In any event, it was too late to overhaul her overall strategy. By Hillary's decree, the campaign was cheap. But it was Mook who allocated the available resources, and many of his subordinates believed he'd left Hillary vulnerable to losing states or delegates that she needed to win.

In Texas, Renteria was quoted saying that the campaign was operating on a shoestring budget, even though Hillary was counting on a massive delegate haul in the Lone Star State to put distance between herself and Sanders. It was a subtle shot at Mook. With the most important day on the primary calendar fast approaching—more than nine hundred of the roughly four thousand pledged delegates to the Democratic convention would be allocated based on Super Tuesday's results—Hillary had a phantom campaign operation in most of the states.

"It was smoke and mirrors," one of her best organizers griped.

Hillary's phone rang and buzzed a lot in the lead-up to Super Tuesday. Friends and outside advisers that she and her husband accrued over the years were alarmed at the sparseness of her operations. In every state after Iowa, her campaign was actually smaller than it had been in 2008. The Bernie armies were all over the ground, and there was no visible Clinton presence. "Where's the staffing? Where's the infrastructure?" she heard over and over.

Mook thought critics like Renteria didn't understand his strategy. The plan for Super Tuesday relied on heavy doses of earned media, meaning television, digital, and print stories that would amplify Hillary's message without forcing the campaign to spend precious dollars on paid organizing staff that couldn't tilt a race by more than a few points. Mook was looking to make the most efficient expenditures possible, and sometimes that meant the campaign would look absent both on the ground and on the airwaves. In his view, for example, it was a waste of money to pay for expensive ads in Houston and Dallas, where most voters were inclined to go with Hillary in the primary. But he loved throwing money at Waco television. The TV stations there reached several congressional districts with odd numbers of delegates where the results were up in the air. Odd-number districts were more valuable in Democratic delegate math because winning by a single vote would produce an extra delegate. In an even-numbered district, a candidate might win by ten or more points and split the delegates with the loser. In his mind, it was a simple calculation of modern campaign targeting. All of it was informed by analytics models that projected how the vote would turn out in each district.

Deep inside the Brooklyn HQ, amid the faux–Silicon Valley hammock, beanbag chairs, and air hockey table, data technicians concentrated on how analytics could maximize delegate numbers. Elan Kriegel and his team had built a "delegate-flip" model that allowed them to target media markets, like Waco, where there was the best chance of bringing in an extra delegate or two for the least amount of money. "The analytics tools, both the surveys that were painting the picture of our prognosis in a state and the targeting and the paid media, played a bigger role because we weren't going to have a robust ground game in all these states," said one Hillary aide.

From Mook's perspective, which amounted to Hillary's view, it didn't make sense to try to flood the Super Tuesday states with paid field staff just a few weeks before an election. That would be costly, and it probably wouldn't work in large states. "You cannot organize your way to a primary victory in Texas," said one operative who was in on the planning.

Mook's tight fists made plenty of Clintonites nervous heading into the biggest single day of the primary campaign. If his methods worked, Hillary would have enough delegates to claim the inside track to the nomination. But he was gambling a lot on those methods. "He is incredibly awesome at figuring out how much money we need to spend," one Clinton adviser said of Mook. "But when you're close to the margins, there's not a lot of room to spare." Mook bet on Kriegel as the professional political class griped.

The decision to hold back on spending and trust his plan was a striking demonstration of discipline. He'd made his name as an organizer and yet essentially determined that organizing was a fool's errand on the short timeline before the March 1 showdown with Sanders.

"It was a ballsy move," said one source familiar with the strategy.

Every time self-doubt began to creep in, Hillary called Mook. She believed in his strategy, to a point. After years of living in a high-stakes political world in which perception often mattered more than reality—and knowing that the media narrative could overtake reality—Hillary understood the potential toxicity of failing to show that she was campaigning hard.

With so many of her friends up in arms, Hillary began to feel uncertain about Mook's ability to get both the delegate math and the politics right. The narrative mattered too. Super Tuesday would be another major test for Hillary's precocious campaign manager, who gambled heavily on the idea that she was better off husbanding her money and trying to win delegates on the cheap—even if it meant sowing doubt throughout her vast network of unpaid advisers and professional skeptics.

Meanwhile, Bernie was burning through money, both in television ads and in paying staffers on the ground. With a wag of his finger, he bragged about asking everyone on his list to match the $27 average donation and then pulling in $5 million or more overnight. His fund-raising forced Hillary to go back to the well of elites time and again at tony dinners and receptions, allowing Bernie to hit her relentlessly for taking money from Wall Street tycoons, Hollywood celebrities, and Georgetown cocktail-circuit regulars.

Hillary was confident that she was going to rack up a lead in delegates on Super Tuesday, but the question that racked her nerves was whether it would be big enough to convince her allies, her donors, and the media that she was on a glide path to the nomination.

Her anxiety turned out to be mostly unwarranted. She torched Bernie in the South, winning Alabama, Arkansas, Georgia, Tennessee, Texas, and Virginia, while dropping contests in Colorado, Minnesota, Oklahoma, and Sanders's home state of Vermont. Those southern Super Tuesday states, full of people of color, delivered what Hillary had projected: a convincing victory that allowed her to take control of the race for the nomination for the first time. Not only had she won big states, but Mook's attention to squeezing out delegates had paid off. Hillary netted more than 150 of them that day. He was struggling to corral all the parts of the sprawling Clinton empire, and his efforts to silence dissent within the campaign rubbed some people the wrong way, but he'd accurately predicted which states she would win and built the delegate lead he'd promised her. If Bernie Sanders was to defeat Hillary, he would have to do it by climbing out of a massive delegate hole. When she looked back at the calendar later, Hillary would know that it was the voters of these states who had truly launched her into a commanding lead.

The only real cliffhanger was in Massachusetts, a state that bordered Sanders's Vermont. Bill Clinton had done a midnight rally in Worcester the night before. Consuming large quantities of beer, pizza, and sundry specialty orders—"the United Nations of food," one HQ denizen said—Hillary's aides were glued to TVs in Brooklyn all night. The sets weren't synced, so hollering and applause would break out from one set of cubicles seconds before the other end of the room knew she had won a state. Massachusetts was the gilding on a primary night that largely matched Hillary's expectations. She ended up winning the state by about 17,000 votes out of more than 1.2 million cast.

BECAUSE HILLARY WAS confident that she'd put more than enough distance between herself and Sanders, her victory speech that night in Miami contained hints of a quick pivot to the general election.

"We know we've got work to do. But that work, that work is not to make America great again," she said, ridiculing Donald Trump's slogan. "America never stopped being great. We have to make America whole. We have to fill in what's been hollowed out."

Hillary had finally turned the corner, rising on the strength of consecutive triumphs in Nevada, South Carolina, and the delegate-laden Super Tuesday states. For the first time that night, she and her team thought they had put the race against an inferior rival away. But the nagging doubts about her strategy and messaging were about to return to the surface, and Mook's surgical, analytics-based approach to spending would start to look far less precise.

Chapter 11

CANARY IN THE AUTO PLANT

ILLARY WAS SO MAD SHE COULDN'T THINK STRAIGHT. She was supposed to be focused on the prep session for that night's Univision debate in Miami, but a potent mix of exhaustion and exasperation bubbled up inside. She'd been humiliated in the Michigan primary the night before, a loss that not only robbed her of a prime opportunity to put Bernie Sanders down for good but also exposed several of her weaknesses. How could she have been left so vulnerable? She knew—or at least she thought she did. The blame belonged to her campaign team, she believed, for failing to hone her message, energize important constituencies, and take care of business in getting voters to the polls. And now, Jake Sullivan, her de facto chief strategist, was giving her lip about the last answer she'd delivered in this prep session.

"That's not very good," Sullivan corrected.

"Really?" Hillary snapped back. The room fell silent. "Why don't you do it?"

The command was pointed and sarcastic, but she meant it. So, for the next thirty minutes, there he was, pretending to be Hillary while she critiqued his performance. Every time the Yale lawyer and former high school debate champ opened his mouth, Hillary cut him off. "That isn't very good," she'd say. "You can do better." Then she'd hammer him with a Bernie line.

It wasn't just Sullivan in her crosshairs. She let everyone on her team have it that day. "We haven't made our case," she fumed. "We haven't framed the choice. We haven't done the politics."

"She was visibly, unflinchingly pissed off at us as a group," said one aide who was in the room for the humiliating scene. "And she let us know she felt that way."

Hillary had been up into the wee hours the night before, agitating over her loss. *This is because we made poor choices about where we traveled,* she thought. She e-mailed Mook to tell him she believed she'd spent too much time in the cities of Detroit and Flint and not enough in the working-class white suburbs around them. Sensing just how angry she was, Mook responded by putting together a morning conference call so that Hillary could vent. But that didn't settle her; if anything, it left her more perplexed and angry, as her debate-prep team witnessed firsthand.

Her aides took the browbeating—one of several she delivered in person and on the phone that day—in silence. They had a lot of their own thoughts on what went wrong, some of which echoed Hillary's assessment: her message was off for Michigan, she had refused to go hard against trade; Mook had pinched pennies and failed to put organizers on the ground; the polling and analytics were a touch too rosy, meaning the campaign didn't know Bernie was ahead; she had set up an ambiguous decision-making structure on the campaign; and she'd focused too heavily on black and brown voters at the expense of competing for the whites who had formed her base in 2008. The list went on and on. The underlying truth— the one many didn't want to admit to themselves—was that the person ultimately responsible for these decisions, the one whose name was on the ticket, hadn't corrected for these problems, all of which had been brought to her attention before primary day. She'd stuck with the plan, and it had cost her.

This reckoning had been coming for some time. Even as Hillary's mood had improved with her victories in Nevada, South Carolina, and key Super Tuesday states, she remained vexed by her campaign's imperfections. Victory had covered up her weaknesses, and now, having lost Michigan, that was undeniable.

"Michigan was the tipping point," said one of her top lieutenants.

Hillary didn't want to dwell on the state, but she needed answers from her team about what they planned to do to make sure she didn't get blindsided again. It was hard enough to run against Bernie Sanders, Donald Trump, the Republican National Committee, the FBI, the House Benghazi Committee, and the national media—plus slippery-lipped Joe Biden on any given day—without her own team screwing things up. The one person with whom she didn't seem particularly upset: herself. No one who drew a salary from the campaign would tell her that. It was a self-signed death warrant to raise a question about Hillary's competence—to her or anyone else—in loyalty-obsessed Clintonworld. Most of the people around her were jockeying to get closer to her, not to make her wonder about their commitment. And many didn't know her very well personally. Even Huma Abedin, who was close to her, had all but given up on guiding her toward shifting course. She had long since started telling Hillary allies outside the campaign to take their complaints and suggestions straight to the candidate. For the mercenaries who had joined the campaign in hopes of finding jobs in the next administration, there was little percentage in getting on Hillary's bad side. They also feared—appropriately—that unflattering words about Hillary or the strategy would be repeated at their own expense by those who hoped to gain Hillary's favor. Concern about being cast out to the perimeter of Hillary's overlapping circles of influence far outweighed the itch to tell Hillary what she was doing wrong. So, on the phone and in person, as Hillary prepared for a crucial debate with Bernie in Miami, her advisers held their tongues.

On one call that day, Hillary pushed for information on why Bernie killed her with working-class whites, the demographic group that had been her most consistent support network in 2008. What was her campaign failing to do to keep them in her column? She had counted on adding parts of the Obama coalition to her white working-class base this time around, but it felt like those once-loyal friends had abandoned her. "Why aren't they with me? Why can't we bring them on board?" she demanded.

Hillary was getting conflicting input from the cacophony of voices that had direct access to her. The younger generation believed in the Obama coalition–plus model, but some of her older allies thought she should have started from the other end of the equation. "Her base should have been where she left off with eighteen million cracks," said one adviser who didn't buy into the idea she could largely replicate Obama's math. "Working class. Not just working-class white—women, firefighters."

Tellingly—and with serious implications for the general election—Hillary couldn't put her finger on the problem. "Is it my stance on guns?" she asked.

The real answer: she'd become the candidate of minority voters on social justice issues while Bernie was hitting her as a corrupt, Wall Street–loving champion of the "rigged" financial system that took advantage of working-class voters. Whether she was perceived as hostile to working- and middle-class whites or just indifferent, it wasn't a big leap from "she doesn't care about my job" to "she'd rather give my job to a minority or a foreigner than fight for me to keep it." She and her aides were focused on the wrong issue set for working-class white Michigan voters, and, even when she talked about the economy—rather than her e-mail scandal, mass shootings, or the water crisis in Flint—it wasn't at all clear to them that she was on their side.

Hillary's attention to Flint was a prime example of this dynamic. While Democrats agreed with her that toxic lead in the water was a problem—and this was a pressing, life-and-death issue for a small subset of the electorate—it didn't address jobs or the feeling of many Michigan voters that their paychecks simply didn't go as far as they used to. But Hillary pounded on the water crisis because it showed empathy for minority voters in the state—African Americans are the majority in Flint—which had an echo effect in communities of color around the country.

Indeed, her overall response to Bernie's more-aggressive-than-expected challenge had been to rely more heavily on African American and Hispanic voters to come to her rescue in Nevada,

Texas, and the Deep South and give her a substantial delegate lead. It was not only what she was doing on the ground but part and parcel of the narrative her advisers pushed to the press: she would win the nomination by collecting big majorities among minorities. The political strategy worked to complicate Sanders's path, but it also began to alienate the very white voters who had picked her over Obama in 2008. The more she became a candidate of minority voters, the less affinity whites had for her—particularly those whites who had little or no allegiance to the Democratic Party. Amazingly, after having been the candidate of the white working class in a 2008 race against a black opponent, she was becoming anathema to them. Even more astounding, the wife of the president who had won on an "It's the economy, stupid" mantra was ignoring the core of the Clinton brand—robust growth that touched every American. *Why am I not talking to the foundation of what the Clinton brand is about?* she thought, time and again, throughout the campaign.

That was certainly Bill's take too. Her belief that she'd spent too much of her time in Detroit and Flint was influenced by his frustration at being closed off from suburban and exurban voters. Bill had been griping about it to anyone who would listen since he'd first set out on the campaign trail in January. Now he was convinced he'd been right. For Bill, "Michigan really baked in this idea that we had pushed him to spend time in the African American communities when he should have been out pursuing white people," said one person who spoke to Bill frequently.

Meanwhile, Bernie had a message tailor-made for working-class whites. He'd take on the rich guys and the rigged game to deliver money and benefits to the working class. He'd kill trade deals like the Trans-Pacific Partnership that workers and their union leaders believed would result in jobs being shipped overseas. He argued that his economic fairness doctrine was color-blind and would help everyone on the lower end of the scale. Trump was hammering home the same message in the Republican primary: He'd be for the white working-class stiff. He'd void or rewrite bad trade deals, and, going beyond Bernie, he'd protect their jobs against the encroachment of undocumented Mexican immigrants.

But by her word and her deed, Hillary gave white working-class voters little reason to believe she was motivated by the issue foremost on their minds. To vote for her, they'd have to ignore their distrust of her intentions and the more alluring promises of Sanders and Trump. The race dynamics told only part of the story.

"There's no doubt that in the primary we noticed a tension" between Hillary's success with voters of color and her attempts to court white voters, particularly white men, one aide said after the Michigan primary. But what neither Hillary nor her aides could identify—what was so plainly and painfully obvious to politicians who had spent time among white working-class voters—was the other fundamental truth about the Rust Belt electorate: populist politics weren't just on the rise, they were becoming dominant. And there's no nuance in the business end of a pitchfork.

It was difficult for Hillary to speak to voters' distrust because her personal credibility had been damaged by the e-mail scandal and she couldn't distance herself from Washington and Wall Street.

Michigan was a wake-up call for Hillary. After the votes were counted there, she began to hammer a mantra about working-class white voters into her team's collective brain: "We've got to re-earn them." She had identified the problem, but her inability to discover a solution would haunt her for the rest of the campaign.

HILLARY HAD REASON to be confident when she first turned her attention to Michigan's March 8 contest, sandwiched, as it was, directly between the March 1 Super Tuesday primaries and the five big "mini Super Tuesday" states that would vote on March 15. As Mook had predicted, she'd amassed enough delegates on Super Tuesday to put Bernie at a nearly insurmountable disadvantage in the race for the nomination. With African Americans constituting nearly 15 percent of the state's population, she thought she could count on a significant minority presence on primary day. While her internal numbers showed a closer race than the public polls, her analytics team believed she was in the driver's seat.

Mook's plan for Michigan, blessed by Hillary, reflected his strategy in other states. He emphasized advertising, focused on turning out Hillary supporters in the cities, and waited until the last possible moment to put a small field operation in place for primary day turnout. When a question about staffing in Michigan was raised in late January, Mook responded by saying he wanted to see how Iowa and New Hampshire went before dropping cash to hire organizers in the state. Hillary, who had caught wind of the concern that she had no presence in Michigan, checked in with Mook about it and was reassured that everything was under control.

But, as she would soon find out, that wasn't the case at all. Some of the political professionals in the state knew not to trust the surveys they saw. There had been no reason to poll a Democratic presidential primary in Michigan in more than a decade—Obama didn't compete there in 2008. It was widely regarded as a "blue" state that would go Democratic in the general election, regardless of which candidate won in March. Its competitive value—or so Hillary's team thought—was limited to the lift it could give her, or the damage it could do, in terms of accumulating delegates and shaping the public perception of the remainder of her race against Bernie.

On the ground, though, there were warning signs. As Sanders and Trump hammered away with clear antitrade messages, both built support among working- and middle-class white voters. They were playing to fears about globalization destroying Michigan's economy, and they were doing it unambiguously. Bernie sprinkled in an unvarnished attack on Hillary as a pawn of Wall Street because she'd given speeches to banks for money and hadn't released the transcripts publicly. "I kind of think if you're going to be paid $225,000 for a speech, it must be a fantastic speech . . . a brilliant speech which you would want to share with the American people," he said. The Sanders and Trump messages were hitting home with voters who could swing either way in the primary or the general. Hillary's message was much harder to decipher.

That was evident to Debbie Dingell, a freshman Democratic congresswoman who represented the working- and middle-class suburbs south of Detroit and the college-kid mecca of Ann Arbor. For months, Dingell rang every alarm bell she could. A former General Motors lobbyist with deep ties to the region's bedrock automotive industry and its union jobs, she wasn't the typical first-term lawmaker. She'd taken over the "Dingell seat" in Michigan from her husband, John D. Dingell Jr., who served in the House for sixty years. He had succeeded his father, John D. Dingell Sr., who was first elected as a "New Deal" Democrat with Franklin Roosevelt in 1932 and promptly introduced a bill that would have created a national health insurance system. A Dingell had represented parts of Michigan for eighty-three consecutive years.

In short, no elected official could claim deeper ties to working- and middle-class white Democrats in Michigan than Debbie Dingell. She knew the men and women who were working harder for less—and who worried that they wouldn't have money for retirement or to send their kids to college. She represented them in Congress. And she saw the peril on Hillary's horizon long before the candidate or anyone in her Brooklyn headquarters. She sent word that Bernie's antitrade message was resonating while voters didn't trust Hillary's late and muddled opposition to the Trans-Pacific Partnership. And she told Hillary that the campaign didn't have enough of a presence on the ground.

"Debbie Dingell will fucking call her twelve times a day and say, 'This is fucked up. This is wrong,'" one admiring Hillary aide said, exaggerating to emphasize that the candidate was hearing the message even if she wasn't taking all of Dingell's warnings to heart.

Between the campaign manager and the analytics team, Hillary was getting the same message: it would be closer than the public surveys showed—her internal polls indicated that—but she would pull it out if she stuck to the plan.

The whole construct was designed to rack up delegates by running up margins in Detroit and Flint, take a majority—no matter how small—statewide, and not waste precious resources on a rout.

No one seemed terribly occupied with the idea that she should appeal to as many voters as possible and win by as large a margin as she could. That was a reasonable strategy for the overall goal of getting closer to the nomination, but it did little to turn the primary into a staging ground for her general-election campaign in Michigan.

In Brooklyn, the collective wisdom held that Hillary just had to hit her marks and continue on her inevitable march to the nomination. The coming victory in Michigan would be a punishing blow—perhaps a fatal one—to Bernie's narrative because it would show Hillary's strength in a big industrial state.

But the wily Vermont senator had a much different view of what was happening on the ground, and his interpretation was shaped by the time he'd spent in the state. Bernie knew he had a real shot at a major narrative-busting upset. He too wanted Michigan to take on outsize significance in the race. This was fertile ground for him and an opportunity to arrest Hillary's momentum. Her aides could point to delegate math all they wanted, but as long as he could pick off big states here and there, neither the enthusiasm for his campaign nor his fund-raising would dry up. His message was resonating with working-class and college Democrats in Michigan, just as Trump's similar themes were gaining traction among the state's Republicans. Importantly, independents could vote in either primary, and Bernie was crushing Hillary among that set.

Rather than fighting on trade, Hillary's advisers thought her best arguments were the broad "Breaking Barriers" line aimed at women and voters of color and taking on specific companies by name. They were relying on polling and analytics, instead of a robust organization in the state, to dictate strategy. In one ad that began running in Michigan on March 1, taken from a town hall meeting she'd held in January, Hillary talked about a woman whose costs for a brand-name drug had risen from $180 to $14,700 for ten shots of the medicine.

"The company is called Valeant Pharmaceuticals. I'm going after them; this is predatory pricing, and we're going to make sure it is stopped," Hillary said in the ad.

She had personally signed off on that spot, and she was surprisingly engaged in the minutiae of campaign tactics at that point.

"What else besides Flint are we running in Michigan?" she asked at one point, using the eponymous short title of an ad aimed at those who cared about the water crisis in the city of Flint. Three more ads, "Johnson," "Valeant," and "Wham," "seem good for there." And she'd nixed the particulars of a spot on debt-free tuition because it didn't do enough to hammer home her point. "I like the humorous skit idea but still think we also have to explain and sell the plan," she told her aides. It would be hard to make the case that she wasn't aware of every little thing her operatives were doing on her behalf.

But for all her attention to detail, Hillary mostly put her fate and her faith in the hands of the professionals she'd hired to run the campaign. The "Valeant" ad was symbolic of her larger challenge in overrelying on data. It tested well with focus groups, but corporate profiteering wasn't the issue animating the working-class white voters Hillary had to fight for to win Michigan. They cared about trade, trade, and trade.

"Bernie Sanders really captured the zeitgeist," said one longtime Michigan politician. And, like Trump, he did it without Hillary's taking notice. The traction they were getting should have been a warning sign to Hillary not just about the rest of the primary but for the general election looming behind it.

Bernie had to elevate the importance of Michigan, but Hillary chose to play into his hands. In large part, that's because it looked like she was going to win. On March 3, analytics chief Elan Kriegel reported that she had a five-point lead, 49 percent to 44 percent. His team ran quick, cheap phone surveys, fed the results into a model of the electorate, and spit out horse race numbers. He would continue to find a similar gap up through the morning of primary day. That is, Michigan looked a lot like Iowa and Nevada had. Kriegel thought he was taking a very conservative approach by assuming an electorate less heavily populated by African American voters and more tilted toward college kids. His analysis, he told colleagues, was more realistic than the public polls that gave Hillary a much larger lead. But even his assumptions showed a cushion for her.

That's why Hillary didn't know quite how much trouble she was in when she arrived in Detroit on March 4 to deliver a speech on jobs and the economy. Dingell, ensconced in working-class white politics, felt in her gut that the race was closer than Hillary's data suggested. She pressed the campaign to ditch a nuanced message on trade and give a clean, clear explanation of why Hillary opposed the TPP deal. It was the only thing white Democratic primary voters in the state were talking about.

But instead of preaching a new brand of fiery populism when she arrived at the manufacturing plant that Friday, Hillary touted a "new bargain" jobs plan. It was classic Hillary. Rather than capturing the politics of the moment, she chose to emphasize why she thought a policy was right. She firmly believed that voters would see the wisdom of her broader economic platform and understand her trade position in context. She led with an arcane "clawback" proposal that would take away companies' corporate tax breaks if they moved jobs overseas. It was Washington-speak. On TPP, the issue that mattered most politically, she punted.

"When it comes to trade deals, here's my standard," she said. "I won't support any agreement unless it helps create good jobs and higher wages for American workers and protects our national security. I need to be able to look into the eyes of any hardworking American anywhere in our country and say this deal will help raise your income. That's why I voted against the big—last big, multinational trade deal called CAFTA. It's why I don't support the Trans-Pacific Partnership trade deal."

It was buried in the speech and given as much attention as a throwaway line about the Export-Import Bank, an institution of which few voters had ever heard. Incredibly, it was noncommittal. Instead of saying why she opposed trade deals, Hillary explained the conditions under which she could support them. Sanders's basic assertion, everywhere he went, was simple: I'm against trade, she's for it. That resonated.

Hillary believed that if she just had time to give her "new bar-gain" message oxygen—to promote it on the air and through a union-driven ground operation—she could steal some Sanders voters. She was offering a solution, she believed, not just antitrade rhetoric.

But while Hillary talked about impenetrable corporate tax pol-icy, Bernie's campaign circulated video of her extolling the virtues of trade in India in 2012. She couldn't have made it any easier for him to draw a contrast on the issue that mattered most to Michigan voters—Democrats, persuadable independents, and a good number of Republicans.

With the margins so close, Hillary was going to have to rely on her team's ability to identify voters and get them to the polls. But Mook had staffed the state thinly. And, as he was starting to discover, television ads were having less influence on voters than earned and social media. That was particularly true if—as was the case with Hillary's ads in Michigan—they weren't aimed in the right direction. The candidate was hands-on with the advertising plan, reviewing pitches, watching spots, knocking down certain ideas, and even suggesting which markets would get the best bang for the buck. Her instincts were off.

"The trade angle that Bernie took paid off," said one of Hil-lary's aides. "For decades, people have been running against trade in Michigan. The fact that her out-of-the-gate conversation wasn't as strong as Bernie's made it hard."

Bill Clinton didn't need polling or analytics to know this race was going to turn on a knife's edge. He'd been hearing all the con-cerns and complaints that had seeped through to Hillary but hadn't convinced her to change direction. When he arrived to campaign for her the day after her speech at the manufacturing plant, he used a much more human bellwether to judge how things were going. As Dingell would later tell friends, Bill took one look at her and drew a conclusion. She had met him to campaign in her district, and she knew that part of her mission was to avoid getting him all riled up. Brooklyn had heard enough of Bill's second-guessing and didn't need the local congresswoman giving him more ammunition. So she kept her mouth shut.

But Bill could see the pending disaster in her blue eyes and drawn lips.

"Do you think I can't read your face?" he asked.

The former president wasn't the only one who felt apprehensive as primary day approached. Neera Tanden e-mailed Podesta to ask how things were going. He replied on Sunday, March 6, two days before voters went to the polls. "Should get a squeaker win but he can still get past us," he replied. That view informed the way Hillary's press team suddenly tried to lower expectations. She was leading but far from comfortable. Too late, she and her team began to hedge on the importance of Michigan. Mook started to argue internally that she should spend primary day in the Deep South and put more emphasis on the same-day Mississippi primary, where she would clean up. But all eyes were already on Michigan, and Hillary believed she could take it. At that point, anything short of a clear victory would be seen as a resuscitating upset for Bernie. The shape of the race—a prolonged brawl or a foregone conclusion—would be formed by the winner in Michigan.

Looking to deal Bernie a mortal blow, Hillary took a desperate stab at undermining his core narrative two nights before the primary. For most of the campaign, she'd shied away from taking direct shots at Sanders. The unspoken rule: if she could find a policy on which Bernie differed from the Democratic base, she could go a little negative. Standing on a debate stage in Flint, and casting aside her practiced caution about negativity, Hillary sensed an opening to go after him hard.

"I voted to save the auto industry," she said with just a hint in her eyes of the roundhouse she was about to throw. "He voted against the money that ended up saving the auto industry. I think that is a pretty big difference." No one was more stunned to hear this than Sanders, who had supported federal money for Detroit's carmakers during the 2008 financial meltdown. Hillary was hanging her claim on Sanders's vote against the $700 billion bailout of the financial industry, which ended up being a source of money that went to the auto industry.

Fact-checkers called Clinton out, and for Sanders's supporters the charge was emblematic of three things: Clinton's willingness to say anything to win, her negativity, and her desperation in Michigan. It's hard to know how many votes moved in one direction or another based on that single moment on stage, but it's safe to say she didn't boost her position much. For the long term, she may have helped cement her negatives in the minds of impressionable Michigan voters.

The night before the primary, Mook called Hillary to update her on the state of the race. "It's going to be very close, but I'm feeling more optimistic," he said. "I think it's more likely that you'll win than lose." He was hedging in the probability-talk of a data guy. But Mook also raised the idea of sending her to Mississippi instead of Michigan to ensure she had victory as her backdrop. That was a nonstarter, but Mook would later kick himself for not being more strident. *I should have laid down the hammer,* he thought.

On primary day, Kriegel sent word that the final analytics showed Hillary winning by six points, 49 percent to 43 percent. His numbers relied on the assumption that African Americans would account for 20 percent of the vote, white men would break 56 percent to 36 percent for Bernie, and white women would favor Hillary 52 percent to 42 percent. Just like Bill, Podesta wasn't sold on the numbers. "Wish us luck," he told a friend that afternoon. "Tighter than public polls indicate."

At the same time, Bernie was riding in a car with his top aides, Jeff Weaver and Tad Devine.

"I think you've done an incredible job," Devine told his candidate. "But I think we're going to come up a little short." Weaver was a little more bullish. The way he saw it, Bernie was surging like he had in Iowa, New Hampshire, and Nevada. The numbers weren't exactly there heading into primary day, but it wouldn't take much overperformance to nail down the state and put Hillary on her heels. Weaver certainly didn't want to be wrong if Bernie pulled it out. He offered up a wide range of possibilities. Bernie could lose by as many as nine points, he said, or win by as many as two points.

Bernie liked what he heard. He knew he was connecting with supporters by the thousands on college campuses and in midsize cities. He would be mildly surprised, but not entirely shocked, if he had closed the deal in the final days.

Still, he was the underdog, and even Weaver's rosier scenario suggested he was more likely to lose than win. He didn't need to stick around for that. He boarded a flight for Miami. Bernie would come to rue that decision later that night. Huddled around a television set in his no-frills South Florida hotel room, about 1,300 miles from Michigan, Bernie, his family, and his top aides watched as Wolverine State voters breathed a new burst of life into the campaign.

"If we had really believed we could have done it, we would not have gone to Florida," one Sanders ally said. "We would have stayed in Michigan and tried to make a much bigger statement about what the hell went on."

As it turned out, Kriegel had been spot-on in projecting African American turnout. It accounted for a hair more than the 20 percent he'd predicted. But he was way off on how white voters would split between Hillary and Bernie. White men went a little harder for Bernie, 62 percent to 37 percent. But the big surprise—one that got little if any public or internal mention given its significance—was that she lost white women. Bernie beat her 51 percent to 47 percent in that demographic, according to exit polls. Also important for the general election, Bernie won independents who voted in the Democratic primary 71 percent to 28 percent.

Overall, Hillary lost the state narrowly, 49.8 percent to 48.3 percent. Sanders netted just four delegates—far smaller than the twenty-six-delegate victory she won by taking Mississippi with nearly 83 percent of the vote that night—but in the media the loss in Michigan played exactly how she and her aides had feared.

"For Sanders—the 'democratic socialist' from Vermont running an insurgent campaign on Clinton's left—the Michigan victory will bring a new energy, after several weeks in which his chances had seemed to fade," David Fahrenthold wrote in the *Washington Post,* pointing to Sanders's two-to-one loss among black voters as a sign that his message on "racial justice and police brutality" had "paid off." That, of course, wasn't the real story—at least not the one that would matter going forward. What had really happened was that Hillary had become disconnected from her 2008 base; she'd alienated white working- and middle-class Democrats. But she still didn't know what to do about it.

In an instant, Sanders was Lazarus.

THE MICHIGAN PRIMARY was the moment when Hillary finally lost all patience with the leadership of her campaign. The failure, and what it would bring from the media and her allies, consumed her. All of the aspects of the campaign had come up short. The flaws that donors and friends had complained to her about were all exposed by Michigan voters. She'd checked in with Mook about not spending more money on a field operation and been told not to worry—he had had it under control. She'd complained to her communications team that her economic messaging sucked, and they'd told her to keep repeating it. But the problem wasn't the way she was selling her economic plan; it was that the voters didn't like her stance on the issue that mattered most to them. Some big staff changes had been in the works for a while, and the Michigan loss accelerated their implementation.

Mook knew he was on the firing line and desperately tried to salvage his job. He turned to chief administrative officer Charlie Baker, Podesta, and Minyon Moore, a veteran political organizer and close Hillary confidante, for help—perhaps forgetting that he'd tried to minimize their influence earlier in the campaign. He even made it clear to others that he was willing to "get rid of" Marshall, his close friend and top lieutenant, "in order to save his own skin," as one colleague put it.

But as much as Hillary was ready to reset her lineup, she still didn't want to suggest to the press and the public that her campaign was in chaos. She wanted to make the right moves with the least noise possible, and the crush of primaries meant that she had to wait for a lull to fully execute the changes. There would be no sharp and obvious shift in direction.

Chief strategist Joel Benenson was among the first in her sights. It was bad enough that he wasn't proving himself as a strategist in her mind. Worse still, he fought back against Hillary and treated the people around him as though they were just plain dumb. "Joel basically alienated himself from everyone because of his personality," said one Clinton adviser. "He has no filter." I don't want him doing my stuff, Hillary had told confidants. We've got to have another structure.

Amanda Renteria, the political director, was also on a hot seat. She was the highest-ranking Latina on the campaign, a good surrogate, and a strong fund-raising draw, but she had clashed with Mook over his allocation of campaign resources.

In a familiar refrain from their State Department days, Hillary told Sullivan she wanted him to take over. You're going to be my traffic cop and my rabbi, she told Sullivan, adding that he would be her de facto chief strategist. His purview would include political strategy, policy, messaging, and debate prep. Halfway through the campaign, Sullivan, who worried that he wasn't the right person to do political strategy, became the official Hillary whisperer. Benenson, who had a $1 million "win bonus" in his contract, was being informally demoted. But he wouldn't be fired either.

Instead, his role reduction was a secret kept inside the most elite offices of the Brooklyn headquarters, and many of the people in the second tier of the campaign and below never knew about it.

"He has almost no role, but they wouldn't fire him," one high-ranking Hillary aide said in May 2016. "We didn't want any press. We don't want anyone to know about it." It wasn't just Benenson. Mook and Podesta had conspired to sideline all three of the main consultants, including the exceptionally well-liked Jim

Margolis and the still-close-to-Hillary Mandy Grunwald. The three of them ended up being reassigned to managing the program for the convention.

The kneecapping of several aides, which wouldn't fully take shape for a few more weeks, didn't mean Hillary intended to let the rest of her staff off easy. She was ripshit over the confluence of calamities in Michigan. Her senior aides and advisers all got reamed—she even made an example of Sullivan—the day after the Michigan primary.

By then, Hillary had transitioned mostly from shock to anger. She had noticed a few other things about the Michigan debacle on her own. Her economic message seemed to resonate when she met with voters, but it hadn't gotten enough lift to get her past Sanders. It was the right forward-looking message about a plan for job growth—or a good enough message, anyway—but it wasn't getting enough oxygen, she thought. She was also pissed that the media narrative out of that primary night was about the Michigan loss and all but ignored the fact that she'd beaten the living hell out of Sanders in Mississippi. In the high-value 2nd congressional district, he'd failed to get the 15 percent of the vote needed to earn a single delegate. Why hadn't her comms team prepared the media for Mississippi? The Delta primary earned little more than a line in stories about Bernie's supposed comeback, even though it loomed much larger in the delegate math.

Most important, though, she felt like she might have beaten Sanders if she hadn't shortchanged her field operation. After all, she'd only lost by a point and a half. Maybe for the relatively low cost of a couple of twenty-something field operatives, she could have won the state and prevented the Democratic hand-wringing and media second-guessing that was now coming her way. She'd signed off on the plans, but they were Mook's and he was on the hot seat.

"Did we run an aggressive enough ground game to go over the edge?" she asked on one call.

Hillary forced her aides to think about their failure. Some of the

questions, like the ones about her ground game, were clearly rhe-
torical. She almost dared them to answer back. This series of calls
and face-to-face talks was reminiscent of a conference call she'd run
after her devastating loss in Iowa in 2008. That time, she'd bullied
her aides in the same marmish way and then hung up on them in
disgust.

But now she also saw an opportunity to push her team to learn
from its mistakes. There was a point to her scolding: get it right, and
do it fast.

In one week, she'd be on the ballot again in Ohio, Missouri, Illinois, North Carolina, and Florida. She'd win North Carolina and
Florida, she knew, and pile up delegates in those two states. But now
Ohio and Missouri, both with big working-class white contingents,
and Illinois, where Chicago mayor Rahm Emanuel, a Clinton in-
vention, had mishandled police-involved shootings, were in play.
And with Trump whipping white working-class voters into a frenzy
across the country, Hillary knew that she had to solve her problem
with them before the general election. These primaries would be a
test run, a chance for her to hone her message and ground game in
swing states before then.

On one call, Renteria, the political director, saw an opportunity
to push back against Mook's tight budgets in the upcoming states.
For her, part of the lesson of Michigan was that Hillary's economic
message didn't have time to sink in with the electorate. She also
needed more people on the ground to organize and turn out voters earlier in the remaining primary states. The come-late, spend-
little mantra that had worked on Super Tuesday had failed her in
Michigan. Back then, there was really just one race on the map close
enough for a field operation to make a difference in determining
which candidate would win.

"Trying that same strategy in Michigan was hard because it
wasn't long enough, especially when you don't have something to
tap into," said one Clinton aide. For Clinton, that would have meant
linking up with the politically muscular United Automobile Workers in Michigan, an existing network that could deploy volunteers

and voters on the ground. But the UAW, whose members were more aligned with Bernie than Hillary, sat on its hands during the primary, depriving Hillary of the kind of institutional support that could have delivered votes, and likely a victory, without her having to spend money on campaign workers.

What Renteria didn't know is that while she could damage Mook, she wasn't helping herself. She'd soon be demoted—without a change in title—too.

One of the lessons Mook and his allies took from Michigan was that Hillary was better off not getting into an all-out war with her opponent in states where non-college-educated whites could be the decisive demographic. In Michigan, they believed, Hillary's hard campaigning had called attention to an election that many would-be voters weren't paying attention to, and given Bernie a chance to show that his economic message was more in line with their views. So Mook's clique looked at the elevation of the Michigan primary—poking the sleeping bear of the white working class—as a mistake that shouldn't be repeated. "That was a takeaway that we tried to use in the general," said one high-ranking campaign official.

The old-school, instinct-driven set drew a different lesson from Michigan: the campaign wasn't making good use of Democrats, like Dingell, who could tap into their own political networks across the states. One of the corners Mook had cut was choosing not to place a political director in each state, relying instead on Renteria at the national level to hold things together. The state directors, a level above the political director position on most campaigns, jumped from location to location as needed and often didn't have ties to the political network in the states where they were organizing. That was in large part a by-product of the emphasis the campaign had put on early states, particularly Iowa, at the expense of paying attention to the rest of the country.

The ad hoc political organizing left a lot of people who wanted to help Hillary—and had the skills and networks to do it—feeling like they weren't being deployed effectively by the campaign. But, after

Michigan, their frustration was hitting home with the candidate. Over and over again, the Clintonworld veterans—including Bill and Hillary—heard that there was no infrastructure in the states and that no one had been empowered to start building ground operations. In the early stages of the campaign, the old Clinton hands told nervous Democrats that if the campaign didn't keep its focus on the early states, the later ones wouldn't matter. But even as they sought to comfort, they knew there was a problem.

"Why are we not using these resources?" Hillary asked.

She turned to old friends Charlie Baker and Craig Smith to solve the problem. While Mook would send more paid staff into the states after Michigan, Hillary would also activate the networks of her allies.

Smith, a University of Arkansas grad, was the first person hired on Bill Clinton's 1992 presidential campaign and went on to serve as political director in Bill's White House. When Clintonworld had needed an adult to supervise the Ready for Hillary operation, Smith took on the task from his Fort Lauderdale home. His Ozark drawl seemed out of place in South Florida, but it was music to Bill's ears. As much as anyone in Clintonworld, he shared the Big Dog's old-school political sensibilities. The two men spoke often, and Smith had been well aware of—and complicit in articulating—the concerns that the campaign had failed to build political units.

Baker too had been hearing the frustrations of Clinton supporters who were racked with concern over the campaign's lack of a presence in their states. He had helped Hillary map out her campaign long before it launched, and wasn't as much rattled by the noise of Democrats complaining about staffing as he was interested in taking advantage of untapped resources. Baker's activation of a political network in his own home state, Massachusetts, had helped deliver the only competitive contest on Super Tuesday. After a quarter of a century of playing the political game at the national level, the Clintons had political allies waiting to be engaged all over the country. Each of them had their own networks to mobilize. It was a no-brainer to get those folks involved, he thought. For Hillary, it meant having a more trusted, more seasoned set of friends doing her politics at the state level. And it meant she didn't have to pay for top-flight talent. Many were longtime Clinton allies who would donate their time, their networks, and their skills.

He and Smith, collaborating with Marshall, set to work on putting together a list of senior friends of the Clintons in each state who could play the role of political overseers. They hammered out a roster of people who had both personal connections to Hillary and knowledge of the political class in the states—folks like Teresa Vilmain in Wisconsin and Tamera Luzzatto, a longtime Hillary Senate chief of staff who knew West Virginia's political community thoroughly from her time as an aide to Senator Jay Rockefeller. Mike Stratton, a Colorado-based strategist, was dispatched to New Mexico, where he'd run Democratic presidential campaigns for Bill Clinton and Al Gore.

These friends of Hillary would operate above the state-level campaign infrastructure and report back to Brooklyn. The idea was to make sure that trusted allies could tap their own political networks and act as a check on the polling, the data analytics, and the field operations. The campaign dubbed the senior political operatives in the states "ubers" and those who moved to other states "traveling ubers." One source familiar with the initiative called them "a second set of eyes and ears." They weren't a formal part of the campaign—they were drafted into volunteering—but rather a shadow political operation and early warning system.

This deployment of outside black ops teams mirrored the way Hillary managed other areas of her campaign. It was reminiscent of the speechwriting construct in which Dan Schwerin was the chief wordsmith but dealt with a coterie of outside scribes who had deeper ties to Hillary and more experience writing at the presidential level.

Before the uber system was developed, inexperienced aides were trying in vain to quickly organize political networks. "People were coming in three weeks out" from a primary, another source familiar with the program said. "It's hard to figure out who the players are. We gave them these more seasoned operatives. They'd done it before."

If the fix worked, it would boost the political operation and cut down on complaints from officials and allies who thought there weren't enough savvy staffers on the ground to run a proper campaign.

The activation of key political leadership outside the campaign wasn't just a de facto demotion for Renteria but also part of a broader rebuke of Mook. The state teams under the control of Marshall, his top lieutenant, would now be shadowed by veteran operatives with closer ties to the Clintons.

Mook had been so focused on the main task at hand—winning delegates without spending too much money—that he had lost sight of the optics and the politics. For weeks, Hillary had been trying to impress on him the importance of finding a sweet spot that honored the delegate-driven strategy without allowing bad story lines to fester. Within the Democratic Party, the perception was that Hillary wasn't putting enough people into primary states, and the media story was that Bernie's ground troops were evidence that he had more support in state after state (even when she won). "There was concern. The narrative was not good," said one of her most senior advisers. "If you look at the narrative versus the results, the results spoke for themselves."

What Hillary wanted to know was "How do we make sure we don't enhance the narrative?" All of the issues she identified were intertwined, but some were more real—she wasn't effectively communicating her economic message to voters, white men were moving away from her, and there weren't enough ground troops to support her in some states—and others were based in the skewed perceptions of Democratic elites and the media.

Having spent a dozen years at the highest levels of an administration, as first lady under her husband and as secretary of state under Obama, Hillary knew better than most of the people around her that both reality and perception could destroy her. And she knew that in order to sell her policies to the American public, from the campaign trail or the White House, she had to master both the policy and how to sell it. That was a hard-won lesson for Hillary. She'd been humiliated after she'd failed to get buy-in for her health care plan in 1993 and 1994—not just from the public but even from Democratic senators on Capitol Hill. Her messaging had been terrible then, and her political outreach had been even worse. And in 2008, she'd been convinced that Democratic voters would choose her experience and policy acumen over what she saw as Barack Obama's cheap sloganeering. But it didn't matter how much she'd mastered the details of policy or how many times she'd been in political and policy meetings at the White House—she failed to sell herself as someone who could bring about the things Obama promised. For decades, she'd worked so damn hard to address her deficiencies as both a policymaker and a politician. There were still rough edges on her, some of which sat in places she couldn't see—like her blindness to conflicts of interest, her own preference for reality over political optics, her paranoia about political opponents, and her love of the dollar. She was committed to addressing her own weaknesses as a politician, but she didn't always know how. She needed her lieutenants to do it—or, she thought, she needed to find new lieutenants. It wasn't enough to get most things right most of the time and dismiss failures. This was the time for honing her operation—for the rest of the primary, the general election, and, she hoped, the presidency.

Soon she would install Minyon Moore as a power in Brooklyn. Mook could never figure out exactly what Moore's job was, which should have been a good indication of her influence with Hillary. If the campaign manager didn't know why she had been placed in his midst, it was at the behest of the candidate. Between Sullivan's taking authority for strategy and Moore's keeping an eye on Mook, Hillary had quietly deputized a new leadership team. Mook would remain in charge of the day-to-day operations of organizing in the states, but his role would look less like that of a campaign manager by the end of March. The Clintons didn't think he could handle the whole job he'd been given, but they didn't want to push him from the upper ranks of the campaign. He had value, they believed, and his plans had put her in position to win the nomination. "Robby was never bad enough at a crucial enough moment" to warrant a dismissal, said one senior aide.

"If they had made a decision to remove him," said another, "he would have been removed."

Chapter 12

DAMAGE

IN THE AFTERMATH OF HILLARY'S NEW HAMPSHIRE DEBAcle several weeks earlier, when white working-class voters ran up the score in Bernie's favor, John Podesta offered Robby Mook an insight that should have sent a chill up the young campaign manager's spine.

"There's more chance that Jeff Weaver," the top Sanders aide, "is going to be running a campaign that's ahead on March 15 than you are," Podesta said. Mook, who already knew his job was in jeopardy, had husbanded the campaign's money—to the frustration of operatives in the states—but knew that donors would stop writing checks if Hillary fell behind, or was even seen as floundering, when the results of the five-state mini–Super Tuesday elections came in on the ides. He knew he'd get fired or "layered over" if she wasn't on a clear path to the nomination at that point.

Behind the scenes, Hillary was already reining him in, but her fate—and his reputation—were on the line as voters in Florida, North Carolina, Ohio, Illinois, and Missouri prepared to go to the polls. To his credit and his detriment, Mook was able to tune out the negativity of people around him and keep his focus on the task at hand rather than his job status. Podesta, the pessimist, was in a funeral mood on one conference call about the states, but Mook, despite his precarious position, was more optimistic.

"Guys, it's pretty likely that we'll win at least three of these states, probably even four," he said. *We're not going to win Missouri,* he thought, *but we're more likely to win four of five than get zero, one, or two of them.*

From Mook's perspective, Hillary was already ahead of the conservative scenario he'd drawn up in 2015. He'd planned for losing Iowa, New Hampshire, and Nevada before winning in South Carolina and on Super Tuesday and March 15. But he also knew by this point that if she'd lost Iowa and Nevada, he'd have already been fired or layered over. Heading into March 15, he was confident that Hillary's delegate lead would hold or expand, and, in his mind, that was pretty much all that mattered. Former Obama campaign manager David Plouffe was in Mook's ear too. He had told the campaign manager to ignore the noise of the Clintons and their coterie of outside advisers and just stick to his plan. Mook firmly believed that thinking too much about his own situation would lead him to run the campaign the wrong way and to spend too much time on internal politics. He was determined not to make what he thought were poor strategic decisions in the service of saving his own hide. So Mook focused on the data and the delegates, and Podesta worried about the narrative and the potential for the race to go sideways if Bernie got a big boost.

The bar for Bernie was low. If he won one or two of the states, it would look like he was building off his Michigan upset. That was particularly true because Ohio, Illinois, and Missouri were all midwestern industrial states with significant white working-class populations, and they all held primaries—the type of election that was supposed to favor Hillary. After Michigan, she needed to deal Bernie a major blow to restore confidence in her own campaign and prevent him from picking up momentum. Her lead in the national polls was widening ever so slightly. On a more granular level, she had big leads in Florida and North Carolina, where minority voters would constitute a major share of the electorate, but the margins were just holding steady. More troubling, Bernie was gaining on her in Ohio, Illinois, and Missouri.

Despite temporary spirit lifters in Nevada, South Carolina, and the Super Tuesday states, Hillary was still stuck in a rut running between frustrated and forlorn, and those closest to her knew it. On the night of March 11, just before she flew to St. Louis for a campaign rally, a special visitor to her plane tried to improve her mood and help her come up with a plan of action. She was aboard her plane at the Peoria International Airport, going over her remarks on criminal-justice issues, when a figure with a puff of white hair, ruddy cheeks, and a toothy smile burst into the cabin.

"I figured it out!" Bill Clinton exclaimed, his blue eyes flashing with excitement. "Trump can build his wall and we can open up slot machines along the wall, and the proceeds from the slots can pay for the wall and maybe could send people to college too." Hillary beamed, laughing and clapping her hands as her husband sketched the preposterous caricature of a way to one-up Trump.

But there was a more serious point behind the quip. They both knew Hillary was failing to connect with non-college-educated whites. It was the reason they had decided to meet together on the tarmac before they went their separate ways. Hillary's inability to break through with these voters had been apparent in New Hampshire, in Michigan, and in the industrial states they had campaigned in that had yet to hold elections. The problem was most pronounced in "coal country," including parts of Ohio, Illinois, and Missouri where voters were listening to Bernie in the Democratic primary and Trump on the Republican side. People were struggling to get ahead economically. They hadn't recovered from the financial crisis, and jobs that had traditionally sustained their part of the country had been disappearing for decades. They feel like they're forgotten, Bill said.

Sitting on a couch as Hillary stood with her palms resting on the tops of two captain's chairs, Bill went through her stump speech, making recommendations. They believed her policy solutions were the right ones to modernize these industrial economies for the long haul, but Hillary hadn't yet connected the dots effectively. She had to explain why the turn-back-the-clock promises of politicians like Sanders and Trump were empty and why voters' anger had to be converted into a commitment to policies that would bring their communities into the future. It was a bank shot compared to a vow to end trade and resurrect coal jobs. Bill was a much better explainer than Hillary, but she had to do something to bridge the distance between what these voters thought they wanted and what Hillary believed would be best for them.

By the time Hillary took off for St. Louis that night, Bill had provided some much-needed energy and levity. She was "clearly uplifted," said a person who was on the plane. More important, he'd given a thorough distillation of where her stump speech was missing the mark. When she arrived at the Nelson-Mulligan Carpenters' Training Center the next day, Hillary made a Bill-style acknowledgment of the validity of voters' anger.

"You have every right to be angry, but anger is not a plan," she said. "You have every right to vent your frustration about the way that our economy and our political system is failing, but venting is not a solution." Then she laid out her economic strategy. It was better, more tailored to the working-class whites in Missouri, Illinois, and Ohio—the industrial states voting on March 15—than a lot of her previous rhetoric on the trail. And the message couldn't have been delivered at a better time.

THE SAME DAY as the St. Louis trip, and three days before the primary, Elan Kriegel sent the candidate an update on the state of the race in each of the primaries. Hillary was going to cruise in Florida, where she held a 59 percent to 29 percent lead, and she had a comfortable margin in North Carolina at 51 percent to 37 percent. But in just a few days' time, her ten-point lead in Ohio had been cut in half, she had gone from up a point or two in Missouri to down a point, and her advantage in Illinois had narrowed from eight points to six points. All over the map, she was losing ground among white voters.

Yet again, Bernie seemed positioned to turn a narrow victory in a big state into fuel for his "revolution" to continue. Hillary was going to extend her lead in delegates, but could she finally stick a fork in Bernie's campaign?

On election night, she quickly racked up wins in Florida, North Carolina, and Ohio. Despite the shifting momentum in Ohio, she won comfortably—by fourteen points—by running up the score with African Americans and taking the white vote 53 percent to 47 percent. Bernie won white men, a continuing source of consternation to Hillary, 57 percent to 42 percent, while 61 percent of white women went with her. With Illinois and Missouri still outstanding, and her aides still concerned that they could tip in Bernie's direction, Hillary took the stage a little bit before 9 p.m. in a West Palm Beach, Florida, convention center and not only declared victory but tried to use the three-state run to pivot away from Sanders and toward Donald Trump.

A few hours earlier, around 5 p.m., she'd phoned Dan Schwerin in Brooklyn. She didn't like the draft of the victory speech she was looking at. It was focused on her contrasts with Sanders, as Podesta and Sullivan had wanted. They didn't like the optics of dismissing Sanders and his supporters. But Mook had been pressing behind the scenes for her to rhetorically turn the page on Bernie and start lining up for the general election. This wasn't just another primary day; it was the moment that any honest appraiser of the race would say Bernie had no chance to win the nomination. Hillary took his side.

"This is a big night," she told Schwerin. "This sounds like every speech I've ever heard. What's new? What can I say?" She wanted something that felt like she was speaking to Trump but could also be seen as a contrast with Bernie. Schwerin had been through the last-minute act before. So, knowing Hillary's lawyerly affinity for numbering her points, he scrambled to put together a framework with "three tests" for the commander in chief that could be applied to both Sanders and Trump. He fired off the new draft about an hour later, and they kept tweaking it right up until she took the stage.

Amid the string of victories at a seemingly critical moment, Clinton seized an opening to declare victory. The underlying message in her speech that night was clear: she wanted the public to believe the Democratic primary had just come to a close and she was on to the general—and she wanted that to happen without her explicitly saying Bernie had lost.

"Our next president has to be ready to face three big tests," she said. "First, can you make positive differences in people's lives? Second, can you keep us safe? Third, can you bring our country together again?"

She hit Trump directly too.

"When we hear a candidate for president call for rounding up 12 million immigrants," Clinton railed, "banning all Muslims from entering the United States, when he embraces torture, that doesn't make him strong—it makes him wrong."

Trump had just thumped his Republican rivals that night, highlighting his powerful performance with a rout of Florida senator Marco Rubio in Rubio's own home state. Trump's victory knocked Rubio—the best hope of the establishment wing of the GOP—out of the race. With each passing primary day, it was getting harder and harder to see paths for candidates other than Trump to win the nomination, and Hillary wanted to start throwing jabs in what she believed would be a heavyweight fight with Trump for the presidency.

When she was done blasting the Donald, Hillary hustled to the airport for a flight back to New York. Now she just had to hope that the results in Illinois and Missouri didn't make her pivot speech look presumptuous. She didn't know the exact delegate count as her motorcade moved toward the landing strip, but Florida, Ohio, and North Carolina would end up netting her one hundred pledged delegates. If Sanders got really lucky in the remaining two states, he might be able to pick up ten or fifteen delegates. She'd hammered him, and yet a loss in either Missouri or Illinois would provide tinder for a Bernie comeback tale, especially with a series of states that favored him looming on the calendar over the next several weeks. "We thought we would surely lose Missouri, maybe Illinois," one Hillary adviser said.

As her pilot prepared for takeoff, Hillary got a quick burst of good news. She was going to win Illinois. There was an understated symbolic importance to that: it was Hillary's native state, and a place she'd been crushed by Obama in 2008. Four out of five was good, but she wanted a sweep. She was tired—both from the grueling primary campaign that was supposed to have been a cakewalk and from having to pretend that this was a real race against Sanders.

Hillary settled into a seat next to Mook and Huma Abedin and lazily listened to updates on the numbers that were still trickling in. Then the exhaustion overtook her; she closed her eyes and dozed off. Over the years of traveling from state to state and country to country, Hillary had developed the uncommon ability to fall asleep anytime she wanted, no matter what else might be going on around her.

But her staff remained anxious about Missouri, too edgy to use the two-plus-hour flight to recharge. Mook and Marshall had a lot riding on a sweep. They were sick of being second-guessed. Michigan notwithstanding, their plans were working just fine, they believed. Hillary already had a delegate lead that Sanders couldn't touch without a catastrophic shift in the dynamics of the Democratic electorate—say, an indictment of Hillary over the e-mail scandal. Even that might not be enough for him. But Michigan had reinforced all of Hillary's concerns about the thin staffing on the ground.

And Bill had been beside himself. The night before the primaries, he came padding down a hallway yelling the name of his chief of staff, Tina Flournoy. He'd been talking to Joyce Aboussie, a veteran Democratic operative in Missouri, and she'd given him an earful about how Brooklyn had rejected her requests for more staff and more money. If things turned sour, it wasn't her fault, she argued. Bill was riled up.

But for Hillary, it was no longer just about being on the path to victory. She was infuriated by the way Sanders had made his attacks against her personal and about her character. His focus now was fully directed at portraying her as a corrupted creature of elitist circles in Washington and on Wall Street, a perpetrator of the sins of the powerful against the powerless. And she was irritated by Sanders's ability to command media attention for pulling off Pyrrhic victories. Each time that happened, it meant she was another set of primaries away from turning her attention to the general election. Hillary was stuck fighting a zombie candidate who could embarrass her and undermine her but not defeat her for the nomination. She wanted to square up with Trump in earnest, not just in rhetoric carefully designed to guard against a backlash from Bernie and his voters. But, to do that, she'd have to convince everyone that Sanders had no shot. That, in turn, meant she had to beat him badly on March 15. Even then, she might not be able to shake him.

From the Clintons' perspective, Mook and Marshall had failed to put organizers on the ground, the communications team wasn't getting the message right, and Benenson's attitude was the only thing worse, they thought, than the strategic advice he gave. Even the vaunted analytics team couldn't predict turnout as precisely as she would have liked. The pitch-perfect component was the delegate plan mapped out by Jeff Berman, who had counted the all-important noses for the nomination of Barack Obama in 2008.

Mook and Marshall had their own tried-and-true method of dealing with the Clintons' frustrations: they'd do just enough to make it look like they were taking instructions to heart. That's why, after Super Tuesday, they'd hired just a handful of staff in the five March 15 states. No matter how furious Hillary was after being humiliated in Michigan, neither Mook nor Marshall thought it wise to flood the zone in the upcoming states with paid staff. They were the professionals, and Clintonworld was full of backseat drivers who didn't understand modern campaigning. Their strategy risked further enraging Hillary if she lost a state she thought she would win, but they were confident in the merits of their plan.

▼

NOW, WITH FOUR of the five states in their pocket, Clinton's young strategists were one state away from silencing their critics—or so they hoped. Missouri, they knew, held outsize importance in the power jockeying that constantly raged behind the scenes in Clintonworld. It would be harder for others to second-guess them if Hillary cruised through mini Super Tuesday unblemished.

As her jet made its way over Long Island Sound, descending toward White Plains, Marshall's phone service kicked back in. He called Aboussie on the ground in Missouri. With 99 percent of the precincts reporting, Hillary held a razor-thin lead. The conversation had been going on for three or four minutes when Aboussie told Marshall to hold on for a second.

"I think the last precinct's in," she told him. Marshall urged his fellow passengers to quiet down. With the plane moments from touching down, a groggy Hillary awoke to the minor commotion he caused by shushing his colleagues. Marshall put his phone on speaker, and Aboussie's voice boomed across the cabin.

"Oh, my fucking God!" she shrieked. "We just won the fucking state of Missouri."

Hillary and her aides erupted as the plane touched down. She smiled, high-fived Mook, and clapped along with the rest of the jubilant crew.

"Oh, my goodness," Hillary said. That was an understatement. This mini Super Tuesday, in the shadow of the Michigan loss and with three midwestern industrial states voting, held so much portent for the rest of the Democratic contest, and perhaps for Hillary's ability to compete for white working-class votes in the general election.

"We weren't talking about Michigan on the plane," one Hillary aide said of the seven-day-old ghost that had all but reserved a seat, "but a lot changed in just a matter of a week."

She'd just knocked Sanders out. She knew it. He knew it—or at least he should have. And so did Mook and Marshall. As the plane taxied, the Clinton team popped a bottle of champagne—a more celebratory drink than the leftover bottle of some previous jet-setter's scotch that Marshall had discovered squirreled away behind a seat earlier in the campaign.

Back at the Brooklyn headquarters, in the dead of night, someone handed brooms to Mook and Marshall. Sweep. Sweep. Sweep. They were cult heroes for the hundreds of campaign staffers removed from the elite level of the operation.

But the five-to-nothing drubbing Hillary delivered to Sanders shouldn't have been such a nail-biter, internal critics and some of Hillary's closest friends griped. The margins should never have been that close. A little extra money and a few more staffers placed in the states earlier in the campaign would have rendered Sanders incapable of contesting states like Illinois and Missouri, these naysayers believed. Victory was covering up the deficiencies in Mook's strategy and tactics, they thought.

"Hillary won because of Hillary, not because of her staff," one of them insisted. Hillary, it turned out, was thinking exactly the same thing.

In the days after the March 15 primaries, Marshall gathered two dozen or so members of his staff at the Brooklyn headquarters. He needed to tell the campaign's organizers that he and Mook and Hillary had heard the complaints about having too few people on the ground in primary states. In truth, that was a source of tension between Hillary and Mook; she wanted more resources campaigning in theater. But for Marshall, this meeting was an appeasement mission. The organizing unit had taken the brunt of the criticism for Hillary's losses and near misses, and he took a stab at accountability.

"We fucked up," he said. In Marshall's mind, it wasn't a true admission of failure on the part of the campaign leadership, but he had to sell it that way to convince his audience. "We didn't have people in the states. Huge mistake."

What Marshall knew all too well was that Hillary was about to go through her worst stretch of the campaign from the perspective of losing states and yielding delegates to Sanders. It wouldn't be enough to put Sanders in contention, but it would knock her off stride.

Mook tried to prepare Hillary for the coming rough patch. "We're going to lose all of these," he told her. "It's going to feel awful." From his viewpoint, Hillary could look at the delegate math and see that she wasn't in danger of losing the nomination. But no candidate likes to be humiliated, whether she's expecting it or not.

More complicated was the challenge with the junior staff, who were going to have to suffer through the pain of losing, the second-guessing of the Democratic donors and elected officials, the sharp-bladed media, and the possibility of more infighting. And they'd have to come out the other side ready to do battle in the remaining primaries and in the general election.

"Robby's learned his lesson now," Marshall said, subtly elbowing his boss and close friend, which suggested to those in the room that he wanted people to believe he'd stopped greedily slurping Mook's Kool-Aid.

"We've got a lot of work to do," he added. "We're going to be different moving forward." He was more right than anyone at this meeting would ever know.

Hillary was hearing all of the second-guessing about her campaign manager, and she did plenty of it herself. He seemed so confident about his way of doing things, always ready with an answer to her questions. But he was good at managing up, and she worried that she was sliding by on too-thin margins in many of the primary states. By keeping him in the campaign manager post, where he'd continue to control the budget and the vote-building operations, she betrayed a lack of confidence in her own political instincts after the 2008 loss. One friend explained Hillary's reluctance to sack Mook this way: David Plouffe and David Axelrod, Obama's successful campaign gurus, believed *she* was the problem, not her campaign manager. That was in Hillary's head. If someone was wrong, she thought, it might be her. "That paralyzed her a little bit," the friend said. Still, by the middle of March, she had all but stopped talking to Mook directly.

By then, Mook was in all but open warfare with Podesta. For starters, their vastly different styles clashed time and again. Mook, with his field-organizing roots and millennial viewpoints, was part manager, part dreamer, part salesman, and part cheerleader. Podesta was more grounded, direct, and pessimistic. He was also furious at Mook for cutting him out of the information loop on major parts of the campaign, including budgets, analytics data, and staffing in the states. It's not that Podesta believed modern campaign tools were useless. He trusted that they had value. He just didn't trust Mook.

When Aboussie had called Bill to raise the alarm that she wasn't getting enough resources from Brooklyn, Podesta told Bill's chief of staff, Tina Flournoy, that Aboussie "was in charge according to Robby."

"In charge?" Flournoy asked incredulously. "As in she was the state director?"

"That's what he [led] me to believe," Podesta replied. Aboussie wasn't officially the state director, and both Podesta and Flournoy seemed to be at a loss as to why the person in charge of the state would get Bill riled up about a possible loss.

The younger man's campaign projections were always rosy, no matter the topic—fund-raising, organizing volunteers, getting votes. He aimed to please. But he also closely guarded the truth.

Since the very beginning of the campaign, Podesta had watched as Mook tried to neutralize potential power rivals—Jen O'Malley Dillon, Adam Parkhomenko, and Charlie Baker among them. Together, they'd boxed out the consultants. But after two stints as a top White House official, Podesta had little patience for playing games with Mook.

The clash had created an environment in which it was impossible for even relatively high-ranking campaign operatives to get a feel for who was making decisions. "Robby felt like 'I'm the campaign manager, I'm supposed to run a campaign.' And John felt like, 'I'm the chairman, I'm supposed to be in charge,'" one top aide said.

By late March, the slow shift of power away from Mook became semiformalized with the creation of a new brain trust. All decisions would now flow through a six-person team: Mook, Podesta, Huma Abedin, Jake Sullivan, Jennifer Palmieri, and Minyon Moore rounded out an executive council known by a variety of nicknames, the most positive of which was "the Super Six." It operated as a board of directors. Podesta and Mook, who had frequently rendered decisions without consulting each other, retained the titles of chairman and campaign manager, respectively. Abedin had control of Hillary's schedule and traveled with the candidate. Palmieri, who had endeared herself to Hillary and would ultimately take on a traveling chief of staff role, was in charge of the sprawling communications department. Sullivan oversaw just about everything else. And Moore was a powerful minister without a portfolio. Hillary charged them with making decisions by committee.

Sullivan, the policy chief and the only one of his generation rising at a time when Hillary was turning to old hands, ran the Super Six meetings. He declined an offer for a bump in title as he was given ever-greater jurisdiction. That decision was a sign of his savvy in not making waves any bigger than he had to internally or externally. He also knew that he was a square peg in a round hole. Hillary had asked him to take on a role that was outside his wheelhouse because she trusted him. Throughout the campaign and after it, Hillary's other aides spoke of Sullivan in reverent terms. Abedin remained Hillary's shadow—a translator and gatekeeper whose influence could never be overestimated. Often blamed, unfairly, when she rendered decisions that had actually been made by Hillary, Abedin had graduated from her longtime post as Clinton's body woman—the aide physically closest to her at all times—and carried the title of vice chairwoman. But no one had greater metaphorical proximity to the candidate.

Moore, who cut her teeth in politics as an aide to Jesse Jackson and who had been the White House political director in the Bill Clinton administration, had a leg up on everyone in Brooklyn: not only did she know electoral politics, but she knew Hillary as well as anyone. Moore was a one-woman Hillary tribe. In fact, Hillary had been pressing her to come aboard the campaign for months, and

Moore had finally relented—giving up most of her responsibilities at the public affairs shop Dewey Square Group to move into an office in Brooklyn with a sign on the door that said "Super Volunteer."

Possessed of a steel spine, Moore served as a fixer in the Super Six meetings, determined to reduce the number of problems that rose to Hillary's level, and as a mentor for many of the mid- and junior-level staffers. What she soon discovered after settling into the headquarters was that Mook's underlings were afraid that he would retaliate against them when they raised red flags. "Everybody was on these eggshells," said one person familiar with the environment when Moore showed up. She became "a spindle" to break down silos and encouraged staffers to "say what they wanted to say in front of Robby or in front of John."

"There just needed to be a forum where stuff was actually hashed out, instead of unilateral decision making," said another person familiar with Hillary's thinking in putting together the Super Six.

Moore was also a specialist in African American outreach and the only black person at the top of a leadership team running a campaign that was relying on African American voters to win the primary and needed them to show up in force in the general election. Most important, she was the one who best understood Hillary's history, motivations, and moods and how they fit into the turbulent political environs of the 2016 campaign. Behind the scenes, Moore had helped Hillary lay the groundwork for this bid for years, going over the 2008 campaign's autopsy, helping her build her team at the State Department, and presenting, along with her Dewey Square Group colleagues, the blueprints for the current campaign years before the election. And it was Moore who was beckoned to the trail after New Hampshire to help Hillary get her arms around why the campaign wasn't working.

At a slightly lower level, though, Marshall was consolidating power over state-by-state operations. Political director Amanda Renteria was stripped of her staff, and they were reassigned to Marshall's organizing team. Mook and Marshall would remain in control of the campaign's fieldwork. Mook also retained power over the all-important analytics team and paid media operations. There was good reason—aside from his skills—for Hillary to keep Mook happy enough. His ability to create a cultlike following within a campaign meant that he could boost morale or kill it. Hillary didn't have the luxury of sparing enthusiasm in her Brooklyn headquarters or anywhere else. The Super Six model, with Moore operating as eyes and ears for Hillary, was supposed to help get everyone on the same page so that decisions could be made and carried out efficiently. But the power struggles and ambiguity in the lines of authority within the campaign would persist.

All of it reflected several truths about Hillary's world. First, she was ultimately running it. Second, she liked to set up rival power centers within and outside her operation, which created no shortage of confusion, angst, and infighting. And third, the campaign was just one piece of a much larger Clintonworld operation that included the Clinton Foundation, Bill's personal office, and the legal team that had been assembled to handle her e-mail issue. She was the only one with full visibility into all the component parts. Having cut off Bernie's chances of staging a comeback and with her new power structure moving into place, Hillary began to think seriously about the major challenges of the general election.

Deep in the shadows of Brooklyn, Podesta was working on a secret project. A few days before the March 15 primaries, he put together a list of potential vice presidential running mates for Hillary. His initial cut was shared with Cheryl Mills, the longtime Hillary confidante who had no formal role on the campaign and yet continued to exercise tremendous influence with the candidate and her top aides. Having worked with Podesta, Abedin, Moore, and Palmieri as far back as the Clinton White House days, and closely with Sullivan at State, she didn't need to be in the Super Six to know what was going on in Brooklyn.

Podesta's first list included three dozen names. They were broken into seven categories: Latinos, female senators, male senators, African Americans, high-ranking military officials, business leaders, and Bernie Sanders. As Hillary was putting away the mini–

Super Tuesday states, Podesta and Mills made edits with Sullivan, Abedin, Palmieri, and Mook. The final version added New Yorkers Mike Bloomberg and Senator Kirsten Gillibrand, and Coca-Cola CEO Muhtar Kent, whose company was a multimillion-dollar contributor to the Clinton Foundation. Michael Bennet of Colorado, a young swing-state senator close to Obama but not to Hillary, was also added. Kevin de León, a leader in the California assembly, was dropped.

Podesta waited until two days after the March 15 primaries to send the list to Hillary—a tacit acknowledgment that the state of the race had turned inarguably in her favor.

"OK, I can breathe again! Congrats on a fabulous night," he wrote on March 17. "I am feeling like it's possible to get back to the longer term again." He also sent her the names of people who would write reports on each of the prospective running mates and a separate team of vetters who would dive deeply into the candidates' backgrounds. "Let me know if there are people you would like to see added or removed before we begin the process," he concluded.

DONALD TRUMP WAS edging ever closer to the Republican nomination. The GOP race had, surprisingly, managed to get uglier over time, with Trump and Marco Rubio engaging in repartee about the sizes of each other's body parts and Trump retweeting an unflattering picture of Ted Cruz's wife and eventually repeating a never-substantiated *National Enquirer* claim that the Texas senator had been unfaithful to her with a series of female aides and acquaintances.

Bill thought Trump was crazy, but he had never expected the developer to become unhinged. He'd watched some of the debates and read the news coverage. Trump's attacks on Hispanics, Muslims, even Fox anchor Megyn Kelly were beyond the pale. But, at that point, he welcomed Trump's success because he had long believed either Rubio or Cruz would make a tougher general-election opponent for Hillary. Keeping one eye on the field, Bill saw Rubio as fresh and polished at the same time. His Cuban heritage would give him an opportunity to court the Hispanic voters that Trump was turning off with his plan to build a wall between the United States and Mexico and with his divisive rhetoric. Now, though, Rubio was out. Cruz, also of Hispanic heritage, would present a different kind of challenge to Hillary, but a strong one nonetheless. Bill wasn't sure how Trump would flip-flop if he were nominated, but he was confident that the Queens-reared billionaire wouldn't stick to the conservative line he was toeing to get through the primary. Cruz, on the other hand, was a true believer with a vision that could be articulated. He could tap into the same anger that Trump was galvanizing on the political right and among fed-up independents. If elected, Bill thought, Cruz would try to make good on his promises to close down the IRS and other government agencies.

As Trump closed in on the nomination, he focused ever more of his fire on Hillary. And, in addition to the bed-wetting within the Democratic Party, Hillary had to contend with the concerns of Democrats who had conflicting interests in individual states. Some wanted to keep their distance from her campaign, and others had specific needs that threatened to hurt her turnout.

From Hillary's point of view, she could no longer afford to take incoming fire from Bernie—it was time for him to start winding down his campaign. The mini–Super Tuesday states had been an inflection point. Bernie's camp was slower to come to grips with that. But, over time, his camp would divide over when and how to ramp down. For now, Bernie, his wife, Jane, and campaign manager Jeff Weaver, knew he could capture several upcoming states and hoped—hoped enough to believe—that he could grab momentum, score a couple of upsets at the end of the primary, and convince superdelegates to abandon Clinton and put him over the top. It was not lost on them that there was a startling irony in Hillary—who had run through fifty states against Obama—wanting Bernie to cease and desist.

That is, Bernie and the people closest to him wanted to rage against the dying of the light. And rage Bernie did. He won seven of eight states between March 22 and April 9, including blow-outs in Washington, Utah, and Wisconsin. During that time, he ramped up his attacks on Clinton, particularly her ill-advised deci-sion to give paid speeches to companies with business before the federal government. For a time, it sounded like Sanders believed his opponent wasn't Hillary Clinton but some guy named "Gold-man Sachs." Though Sanders had refused assistance offered from the Democratic National Committee, he accused the party ma-chine and its chairwoman, Debbie Wasserman Schultz, of tilting the playing field in Hillary's favor. It wasn't a baseless charge—Hillary's campaign had been in close communication with Was-serman Schultz throughout—and it reinforced the idea that she was a candidate born of the establishment at a time when voters in both parties were as angry as they had been in generations with the nation's major institutions. Bernie was taking a family fight to new levels.

In so many words, he kept calling her corrupt. It was one thing to hit her on policy, but his increasingly favored brand of personal attacks would deepen some Democrats' distrust of her and could easily spill over into the general election. It was terribly damaging to have a fellow Democrat (or at least someone running for the par-ty's nomination) highlight the very weaknesses most voters already saw in her.

Moreover, Hillary thought it was unfair. She'd ignored warn-ings from friends not to give the paid speeches, but she truly be-lieved she couldn't be corrupted and that she hadn't done anyone favors for money. Her platform, she thought, was proof positive that she would regulate big banks, and she had promised to make it easier to prosecute wrongdoing at a time when liberals believed the Obama administration had gone too easy on bankers in the wake of the 2008 financial crisis.

"The whole bought-and-paid-for thing came from Bernie," one Clinton aide said in the fall of 2016, lamenting that it hadn't really been a knock against her among Democrats coming into the campaign. "That did her damage." Her overall national favorability rating had actually held fairly constant in the low forties—a sign that most Democrats still approved of her—but it had slowly moved downward while her unfavorability percentage had moved from below fifty in mid-December 2015 to the midfifties by early April 2016.

"The idea that she was in the pocket of big banks bothered her," said another staffer, who nonetheless maintained that it was a "horrible mistake" to give the speeches in the first place.

But, as with the e-mail scandal and the dealings of the Clinton Foundation, she couldn't turn back the clock. She could only pledge to be a strict regulator and hope that Bernie would back off. Democrats worried that Bernie would just keep turning the knife in a vain effort to win the nomination by destroying her. Ironically, Hillary had made changes in her campaign just in time to lose a string of states that favored Sanders simply because they were caucuses, or allowed independents to vote in Democratic primaries, or had few voters of color—or some combination of those factors. And, equally ironically, Bernie looked like he was gaining momentum when five nails had been driven into his campaign's coffin on March 15. But because they could write off Bernie's wins as coming in states tailored to him—and because they were so hyperfocused on delegates—Hillary and her team didn't pay enough attention to the fact that working-class progressives, particularly the white ones, were voting against her at alarming rates.

As Sanders reeled off a string of sizable victories—including a double-digit blowout in the white, working-class haven of Wisconsin—Democratic allies continued to tell Hillary she wasn't putting enough money and energy into each of the states. On April 5, for example, Bernie had beaten her 59 percent to 40 percent among white voters in Wisconsin. The numbers were a little bit more stark in the set of voters with household income between $50,000 and $100,000 per year: 60 percent to 39 percent. And gender continued to have a high correlation with her performance. Despite getting thrashed in the state, 57 percent to 43 percent, Hillary had edged Bernie 50 percent to 49 percent among women. But, among men, he crushed her, 63 percent to 36 percent.

The myopia was striking. Hillary had blinders on because she had always thought the primary would be tougher than the general election. Where she had misunderstood the importance of delegate accumulation in 2008, she was now so driven by math—and the message that she would win by sheer numerical force—that she couldn't, or wouldn't, see that she was doing nothing to inspire the poor, rural, and working-class white voters who had so identified with her husband. She was aware of the problem, but she didn't act effectively to fix it. After all, she was racking up delegates.

Rather than vying for their votes, the campaign dismissed their impact in the primary. That attitude was evident in a memo Mook posted on Medium in early April. It was designed to point out to the press and the public that Sanders was no longer in contention for the nomination—an idea that, if it took hold, would start to build pressure on Bernie to either get out or simply stop attacking Clinton. But it was bloodless in its analysis.

"The math being what it is, the Sanders campaign has struggled to explain their path to the nomination," Mook wrote. "Their latest strategy involves a combination of trying to flip pledged delegates at state and county conventions, while also convincing superdelegates that he deserves their support—despite the fact that Hillary Clinton has won 58 percent of the popular vote and a majority of pledged delegates thus far."

He was basically making the delegate-side argument that Hillary had been constructing against Sanders's policy: it was pure fantasy. That had everything to do with who was going to win—and it was a reasonable measure of which candidate voters had favored so far—but it was hardly an argument that her platform or her values were better than Bernie's.

Bernie was just one of the problems Hillary faced in the spring, down the homestretch of the Democratic primary season.

But he was still foremost on her mind after he thwacked her in

Wisconsin. He only picked up ten net delegates from the voting re-sults. Even when Bernie won a state by a big margin, he couldn't count on substantially cutting into Hillary's lead. Her delegate-hunting team was the most consistently effective part of her campaign—and, to her credit, the lesson she'd most fully learned from 2008 was to make sure her delegates were in line. To put a finer point on it, nine of the ten superdelegates in Wisconsin went to Hillary, meaning that his overall edge in the state was forty-nine delegates to forty-seven delegates despite his overwhelming victory in the popular vote.

For the data lovers in politics, this meant that the trajectory for him to win the nomination was even steeper than it had been before. Hillary was getting closer to winning even when she was losing—because there were states left on the map that she was sure to win big and the window for Bernie to make a move closed with each passing primary day. The prospect of a long, slow march to an inevitable Clinton nomination frustrated Sanders and his support-ers no end, and it made them much more aggressive.

Bernie's attacks on Hillary's character and the Clintons' record, repeated by progressive activists, were dividing the Democratic Party and getting under Bill's skin.

A few days after the Wisconsin primary, he got into a protracted battle with two Black Lives Matter protesters who interrupted him at a recreation center in Philadelphia. One held a sign with the word "superpredator" on it, a reference to Hillary's mid-1990s remark about putting "superpredators" away. They called her a murderer too, for her role in the bombardment of Libya that eventually led to Muammar Gaddafi's death.

Bill went back and forth with them for ten minutes about his 1994 crime bill and a variety of other topics. "I don't know how you would characterize the gang leaders who got 13-year-old kids hopped up on crack and sent them out into the street to murder other African American children," he charged in reference to the "superpredator" sign. "Maybe you thought they were good citizens. She didn't."

The tense confrontation, an echo of a private South Carolina event at which Hillary had been verbally accosted by a BLM protester, seemed way off message for a campaign reliant on support from African Americans and worried that younger black voters were more likely than their older counterparts to support Bernie. Hillary had already apologized for her choice of words, and here Bill was defending his policy, his legacy, and her original sentiments.

Bill thought he'd "turned in" effectively, countering the BLM protesters with context, history, and facts about the Clinton Foundation's work on behalf of black lives in Africa. His answer was the right one for his old political frame—a throwback to his "Sister Souljah" moment—and for many working-class whites who neither saw themselves as racially insensitive nor had a problem with the "superpredator" description for gangbangers. He believed he was in the right and that he was helping his wife. No one else did. For many in Clintonworld, it was a flashback to his clumsy handling of race issues in the 2008 campaign, a clue that he no longer had a pitch-perfect sense of the American electorate or the Democratic Party's values.

As his small motorcade left the Dorothy Emanuel Recreation Center in a heavily African American neighborhood and rolled through northwest Philadelphia, Bill's aides lit into him. Whether you're right or not, they told him, you went about this the wrong way. His little campaign team, led by chief of staff Tina Flournoy, made no bones about telling him when he'd messed up. This had been his worst foul-up of the campaign, they told him. It was too late in the cycle, and they were too close to a string of May primaries in which Sanders was expected to do well, for Bill to still be shaking off rust. He had been in Philadelphia because polling showed that the upcoming April 26 Pennsylvania contest offered Sanders an opportunity to steal a big state from underneath Hillary's feet.

Afterward, the campaign essentially sided with the protesters, reiterating that Hillary should have picked different terms to describe gangsters. The feeling inside the campaign was that Bill had helped Bernie in a state where African American turnout and support were key to Hillary holding off the surge. He was going to have to stay focused.

Before Pennsylvania, though, Hillary and Bernie would sprint to the finish line in New York on April 19.

On paper, it was a home game for Hillary, who had been elected statewide there twice. But Brooklyn-born Bernie had a claim on the state too, and he and his aides began to portray it as a last chance for him to turn the race around. He was going to fight her, and fight hard, on her own turf. Damaging Hillary in her backyard would not only signal her weakness in the primary but ingrain the narrative that he was the stronger general-election candidate versus an opponent like Trump.

If Bill was feeling frustrated with Bernie's attacks, Hillary was feeling worse. She wanted to go negative. She was the one who had been absorbing his ever-heightening broadsides—and she was pissed that the news media always portrayed him as running a positive campaign on the issues. *Bullshit,* she thought. Bernie's entire campaign was a character assassination—a moral-high-ground argument that she was less pure than he was. Of course, that was true in the sense that she believed in moving forward by building political coalitions. Bernie didn't work with anyone. He didn't do it in the House. He didn't do it in the Senate. His "coalition" on the campaign trail was almost entirely white and disproportionately male. Hell, he was only competitive in states where just a handful of people showed up for caucuses or large portions of the electorate were independents, not Democrats.

His platform was fantastical, and it wasn't nearly as well thought out as hers. Unlike Obama, whom she'd painted that way in 2008, Bernie really didn't make any effort to explain realistic scenarios in which his agenda could be enacted. Obama worried about the costs of his proposals and their real-world impact. Bernie relied on rhetoric about a "political revolution"—that even electing him president would only be the beginning. His followers would have to rise up and remake the entire political map over a series of elections, convincing America of the rightness and rectitude of his brand of socialism. After stepping up the attacks and creating an unforgettable narrative about Hillary's lack of integrity, Sanders framed her to his supporters as the problem, not the solution. She would never be for them because she was nothing like them.

For the most part, Hillary and her campaign aides were fearful that attacks on Bernie would just backfire, but New York was different. These voters were accustomed to bare-knuckle politics. She had better standing with them, and there were issues—Israel, for example—on which they were much more aligned with her than with Bernie. On conference calls, she and her aides talked about getting a little tougher with him.

ON THE OTHER side, Bernie and his top strategist, Tad Devine, split over how to approach New York. Devine wanted to run a campaign in the state that focused on Bernie's roots there. He would out–New York the New Yorker. Devine even cut an ad, narrated by Susan Sarandon, that focused on Bernie's Brooklyn upbringing. But Bernie and Jane Sanders weren't sold on the risk of sacrificing his national brand to sell himself in the state. Devine thought New York was make-or-break. But they all agreed that it was time to turn up the heat even more on Hillary.

"We were really going to get much more aggressive about her weakness as a candidate," said one Bernie ally. Every single time Bernie ridiculed Clinton's six-figure speeches ("Not a bad day's work," he would say) and her ties to Wall Street, he planted doubt in the minds of even the staunchest Democrats. His thinly veiled allegations of corruption, coupled with the unrelenting crush of the still-unfolding e-mail scandal, kept the pressure on her. And Trump did his part to reinforce Sanders's message, debuting the nickname "Crooked Hillary" at a rally in Watertown, New York, just before voters went to the polls.

An athlete hasn't proved his mettle until he has survived New York sports fans. It's the same in politics, and Bernie wasn't ready for the playoff-style atmosphere in the Big Apple. He choked. The first hands around his throat belonged to Art Browne, the top dog in his meeting with the editorial board of the *New York Daily News*. Browne, a slim, balding Pulitzer Prize winner with about forty years logged at the paper, tried to nail him down on a basic question that had eluded most of the media for the entirety of the campaign. Bernie liked to say that he would break up the big banks. In the interview, Sanders acknowledged two important substantive matters that undermined his favorite talking point: he didn't have a plan for what to do with the banks once they were broken up, and there was already existing authority under the Dodd-Frank law to wind down banks that posed too much risk to the system.

He was calling for new authority that already existed! And beyond that, he couldn't say what would happen to all of the assets once a bank was required to break apart. He was flirting with increasing the risk to consumers, rather than decreasing it. It was a demonstration of exactly what Hillary had been saying about him: his plans weren't real.

"That is their decision as to what they want to do and how they want to reconfigure themselves," he said. "That's not my decision. All I am saying is that I do not want to see this country be in a position where it was in 2008, where we have to bail them out. And, in addition, I oppose that kind of concentration of ownership entirely." On his number one issue, he sounded lost on the specifics.

Hillary seized the opening immediately, using an appearance on *Morning Joe* the following day to pounce. "Well, I think he hadn't done his homework and he'd been talking for more than a year about doing things that he obviously hadn't really studied or understood, and that does raise a lot of questions," she said. Asked whether he was qualified for the presidency, she demurred.

Bernie was furious. He hadn't gone so far as to say she was unqualified. And to him, she'd done just that to him. He thought he needed to throw a roundhouse, and he overswung at a campaign rally later that day. Clinton said "I am quote-unquote not qualified" to be president, Sanders told the crowd. She'd never said it that way. Maybe he'd been misinformed by a staffer. But it was untrue.

Honest Bernie was lying about dishonest Hillary. Then he went on: "I don't believe that she is qualified if she is, through her super PAC, taking tens of millions of dollars in special-interest funds." He sounded out of control.

The touchstone for Hillary's approach to whaling on Sanders was a bank-shot ad she began running in New York about a week before the primary that hit both Bernie and Trump. It showed clips of Trump's most outlandish statements—women should be punished for having abortions, Mexico sends the United States its rapists, and Muslims should be banned from entering the country—to contrast Hillary's values with those of the likely Republican nominee. At the end, an announcer proclaims, "She's the one tough enough to stop Trump."

"Trump was emerging as the front-runner, and it was a way for us to put our flag down and reiterate what was at stake," one aide said.

In her telling, Trump was the enemy of all Democrats, and Bernie was the candidate too frail to fight him. The title of the ad: "Stronger Together." Bernie had played right into her hands when the heat had been turned up on him. "He did more of his own damage than we really did on him," said one top Hillary aide. "That was his worst couple of weeks, but it was really self-inflicted."

Hillary ended up whipping Bernie 58 percent to 42 percent, even as his massive, enthusiastic crowds dwarfed her much smaller and more sedate campaign events. "That was kind of our last hurrah in terms of actually trying to win the thing," said one Bernie adviser. "After that it was a question of how much ground we were going to capture between that and the end" of the primary season.

But Bernie didn't see it quite that way. While he always knew he was a long shot to win, his drubbing in New York didn't dissuade him from campaigning hard. He was a better candidate than Hillary, he believed, and there was still a chance to convince Democratic superdelegates of that. If he could just keep it close and win a big state like California, maybe, just maybe, others would see the flaws in Hillary that were so obvious to him and to Trump. Besides, even if he couldn't supplant Hillary, each additional delegate he won would give him more leverage in negotiating the Democratic platform, he thought.

Hillary and her team believed New York had finally and conclusively ended the competitive phase of the primary. "For the fourth time," one aide joked with a sigh.

Whether the press would give her the title or not, Hillary now knew she was the presumptive Democratic nominee, and she expected the trappings of that standing. It was time to force fellow Democrats to declare their allegiance and help her put Bernie away once and for all. Her state of mind was evident to those around her during a visit to Maryland in advance of the April 26 primary there.

Representative Chris Van Hollen, who had scored a maximum seven on a hit list of enemies she'd kept after the 2008 campaign, was locked in a tough Senate primary fight with Representative Donna Edwards. Van Hollen, the choice of Senate Democratic leaders Harry Reid and Chuck Schumer, worried throughout the campaign that Hillary's ability to turn out black voters in Maryland could put Edwards, who is black, over the top. He had support from some major unions, and, at a rally in Baltimore, Hillary learned that those unions planned to help Van Hollen by not pushing black labor voters out to the polls. If their members voted in force, many of them would pull the lever for Edwards. Rather than directly suppressing the black vote, which could be lethal in a Democratic primary, Van Hollen banked on his union allies just going through the motions.

Hillary was outraged. She wanted to win Maryland and win it big. She needed to show Sanders just how futile his efforts were at a time when he still hadn't given up the ghost of defeating her and was now responding to her with the indignation of a candidate who had been humiliated in his native state of New York. She was also feeling entitled to the kind of fealty typically accorded the party's nominee for president. As an aide walked her out of the event, Hillary smiled and waved at a crowd of supporters. But her broad grin belied the anger behind it. Through bared and gritted teeth, vengeance slipped out.

"Who gives a fuck about Chris Van Hollen?" she said to her aide. "What the fuck are we going to do to fix this?"

The aide said he would deliver a message to the unions: Do you want another friend in the Senate or do you want one in the White House? The threat was pretty explicit: Hillary, who kept careful track of friends and enemies, wouldn't look kindly on anything less than a full-throttle effort to drive black voters to the polls in Maryland.

"Good," she said to the aide. "I'm not going to let his campaign suppress the vote in Baltimore."

All the while she kept smiling and waving. On the verge of capturing the Democratic nomination, Hillary was sick of other people's priorities getting in the way of her path to the presidency. In the end, the unions did enough to appease Hillary without jeopardizing Van Hollen. "They really did the bare minimum," said one political observer familiar with the state's labor politics. Hillary cruised to victory anyway in Maryland and won three other states on April 26.

But the fact that she'd had to push unions to whip up their members to vote was indicative of how little natural support she had in the ranks. The lack of enthusiasm for her candidacy among labor's foot soldiers in Maryland should have been one of that day's major warning signs. She also lost Rhode Island, a haven for working-class whites. But the outcome there was overshadowed by Hillary's victories in more populous states, including Pennsylvania.

It was high time, Hillary believed, for Bernie to back off. A few days later, at the White House Correspondents' Dinner, a black-tie affair for the president, the White House press corps, Washington's self-important political class, and a smattering of Hollywood elites, Hillary ad-maker Jim Margolis bumped into Devine. They'd known each other for more than three decades, having both worked for 1984 Democratic presidential nominee Walter Mondale. Margolis pulled Devine aside. Bernie was hurting Hillary with his emphasis on her ties to the banking industry. One ad in particular was really excruciating, he said.

"Can you please stop running the Goldman Sachs ad?" Margolis asked. The spot came down.

Chapter 13

"TOO EASY"

A S DONALD TRUMP TOOK CONTROL OF THE REPUBLICAN
race, one of Hillary's longtime advisers circulated a memo.
The very top read "FACT: Donald Trump can defeat Hillary
Clinton and become the 45th President of the United States." Hillary, the memo went on to say, should not "underestimate his capacity to draw people to the polls who normally do not vote." That
could "tip the scales in key states (and put certain states in play that
would otherwise be more safely Democratic)," the adviser wrote,
adding that in assessing polls, "I'd routinely add three or four
points to whatever they say about his support."

For a Brooklyn command that worshipped hard data, such
musings were the kind of misguided old-school hocus-pocus that
had very little to do with winning modern campaigns. So perhaps
it shouldn't have been surprising that the adviser's memo never
gained traction. This campaign engine, driven so much by the science of analytics and so little by the art of political persuasion, was
really starting to hum. Mook had tuned out his internal and external critics, focused on the numerical path to victory, and now it
had paid off. Hillary was poised to become the first woman ever
nominated for president by a major political party. Better yet, she
was going to draw Trump—the clown prince of the Republican primary field—as a general-election opponent. Soon the increasingly

popular Barack Obama would join her on the campaign trail and bless her as the natural heir to his historic presidency.

These young data warriors, most of whom had grown up in politics during the Obama era, behaved as though the Democratic Party had come up with an inviolable formula for winning presidential elections. It started with the "blue wall"—eighteen states, plus the District of Columbia, that had voted for the Democratic presidential nominee in every election since 1992. They accounted for 242 of the 270 electoral votes needed to win the presidency. From there, you expanded the playing field of battleground states to provide as many "paths" as possible to get the remaining 28 electoral votes.

Adding to their perceived advantage, Democrats believed they'd demonstrated in Obama's two elections that they were much more sophisticated in bringing data to bear to get their voters to the polls. For all the talk of models and algorithms, the basic thrust of campaign analytics was pretty straightforward when it came to figuring out how to move voters to the polls.

The data team would collect as much information as possible about potential voters, including age, race, ethnicity, voting history, and magazine subscriptions, among other things. Each person was given a score, ranging from zero to one hundred, in each of three categories: probability of voting, probability of voting for Hillary, and probability, if they were undecided, that they could be persuaded to vote for her.

These scores determined which voters got contacted by the campaign and in which manner—a television spot, an ad on their favorite website, a knock on their door, or a piece of direct mail. "It's a grayscale," said a campaign aide familiar with the operation. "You start with the people who are the best targets and go down until you run out of resources."

Mook, always attentive to cash flow, knew that it was much more costly to try to persuade undecided voters to back Hillary than it was to register her supporters or to make sure they went to the polls. The analytics team could also conduct less expensive surveys than the pollsters to get a snapshot of the horse race in a given state. Separate from the three scores, the analytics experts would do quick surveys with a small universe of voters and then extrapolate how many other voters with similar demographic profiles were likely to vote and for whom they would cast their ballots. The same methods had been used in the primaries, when adjustments could be made based on the outcome of a string of contests. The general election was different, in part, because there was only one Election Day. The analytics were also thought to be more precise at predicting general-election outcomes in each state than primary outcomes because the exact shape of the electorate could be harder to project in lower-turnout contests. But in both cases, Mook relied heavily on the data to figure out where the campaign could get the most bang for its buck. Like a baseball executive in the *Moneyball* era, Mook looked at the data as the means for taking the least costly route to victory.

"Every investment decision we made—like how many staff to put into a state, how frequently she would visit some place—was all driven by analytics," said one high-ranking campaign official. Mook had taken a lot of incoming fire for those decisions from insiders and outsiders who believed he'd relied too heavily on the data to slice and dice the electorate rather than reaching out beyond those most likely to vote for Hillary. Mook used analytics "not as a tool but as a decider," said the high-ranking official, who wanted the campaign manager to rely less exclusively on analytics.

Jen O'Malley Dillon, the runner-up for manager who worked with the campaign for many months, pushed Mook to spend more on persuading voters by knocking on their doors, a traditional method of building vote count. But the combination of a shorter-than-anticipated window for focusing on the general election—because of the length of the primaries—and the relative cost of on-the-ground persuasion efforts pulled Mook in a different direction. He chose to focus on turning out voters who already preferred Hillary with his staff in the states and on using television and digital advertising to change hearts and minds.

"We did not have the choice to take a path off the table," said one person who disagreed with Mook's approach. "It wasn't enough to say that we could just do voter registration and turnout and that would be enough to win. And I never believed that advertising and digital alone is enough to do your persuasion." Mook quieted the dissenters and moved forward with his plan. But he had plenty of defenders too. "That team really helped drive the campaign, which is how it should work," said one ally. "It ends up being right more than it's wrong."

By the tail end of the primary calendar, he had reason to believe his methods had been validated. Hillary had racked up the delegates she needed to capture the nomination, she hadn't really been surprised anywhere but Michigan, and her bank account had never been empty.

The success emboldened him. Between the built-in advantage her campaign team believed Democrats had in the Electoral College, the data squad's ability to target voters in such a sophisticated fashion, and the Republicans' impending nomination of Trump, Mook began to think about expanding the electoral battleground into traditionally Republican states. Toward the end of the primary, he would commission the data analytics team to conduct surveys not just in battleground states but in traditionally Democratic places like Washington and Oregon and the Republican strongholds of Arizona, Georgia, and Texas so that he could get a feel for just how much he might try to flex Democratic muscles across the map. The analytics surveys were quicker and cheaper than traditional polling, and, in Mook's view, they were just as accurate about candidate preference.

At the same time, Trump was taking the opposite tack. Instead of trying to increase the number of competitive states, he concentrated intently on a handful that carried large numbers of electoral votes. Trump focused, in particular, on Rust Belt states Obama won, where his tough-talking Queens bravado and isolationist message played well with working-class whites, and Florida, where Obama had prevailed by less than one percentage point in 2012. Together,

Ohio, Pennsylvania, Michigan, Wisconsin, and Florida accounted for ninety-three electoral votes. If Trump won any four of the five and held on to Romney's states, he would be president. In some scenarios, he only needed three of them. And of all the states that Romney had won, Obama had only come within five percentage points in one: North Carolina. There was good reason for Trump to have some hope. He had several important tailwinds: only twice since 1828 had a Democrat won a third consecutive term for the party; populist movements on the right and the left had arisen from the ashes of the 2008 financial crisis and gathered steam throughout the intervening years; and the states he needed to flip had all elected Republican governors.

By early May, Trump was galvanizing the GOP and rising in head-to-head polls against Hillary. More worrisome for some Democrats, the plain-talking Trump was striking a chord with working-class white voters who felt like they had been left behind. With the exceptions of Ohio, where favorite son Governor John Kasich won, and Wisconsin, where Ted Cruz was the victor, Trump had carried all of the Rust Belt and Appalachia in the primaries.

"He's tapped into the real and understandable frustration that's felt among working people," AFL-CIO chief Richard Trumka said that month.

Once Cruz and Kasich dropped out of the race following the Indiana primary on May 3, Trump's inner circle—including campaign manager Corey Lewandowski and convention chairman Paul Manafort—visited the belly of the establishment beast, the headquarters of the Republican National Committee in Washington. His aides huddled with party officials for a daylong series of meetings that amounted to a 101 class on the party machinery. There, in the "Ronald Reagan" room, with TV monitors affixed to three of the four walls, RNC officials taught the rookies on Trump's team about budgets, data, strategy, messaging, and other aspects of the campaign. Some wrote on the room's whiteboard walls, leaving their scrawls visible during the next department's presentation.

Trump's team was particularly enthralled with a communications presentation that focused on the RNC's strategy for hammering Hillary. Raj Shah, the party's research director, outlined the buckets of messaging against Clinton: a creature of Washington, a corrupt insider influenced by foreigners, untrustworthy, unaccomplished at State, and a liberal Democrat after eight years of the liberal Democratic Obama presidency.

"Our goal was to make sure that we made them understand the contrast we could draw," one GOP source said. "He would be the agent of change, and she would be the status quo." From the RNC's perspective, Hillary was a godsend. Everyone in the country knew the former first lady, and the majority of Americans didn't trust or like her. The primary had only served to deepen voters' antipathy toward her. Half of the messaging job for Trump and the RNC was already done. "With Hillary, the beauty was she was already defined, and we just needed to reinforce it," the official said. The challenge, even at that early date, was figuring out how to "create the drip-drip-drip to reinforce the existing narrative."

RNC officials had been surprised when polling in 2015 had shown that voters didn't care nearly as much that Hillary would be the first female president as they had in 2008 that Barack Obama would be the first black president. Whether that was because voters were misogynistic or just didn't care for Hillary was irrelevant; it only mattered that Hillary's gender wasn't going to sweep her into the presidency. That said, they had also learned from early surveys that most voters didn't hold Bill's infidelity against Hillary.

While Democrats were convinced they had the math and a strong enough candidate to win the presidency, Republicans saw that the mood of the country created a landscape that should have suited them well: Hillary was deeply unpopular and well defined, she was running for the Democratic Party's third consecutive term, and there was little reason to think her gender would be an asset. But they knew Trump was his own worst enemy, and they had little faith that he could be contained. "If Trump went on vacation for the next six months," one Republican official observed, "he would be the next president of the United States."

The RNC's strategy and communications team explained the messaging that had been taking shape during the primary and shared the party's polling with a Trump operation that didn't spend much time or money on surveying public opinion. At a time when Hillary was supposed to be cruising to her nomination while a mess of Republicans battled to bear their party's standard, the reality was that the GOP was instead getting the jump on her.

SUDDENLY, HILLARY COULDN'T afford to lose any time. For months, years even, she had been secretly outlining plans for the general election. She hadn't known for sure that she would face off against Trump, but, as he gathered steam during the primaries, the campaign, the Democratic National Committee, and an assortment of political action committees supporting Hillary increasingly turned their attention away from the other Republican candidates and homed in on the billionaire. While she battled Bernie, Hillary had to keep up the public appearance that she wasn't looking past him to the general election. At the end of April, she could wait no longer. She instructed aides to begin filling out staff rosters for the big battleground states, moves that would show she was now focusing on how to win in November.

"That's when we started feeling like we needed to put people on the ground," said one Hillary aide. That would position her to take on Trump but "not so early that you look like you're taking the primary for granted."

But for Mook and the data analysts, it was already too late to build the kind of ground forces required to knock on doors and persuade voters to back Hillary.

"TV was persuasion. Mail was largely persuasion," said one high-ranking aide. "The place where we didn't have as much opportunity to do persuasion was more a function of the primary than a decision. The thing with the field operation—unlike a TV ad or a piece of mail, a field operation takes several weeks to build. And the people knocking on doors aren't staff."

Many of Hillary's field organizers had cut their teeth on Obama's 2012 campaign, when he had been able to build his battleground field operation without worrying about a primary. But the window was much shorter this time around precisely because Bernie had stayed in the race until the very end.

"The best way to fund organizing is through the state parties and coordinated campaigns, but that's not available until there's a presumptive nominee," said one person familiar with the campaign's field operations. It takes about two months to find and train talent for a state-coordinated campaign—which works on turnout up and down the ballot for the party. Obama had been able to begin that process much earlier. Mook didn't have the time or the cash to ramp up in the same way. Time was "unequivocally" a factor, this person said, but, contradicting those who said the length of the primary was the only reason, he acknowledged, "there was a strategic decision to do more voter registration work in the summer and not persuasion."

Persuasion would turn out to be a key factor in 2016 because there was a lot of volatility in the electorate. Many voters were up for grabs. And Mook's critics believed he was ignoring an essential piece of the puzzle for building Hillary's coalition. Whether persuasion would work with voters who already had a wealth of information and well-formed opinions about the former first lady was another question—one that would be impossible to answer without an earnest attempt. But Hillary and her aides weren't heeding warnings from the electorate. The self-assuring nature of taking primaries, coupled with Hillary's belief that her younger generation of organizers and data scientists understood the math and mechanics of winning, prevailed over her doubts about strategy and tactics. It was as if victory hinged solely on painting by the numbers revealed through analytics.

Fundamentally, she was misreading the mood of the voters. Trump was winning primaries because he was a torch-bearing outsider ready to burn the nation's institutions to the ground. Bernie was offering the same thing on the Democratic side, and he had flown in from off the political radar screen to give Hillary fits. In January 2016, Democratic pollster Stan Greenberg, a former Clinton White House aide and sometime critic of both Clintons, had beseeched Podesta to open Hillary's eyes to the changing world around her. With Bernie and Republicans attacking her as an agent of the establishment and an avatar of the status quo, Greenberg argued, Hillary had to make political reform a central part of her campaign.

"With Trump and Cruz attacking crony capitalism, do not assume we own reform in the general election," he advised. "With people struggling financially, they want to make sure government works for them and they want to make sure taxpayers get their money's worth. That includes many base Democratic voters." Hillary was running in the wrong year to ignore the power of promises to rein in establishment excesses. But she would never put forward an ethics agenda.

THE RISE OF populism, and particularly right-wing populism, wasn't a phenomenon limited to American politics. Brits were locked in a tense battle between those who wanted to exit the European Union and those who wanted to remain. Populist figures with nationalistic tendencies—like Nigel Farage in Britain, Marine Le Pen in France, and Norbert Hofer in Austria—were on the rise across Europe. By ceding the reformer mantle to Sanders—and to Trump—Hillary was dismissing a whole world's worth of evidence that she was running into the headwinds of history.

"If you look at the absolute collapse of the establishment of the Republican Party, the fact that we survived through our primary process was actually a minor miracle," one of her senior aides told friends in the spring of 2016. Instead of shifting, she was locking in a general-election strategy based on the assumption that the 2016 electorate would look a lot like those of the previous two elections. Having defeated Bernie's surge, Hillary was reassured that the national political firmament would hold.

Interestingly, both Bill and Hillary were paying attention to

British politics. In 2015, when conservatives thrashed the liberal Labour Party, Hillary confided in aides that former prime minister Tony Blair had predicted to her that the left would lose if it ran a "base" election. She appeared to worry about being drawn too far to the left, rather than seeing the conservative takeover as an affirmation of nationalistic populism. Bill believed the push for Brexit—and its eventual approval by voters—showed a strong contempt for existing power structures that reflected the mood of the American electorate. You guys are underestimating the significance of Brexit, he told Brooklyn and his own advisers over and over. He'd come to power by tapping into similar frustrations in 1992, convincing voters that a reasonably good economy was swirling down the drain—and that he was the only guy who could fish it out and revive it. Bill had a better feel for the working stiff, whether American or British, than anyone else in Hillary's orbit. He knew that, and he felt like he was being heard. But he couldn't figure out why Hillary and her team weren't executing.

He liked Mook enough, and appreciated the explanations he'd get for why the campaign was pursuing particular tactics and not others. It was a familiar feeling. Throughout the primary, he'd report back from the field on what he was hearing at campaign events and from friends across the country. Mook's response was always a variation on the same analysis: the data run counter to your anecdotes. Bill liked data, but he believed it was insufficient. To him, politics wasn't just about finding people who agreed with you and getting them to the polls. He felt that it was important to talk to voters individually and get a real sense for what they were feeling. He also believed that a candidate could persuade voters with the right argument. And in pursuit of that, the on-the-ground feel for how hopes and fears were motivating voters was invaluable.

For Mook and the Brooklyn number crunchers, it held little value. Hillary, the policy wonk, leaned heavily toward hard evidence too. And, because she didn't want to expose herself to unscripted interactions with voters, she wasn't getting much retail political information. From the very beginning of the campaign, Hillary had met with preselected groups but tried to avoid chance encounters with voters who might heckle her. She took the same approach to members of the media, who sometimes relayed the concerns of voters to candidates. She was running a variation on a "Rose Garden" strategy—the term for an incumbent president who stays at home and uses the trappings of the office to campaign rather than getting out on the hustings. For years, she'd been in the bubble of elite circles in Washington, New York, and foreign capitals. Whether or not she understood their concerns, she was literally out of touch with voters. Bill hungered for, and sought, more casual discussions with them.

"He felt like they weren't talking to and hearing from actual people at events," one of Bill's confidants said.

As they began to plot in earnest for the general election, Hillary and her aides thought things were finally starting to go their way. They believed Trump offered them the perfect foil against which to run a base-focused campaign with a dash of outreach to centrist Republicans fearful that he would be intemperate in an international crisis. Trump was dividing the Republican establishment from its base in the primary, and the Clinton campaign saw an opportunity to take advantage of that rift. If everything went right—and they thought there was a good chance of that happening—Hillary would be able to expand Democrats' dominance of the electoral map. They couldn't or wouldn't see that Trump had spent the primaries courting voters in their backyard.

In a traditional campaign environment, Mook's plan to reach into more Republican states made sense not just as a means for giving Hillary the most chances to win or even a possible mandate with a sizable Electoral College victory but because it would force Trump to play defense in places where the Clinton campaign could get more bang for the buck. Every day you make Trump go to Arizona, he liked to say, is a day he can't be someplace else. "What you're always trying to do is to spend fifteen cents if someone else has to spend seventy-five cents," one source familiar with Mook's thinking said. "The problem is we're dealing with a nonconventional campaign."

But it was Trump who figured out how to compete without spending as much as Hillary.

It would be some time before Hillary, Mook, and the rest of Clintonworld discovered that Trump's ability to run a campaign on the cheap was a sign that he didn't have to run everywhere. They already knew that he could rely on earned media—his mastery of Twitter and his ability to orchestrate free coverage from television, digital, and print outlets—to carry his message. They knew he didn't need to invest in field-organizing programs in the primaries or raise much money from donors to sustain himself. What they didn't fully grasp is that Trump had tapped into a vein in the electorate that Hillary couldn't locate—and, just as important, that his much narrower focus within the Electoral College provided a viable path to victory.

Beyond her confidence in the blue wall and her own data-driven strategy and tactics, Trump was giving Hillary reason to feel good about the possibility that he would implode. She was counting on strong support from women; there were endless stories about his mistreatment of them. She was courting diverse constituencies; Trump was attacking a Mexican American judge, Gonzalo Curiel, over his heritage; and Trump's paeans to social conservatives—like a formulation that women who had abortions should be punished—bore all the hallmarks of a candidate who was overcompensating. Cruz, the conservative Texas Republican and a rival of Trump's for the nomination, criticized him harshly for that statement, contending that Trump "hasn't seriously thought through the issues."

Trump's campaign appeared to have other fundamental flaws, particularly when it came to fund-raising. The billionaire businessman had only raised $3.1 million in May, typical of a rainmaking Senate candidate, not one running for president. By every traditional metric, his campaign was insufficient to win a primary, much less a general election. Despite all that, Trump's ascent in the Republican primary had been a pretty straight line, and by May 23 he led Hillary by two-tenths of a percentage point. Once he captured the nomination, Republican voters began flocking to him. In the final stages of the primary season, it was Trump who was gaining strength for the general election.

FROM THE WHITE HOUSE, Obama chose to remain neutral in the primary. Early on, it made sense for him to stay above the fray of an intraparty contest. As the calendar wound down, there was a risk that weighing in would backfire, bolstering Bernie's claims that the Democratic Party had rigged the nomination process for Hillary. Obama could end up alienating Bernie supporters in his own coalition and reenergizing their complaints against Hillary.

So it wasn't until about a week or so before the June 7 California primary that Obama gave White House officials the nod to begin putting together a plan for the president to endorse Hillary in a video—a piece of shareable content that could bounce around and through the warrens of the Internet and reach every last voter who was interested in watching it.

Over the weekend before the primary, aides arranged for Obama to speak to Bernie from a fund-raising and golfing trip in Florida. When they connected by phone, Obama congratulated Bernie on running a tough campaign. But it's the end of the road, Obama told his former Senate colleague. It's time to unify the party. And, the president added, I'm going to endorse Hillary after California.

As leader of the party, it was Obama's place, and only Obama's place, to tell a Democratic presidential candidate when to exit the race with grace. That's what he was doing now.

Bernie got it. I appreciate your neutrality through the primary, he replied, adding a small request: Let me come to the Oval Office for a meeting before you endorse her. Obama agreed.

On June 7—while California voters were still at the polls—Obama walked down the majestic colonnade near the Rose Garden and into the White House residence to put the finishing touches on an unspoken pact he'd made with Hillary the day he'd asked her to serve as his secretary of state. They had become close enough personally not to think of his endorsement of her in the transactional terms of a final payment on the deal. But that's what it was—one of the last big mutually beneficial acts of a political partnership for the ages. For Hillary, who was eager to have Obama on her side as soon as possible—and who would have liked an endorsement before the primaries began—it was the validation she'd been waiting on. For Obama, it was the ultimate insurance policy on his legacy.

He settled into a wood-backed chair in front of a red patterned sofa in the Map Room, oddly enough the same room in which Bill Clinton had given grand jury testimony during the Monica Lewinsky scandal. By recording a video in the residence, Obama was able to keep his endorsement under wraps. As the president prepared himself, he thought of the journey he and Hillary had undertaken at the highest levels of policy and politics—the 2008 primary, the raid that killed Osama bin Laden, her quiet assistance in passing his health care law, and the many stops where they'd shared exhausted laughs as they tried to leverage American power around the globe.

With the camera rolling, Obama testified to Hillary's judgment, celebrated the history she was making, and urged his supporters to build the rest of his blueprint by electing his former rival president. "I don't think there's ever been someone so qualified to hold this office," he said in the relaxed, confident, and upbeat tone Americans had become familiar with over the previous decade. "I want those of you who have been with me since the beginning of this incredible journey to be the first to know that I'm with her."

With the film in the proverbial can, the only question for the White House was timing its release. But that process ended up being driven not by Obama or Hillary but by Sanders, who wanted his Oval Office meeting before Obama signaled the end of the primary campaign. That was very important to Bernie, and, because Hillary wanted to smooth the path for him and his followers to unite with her, it was important to her. And, because it was important to Hillary, it was important to the White House. In addition, the president admired the way Sanders had mobilized the progressive grass roots and didn't mind doing Sanders the small courtesy of waiting a couple of days to put the exclamation point on Hillary's victory.

Beating expectations, she won California on the night of Obama's video shoot by about seven points and also picked up New Jersey, New Mexico, and South Dakota.

Hillary had gone home to New York to address her supporters. For most nominees, the victory speech at the end of the primaries is the time to honor defeated rivals, start to bring the party together, and punch the other side's candidate. Hillary's team had written all of those themes into her remarks at the Brooklyn Navy Yard. There was also a nod to the history she and her voters had made. But it wasn't enough for Hillary. Just before she took the stage, she told Dan Schwerin she wanted her words to be big enough for the moment.

"Put in brackets 'Seneca Falls,'" she said. Hillary didn't need a script to riff on the famous women's rights conference. After acknowledging the milestone of becoming the first woman to win a major-party presidential primary, she said the victory belonged "to generations of women and men who struggled and sacrificed."

"In our country, it started right here in New York, a place called Seneca Falls, in 1848. When a small but determined group of women, and men, came together with the idea that women deserved equal rights, and they set it forth in something called the Declaration of Sentiments, and it was the first time in human history that that kind of declaration occurred. So we all owe so much to those who came before, and tonight belongs to all of you." Hillary hoped to make more history before all was said and done, and yet she recognized the importance of pausing to call attention to the progress that she and the nation had made.

But Bernie, speaking that same night in California, still wasn't ready to release his supporters from the thrall of the campaign. "I am pretty good at arithmetic, and I know that the fight in front of us is a very, very steep fight," he said. "But we will continue to fight for every vote and every delegate we can get." Even when the primary calendar had come to a close with Hillary holding an insurmountable number of delegates, she couldn't have one night of relief from the battle. At some point during the campaign, Jennifer Palmieri, the communications director, had coined a phrase to describe the punishing pattern in which there never seemed to be an unadulterated triumph. "We're not allowed to have nice things," she'd said. The interminable fight with Bernie, in the midst of Trump gathering his party, certainly qualified. But the pattern would soon repeat in an unpredictable and unfathomable fashion.

WHEN BERNIE RETURNED to Vermont after the June 7 primaries, he huddled with Jane, Jeff Weaver, and Tad Devine. "The race is over," Devine told Bernie. "This thing with Trump is very serious. It's not going to be a blowout. The sooner you can put it together, the better. Call her. Tell her how important it is to win the election, and that you'll do whatever she needs you to do to win."

But Bernie didn't want to give up the leverage created by the number of votes and delegates he'd won. As soon as he conceded the political battle to Hillary, he'd have no way to force substantive concessions from her in the formation of the party's platform. He was committed to making his political revolution mean something.

"If I don't get what I need," he told Devine, "I'm going to have to negotiate harder." Jane and Weaver stood with him. Devine left town.

Sanders ended up in the West Wing of the White House on the morning of June 9, two days after the California primary. He knew that an endorsement of Hillary was coming, but he didn't know when it would come or how—just that it would be after he left. Obama started to soften the blow for Bernie by talking about the parallels between their campaigns and their visions for the country.

In the sense that they both ran outsider campaigns built on the promise of reforming Washington, Bernie and Obama had something in common. But comparisons with Bernie irritated Obama no end, and he could be heard grumbling about them in the West Wing. *No serious person would really compare me to Bernie,* Obama thought—and hoped. It probably wouldn't have bugged him so much if there wasn't at least a kernel of truth to the idea. But he believed that it was a fundamentally unfair comparison. He thought he'd put meat on the bones of his own proposals in 2008 and that Bernie had not done the same in 2016. Bernie might be able to hit a high note or two, but he couldn't sustain a melody. Whenever the subject came up privately, Obama would talk about his respect for what Bernie had done to make it a race against Hillary, but he seldom failed to let his annoyance show. For Bernie's visit, he was going to have to hold it back.

Obama told Sanders that he'd been impressed with the Vermont senator's energy and his ability to tap into compelling arguments that resonated with voters. More important, the president said, he didn't want Democrats to lose what Bernie had brought to the table—and not just because he wanted Hillary to win. Obama and Sanders shared a capacity to bring more people into the political system. The two men spent some of their hour-long meeting brainstorming ways that the Democratic Party could sustain the energy of Bernie's campaign both in the election and in helping to move public policy debates with grassroots engagement. Though he'd tried with a group called Organizing for America, Obama had been unsuccessful at converting his campaign into a non-election-year force in public policy. Bernie had a chance to use his own movement to affect policy.

Bernie's reservations about aspects of the administration notwithstanding, he'd always admired Obama's cool handling of crises. It was a trait that eluded Bernie at times. He got fired up too easily over little things. Indeed, the rigors and stresses of the campaign trail put Obama's skills into sharper relief for him. Now Bernie knew firsthand how hard it was to project composure on the big stage of national politics, where scrutiny from an opponent and the media exaggerated every Brooklyn-accented word and every finger jabbed in the air to emphasize a point. Obama made it look so damn easy.

Following the one-on-one with the president, Sanders held an ad hoc press conference in the driveway outside the West Wing. The campaign that had begun in the Senate Swamp fourteen months earlier was ending, as Bernie had hoped, at the White House. But, despite his best efforts, it was coming to a close on the wrong side of the doors. He still wasn't quite ready to say anything close to "I'm with her."

"I look forward to meeting with her in the near future to see how we can work together to defeat Donald Trump and to create a government which represents all of us and not just the 1 percent," Sanders said.

White House officials didn't give the media time to dissect what Sanders had said or to report that his the-enemy-of-my-enemy-is-my-friend acknowledgment of his preference fell short of the kind of endorsement Hillary would have liked. Bernie was hardly out of the driveway when they pushed out Obama's endorsement video, wiping out what had been the big story of the morning: the Democratic Party's effort to bring Sanders inside the Clinton tent. Instead, all of the headlines pointed to Obama's endorsement of Clinton and their upcoming joint appearance in Wisconsin that had just been announced.

On the one hand, it was a great day for Hillary. Bernie had gotten out of the race, and Obama had endorsed her. But it was telling that the White House had needed to step on Bernie's departure to quell news stories about the deep divisions that remained in the party.

White House officials and Clinton campaign aides had settled on Green Bay, Wisconsin, for the president's first joint appearance with Hillary. The location had been selected in part by process of elimination. Mook wanted Obama to go to North Carolina to rally Democrats, but the White House didn't want to get in the middle of the fight over the state's "bathroom" bill. Pennsylvania and Michigan were out because Mook was reluctant to give Trump a reason to think Hillary was worried about those states. They settled on Wisconsin, but Mook wasn't a fan of going to Green Bay. The voters there wanted change and Obama's presence would suggest that Hillary was running for his third term, he thought. Mook argued that it was better to send Obama to a place where he could mobilize millennials and register African American voters.

But there were reasons to think that Green Bay was exactly the kind of place where Hillary should be campaigning—with or without Obama. The National Football League's poster town for hardscrabble working-class values, the city and surrounding Brown County were chock-full of the very working-class white voters who had supported Obama in 2008, were deeply ambivalent about Hillary, and were open to the siren song of Trump's promise to restore American greatness. It was a part of the country that was competitive but trending in the wrong direction for Democrats. In Brown County, Obama had won with 54 percent of the vote in 2008 and then lost with 48 percent in 2012. It was the kind of national bellwether county where Democrats couldn't afford to cede much more ground if Hillary hoped to win the presidency.

But she and Obama never made it there. Three days before they were set to visit, a twenty-nine-year-old security guard killed forty-nine people at Pulse, a gay nightclub in Orlando, Florida, in a lone-wolf attack. The shooter had placed a call to police beforehand in which he swore allegiance to ISIS, the terrorist group wreaking havoc across Syria and Iraq. Rather than shrouding the nation in solemnity, the specter of a heavily armed Muslim man opening fire with an assault weapon in a gay club created a political firestorm.

Trump charged in a statement that Obama should resign and Hillary should bow out of the race if they refused to say the words "radical Islamic terrorism." He reiterated his call for a ban on admitting Muslims to the United States and boasted of his prescience in predicting that there would be another mass killing in America. "Because our leaders are weak, I said this was going to happen—and it is only going to get worse," Trump said.

Hillary and Obama called off their rally in Green Bay, postponing their first big event until a more appropriate time. A big moment was again being stolen by events outside her control. Their staffs went back to the drawing board and, at the end of June, settled on a familiar setting. Charlotte, North Carolina, had played host to the

2012 Democratic National Convention, where Bill Clinton delivered a magnum opus that even many Obama loyalists considered the defining speech of the president's reelection campaign.

Forgoing Wisconsin, widely perceived as home turf for Democrats, they decided to go into tougher territory to try to expand the electoral map. "We agreed that North Carolina would be a good on-offense trip to do," said one official involved in the planning. The shift was evidence of the Clinton camp's growing confidence.

ON JUNE 27, as the White House and Brooklyn were putting the finishing touches on the plan for the trip, the administration and the Clinton campaign collided, metaphorically, on a tarmac in Phoenix, Arizona. Bill Clinton was in one plane when he found out that Attorney General Loretta Lynch was sitting in another plane at the same airport. He walked over for a visit with the official who held authority over whether Hillary would be charged in the e-mail scandal. Lynch felt that she couldn't refuse a quick greeting from Bill, a former president. He had picked her to serve as the United States Attorney for the Eastern District of New York in 1999, a job that had helped catapult her through the prosecutorial ranks and eventually into the role of the nation's chief law enforcement officer. But this discussion was more than a quick hello. It went on for thirty minutes. She would later say they talked about their families, golf, travel, and Bill's favorite topic of the moment—Brexit. Bill didn't have to say anything about Hillary's e-mail case for the meeting to create havoc. It could be read as a message to Lynch that she'd better not charge Hillary if she expected to keep her job, or as a sign to the public that Lynch had already decided not to prosecute. Clinton critics said it could have a chilling effect on the FBI, which was still investigating Hillary, or Justice Department officials involved in the prosecution decision.

The ex parte chat set off a flurry of punditry and headlines questioning Lynch's impartiality. It also reinforced the idea that Hillary could pull establishment strings to rig outcomes in her favor. Lynch backed off as if scalded by a hot stove, publicly stating that she would follow the recommendation of the FBI and the career lawyers at the Justice Department on the Clinton e-mail probe. She never went so far as to say that she would give up her right to intervene if she didn't agree with the FBI's recommendation on whether or not to prosecute. But FBI director James Comey would soon seize on Lynch's quasi-recusal to step into the spotlight.

West Wing and Clinton campaign aides had the same collective reaction to the meeting, according to one Democratic source who talked to officials in both places: "What the fuck?"

Bill Clinton didn't have an impulse-control button. Everyone knew that. And still, this stood out as colossally high-risk and low-reward. Hillary's aides would insist that he was just being friendly and cordial. It was plausible that Bill hadn't even thought of the e-mail investigation, one campaign official said, because the Clintons and their aides never took seriously the possibility that she could be charged with a crime. "We always thought it was a joke," the aide said.

The White House didn't think it was funny. Obama and his aides knew they couldn't account for Bill Clinton's behavior, but they were dismayed with Lynch. She had a well-earned reputation as one of the shrewdest, and most mistake-averse, members of his team.

The tarmac debacle couldn't have happened at a worse time. Less than a week before Obama's first stump speech for Hillary, conservatives were charging that his Justice Department was on the verge of letting her off the hook on the e-mail scandal. They had pretty good circumstantial evidence that the Obama Justice Department and the Clinton operation were coordinating on the e-mail scandal (even if it wasn't true—and both sides insisted it wasn't—how could anyone be certain?). For Comey, a former federal prosecutor who had been the deputy attorney general during President George W. Bush's administration, the flow of events created an opportunity to play the roles of FBI director and attorney general at the same time.

▼

ON JULY 5, the very day Obama and Hillary were scheduled to fly to Charlotte for their first joint event, Comey stepped to a podium at the J. Edgar Hoover Building in Washington. Wearing a gold tie pinched tight at the knot, and standing in front of two Justice Department banners and an American flag, the FBI director began reading an indictment of Hillary Clinton's conduct.

She and her aides were "extremely careless in their handling of very sensitive, highly classified information." It was possible, he said, that hostile actors gained access to her e-mails, including those containing sensitive information. And, he added, it was possible that she had broken the law. But, he said, the Justice Department had never prosecuted someone under similar circumstances before. He would recommend against filing charges in the case. It was highly unusual, if not unprecedented, for the FBI director to read out the findings of an investigation when the target wouldn't be charged.

The e-mail scandal was over, and everyone was unhappy with the outcome. Conservatives looked past Comey's public shaming of Hillary and faulted him for letting her off the hook. Liberals were furious that he'd paired his recommendation against prosecution with a stinging rebuke of Hillary's character and judgment.

While Comey was delivering his verdict, Hillary was giving a speech less than a mile away at the National Education Association's representative assembly at the Walter E. Washington Convention Center. Backstage, her aides hopped onto a conference call with her lawyers that would last for forty-five minutes. Members of her press staff fielded what one insider called "relentless 'fuck yous'" from reporters who believed they'd been lied to about how she'd handled her e-mail as secretary of state.

It was hard to keep track of how many times Hillary and her press team had said things on the record that were contradicted, either directly or by implication, in Comey's statement about why a case was not moving forward.

At the end of the NEA event, Hillary slid into an SUV with John Podesta, Huma Abedin, and Jake Sullivan. As her motorcade navigated through the city toward Joint Base Andrews, the suburban Maryland military installation where Air Force One sat waiting to take her and Obama to Charlotte, Hillary processed what Comey had done. While it was a relief to be in the clear—the outcome she'd always expected—it was infuriating to be subjected to Comey's clear attempt to explain himself to the public, and to Republicans in Congress, by whacking her.

Hillary's goal was to starve, not feed, a media frenzy that threatened to distract from Obama's first campaign appearance for her. Attacking Comey directly was out of the question. Though he was a Republican, no one in Washington had a better reputation for executing his or her duties without fear or favor. Obama had picked him to run the FBI, even though he had been a high-ranking political appointee in President George W. Bush's Justice Department. She and her aides knew that she'd lose in the court of public opinion if she got in a fight with the highly regarded and widely respected FBI director.

So her campaign spokesman, Brian Fallon, a former Justice Department official, issued the most vanilla statement he could possibly serve up. "We are pleased that the career officials handling this case have determined that no further action by the department is appropriate," he said. "As the secretary has long said, it was a mistake to use her personal email and she would not do it again. We are glad that this matter is now resolved." It didn't address any of Comey's allegations of carelessness, evasion of open-records rules, and possible exposure of government secrets to America's enemies.

It can be hard to fully appreciate just how much Hillary could have been buffeted by the events of that early July day. Comey's statement in and of itself was a heavily stirred good news/bad news cocktail of reprieve and reproof that bolstered her legal case while laying bare the lies of her political spin. She didn't have much time to sort through all that before the most important stop of her campaign to date, a debut appearance with Obama that she saw as a crucial piece of her effort to begin the postprimary unification of a still-fractured Democratic Party.

Inside the Clinton campaign and at the White House, there were two basic reads on the awkward timing of Comey's making his statement just hours before the Charlotte campaign stop: (1) it ensured that Obama's first appearance for Clinton wouldn't monopolize newscasts and headlines, and (2) by juxtaposing the two news-driving events, the attention paid to the onetime rivals appearing together again on a campaign stage would dampen the impact of Comey's statement.

"For the day-of news coverage, would it have been more ideal had that not been yesterday?" one Obamaworld source asked rhetorically the next day. "Yeah, because it would have been about the president and Clinton campaigning together instead of it being four hundred malice pieces about what Comey said." But, this official said, "if you were to pick between either that, or in a week her being indicted, yeah we'd go with that."

Still, the inescapable doom that shadowed Hillary's campaign had reared its head again. On the day Obama would endorse her, and at the same time she was being let off the legal hook for her e-mail scandal, the FBI director affirmed she'd done something wrong—just nothing he could pin on her.

HILLARY'S SMALL PROCESSION of SUVs pulled up at Andrews at 12:35 p.m., forty-five minutes before Obama's scheduled arrival and the near-immediate departure of Air Force One. She and her aides boarded the bird and waited for Obama in the plane's senior staff cabin. Comey was still on her mind. "She's frustrated because it dropped like a hammer," said one of her senior staff members. She was "digesting" the news and "inscrutable," said another aide.

When the commander in chief bounded into the cabin and plopped down into one of the four facing leather captain's chairs,

Hillary was still quietly cursing Comey. But Obama helped turn her mood around. He was relaxed and excited about the chance to deliver a campaign-style ass kicking to Trump. His energy was infectious, helping Hillary shove Comey to the back burner. It wasn't the first time she'd had to compartmentalize bad news and push through it with a happy face.

"It wasn't a given that we were able to bifurcate these two things," said one Hillary aide. But "the president was so happy."

On the quick hop to North Carolina—less than an hour in the air—Hillary showed Obama pictures of her grandchildren, Charlotte and Aidan, and they discussed their shared chagrin about Trump's ability to foment anger in the electorate.

But there was meat to their discussion too. With White House communications director Jen Psaki and Huma Abedin floating in and out of the small cabin on Air Force One, Obama, Hillary, Sullivan, Podesta, and White House deputy national security adviser Ben Rhodes dissected the president's policy in the Middle East. Obama quizzed Hillary on her take on Syria, in particular. In a break with the president, she had recommended implementing a no-fly zone to try to protect innocents from the wrath of President Bashar al-Assad. One participant likened the rhythm and substance to the kind of conversation Obama would have had with a columnist who had a different point of view. He wanted to know whether she thought it would really make sense to threaten Syrian regime assets in order to force a negotiation, for example. The contrast in their positions was "almost as dramatic a departure as you will see in the national security space" among two people in the same party, the participant said. They also discussed how Hillary would continue to implement the Iran nuclear deal that her aides had first negotiated, and talked a bit about Asia—anything to avoid the Comey elephant in the room.

At one point, Obama took on the role of pep-talking coach, dispensing a little bit of wisdom to the woman he defeated on his way to the presidency.

"It's a four-month sprint to the end, and it will go quickly," he said, betraying a hint of nostalgia. "It's hard and it's tiring. But this is a different stage than the primary."

The e-mail scandal, and Comey's just-delivered indictment of Clinton's behavior, could have occupied half of Air Force One, but they were unwelcome visitors. Obama had been briefed on the Comey statement, seemingly just the latest turn in an unfolding story he'd kept up with from the Oval Office. And, of course, he'd been asked about the e-mail issue more times than he would have liked. Publicly, he toed the company line and said he knew Hillary wouldn't intentionally mishandle information—and he believed that. But inside the secluded confines of the West Wing, he confided his true feelings. He couldn't understand what possessed Hillary to set up the private e-mail server, and her handling of the scandal—obfuscate, deny, and evade—amounted to political malpractice. He wanted his friend to win, and yet she was exhibiting, again, some of the very qualities that had helped him defeat her in 2008. It was a classic unforced Clinton error, and he couldn't believe that she and the people around her had let it happen. When would they learn?

He said nothing of this to Hillary. When he scratched his head or rolled his eyes, he did it in the privacy of the West Wing.

When Obama and Clinton arrived at the rally, two seemingly conflicting dynamics took hold: Comey dominated news coverage and Clinton and Obama effectively communicated to Democrats and independents that she would be leading a unified party into battle in November. Comey distracted from the message Hillary and Obama tried to send, but he didn't prevent it from getting out.

Obama was thrilled to take on Trump, but he was also getting his first chance to really lay out his argument for why Hillary Clinton should succeed him. The night before, he had studied drafts of the speech to ensure he got the tone just right. Both Obama and Hillary knew that his power as an advocate for her lay in his knowledge of the job she sought and in his own personal approval ratings. Where she was seen as dishonest, he had much more credibility with the public—and nearly universal trust within the Democratic Party. His job was to talk about her credentials, temperament, and credibility—and she sorely needed a character witness on that latter trait. He could speak to Clinton's character in moments when the public couldn't see what she was doing.

With his legacy in mind, Obama told the crowd in Charlotte that he was ready to "pass the baton" to a fuchsia-suited Clinton, who sat behind him on a stool and nodded approvingly throughout a partially improvised speech that lasted more than forty minutes. It was the wording of his testament to her that he had played with at the White House the night before.

"I saw how she treated everybody with respect, even the folks who aren't quote/unquote 'important.' That's how you judge somebody. . . . How do they treat somebody when the cameras are off and they can't do anything for you?" he said. "Do you still treat them right? Do you still treat them with respect? Do you still listen to them? Are you still fighting for them?" For a candidate beset by the perception that she was operating dishonestly in the shadows, it was an important validation of her values. But the speech would be remembered for Obama's off-the-teleprompter riffs on Trump. He liked to needle the Donald almost as much as he liked firing up a big crowd. This moment gave him the opportunity to do both.

"Everybody can tweet, but nobody actually knows what it takes to do the job until you sit behind the desk," Obama chided as the crowd cheered. "I mean, Sasha tweets, but she doesn't think that she thereby should be sitting behind the desk."

Obama was feeling it. And because he was feeling it, so was Hillary. For a couple of hours, at least, James Comey faded into the background. On a rope line after their speeches, Obama and Hillary put their arms around each other's waists and whispered to each other as they greeted voters. Afterward, in a holding area, Obama walked up to Podesta and Sullivan, both of whom had worked at the White House in his administration.

"This is too easy," Obama said, flashing a toothy grin.

Podesta looked up at his former boss quizzically. *Are you fucking kidding me?*

"All right, all right, all right," Obama conceded. "There's just so much material."

Chapter 14

"HILLARY JUST CAN'T MAKE UP HER MIND"

ILLARY WAS DISSATISFIED WITH HER OPTIONS. SHE WANTED a vice presidential running mate who would electrify her campaign. It was late June or early July when one of her senior aides described her conundrum: "Hillary just can't make up her mind. She doesn't have a good list." And that's how Elizabeth Warren made an eleventh-hour climb up the ranks of Hillary's short list.

The Massachusetts senator—a liberal darling, Trump antagonist, and unrelenting populist who had won her Senate seat in a state full of working-class whites—had the potential to mainline progressive enthusiasm into Hillary's ticket. And she would reinforce the history-making aspect of Hillary's narrative if America elected not one but two women to executive office in the same year. Warren had precisely the sizzle Hillary was looking for to juice up the campaign, but Clinton wanted a governing partner, someone who saw the world in a similar way and could help her run the executive branch. She just didn't know if she could trust Warren to be pragmatic and constructive. The decision would pit Hillary's natural caution, focus on policy making, and thirst for loyalty against her desire to give her ticket fresh appeal.

That Hillary would even consider Warren, who had pilloried her for flip-flopping to vote in favor of a bankruptcy reform bill, stunned some denizens of Clintonworld. For most of the campaign, Hillary's aides had frantically exchanged concerns that Warren would endorse Sanders, an ideological brother. Huma Abedin, in particular, was obsessed with the idea that Warren was always on the verge of backing Bernie, an anxiety that may have reflected Hillary's own worry. But throughout, Warren maintained studied neutrality, even as she pushed Hillary to the left publicly and privately via mutual friends Gary Gensler, a former Commodity Futures Trading Commission chairman and the campaign's chief financial officer, and Mandy Grunwald. As the primary drew closer to its end, the fiery, populist former Harvard professor tangled with Trump in speeches and on Twitter. Warren respected Hillary and appreciated her ability to work with colleagues to get things done. Hillary began, for the first time, to see Warren as a pragmatist with a steely backbone. She liked what she saw. Both women recognized that their commonalities far outweighed their differences.

Hillary also knew that Warren had been back-channeling with her policy aides since the beginning of the campaign. The open line, usually Gensler's cell phone, enabled Warren to make her views known before planks of the platform were rolled out, and allowed the campaign to avoid surprising a potential ally. Liberals had initially begged Warren to jump into the primary, labeling themselves members of the "Elizabeth Warren wing" of the Democratic Party. She had declined, but retained a hold on the party's economic progressives, a set that was disappointed in Hillary even when she moved toward them. There was no question that Hillary would please the Democratic base if she picked Warren.

Hillary invited Warren to a meeting at the Clinton family home on Whitehaven Street in the nation's capital on the morning of June 10. Warren issued an endorsement of Hillary the night before their sit-down, clearing the way for a more serious discussion. Their chat "catapulted Warren into real consideration," said one high-ranking Clinton campaign official. "They connected at a policy level," said a second official familiar with the conversation. "They like to get into the details." Hillary decided from that meeting, and an earlier joint rally, that Warren was someone who should advance into the final round of consideration. "It gave Hillary comfort that was a choice that should really be seen from all sides, and that she can move forward," the second official said.

Inside the campaign, some of the younger aides were pulling for Warren, and Brooklyn fielded plenty of testimonials from progressive groups and Bernie supporters. If it wasn't going to be Bernie—and it wasn't—selecting Warren would show that Hillary had learned from the primary that she needed to address the populist clamor within the party.

Some of the veteran hands in Brooklyn worried that two women would be too much for voters. That wasn't the deciding factor for Hillary, though. Ultimately, Hillary hadn't been through enough political transactions with Warren to feel comfortable that they would be a good match. After all, Obama had become deeply frustrated with Warren, a onetime ally, for what he saw as demagoguing against him on economic issues and for wreaking havoc when he nominated a banker, Antonio Weiss, as an undersecretary at the Treasury Department. "It's safe to say she's not a favorite person in this building," one White House official observed.

Throughout the selection process, Hillary picked the brains of a close circle of aides as well as other Democratic officials. She'd ask what they thought but played her hand very close to the vest. Bill Clinton, who was once reported to favor Secretary of Agriculture Tom Vilsack, told Podesta at one point that it was Hillary's choice to make. Podesta, the founder of the liberal think tank Center for American Progress, favored a Kennedy/Johnson–style pick of a progressive to balance the ticket—though not necessarily Warren. And he too was careful not to push his preferences on Hillary.

Another potential candidate who had surfaced during the selection process—largely under the radar—was Joe Biden. The vice president's name was tossed around by members of Congress and some top Hillary aides. Sullivan, who served as Biden's national security adviser before ultimately returning to work on Clinton's campaign, was particularly intrigued by the idea.

"No constitutional bar to it, so why would you take it off the table?" one Hillary adviser reasoned.

Missouri senator Claire McCaskill provided a light push for Biden from Capitol Hill, but the suggestion was never taken very seriously by the campaign. Hillary didn't want or need the vice president, who had flirted with running long enough—and said enough unflattering things about her—to injure her when Bernie Sanders's campaign was gaining steam in the latter part of 2015. Barack Obama might be able to count Biden as an unfailing loyalist, but Hillary never would. And nothing would have screamed status quo louder than keeping Obama's vice president in his job.

Throughout the process, Podesta demanded secrecy. A small group of senior aides met frequently in the Brooklyn headquarters to discuss Hillary's options. Everyone in the office knew what they were talking about, but little leaked. Podesta even sent an e-mail to those involved in the process warning them not to talk to the media about the deliberations. Some of the candidates made joint appearances with Hillary on the campaign trail so she could assess their skills in person, and others—like Secretary of Labor Tom Perez—had auditions with Bill, who gave his opinions freely to his wife. Perez didn't make the cut.

By mid-July, it was basically down to Virginia senator Tim Kaine, New Jersey senator Cory Booker, Vilsack, and Warren. Vilsack was milquetoast. Booker, the only minority to make the final cut, was seen as a future star, but he didn't have much history with Hillary and the campaign's consensus was that she didn't need an African American running mate. And she didn't know much about Kaine, other than the fact that he'd endorsed Obama out of the box in 2007. Sherrod Brown, an Ohio senator who could rally party populists and with whom Hillary always had a strong personal bond, had a cheering section within the campaign and among some of Hillary's outside advisers. But he also carried a unique disadvantage: if he was picked and Hillary won, the state's Republican governor, John Kasich, would get to choose his replacement in the Senate. While Massachusetts also had a Republican governor, state law called for a quick special election and Democrats weren't terribly worried about holding Warren's seat. But they were concerned that a Republican could win and keep the seat for a long time in Ohio if Brown were no longer there to defend it.

Obama had told Hillary that he liked Kaine, and the Virginia senator's selection would allow a pal, Governor Terry McAuliffe, to appoint a replacement to the Senate. Kaine was also the only one with a résumé that boasted both domestic and foreign policy experience—he was a former governor of Virginia and a member of the Senate Armed Services and Foreign Relations Committees. But Hillary hardly knew Kaine, a real consideration for her, and the public perception of him—to the extent there was one—was that he was as dull as a month-old razor.

Still, Kaine, the man political handicappers had identified early as the likeliest pick, had emerged as the leading contender by Thursday, July 21. He filled the most boxes on her checklist of considerations. "The fix wasn't in for Tim Kaine," said one of the advisers who participated in the vetting process, but he was always the frontrunner. Kaine didn't give her a state she couldn't win on her own, add populist progressive flavor to the ticket, or excite anyone—including the candidate herself. Instead, she'd worked through a process of elimination, even as she'd complained that her options were suboptimal. The bench was thin, in part because Hillary herself, one half of the Clinton political empire, had been a candidate or potential candidate since the 2004 election cycle.

"Kaine was someone she didn't know well but felt a very strong rapport with once the four of them [the Clintons and the Kaines] really started to get together. Liked his values. Similar stories. Reinforced each other's stories," said one of the people familiar with her decision making. "She felt, on balance, that Tim would be a very solid person on the campaign trail, would be a really good partner."

But even after settling on Kaine, Hillary wasn't quite ready to pull the trigger until the afternoon of Friday, July 22—the day before a planned rollout event with the VP pick in South Florida and three days before the start of the Democratic convention. She'd waited until the last possible minute to tap her running mate.

While campaigning in Florida that afternoon, she called Podesta at the Brooklyn headquarters. "I feel confident about this decision," she told him. "Let's put it in motion." Podesta had to move fast. Once he got off the phone, he executed a black ops mission to grab the Virginia senator surreptitiously, sequester him from the view of the media, and get him ready for the next day's rollout. His chief of staff, Sara Latham, gave the high sign to speechwriter Megan Rooney and former Iowa state director Matt Paul, who had been tapped to work for the vice presidential nominee. Rooney and her colleagues had prepared speech drafts with personal details for Kaine, Vilsack, Booker, and Warren. They also had biographical sketches on hand for several other candidates in case Hillary had chosen a wild card. Before leaving, Rooney wrote out a list of speeches for her team to have ready, with "TK" in the number one position; then Podesta, Latham, Rooney, and Paul headed to a back elevator to ride down to the garage. When they got there, a black Suburban was waiting with the doors open. It took them to the airport in Teterboro, New Jersey, where they boarded a private jet for a flight to Quonset State Airport in North Kingstown, Rhode Island.

Once they landed, a flight attendant was dispatched to acquire a bottle of champagne, as Podesta and Latham sped off in an SUV to meet Kaine, who still didn't know he'd been picked. The Virginia senator was in Rhode Island to headline a fund-raiser for Senator Jack Reed, a fellow member of the Armed Services Committee, at the Newport Shipyard, and Podesta and Latham pulled up outside the event. From there, Podesta dialed several of the also-rans to inform them they wouldn't be on the ticket. Hillary was doing the same thing from Miami. When the call lists were exhausted, she dialed Kaine.

Inside the event, Kaine's phone rang. He answered and heard Hillary on the line. Seeking privacy for the call, Kaine ducked into an empty office. With dockworkers trying to gain access to the space, Kaine spent fifteen to twenty minutes on the phone with Hillary, who secured his commitment to run and advised him of one more important logistical detail.

"I don't mean to alarm you," she said, "but John Podesta is outside your building right now." The campaign chairman, still undetected by the media, would drive Kaine away from the fund-raiser. Podesta then called Kaine, who said he wanted to go back to his nearby hotel and tell his wife, Anne Holton. "Give me five minutes," Kaine said. Getting into a Volvo, which would attract less attention than the SUV, Podesta drove Kaine to the hotel. The new VP candidate went upstairs to talk with his wife and then Podesta, Latham, and Kaine aides Mike Henry and Amy Dudley joined them. Podesta sat on the bed and went over the plans for the next twenty-four hours. While they were there, Obama congratulated Kaine by phone. Having been the runner-up to Biden in Obama's VP-selection process in 2008, Kaine had never allowed himself to get overexcited at the prospect of joining Hillary's ticket. Now, though, he was suddenly full of energy. "He was juiced," said one of the people in the room.

The small party headed back to the airport for the flight to Miami. When they pulled up, Rooney and Paul were waiting by the staircase to a second jet. The whole process of calling the also-rans and gathering Kaine had taken so long that Hillary's longtime scheduler, Lona Valmoro, had to arrange for a new plane because the flight crew for the first one had worked too many hours to make the trip. As lightning lit up the night sky, the Kaines, Podesta, and the small cluster of aides boarded the plane. His and hers Hillary Clinton for President swag bags—one with a blue strap and the other with a red strap—sat waiting in the Kaines' seats. With the champagne ready to flow, Holton interrupted. "I know someone who would prefer bourbon," she said of her husband. So, they toasted with a small bottle of Maker's Mark.

THE OFFICIAL ANNOUNCEMENT of her vice presidential running mate was one of the days on the calendar that Hillary should have been able to count on as a Yale lock for excitement, enthusiasm, energy—and relentlessly positive press coverage. Instead, as she made her way toward Florida International University in Miami for what should have been a squeaky-clean event, more controversy was brewing. Hillary was in danger of getting drowned out by her own party's blemished national chairwoman, Debbie Wasserman Schultz.

The South Florida congresswoman, a Queens export who lived in the gated-community haven of western Broward County, was impossible to miss sitting in a spacious backstage holding room at FIU. Aside from the signature heap of dyed, dirty-blond curls that called attention to her even on the very rare occasions when she wanted to fade into the walls, Wasserman Schultz was throwing a full-on fit.

This was supposed to be a big moment for "DWS" too. It had been circled on her calendar as the day that Hillary would sweep into her home district and say kind words about her—which wouldn't have mattered so much in a year in which Bernie Sanders hadn't encouraged his supporters to fund her primary opponent's campaign. But Wasserman Schultz was now at the center of the internecine Democratic war over the presidential primary.

The day before this Saturday rollout, WikiLeaks had released a trove of damaging internal DNC e-mails that suggested anti-Bernie bias on the part of Wasserman Schultz and her aides. A cyber-attacker going by the alias Guccifer 2.0, a name that would crop up again later in the campaign, claimed credit for swiping the e-mails and giving them to WikiLeaks. They had been published just before the Kaine event and a few days before the start of the party's convention. It didn't take a political pro to know that the leak was designed to sow dissent within the party just as Hillary was trying to bring Democrats together. As a bonus for the GOP, many voters wouldn't make a distinction between headlines about the DNC e-mails and those about Hillary's private e-mail server—even though they were totally unrelated.

On one level, it shouldn't have been surprising if the official political arm of the Democratic Party was more supportive of Hillary against an outsider who was reluctant to even run as a member of the party. On another, though, it was proof-positive to Sanders's supporters—and to Clinton's critics inside and outside the

Democratic Party—that Hillary was an establishment creature who rigged political outcomes. Operating in the shadows, Washington insiders like Wasserman Schultz were working to frustrate the will of the people and they had been caught red-handed. At least that's how the Bernie crowd saw things. Wasserman Schultz had become the face of Sanders's argument that the entire party had manipulated the outcome for Hillary. In fact, there was no more controversial figure in the party at that exact moment than the DNC chair, who had just become exponentially more toxic. Hillary needed to focus on reaching out to the Democratic base, not repelling it.

This was always supposed to be the day that she introduced her running mate to the public. Now, during one of her campaign's most important hours, she had to answer the looming question for all the Bernie skeptics about how she would treat the local congresswoman amid the rapidly unfolding DNC e-mail scandal. The answer in Brooklyn was simple: they wanted to keep Wasserman Schultz as far away from Hillary as possible.

As much as Sanders saw Wasserman Schultz as a semisecret agent for Hillary, the Clinton campaign didn't like the DNC chairwoman much either. "Hillary genuinely likes Debbie. I think she's the only one in the orbit who does," one Democratic source said early on. "The campaign does not like Debbie."

Part of that disdain stemmed from Wasserman Schultz's tendency to make decisions without the input of the campaign, like when she hired the party convention CEO—Leah Daughtry—without consulting Mook or the candidate. Mook characterized himself as "distressed" and "dumbfounded" over this lack of coordination and told Podesta that they "may need to sit down with Debbie to make clear how we want things to change/improve before we are willing to consider playing ball with them." He told Hillary he would keep his mouth shut until she had a chance to talk to Wasserman Schultz but noted that "this concerns me a lot."

Hillary's hair was considerably less aflame. "I just talked to her and she told me she had hired Leah after an 'exhaustive' interviewing process," Hillary reported back to Mook and Podesta. But

Hillary's top two aides would keep Wasserman Schultz in their crosshairs. Later in 2015, Mook presented Hillary with options for taking operational control of the DNC, at least one of which included replacing Wasserman Schultz. Hillary didn't bite then or later when Podesta made similar entreaties to find a new chair.

"She felt loyal to her," one top aide said of Hillary's reasoning for sticking by Wasserman Schultz when so many of her senior advisers felt differently. That loyalty had been tested mightily throughout the primaries. Wasserman Schultz had first become a flash point and political cudgel for Sanders in the summer of 2015 when the DNC scheduled fewer debates than he wanted. Sanders and his supporters earnestly felt that they weren't getting a fair shake from Wasserman Schultz, but all things considered, she was a convenient foil for a candidate running against the Washington establishment.

Hillary's aides had been agitating for some time to make a substitution at the DNC because they didn't have faith in Wasserman Schultz to do her job well. When the subject came up during a debate-prep session, Hillary told Podesta it was a nonstarter to go after an ally who had supported her in 2008 and was taking incoming fire. "I'm not going to be the one who chops off her head," Hillary said then.

Ironically, on a personal level, Wasserman Schultz was in much closer contact with Bernie than with Hillary, having directly dealt with Sanders and his wife, Jane, on debates, party rules, and platform issues, as well as the Sanders campaign's breach of DNC data—over which Bernie filed and then withdrew a lawsuit against the party. The idea of a biased DNC was part and parcel of Bernie's political argument against Hillary, making it difficult to distinguish the real injuries to him from the perceived variety.

Even so, by the time the DNC e-mails came out, Brooklyn had plenty of preexisting reason to put distance between the DNC chair and Hillary. The hacked e-mails might even present the opportunity Mook had been looking for to get rid of her once and for all. But the main concern at the moment was preventing DWS from poisoning Kaine's rollout.

Brooklyn didn't want the candidate to appear on stage with Wasserman Schultz. The problem was that Wasserman Schultz previously had been given a vague promise that she would have a prominent role in Hillary's next visit to South Florida. As it turned out, this visit was that next time. But for Brooklyn, DWS was a net negative on this day. Wasserman Schultz was told that she wouldn't be able to appear on stage with Hillary. That really pissed her off. She scrambled to reverse the decision, bending the ears of Hillary's Florida state director, Simone Ward, her political director, and anyone else who would listen. She needed a vote of confidence, and she was determined, according to one source, to take her case directly to Hillary.

Hillary's aides thought Wasserman Schultz was on another planet, somehow detached from the reality that her days as DNC chairwoman were numbered. She couldn't see that even the decision to give her a few minutes to speak long before Hillary and Kaine arrived carried risk for the campaign. Her mere presence—much less photos of Hillary and DWS together—threatened to completely overshadow the main event. Already, the DNC leaks were depriving the Kaine announcement of some of its oxygen.

By the time Hillary's political director, Amanda Renteria, arrived on the scene, Wasserman Schultz was fuming. Renteria conferred with Ward to get a feel for what they were dealing with and then sat down with Wasserman Schultz in the main holding room, which was adorned with big-screen TVs and would soon house Clinton, Kaine, and their families.

Having worked as a Senate chief of staff, Renteria was well versed in how to carefully manage a political principal.

"How are you feeling?" she asked quietly.

To her credit, and to her political disadvantage, Wasserman Schultz wears her heart on her sleeve. "Not well," she huffed.

"We're obviously figuring it out," Renteria tried to reassure her.

"I know," Wasserman Schultz shot back. Hillary's aides concluded that it had not yet hit Wasserman Schultz just how bad the DNC leaks story was and how much worse it was going to get.

"Her whole style and way was going to be on display very, very soon," said one of Hillary's lieutenants. "We felt that we very much knew what was coming, that this wasn't getting better. She was definitely stuck in her world. Here's this key moment and she was really self-absorbed."

Wasserman Schultz caused such a stir that campaign aides didn't even want her backstage when Hillary arrived. They worried that Wasserman Schultz would get in Hillary's face and finagle a spot on the stage, so they banished the party chairwoman to the audience for the big speeches. If Wasserman Schultz didn't understand then that she was finished as a face of the Clinton campaign—and she didn't—she certainly should have.

For years, a loose confederation of White House aides and senior lawmakers, including New York senator Chuck Schumer and Missouri senator Claire McCaskill, had been trying to push Wasserman Schultz out of the DNC post. Some Democrats believed she'd been an ineffective manager at the committee and that she put her personal priorities ahead of the party's when they came into conflict.

But DWS had a tight relationship with Vice President Joe Biden, Senate majority leader Harry Reid liked her spunk, and Obama didn't want to go through the pain of replacing her. He believed the party's nominee should determine the fate of the sitting DNC chair—a position that conveniently absolved him of responsibility for making a decision. The problem was that Hillary didn't want to make that call either.

Now, though, the bill of particulars against Wasserman Schultz had just grown longer and more damning. And, in throwing what Clinton aides described as a tantrum over the campaign's effort to sideline her for the VP announcement, she was doing nothing to instill confidence in the small set of people who stood between her and an unceremonious sacking.

By moving her out to the crowd, Hillary's team cleared the way for the candidate and her running mate to enter a party rather than a political funeral. The backstage area was set up with separate holding rooms for Hillary and for Kaine, but everyone just hung out in Hillary's space as they waited to take the stage together for the first time as the Democratic ticket. John Podesta quietly brought Hillary up to speed on the Wasserman Schultz situation, but, for the most part, the mood was jubilant.

Greg Hale, Hillary's staging guru, walked the candidates through the blocking of going on stage and where they were to stand. They were awkwardly excited, like teens on a first date, and they were eager to pull out of the driveway.

"Are you ready?" Hillary asked the preternaturally smiling Kaine. He was. And with that, they walked out on stage together for the first time as running mates.

Kaine, who worked in Honduras as a young man, charmed Spanish speakers at a school where 61 percent of the student body is Hispanic by mixing fluent Spanish into his speech. His decision to do so created a not-so-subtle contrast with the anti-immigrant rhetoric of Donald Trump. If Hillary could pull off a win in Florida, where a quarter of the population is Hispanic, she would be all but certain to capture the presidency. She would need both a big margin of victory and heavy turnout among Florida Hispanic voters—a group distinguishable from Latinos in other parts of the country because of its large Cuban and Puerto Rican populations—to offset an influx of white voters who were listening to Trump's pitch.

Though the VP rollout would generally garner good headlines, the choice of Kaine infuriated Bernie supporters who had hoped Sanders's campaign would force Hillary into picking a more liberal running mate. Kaine, an early endorser of then senator Barack Obama in 2007 and later a chairman of the DNC and governor and senator from Virginia, reflected Hillary's comfort with the business community and free trade. He had campaigned in Virginia as an opponent of abortion but had since made clear that he would support abortion rights in office. The movement of Hillary toward Kaine, and the inability of Bernie's supporters to get everything they wanted in the party's platform, did nothing to take the focus off Wasserman Schultz, who suddenly became the most visible and vulnerable target for their outrage.

In her remarks that day, Hillary thanked Wasserman Schultz—a throwaway line that surprised and disappointed many Democrats, including some on the campaign. It was a flash of loyalty that came at the risk of refocusing attention away from the event and toward the implosion of the DNC and its chairwoman.

As the rally was coming to a close, Podesta asked to see Wasserman Schultz in a private room, and Hillary's aides retrieved her from the crowd. Wasserman Schultz was fit to be tied. Her time-out in the audience had done nothing to temper her anger, and Podesta wasn't having it. He soon emerged from the room and waited at the door for her—perhaps making sure that she left the scene without trying to get to Hillary. After a few seconds, Wasserman Schultz came out, composed and solemn-faced, and walked away.

Podesta turned to one of his colleagues and summed up his conversation with the ambitious congresswoman this way: "If she's ever Speaker of the House, I'm done with politics."

Chapter 15

BUT IT LOOKED GREAT

A S THE DELEGATES AND OFFICIALS OF THE DEMOCRATIC Party from all over the country descended on Philadelphia the weekend before their national convention, Hillary faced a daunting task in unifying the disparate factions into one force that could defeat Donald Trump and the Republicans. She still had problems with millennials, progressives, and working-class whites. And she knew that the African American base that had carried her through the primaries was unlikely to show up on Election Day in the numbers that had boosted Barack Obama twice. Trump, on the other hand, was profiting from a postconvention bounce that had brought him within the margin of error in national polling. His party was coming together, just as the wounds of her primary were being reopened by the devastating DNC e-mail hacks. Before Democrats could turn their attention to unifying in the convention hall, they would have to take down a lightning rod for much of the negative energy.

HOLED UP IN a suite at the Marriott in downtown Philadelphia on Sunday, July 24, the eve of the Democratic convention, Debbie Wasserman Schultz started to negotiate the terms of her surrender. The DNC chairwoman had long since become a walking symbol of the deep divisions between the Clinton and Sanders wings of her party.

But now, with the release of stolen e-mails showing anti-Bernie sentiment at her DNC, she was becoming a serious threat to destroy Bernie's and Hillary's joint efforts to project and cultivate party unity heading into the November election.

That's the essential function of a party convention—to show that the wounds of the primary season have healed and that the leaders of major factions fully support the nominee, whether those things are true or not. Of all the obstacles to Bernie's most ardent backers coming around—the selection of centrist Tim Kaine, rather than Bernie or Elizabeth Warren, for the VP slot among them— the most visible and aggravating was the prospect of Wasserman Schultz presiding over Hillary's nomination. Earlier that morning, Sanders had publicly called for her to resign. A Clinton campaign that didn't want her in the job in the first place was besieged with calls from panicked Democrats who worried that the whole convention could go down in flames if Wasserman Schultz wasn't removed from her post immediately.

But DWS held an important card. If she didn't resign, it would take a vote of the DNC to oust her. That would create a destructive and indelible scene of division at the convention. It's not clear that she ever raised that issue, but the Clinton campaign was painfully aware of the party rules and the need to get Wasserman Schultz to walk away without a fight.

The comfortable hotel suite had room for a small coffee table between chairs and a couch, but Wasserman Schultz sat at the dining room table as Charlie Baker, the chief administrative officer of the Clinton campaign, gently laid out the bleak scenario facing her. If Wasserman Schultz stayed in her job, Bernie's supporters would stage protests and try to shout her down from the convention floor. They were angry that Hillary had won, and now they believed they had evidence that DWS and her staff had rigged the primaries. Hillary's crowning moment was in danger of becoming a fiasco. Baker didn't have to say that it would be selfish—that Wasserman Schultz would be putting her own interests above Hillary's, those of the party, and those of the country—if she didn't just step aside.

Try as she did to hold back her anger and frustration, DWS made them evident as she issued demands in return. She wanted an endorsement from Hillary and one from Obama, along with a guarantee that the party would be there for her on primary day in her home district. Furthermore, she didn't want to leave town, as some Democrats urged, and, if she did, she wanted the party to pay for her to fly. It wasn't an unreasonable request: she had a number of family members in town for what she had expected would be a big moment for her, and it would be expensive for her to foot the bill to bring them all back to Florida early.

Unfailingly transactional, Wasserman Schultz was worried that if she didn't have a deal in place, Obama and Clinton might withhold their support for her reelection—or say something so tepid as to be counterproductive. One DNC source who was not in the room said that DWS spent much of the day trying to negotiate the language Obama and Clinton would use in praising her if she resigned. By early afternoon, though, it was becoming clear to Wasserman Schultz that she had no way out.

Obama spoke to her by phone, according to a White House official. He thanked her for serving as DNC chair but declined to urge her to go—or to stay. That was telling enough. Obama had never been a big fan of the DNC, and he had let the organization atrophy under DWS with all the concern of someone who didn't like the muck of party politics.

There was no real choice for Wasserman Schultz, but she was the last to realize it. "Her best friends were telling her she had to leave," said one source involved in the discussions. "It was the only way."

Finally, assured that Obama and Hillary would support her reelection, she acceded to the pressure.

Baker, still operating out of Wasserman Schultz's hotel room, called Donna Brazile, the party vice chairwoman who had long before been designated to take over in the event of a vacancy. Brazile wasn't thrilled. To take the job, she'd have to detach from her lucrative business as a consultant. But she told Baker she knew that she couldn't turn it down. Brazile would present another set of challenges for Mook because she was, as one ally put it, the "polar opposite" as a political operative—someone who trusted her gut and intuition. But, as a longtime operative in the matrix of party politics and a high-profile advocate for Democratic candidates and values on television, she was a choice that would be acceptable to all sides.

THE DWS AFFAIR was just one high-wire act in a full-on backstage circus that Hillary's campaign tried mightily, and with mixed success, to hide from public view throughout the course of the convention. The truth was ugly: The die-hard Bernie backers, including a good number of delegates to the convention, still hated Hillary, and she was struggling to win over the factions they represented—progressive whites, millennials, and a small but committed set of people of color. She needed voters across the country to view her as the unchallenged choice of the delegates of the Democratic Party, and that would take a lot of doing. In her arsenal, she had shiny objects to distract from the mess—Barack Obama, Bill Clinton, and Katy Perry among them—as well as a ground force of allies culled from an unlikely source: the Sanders campaign.

Behind the scenes, the Hillary and Bernie camps had been working together from early June through late July to try to ensure a smooth convention. It was a rocky process that included fights over the party's rules and its platform, but Hillary, who needed Bernie's voters, and Bernie, who didn't want to get blamed for electing Donald Trump, found common ground.

The two campaign managers, Robby Mook and Jeff Weaver, opened a running dialogue before the California primary in early June. Because Bernie's supporters were such dead-enders—and because the candidate himself wasn't really ready to give in until the last votes had been counted—it had taken a long time for Hillary and her team to figure out exactly what concessions Bernie was looking for and which ones could be accommodated. "They outperformed, and they had huge expectations from their core political base that they couldn't walk away from," said one Democrat involved in the reconciliation process.

Publicly, the Clinton camp tried to stay patient, sensitive to the backlash that could come from pushing Bernie too hard. But Hillary and her friends were also frustrated that Sanders wasn't able to snap his followers into line. In Brooklyn, Clinton aides joked about Bernie being the last Japanese World War II soldier tromping through the Philippines in the belief that the war was still being fought decades after it had ended.

The period of détente had begun humbly, in a suite at the Capital Hilton in Washington, down the street from the White House. Bernie arrived for the June 14 meeting with his hallmark yellow legal pad. "Congratulations, you've won the primary," he said as he sat down with Hillary in the living room. "I want to talk to you about some areas that I care about."

Hillary said a few laudatory words about the campaign Sanders had run. And, with that, they dived into the weeds of policy. Bernie believed that he couldn't just turn on a dime and endorse Hillary the way most politicians would. He felt that he owed it to his supporters to use the power of their votes to squeeze concessions from her. If he could make the case to them that she was incorporating their views into her agenda, they would be more likely to see his conversion as earnest and follow him into her fold.

As he'd told Devine a week earlier, he saw this period before his formal endorsement as a moment of maximum leverage. Hillary listened carefully and followed her defeated rival into a thicket of complex issues. They talked about resolving doctor shortages at community health centers and college affordability—he wanted free tuition, while she favored a debt-free graduation plan. "These are the things I care a lot about, and I'd like to be able to jointly produce policy and talk about these to my supporters," he said.

Hillary was polite and sympathetic, but noncommittal. She needed Bernie, but many more people had voted for her and her agenda. "It wasn't a lovefest," said one person familiar with the discussion. "It was like two senators."

Bernie had presented his wish list, and Hillary hadn't rejected it out of hand. But the real test of the ability of the two sides to make peace would come in the drafting of a party platform and the rules of the convention. Bernie was determined to affect the platform, and he believed that his showing in the primaries had earned him that right. Hillary had a different view: she won. But she also knew she needed to make enough accommodations to placate him. Moreover, even as Bernie and his top aides softened, his supporters didn't always follow suit. "They were trying to get their people in line," one Hillary source said.

HER PLATFORM TEAM, led by Sullivan, had put a lot of time and energy into her policy positions. It was the part of the campaign that mattered most to Hillary, and there was a deep reluctance to retreat from her goals. Hillary instructed her aides to "maintain the principles that we successfully won the nomination on and not give ground," as one adviser put it. So they took the stance that they would compromise on the means of achieving policy ends but not on the overall aims. Ultimately, though, the Clinton team negotiated on the minimum wage, fracking, and marijuana legalization, adopting more Bernie-esque approaches to each of those questions, and, in the process, drafted what was widely described as the most progressive platform in modern Democratic Party history. But she would only bend so far. When Bernie's delegates tried to put a full moratorium on fracking, Hillary's beat them back.

"We don't bluff," one of her aides said. "If we're telling you this is our bottom line, this is our fucking bottom line."

Bernie's top advisers began to understand they could win concessions on the details, but many of his supporters were furious with each loss in the development of the platform. Meanwhile, Clinton's aides started to view the Sanders contingent as split between a set that would follow him in trying to bring the party together and a set that was more interested in disrupting the political order than it was loyal to Bernie. It was this second set that the leadership of both campaigns worried about on the eve of the convention.

"There was an overall strategic imperative to see if we could avoid a platform fight at the convention and a rules fight at the convention," said one Clinton campaign source who was involved in the discussions. The secondary and tertiary goals were to avoid a minority report full of pro-Bernie items and to prevent Sanders's forces from handing Republicans platform planks with which to whack Hillary in the general election. In the end, the platform threw enough vague concessions to Bernie that he could support it without locking Hillary into detailed promises on policy.

"We pulled it off," this source said. "We didn't know that we would. But we did."

Between the platform debate and the DWS denouement, the Clinton and Sanders camps had averted two major potential catastrophes before the convention even opened. But there was good reason for them to fear a full-scale revolt from Bernie's delegates. The platform talks had demonstrated goodwill on the part of Bernie and his top aides, but they'd also shown just how recalcitrant many of his supporters remained. Both sides knew that Bernie didn't really control them, and that meant they could sow chaos inside the hall and on television screens across the country.

Heading into Monday, July 25, the first day of the convention, Mook was nervous. "Absolutely shitting my pants" is how he described it to others.

WHILE HER PARTY's national convention was on the brink of disaster, Hillary was in Charlotte, North Carolina, addressing the Veterans of Foreign Wars convention. And things weren't going much better there. If there was ever an audience that needed persuasion to support Hillary, this was it. As she went through a version of her stump speech tailored for the veterans, Hillary looked out at a sea of blank stares. Of course, the VFW members applauded politely when she paid homage to the sacrifices of men and women in uniform, but she could tell they didn't care much for her or what she was saying.

There was an invisible barrier between Hillary and her audience, and she thought it ran along the gender line. Having spent time with flag officers, soldiers, and veterans as a member of the Senate Armed Services Committee and as secretary of state, she knew that some of them had a hard time accepting the idea of a female commander in chief. *That's the elephant in the room,* she thought, and she decided to expose it.

"I know this is the first time that one of our two major parties has ever nominated a woman," she said, deviating from her prepared remarks and earning a round of applause. "I know that it takes a little getting used to, even for me. But here's what I want you to know: I will get up every single day in the White House, doing everything I possibly can to protect our country, to treat our men and women in uniform with the care and concern and respect they deserve, to make good on our nation's promises to our veterans. That's the way I was raised."

On the flight out afterward, Hillary offered a rare review of an audience to speechwriter Megan Rooney. "They weren't feeling it," she said. "Tough crowd."

Rooney, wanting to know if the improvisation was a sign that Hillary would talk more about her gender on the campaign trail, prompted Hillary to explain the decision to go off script.

"I noticed that thing you added about women," the speechwriter said.

"I've been thinking about this," Hillary replied. "People are interested in it, and this seemed like the right place to do it."

Hillary knew she hadn't won over a lot of the veterans. No matter what she tried, it was hard to convince people who didn't want to envision her as president that they should vote for her anyway. This was as true for a group of mostly conservative veterans as it was for many other Americans, including a lot of less-educated whites who had long ago made up their minds about her. For some, her education, privilege, and perceived sense of entitlement were more off-putting than her agenda, her secrecy, or even the way her voice hit their ears. She wasn't like them. And that made it harder, if not impossible, to get them to listen with an open mind. While her campaign aides had long recognized that many voters simply didn't like Hillary or what they thought she stood for, she had just been subjected to that painful truth herself.

IN PHILADELPHIA, Hillary's team would have to put on such a dazzling show in front of the curtain for four days that no one could see the crises unfolding behind it. She faced two major conflicts as the convention opened: papering over her differences with Bernie and delivering an acceptance speech that would convince voters she had a better vision for America than Donald Trump. On the surface, the former would be a tougher challenge, but the absence of a motivation for her candidacy remained the biggest obstacle on Hillary's path to the presidency. Without that, her speech would be what she'd once derisively referred to as "just words."

Two things happened early Monday that illustrated the major tension points. First, Bernie's supporters booed Wasserman Schultz, House minority leader Nancy Pelosi, and every mention of Hillary Clinton's name at events outside the perimeter of the Wells Fargo Center convention hall. As he watched the Bernie contingent wreak havoc, with formal protests outside the arena and sporadic bursts inside it, Mook's nervousness turned to agitation. Then, when Bernie delivered a speech to his delegates in a ballroom at the nearby Philadelphia Convention Center, they booed lustily when he spoke of his rival. Mook lost his temper. He picked up his phone and dialed Weaver.

"What the fuck are you doing?" Mook demanded. But Weaver wasn't doing anything. The two campaign managers' worst fears were being realized. There was a segment of Bernie's constituency that was so angry they couldn't even stand silently by when he talked about his support for Hillary—and the television news cameras had a knack for giving every last dead-ender his or her moment of fame. The convention, they knew, could turn sideways fast. Fortunately for Hillary, for Bernie, and for the Democratic Party, Mook and Weaver had a contingency plan.

About a week before the convention, they had put together a joint command operation behind the arena's main stage. The boiler room, a big open space filled with long tables, folding chairs, and telephones, functioned as a nerve center from which the two camps could exert control over their delegates during the four-day program. On one side sat an office for Clinton's senior staff and on the other a matching space for Bernie's top advisers. The phones, staffed by a mix of Hillary and Bernie aides, connected directly to phones on the convention floor designated for each state's delegation. The big unions, which had been divided in the primaries but would support the Democratic nominee, had their own whip operation humming nearby.

The boiler room proved a physical nexus for the Bernie and Hillary brain trusts, but an electronic connection kept them in sync throughout the convention hall. The two teams created a text-messaging distribution list that allowed for constant communication about potential problems during the four-day convention. When a Bernie supporter raised an anti-Clinton sign, a whip team member in the convention hall could relay the message quickly to the boiler room. The team there would send a note to Bernie and Hillary aides on the floor, who would ask the person to take it down. The flash-speed communications network would turn out to be a major factor in transforming what was a tumultuous convention inside the hall into a unified one on television. That is, it looked a lot different to folks watching at home than it did to participants inside an arena with plenty of anti-Clinton Bernie delegates.

The system got off to a rocky start. When Ohio representative Marcia Fudge gaveled the convention to order on Monday afternoon, Bernie's delegates booed her. They chanted "Ber-nie, Ber-nie, Ber-nie." With his own speech scheduled for that night, Sanders sent a text message to his delegates imploring them to behave themselves on the floor. "I ask you as a personal courtesy to me not to engage in any kind of protest on the floor," he wrote. By this point, he had a lot of skin in the game. If he was seen as failing to unify a party that he had helped divide during the primary, his reputation would be permanently damaged. That didn't matter to his diehards. By the time Bernie left the stage that night to a roaring ovation, the story line for the first day of the convention was simple: chaos. But Hillary would soon be the beneficiary of an Obama intervention.

IF THE BEHAVIOR of the Bernie contingent was one big tension point as the convention opened, the other was how Hillary would perform when she became the first woman to deliver a speech accepting the nomination of a major American political party. In addition to her own propensity for turning great prose into bland rhetoric, Hillary would be following an all-star cast of Democratic orators, including Barack and Michelle Obama, Bill Clinton, and Joe Biden. Indeed, the four-night extravaganza in Philadelphia would essentially be a parade of top Democrats coming to the stage at the Wells Fargo Center, on the outskirts of the nation's first capital, to lend their personal and political credibility to a candidate who badly needed praise from more trusted and liked figures.

And Hillary would be delivering at a time when she had very little faith in her campaign's ability to produce speeches worthy of big moments. In victory and defeat, primary election nights had often been punctuated by the last-minute rending of her prepared remarks so that better text could be substituted.

Hillary knew she had struggled to define herself and her campaign in ways that appealed to voters. She didn't like taking issues she'd been working on for years and boiling them down into little sound bites. She lived for the complexity. This wasn't a new problem. What was so frustrating is that it still hadn't been resolved. More than a year into the campaign, her staff didn't know her well enough to turn her candidacy into a compelling narrative for her. That wasn't exactly their fault. She'd been in the public eye for a quarter of a century and voters didn't trust her. But in search of answers—ways to convince voters that she was not only better than Trump but worthy of their trust, respect, and even sympathy—she had turned, once again, to outside help.

Hillary had secretly tapped Lissa Muscatine months earlier to develop a memo that would serve as the blueprint for the convention speech and her general-election messaging. First and foremost, the goal of the speech was to illustrate Hillary's deep contrasts with Donald Trump. Given her own poor approval ratings, her top priority was to disqualify Trump in the minds of voters. She and her team presumed that if Americans believed Trump was unqualified for the presidency, she would win by default. Her team thought of the core of her argument as three hinges: unity versus division; an economy for everyone versus Trump being in it for himself; and her steadiness versus the risk of Trump.

The campaign's slogan, "Stronger Together," was a consensus point among a series of independent working groups inside and outside the campaign. It was poll-tested and grounded in Trump's negatives—the opposite of the division he sowed—rather than being a true shorthand for Hillary's approach to improving the country. She didn't love it when it was first presented to her at a meeting in a hotel in Westchester in the late spring. It was the best of the slogans she'd seen, she said. After letting it sit for a couple of days, she gave the go-ahead.

Hillary understood the imperative of disqualifying Trump, but she also wanted to turn the public's perception of her in a more positive direction, and that meant focusing more on how her personality and values drove her to public service. That was a tall order for a woman who was so preternaturally private and inaccessible to the public. To help with the task, Muscatine assembled a small team—Jeff Shesol, Vinca LaFleur, Jen Klein, and Judith McHale—that mixed veteran speechwriters and people who knew Hillary well on a personal level.

As usual, Dan Schwerin had the unenviable task of running the formal speechwriting process. In June and July, he cast a wide net for input on what Hillary should say. He spoke to Bill Clinton and former White House speechwriter Don Baer and branding specialist Roy Spence, as well as Jim Kennedy, a News Corp executive and Clintonworld veteran who had crafted the famous "18 million cracks" line in Hillary's 2008 concession speech. Schwerin huddled with Kennedy several weeks before the convention at the Coliseum, an Irish bar near Columbus Circle on New York's Upper West Side. There, for the better part of two hours, over appetizers and beer, Kennedy gave Schwerin advice. Schwerin was eager to hear Kennedy's ideas on elements of both process and substance, and he knew that Hillary loved Kennedy's way of refining complicated concepts into a handful of words.

In hallmark fashion, Hillary had set up two separate and isolated teams to write her convention speech. Muscatine's pros worked under the cover of darkness. Schwerin represented the official campaign apparatus, which had failed, over the course of a year, to supply Hillary with the words that could connect her personal story to the aspirations and needs of voters. This wasn't lost on Schwerin, who had complained repeatedly about the challenge of getting Hillary to find her own vision. For this speech, Kennedy, Philippe Reines, Jon Favreau, and the consultants—Benenson, Grunwald, and Margolis—chipped in their thoughts. Schwerin also consulted with economic policy experts Neera Tanden and Gene Sperling, as well as former State Department officials Nick Burns, Kurt Campbell, and Anne-Marie Slaughter. In part because so many of his colleagues were occupied with other tasks at the convention, Schwerin thought the process was going much more smoothly than it had on major speeches earlier in the campaign.

It was. But that didn't mean the product was strong. When he unveiled his first full draft on the opening day of the convention, even some of his closest friends thought it was in embarrassingly rough shape. "If you want to share a draft because you want input, sometimes you share it when it's not formed yet," said one of Schwerin's colleagues who sympathized with the difficulty of the process. "Dan wants to bring people into the process and be solicitous. He has a very low ego when it comes to edits and ideas. There's a cost to that."

The outside speechwriters criticized it as a cut-and-paste job of previous work that sounded as dry as a State of the Union address. They thought it lacked both personal detail and that elusive commander-in-chief vibe. Where she'd been too ironclad in her 2008 run, there was a danger that she would be too soft now. This first draft had a lot of talk about love and kindness, but if Hillary wanted to be believable as president, she couldn't promise to take on ISIS, Vladimir Putin, Iranian mullahs, and North Korea by talking like a PTA leader. They went straight to Hillary to make sure the candidate knew the pros would have to quickly apply thick layers of foundation to obscure a blemished draft.

"They were really critical, and it was tough," said one campaign aide. "I think they wanted to be constructive. I don't think that was the end result."

As the first night of the convention drew toward its close, Hillary's speech was a disaster, Bernie's delegates were waging war against her, and the underlying level of unrest was even more pervasive than the flashes of protest visible on television.

AND THEN, IN a few minutes at the end of the night, Michelle Obama turned the narrative on its head. The first lady had flown in to Philadelphia that night in the middle of a violent thunderstorm. The plane she was traveling on, a Boeing C-32 often used by Vice President Joe Biden, was rocked by turbulence and had to circle several times before it landed. Others on the flight felt sick to their stomachs, but Michelle Obama strode off the plane as if nothing had happened, knowing all too well what she was there to do that night.

More than anything that evening, Michelle Obama's powerful address would offer an echo of one particular speech from 2008: Hillary Clinton's concession. It was no coincidence, either. The speechwriter who had so powerfully crafted Obama's speech, Sarah Hurwitz, had been the lead writer for the concession address

Clinton delivered in Washington's National Building Museum eight years earlier.

In Michelle's speech, Hurwitz described Clinton as someone who "has the guts and the grace to keep coming back and putting those cracks in that highest and hardest glass ceiling until she finally breaks through. . . . And because of Hillary Clinton, my daughters—and all our sons and daughters—now take for granted that a woman can be president of the United States."

That line recalled one Hurwitz wrote for Hillary in 2008: Because of the abolitionists and suffragists, "children today will grow up taking for granted that an African American or a woman can, yes, become the president of the United States."

Hillary's primary victory—and, her top aides believed, her path to the presidency—relied heavily on an Obama-like coalition driven by African Americans and women of all races and ethnicities. Hurwitz's words, a circle connecting the Obama and Clinton coalitions, illustrated the perfect distinction between enlightened homage and pure plagiarism—the route Melania Trump had taken the week before in repeating Michelle Obama's words from the 2008 Democratic convention as a testament to her own husband. The Melania debacle had so worried Michelle's aides that they Googled clips and phrases of her speech repeatedly to make certain that nothing she said had been uttered before. Even something as anodyne as "There but for the grace of God, go I" was flagged by the staff. Hurwitz assured them that such an aphorism was perfectly fine. Unlike Hillary's chaotic speechwriting process, Michelle Obama's had been elegant and efficient. Her address was signed and sealed a couple of weeks before it was delivered.

And the delivery was a showstopper. The first lady gave a positively glowing endorsement of Hillary and slapped Trump without ever mentioning his name, speaking about the difficulties of raising two young girls in the White House amid a twenty-four-hour news cycle that spewed vicious criticism of their father and how they taught their girls to cope. "How we urge them to ignore those who question their father's citizenship or faith. How we insist that the hateful language they hear from public figures on TV does not represent the true spirit of this country. How we explain that when someone is cruel, or acts like a bully, you don't stoop to their level," she said. "No, our motto is, when they go low, we go high."

Michelle Obama's concise and powerful endorsement of Hillary reset the narrative of the convention from one of chaos to one of lockstep unity at the top echelon of the party. The two women, with their vastly different styles, were not close personally, which made the moment of validation that much more persuasive. On the question of whether Hillary was a better choice for president than Donald Trump, there wasn't a millimeter of daylight between them.

THE TESTIMONIALS WOULD flow forth over the course of the week, but Hillary's case for herself was not coming together. Shesol and LaFleur—who ran Washington's most prominent political and corporate speechwriting shop—were the invisible hands that drafted and delivered the backbone and much of the meat of the full speech by the time the convention got under way. But the first full version had Schwerin's fingerprints all over it. He was fighting them with the power he had: control over the keyboard. "There were two different drafts going back and forth," one Hillary aide said of the confusion. So, several times a day, new drafts, with significant changes, would appear in the in-boxes of the dozen or so people tied to the process. Most of them had little or no idea whose hands, other than Schwerin's, were on the speech.

Favreau, the former chief Obama speechwriter, thought the first version he'd seen, before the start of the convention, was long and meandering at best. But, as Schwerin incorporated the thoughts of the committee, it seemed to be getting worse—and quickly. Panicked, Favreau shipped Schwerin his own revisions, mostly just line edits. In his view, the speech was classically Clintonian in its 1990s feel. Even though Hillary didn't like sound bites, she and her husband were always looking to insert something that would lead the news in the next day's paper. That, Favreau thought, is what made

Hillary sound fake. And when she and her team hit on something great, they'd kill it with overrepetition.

In one early version, though, Favreau saw the seeds of a powerful argument against Trump's temperament. He sanded down the words, first written by Shesol, to "A man you can bait with a Tweet is not a man we can trust with nuclear weapons." It would end up being the most memorable line of Hillary's speech. Still, Favreau's involvement—and the belief that he promoted his work to reporters—would leave lingering bitterness on the palates of some of Hillary's top supporters.

INSIDE THE BOILER room, and around the convention hall, Clinton and Sanders aides worked to quiet the recalcitrants. On the first day, their text-messaging coordination system hadn't prevented pro-Bernie delegates from making a scene, but by Tuesday, after Bernie had called for Hillary's election from the podium the night before, the two camps found more success in tamping down dissent. The haters were harder to find by the time Bill Clinton took the stage Tuesday night with the express mission of acting as a character witness for his wife. It was the right role for the spouse of a presidential nominee, though an unusual one for a former president and for someone whose own character flaws were part of the Republican case against Hillary. But since her mother had died a few years earlier, no one on the planet could claim to know Hillary better than Bill.

He had begun thinking about how he wanted to describe his wife to the country a month or more before the convention. The ask from Hillary was to give the country a window into her core, the very thing she had so much difficulty doing. America knew her—or thought it did—but Bill could give voters more information. He would sketch a biographical narrative of his wife, and he asked a series of people close to her to offer their thoughts on what should be included.

The actual writing started about two and a half weeks out, as

Bill huddled with his personal speechwriter, Steve Rinehart. Bill would occasionally ask other aides for a few facts and figures that could be sprinkled into his draft, but it was very closely held until just before the convention opened. On Sunday night, about forty-eight hours before he was to take the stage, Bill distributed the first four or five pages of the speech to a wider group of aides and advisers. But he kept the rest to himself.

During the commotion of Monday's chaotic opening of the convention, Bill sequestered himself in the presidential suite at the Logan Philadelphia, overlooking a stately fountain, with a downtown view. The former president is a gifted writer, according to people who have seen his raw copy, if prone to cliché and a little in love with his own words. Crooking his left hand, he scrawled out his thoughts on a yellow legal pad.

Bill would deliver pages to Rinehart, who offered his own opinions on structure and phrasing and then dutifully typed the draft into his computer. They worked all day Monday, and Bill shared the full speech with his core group of personal aides on Tuesday during the day. It was running long—no surprise to anyone who had spent any time around the former president—and he worked with his team to try to trim it back under forty minutes. They made a few tweaks, but it was mostly what Bill had put to paper. How could anyone else really tell the story of Hillary Clinton better, or more accurately, than he could? No one dared to tell him that he'd glossed over her loyalty in the face of his publicly revealed sexual dalliances—a fact that would be obvious to anyone who listened to the speech when he delivered it. It wasn't their place to get inside his marriage, even if it meant letting him expose himself and his wife to a lot of chatter about the Monica Lewinsky affair.

Bill took the podium to a raucous standing ovation on Tuesday night, a grayer, more frail returning champion. If there was one thing Bill's fans and sworn enemies could agree on, it was his ability to compel an audience. He opened up with an anecdote, the kind that only he could tell and that no opposition researcher could hope to unravel.

"In the spring of 1971, I met a girl. The first time I saw her, we were, appropriately enough, in a class on political and civil rights. She had thick blond hair, big glasses. Wore no makeup. And she exuded this sense and strength of self-possession that I found magnetic," he began. "After the class, I followed her out, intending to introduce myself. I got close enough to touch her back, but I couldn't do it. Somehow, I knew this would not be just another tap on the shoulder, that I might be starting something I couldn't stop."

"Everyone's mind went to the same place," a confidante of Hillary's later confessed—no one else could ever know whether it was Hillary's back that Bill had chosen not to touch.

But, in Bill's telling, it was a sweet story of innocent fascination. He spent the next forty-five minutes talking about the Hillary he knew—the one he'd walked and talked and laughed with for nearly half a century, the one who threw herself into social justice and child welfare issues, switched parties over the Vietnam War, registered Mexican American voters in Texas, repeatedly refused his entreaties to marry him before finally acceding, took Chelsea to T-ball, volleyball, and ballet, took up controversial policy initiatives on his behalf in Arkansas and Washington—including the federal Children's Health Insurance Program—and served the nation as first lady, senator, and then secretary of state.

"Now, how does this square? How did this square with the things that you heard at the Republican convention? What's the difference in what I told you and what they said? How do you square it?" Bill asked the convention hall. "You can't. One is real, the other is made up. And you just have to decide, and you just have to decide which is which, my fellow Americans. The real one had done more positive change-making before she was thirty than most politicians do with a lifetime in office."

It came off as sincere—coming off as sincere is one of Bill's specialties, even when he's lying—and served its purpose. But it was hardly Bill's most passionate or effective address. He wanted Hillary to be president, and he was playing his role. The Big Dog still had a little magic left in him, but not enough to be the star of the convention.

HILLARY ARRIVED IN Philadelphia on Wednesday, July 27, in time to hear Barack Obama, her former boss and the most popular politician in America, praise her to the heavens. She was there, but her speech wasn't, nor were two of its authors. Shesol and LaFleur, who along with Muscatine and Klein, had written a significant portion of the address, weren't originally given credentials for the convention by the campaign. Muscatine and Klein had to scare up a couple of passes so the pair could be there to hear the words they had written. The snub reflected the tension between the campaign and these outsiders. In the final week or so, drafts had been flying back and forth, with Muscatine and her group delivering big chunks from Washington and Schwerin assembling their work and that of others.

Schwerin was still trying to stitch it all together when Hillary landed in Philadelphia the day before her big moment. He gave her a copy of the latest draft that day, and she would spend much of the next twenty-four hours going over it with him, Megan Rooney, Jake Sullivan, and her husband. Her granddaughter played in the suite as she went through her remarks line by line.

Meanwhile, Barack Obama was excited about hitting the convention stage one more time. For his reelection in 2012, he had leaned a little on Bill as his explainer-in-chief, and he was eager to repay the favor by boosting Hillary.

Inside the White House, the speech was treated with the reverence of a State of the Union, only the draft of this testimonial was kept mostly between Obama himself and his chief speechwriter. Cody Keenan had written some of the president's most poetic speeches, including the one he delivered in the wake of the Sandy Hook school shooting. Obama's aides solicited input on the themes of the speech from Hillary's camp, but they never shared the text. Hillary didn't ask for it—a sign of the deep trust that she and Obama had developed since he'd first asked her to serve as secretary of state.

The main aspect of Hillary that Obama could speak to that not even Bill could was the way she responded to a crisis in the White House Situation Room. As first lady, she had been kept in the loop about many of Bill's policies and decisions, but she had served at Obama's elbow and helped guide him through war, diplomacy, and the raid that killed Osama bin Laden. She had recommended he launch that strike against the advice of Vice President Joe Biden and Secretary of Defense Robert Gates at a time when everyone understood a failure could spell doom for Obama's reelection hopes the following year. By adding her signature to bin Laden's death warrant, she assured Obama that his main intraparty rival would be by his side on the most audacious act of his presidency. Hillary was uniquely prepared to make those decisions, he told the nation. But even Obama struggled to get past Hillary's shell and find the core humanity that voters would seek. He knew her well and yet his endorsement rested on her capacity to handle the job.

"You know, nothing truly prepares you for the demands of the Oval Office. Until you've sat at that desk, you don't know what it's like to manage a global crisis or send young people to war," he said with hallmark authenticity. "But Hillary's been in the room; she's been part of those decisions. She knows what's at stake in the decisions our government makes for the working family, the senior citizen, the small business owner, the soldier, and the veteran. Even in the middle of crisis, she listens to people, and keeps her cool, and treats everybody with respect. And no matter how daunting the odds; no matter how much people try to knock her down, she never, ever quits."

It was the following line that caught Bill Clinton's attention.

"That's the Hillary I know. That's the Hillary I've come to admire," Obama testified. "And that's why I can say with confidence there has never been a man or a woman more qualified than Hillary

Clinton to serve as President of the United States of America."
Obama wasn't much for humility, and neither was Bill. The current
president had just said that neither of them came to the Oval Office
with Hillary's know-how.

After Obama laid out the case against Donald Trump, Bill met
him backstage to offer his thanks. "I enjoyed what you said," the former president drawled, making a reference to the line. It had been
eight years since Bill had tried to cajole superdelegates by insisting
that Obama wasn't prepared for the office, that he wouldn't be able
to handle it.

Now, Obama had revealed that he believed Hillary was better
qualified than Bill had been.

"It happens to be true," Obama said, keeping any hint of ironic
smugness to himself.

He saw Hillary backstage too, and she looked worn around the
edges. The look was familiar to the president. Early in his first term,
he'd noticed that his secretary of state had only one gear, and he
worried that she would burn herself out—that she couldn't keep up
her pace and remain in good health. The month before the convention, Obama advised her that she was in a sprint to the finish line.
But now, as he took stock of his former secretary of state and would-
be successor, he sensed that she still wasn't taking good enough care
of herself. Obama had shown, in the face of criticism, that he understood the importance of downtime—a round on the golf course,
even a smoke break—but that just wasn't in Hillary's DNA.

It's quite a stretch from now to November, Obama said. You've
got to make sure you rest. Take a vacation.

I know, Hillary said. I know, I know. I've got to do that.

But she didn't really know how to slow down; left to her own
devices, she would run herself into the ground.

HILLARY'S OWN SPEECH still wasn't set by late Wednesday night,
less than twenty-four hours before her crowning moment as the

first female presidential nominee of a major party. Having watched the Obamas wow the convention crowd, Hillary told Schwerin they needed to turn things up a notch.

"OK," she said, "we've got to make this really good." As Schwerin was well aware, his candidate was following not only both Obamas but also Bill Clinton. And the nominee's speech isn't usually the most memorable of a convention. At the GOP's confab the week before, it was Ted Cruz's admonishment to "vote your conscience" that had captured the attention of the political world. Ted Kennedy had stolen the show at the 1980 Democratic convention, and Barack Obama had first risen to prominence in 2004, when John Kerry was accepting the Democratic nomination. Other speakers could give tight, focused speeches, but the nominee was always trying to do a lot of things at once. It would be a tough feat, he thought, to make Hillary stand out. Some of the others had been brilliant; Schwerin was hoping Hillary would be good. He went to work with Sullivan and Rooney into the wee hours of Thursday morning trying to sharpen Hillary's lines. Overall, the structure of the speech was set, but there was too much flab. Later Thursday morning, they felt they had whittled it down enough to show Hillary again. After she and Bill had taken a look, Schwerin e-mailed the near-final draft to his colleagues.

Muscatine, Shesol, and LaFleur were shocked at what they saw. They had worked on a few different endings for the speech, but the draft they were looking at was completely different from all of them. It wasn't clear whether Schwerin had messed with it, or whether it was Bill or Hillary, but it didn't sound like Schwerin. They didn't think it was right, but it was highly professional. "He could never have done that," said one person who saw that version of the speech.

All the pros could see from the text was that many of their favorite words were absent from the final run of the speech. In their place stood a handful of paragraphs that the three wordsmiths found jarring, not only in the context of the rest of the narrative but really on all levels. They sent slack-jawed e-mails to one another and even hopped on the phone. Muscatine said she would take a shot at a replacement.

Shesol and LaFleur were just arriving by train to New York's Penn Station when Muscatine sent them seven or eight lines as the dough for a new ending. There, two of the most successful speechwriters in the business refined Muscatine's ideas in thirty minutes and fired the new section off to the campaign. Schwerin put three different endings on the table—his own, one from Muscatine, Shesol, and LaFleur, and one from Kennedy—and melded them. The pros took a look at the compromise and thought a pretty powerful speech would now end the way Hillary's launch speech had landed—with a whimper.

The day of the address, she set up two sessions with Michael Sheehan, a veteran speech coach, in a conference room. Bill sat quietly in the back, as Hillary took her place behind a podium and looked up at the teleprompter. After the first run-through, Hillary seemed pleased. "That's pretty good," she assessed. "I like it."

Hillary was comfortable with the text, but Sheehan gave her a handful of pointers on pacing and tone. He showed her the best way to emphasize certain words, especially those that might be punchier than they seemed on paper. He instructed her on how close to stand to the podium so she could put her hands on it and use it but also give herself a free range of movement for gestures. One person in the room noticed a change in how easily Hillary could be coached around Sheehan. He had a way of connecting with her that many others did not. She could often be dismissive of suggestions when she was sensitive to the criticism, as she had been in debate prep the day after the Michigan primary. But now she had the confidence to take in what Sheehan was saying. Rather than her standard yeah-I-got-it response to instruction, she was asking Sheehan to give her more. And her delivery was a full dress rehearsal. "She really brought it," the aide said.

When Hillary became impassioned behind a microphone, she often came across to some listeners as shouting or strident. It was

a gender-loaded complaint, but one she had to deal with in rallying her own troops and trying to persuade undecided voters to
join her side. As she practiced, her tone had urgency. But Sheehan
wanted her to slow it down, to anticipate the audience and pause
for applause lines. He also told her that she should lower her voice,
rather than raise it, at important moments. It was a technique Bill
had perfected: quieting down so that an audience had to lean in to
hear what he was saying. That, Sheehan explained, would give more
power to her words. It was the way to put listeners in the palm of
her hand.

Perhaps the most important insight he gave her, though, had to
do with her expression. Too often, she didn't have one. She didn't
look like she was having any fun. This speech, the convention, and
the entire campaign were a show, and the performance aspect didn't
come naturally to Hillary. Smile, Sheehan reminded her. With a few
final tweaks, the final draft was ready to go at 9 p.m., more than an
hour before Hillary would take the stage.

As she waited for her big moment, an unlikely Democratic
Party hero was emerging at the Wells Fargo Center. No one knew
ahead of time that the person who would steal the show at the
convention wasn't Clinton herself or her husband or the man she
hoped to replace at the White House. Instead, it was Khizr Khan,
a Muslim Gold Star father whose son had been killed in the Iraq
War. The campaign had put together a long roster of what might be
considered "regular Americans" to illustrate certain arguments for
Hillary or against Trump. Mook thought the most powerful of that
set would be a woman who used a death benefit from her husband
to attend the much-maligned Trump University. Khan had first
become a feature of the campaign in a much more modest fashion
in December 2015, when Hillary called attention to his family in
a speech in Minnesota—right after Khan had bashed Trump in a
story in Vocativ. She had referred to his son, Humayun, as the "best
of America." For convention purposes, Khizr Khan was considered
a "second-tier player," according to one Hillary aide.

That is, until he began speaking. Bald, bespectacled, and grim-faced, Khan took Trump to task for anti-immigrant policies, particularly a proposed temporary ban on Muslims traveling to the United States. With his wife standing beside him, Khan pulled a copy of the Constitution out of his pocket, brandishing it as he lectured Trump from the podium.

"Let me ask you: have you even read the United States Constitution? I will gladly lend you my copy," the Pakistani-born lawyer boomed as the crowd in the convention hall cheered. "Have you ever been to Arlington Cemetery? Go look at the graves of the brave patriots who died defending the United States of America. You will see all faiths, genders and ethnicities." Then Khan made it more personal. "You have sacrificed nothing and no one," he lectured, pitching his body forward and jabbing his index finger toward the camera to punctuate his words.

Hillary watched in amazement from her holding room backstage. Democrats in the hall and around the country exulted in the powerful illustration of their values and the shaming of Trump. Most Republicans immediately grasped the value of the moment. "Whoever found the Khans should be an ambassador to something," one senior GOP official said after the convention.

Khan's conclusion that Trump had sacrificed nothing in his life tied perfectly into the major contrast point Hillary hoped to draw with the most full explication to date of the twining of her values, the party's values, the nation's values, and her record of public service. She and her speechwriters were very mindful of the idea that no matter how long she had been in the public eye, she had still not effectively explained to voters how her life story fit into their ideals of America.

The speeches delivered by Bill and Chelsea Clinton during the convention had a single aim: to help voters understand Clinton at a time when she was drowning in the polls on the issue of likability. "People don't know who my mom is and I want to speak to that," Chelsea had told Rooney in the early summer, when they started working on Chelsea's remarks that would lead in to Hillary's acceptance of the nomination. She knew she had a unique perspective on her mother, and the lineage of women from her grandmother to Chelsea herself was an important, if underappreciated, aspect of Hillary's narrative. Lots of people spoke about Hillary's resilience, but very few of them had a front-row seat to it. "I saw the tough times," Chelsea told Rooney.

The two of them e-mailed thoughts over the course of the summer, and Rooney found that Chelsea was ruthlessly accurate about the details of her childhood. When Rooney tried to gloss over an anecdote about Chelsea's parents asking her about her day at the dinner table before they discussed their own days, Chelsea objected. No, she said, this is telling about my mom. During the convention, Rooney had visited Chelsea in her suite. As Chelsea nursed her infant son, Aidan, and asked her daughter, Charlotte, whether she wanted *agua*—Clinton and her husband, Marc Mezvinsky, were raising their kids to be bilingual—they went over the final edits.

Chelsea would do her best to "humanize" her mom, just as both Obamas, Bill Clinton, Joe Biden, and others had done over the course of the four-day convention. It was up to Chelsea to soften up the audience for her mother's biggest political moment yet.

STANDING IN A retrofitted locker room backstage that served as her holding area, Hillary beamed with pride when Chelsea appeared on a flat-screen television. Her personal photographer, Barbara Kinney, snapped a quick shot of mom watching daughter and then left the room. In the final moments before her own historic speech, Hillary was left in solitude.

When Chelsea announced her mom to a thunderous roar from the convention hall, Hillary stepped into public view for the first time that night wearing a white suit that seemed to scream "I'm pure of heart"—an homage to suffragists who wore white to symbolize the sanctity of their purpose.

As Hillary embraced Chelsea, the emotional crest of the moment hit her hard. Decades of battling at the highest levels of public life, two presidential primary campaigns, her role as the first woman ever nominated by a major party, and her love for Chelsea washed over her.

With her campaign anthem, "Fight Song," blaring in the background, Hillary walked across the stage waving to the crowd, pointing to friends in the first few rows on the floor and mouthing "Oh my gosh." She looked as happy and confident as she had at any point in the campaign, and, to her close friends, a bit overwhelmed. As she finally stepped toward the podium, her hand rested over her heart.

Now Hillary would have another chance—perhaps her last chance—to persuade voters that what Chelsea Clinton said was true, that, despite public perception, she really did wake up every morning trying to figure out how to fight for other people.

The party's leaders had all lent their credibility to her cause in the preceding three days, and she thanked them for it—even Sanders, who wore a disgusted look in a skybox above the convention floor. He'd had a shot, and he'd missed, and now he had to listen to Hillary Clinton's generated graciousness. The scowl on his face read as though it grated on him, and the whole idea of Hillary infuriated many of his supporters who were still in the hall.

Throughout her speech, pockets of die-hard Bernie backers screamed slogans at the stage. Each time, the joint Clinton-Sanders whip team jumped into action, and chants of "U-S-A" drowned out the dissidents. Recalcitrant Bernie supporters who left the hall to get a soda or go to the bathroom found that their seats had been occupied by pro-Clinton forces when they returned. Schwerin, Rooney, and Sullivan had tailored the speech with the aim of including a lot of applause lines, fearful that any lulls would encourage outbursts from the pro-Bernie delegates. They had reassured Hillary that there would be plenty of cheering to cover up any dissent. It turned out to be a prescient concern.

The interruptions were more disruptive in the hall than they seemed at home, and several of Hillary's longtime advisers said that the cadence of her delivery was thrown off. Schwerin, who had walked into the audience to watch the speech, was annoyed by the distractions. So was Rooney, who sat in a family section up front. They worried that all of it—the protests and the oddly timed cheers engineered by the campaign floor operation to stifle dissent— would translate on television and take the air out of Hillary's acceptance. There was nothing they could do but hope that it would come off better to the home audience than it did inside the Wells Fargo Center.

Hillary picked her way through the beginning of the speech. She sounded out the notes that she and her small army of speechwriters had prioritized. And then she turned personal, leaning on words drafted by Muscatine, who had been her first speechwriter.

"I've been your First Lady. Served eight years as a senator from the great State of New York. I ran for president and lost. Then I represented all of you as secretary of state. But my job titles only tell you what I've done. They don't tell you why," Hillary said. "The truth is, through all these years of public service, the 'service' part has always come easier to me than the 'public' part."

It was an acknowledgment, however subtle, of her guardedness—of her reluctance to keep opening her armor to absorb the arrows of public life. Though she didn't mention the e-mail server, her words were a nod to a frustration that many Democrats shared with her Republican critics about her lack of transparency.

She talked about her mother's influence on her and her Methodist faith, about how she learned as a young activist that it takes a lot of hard work to alter the political landscape.

"To drive real progress, you have to change both hearts and laws," she said.

As much as anything she said on the campaign trail, that one sentence explained Hillary's strength and weakness in the public sphere. She wasn't good at the former, so she concentrated on the latter. One of the toughest moments of the 2008 primary campaign for her came when she had accused Obama of using flowery words without having the record to back up his promises. Obama used her formulation—"just words"—to compare himself to Martin Luther

King Jr. Hillary had countered by noting that King wouldn't have won civil rights legislation without Lyndon Johnson working the system from the inside in the Senate and the White House. It had been received as a knock on King. But it was a clear-eyed distillation of the yin and yang of outside activism and inside power. In her Philadelphia speech, Hillary tipped her cap to the civil rights and labor movements, saying to Donald Trump, "We are not afraid"—the hook of the fourth stanza in "We Shall Overcome."

A substantial portion of her address was devoted to knocking down Trump, and she hit the most memorable line of the night—about baiting Trump with a tweet—right out of the park.

Like most of her major speeches, though, Hillary tried to squeeze in too many ideas. It remained impossible to decipher her priorities or her theory for her candidacy. "She genuinely cares about a ton of different things," said one aide. "She has plans for a ton of differing things. It's hard to come up with the three things." Additionally, the aide said, nominees' convention speeches are famous for being stocked with too many ideas. "As a form it's a tough speech," said the aide, who rated it "solid."

She foundered at the end with a sappy wrap-up that borrowed from the musical *Hamilton,* a production that connected with her liberal donors and cosmopolitan millennial aides but perhaps not the rest of the country. It was Kennedy who had come up with the *Hamilton* line, and Hillary, who had seen the show twice, had immediately fawned over it. There was no use in trying to talk her out of it, even though several speechwriters involved in the process thought it was the wrong message to send.

One of the clearest lines of distinction between a great political speech and a pedestrian one is the ability of the speaker to turn the peroration—the final run—into a big call for action. Hillary's fell flat. Her pro speechwriters knew it would. They tried to save her from being hokey and timid. But she'd ignored them.

"America's destiny is ours to choose. So let's be stronger together," she said, repeating her slogan. "Looking to the future with courage and confidence. Building a better tomorrow for our beloved children and our beloved country. When we do, America will be greater than ever." One person who worked on the speech summed up the consensus within Democratic ranks: "Her delivery was better than it usually is." But Hillary was in a celebratory mood backstage— "on cloud nine," one of her aides said.

Given what the convention could have been—a four-day Dumpster inferno—Democrats rated it as a rousing success, with some going so far as to say it was the best in recent memory. Just a few days earlier, the party chairwoman had been ousted without ceremony. Hillary's speech had been rescued from the jaws of disaster and turned into an effective, if uninspiring, contrast with Trump. And the many Bernie delegates who had come to the convention determined to disrupt it with shows of disdain for Hillary had run into a unified phalanx of Sanders and Clinton aides even more committed to shutting them down.

Over their text-messaging system, those aides congratulated one another after all was said and done. They knew all too well that they had narrowly averted the catastrophe of television cameras around the country showing a party still riven by its brutal primary.

"Despite the fact that sometimes it got contentious, we always figured it out and we all wanted the same goal overall," Marlon Marshall wrote. "Nothing like a little skirmish to make folks a family," Charlie Baker replied. Bernie adviser Mark Longabaugh weighed in for the Sanders camp: "The disagreements were passionate but always in good faith," he wrote. "In the end, one of the best conventions in history. Now, on to victory in November!"

Mook was most keenly aware of the optical illusion the two camps had pulled off, as he revealed to friends in a story he would tell later. During the convention, a woman approached him and said that the American flags in the arena were beautiful. *That was to hide the crazy people shouting things,* he thought. *But it looked great.* Similarly, the campaign looked a lot better in front of the curtain than behind it.

Chapter 16

"IT'S SO PHONY"

HILLARY MINGLED WITH OLD FRIENDS IN SAG HARBOR under a tent on the night of August 30: Calvin Klein, Harvey Weinstein, Jimmy Buffett, Jon Bon Jovi, and Sir Paul McCartney. Buffett and his wife, Jane, were the hosts of this extravaganza, which capped a multiday fund-raising blitz through the Hamptons. For a minimum of $100,000, VIPs were treated to dinner, "premium seating," and the option to dance the night away with Hillary, Bill, and a few of their A-list pals. Hillary put on a brave face, reveled with her donors, and even joined in singing "Hey Jude." But, below the surface, she was tense. Her closest aide's personal life was blowing up in a fashion so spectacular that the campaign was at risk of becoming collateral damage.

"It was a day that was very trying because Huma had to go back and deal with the latest crisis," said one friend. Forty-eight hours earlier, the *New York Post* had reported that Abedin's husband, Anthony Weiner, had not only resumed sexting other women but published a photo he had taken of himself, clad only in underwear, with the couple's young son sleeping in the bed next to him.

Years earlier, when Weiner's first sexting scandal erupted, Hillary had told her closest aide that she had "some big decisions to make." Huma had opted to stay with Weiner, both then and when new revelations of his lewd texting had surfaced during his 2013 mayoral run. Huma viewed her husband as a good parent and a necessary partner in caring for their son while she traveled with Hillary. But this time was different. It wasn't just his own political career that he'd put in jeopardy. His exploits were now a problem for Hillary because Abedin was so close to her. Abedin announced the day before the Buffett fund-raiser, and the day after the news broke, that she was separating from Weiner, and she dropped off the campaign to go home and be with her son. "I think I shouldn't come with you guys for a few days," she told colleagues, preempting an uncomfortable internal conversation about whether she should be photographed by Hillary's side while her family life was imploding.

"All of us saw that she was a liability," the friend said. But Abedin was Hillary's intimate, the right-hand aide who anticipated her needs, followed up on her promises, and handled sensitive political and personal issues with discretion and grace. One longtime adviser explained the candidate's fidelity to her aide this way: "Some of it is sheer loyalty. Some of it is empathy."

But the Huma story line had begun to get old for staffers on the campaign who felt like she not only had a firm hold on access to Hillary but also involved herself in making decisions outside her purview. "Everybody wants access, and she's always around, and what happens is you have her speaking for HRC at times," said one colleague, "making decisions she shouldn't have been or simply playing just a protective role. That gets read as she's trying to hold on to her power."

Separately, with her *Vogue* centerpieces and her participation in a revealing documentary on Weiner's mayoral bid, Abedin had broken the old political rule that aides should never overshadow their bosses.

The newest Weiner fiasco was a double blow to Hillary: a painful episode for the woman closest to her and a political bombshell that could cost her in the campaign. It was also yet another subtle reminder for the public of Bill's infidelity. The sexually salacious headlines came at a terrible time for Hillary, in the midst of a slide in the polls that erased her convention bounce. "I think she wished that Huma had left Anthony earlier," the friend said. "But she would not have imposed."

THREE WEEKS EARLIER, after the Democratic convention and at the tail end of a national jobs tour, Hillary's lead had jumped. On August 9, it stood at 7.9 points in the RealClearPolitics average of public polls. She was enjoying the afterglow of the Democrats' show of unity at their convention and Donald Trump's decision to attack Khizr and his wife after it.

She and her team felt good about getting some separation, but the numbers also should have been a red flag. After pouring tens of millions of dollars into the states, watching Trump insult nearly every imaginable group other than white men, and pulling off a convention that could easily have melted down, the Republican nominee was still well within striking distance. The failure to put Trump away would become all the more apparent as Hillary's advantage evaporated over the next six weeks.

The back end of August had always been viewed as a sweet spot in the calendar for Hillary to stock her campaign treasury. She hadn't raised money for the general election in the throes of her primary with Bernie Sanders—a lesson learned from 2008, when she'd piled up cash that she couldn't legally use in her contest against Obama. June and July had been devoted to campaigning and preparation for the convention. After Labor Day, she'd be in a dead sprint to the election. So, with an overall fund-raising goal for the campaign of $1 billion, August represented her last, best chance to collect six-figure checks from "high touch" donors—the kind of contributors who expected real face time for real money.

Hillary didn't love fund-raising, but she understood that she relied more on the wealthiest donors than did passion candidates like Sanders and Obama, who could use digital and grassroots fund-raising techniques to fill their coffers. And she knew her contributors, in particular, needed a lot of hand-holding.

She shared with Mook a fear of plunging into debt, another residual effect of the 2008 campaign. For the campaign manager, rebalancing his candidate's schedule to do more fund-raising and fewer swing-state rallies constituted a necessary evil. He felt that he and Hillary were alone in the view that the campaign didn't have enough cash—a function, in part, of the fact that he didn't always share detailed budget information with other campaign officials. But it was also a telling feeling, given how much less Trump was putting into his campaign. Mook had much more money to spend, but the cost of running Hillary's campaign was high. She'd spent $37 million to Trump's $18 million in July, and she had $58.5 million in the bank—$20 million more than Trump, according to Bloomberg. Yet, at the end of August, she would have 800 paid staff, compared with 130 for Trump. At the same time, the low-spending Trump was starting to rake in contributions at a pace—$80 million in July alone—that grabbed the Clinton campaign's attention. So Hillary was both extremely well funded in comparison to her opponent and nervous that she wouldn't have enough money to sustain her campaign.

This combination of being flush with cash but phobic about expenses put a hammerlock on Mook's budget, and it guided his decision making. Early on in the general campaign, he'd given some of his state directors money to play with, and, from his perspective, they'd burned through it with the expectation that more was coming. He was constantly turning down requests for more paid staff in the states. *You don't understand how big our payroll is now,* he thought each time one of the flock complained that his fists were wrapped too tightly around the campaign's cash. *This is an Obama problem,* he thought, remembering how freely the 2012 campaign had spent money. So many of Hillary's field operatives had worked on that bid, and they expected this one to be as well funded.

Hillary had built a massive operation with an insatiable appetite for cash. Trump's leaner beast was fed with relatively small morsels from his personal treasury and contributors. And he still was trailing by only single digits.

Mook was surprised that Trump and Republican super PACs hadn't flooded the airwaves with ads during the summer, but he couldn't count on that to continue. Sending Hillary to posh fundraisers like the Buffett affair in the Hamptons was the function of a simple truth, said one person familiar with his strategy: "We didn't have the money." It was harder for Hillary to raise money, this person said, "because people thought we were going to win." (Mook was confident enough in that prospect that he had begun to tentatively explore the possibility of taking over at the DNC after the election—a move that gained no traction because of the number and clout of his critics in Clintonworld.)

With regard to the donors, "It was harder to get them to take action when things were going well," said one person familiar with her fund-raising operation. "The times that people thought she was losing or something challenging happened, that's when people would rally behind her." That was the opposite of the experience of many political candidates, including Obama, who could raise cash off their successes.

The problem cut in both directions. Small-dollar donors didn't think Hillary needed their contributions, and, with the exception of her longtime friends, the elites who could bundle hundreds of thousands of dollars believed that they could never give enough to get truly close to her. "You have people who have known her forever who believe she walks on water, she can do no wrong," said one donor who became disillusioned during the campaign. "They work hard; they get invited to all the cool stuff. But for all the new people that have come on board recently, they're going to events, but there's nothing special being done for them."

So Hillary carved out time in August to visit the moneyed set in the elite East Coast summer destinations of Martha's Vineyard, Nantucket, and the Hamptons. The new infusion of cash would help fund her operations through the remainder of the campaign, but not the extra resources that her state directors thought she so desperately needed to compete with Trump on the ground in the most important battlefields.

▼

EARLY ONE MORNING at the beginning of August, Emmy Ruiz fielded a troubling phone call from Allison Zelman, Brooklyn's "regional director" for a handful of battleground states, including Colorado, Nevada, and Florida.

Ruiz, who engineered Hillary's caucus victory in Nevada in February, had since moved to Colorado to set up the general-election campaign there. She thought of herself as a storm chaser—a state-level specialist who had delivered against the odds for Hillary and Obama—and she relished a shot at taking a state that had voted twice for Obama and twice for George W. Bush. From the very start, though, Ruiz viewed Colorado as a tough challenge for Hillary. To win, she thought, Hillary would need a full-court press, complete with significant spending on television ads. But Brooklyn didn't see it that way.

The campaign would be "taking a break," Zelman said. There would be no television advertising.

WTF, Ruiz thought. Hillary was up in Colorado, but only by half a dozen points, and Trump clearly intended to compete heavily there. He'd appeared in the state twice in July. It felt like he was closing ground. Easing off the gas in a true swing state didn't make much sense from Ruiz's perspective on the front lines. She pushed back a little bit. "You wanna do it, go for it," Ruiz replied. "But what you're saying is that you're OK with putting all your eggs in one basket, and I hope you're not wrong."

Zelman, who had worked as the field director for Obama's 2012 campaign in Pennsylvania, said Mook was making the right move based on the analytics. Reviewing Elan Kriegel's data, and having watched Trump cruise through the primaries on the power of Twitter and free coverage from news outlets, Mook came to believe that television ads were less effective in 2016 than they had been in any previous cycle. As he did in Colorado, he directed spending in other battleground states based on what was most efficient, with little regard for the possibility that allocating resources to less efficient methods of reaching voters could also work to build Hillary's coalition.

Brooklyn had reeled back advertising in both Colorado and Virginia at the same time. It was expensive to run TV ads in Denver and the DC market that reached Democratic-rich Northern Virginia suburbs. Trump wasn't on the air, and neither were Republican super PACs. The view of Mook and his paid media guru, Oren Shur, was that the electorate in both states was tailored well for Hillary to win: significant minority populations and a high number of college-educated voters.

"The genetic makeup of the states was beneficial to us," said one aide familiar with the rationale for pulling back on television spending.

The anxiety over money had driven so many decisions, including tailoring primary campaigns to win just enough votes and delegates for Hillary to take a commanding lead without spending extra to convert Bernie supporters and undecided voters. Mook's plan for the primaries had worked. Hillary won the nomination, and she did it even as Bernie raised more money than she did during a crucial period in the spring. But on another level, Bernie's resilience and his appeal to groups that didn't find Hillary inspiring—working-class whites and millennials—had damaged her badly. Had she fought harder for those voters, she might have dispatched Bernie earlier and saved herself some of the pain of a long, divisive primary. That, in essence, was what Bill Clinton and the older set within the campaign were arguing for during the early months: more contact with voters outside the demographic wheelhouse that created the safest path to winning the nomination.

During the primaries, Mook's obsession with efficiency had come at the cost of broad voter contact in states that would become important battlegrounds in the general election. It led him to send the Clintons to big cities, where black and Latino voters would produce major delegate hauls. Putting Hillary in Detroit, for example, was the most efficient way of building votes for the primary and the general election, but it meant that she wasn't in mostly white

Macomb County, just outside the city. "If you're a white voter in Macomb County, that means something," said one high-ranking campaign aide. Some of Hillary's top brass would eventually theorize that this was a major difference between Hillary and Obama: white voters punished her for running a campaign so focused on minority voters, whereas Obama was able to spend time in the white-heavy suburbs of major cities without alienating his African American base. Mook was giving up on persuading voters who weren't inclined to support Hillary because it was less efficient to go after them.

"It's hard if you try; it's even harder if you don't try," one senior aide said of the decision to forgo appearances in white suburbs. "This is where the analytics can mislead you."

A couple of weeks after that first phone call with Ruiz, Zelman sent word of even deeper cuts: the campaign wouldn't spend money on direct mail or digital advertising in Colorado. The former was one of the best ways to reach older voters, and digital was the key to a millennial constituency that didn't like Trump but was very open to voting for a third-party candidate. Taken together, the decisions to go without television, direct mail, or digital advertising amounted to a judgment from Brooklyn that the campaign should focus on turning out supporters rather than trying to persuade fence-sitters. Brooklyn had provided Ruiz with warm bodies—the Colorado field force would number 245—but how was she supposed to win without protection?

"You guys are sending me into war without armor," she complained.

At one level, as Mook understood, it was the job of a state director to ask for more resources and his role to allocate them with a view to the national playing field. But similar conversations were playing out across the dozen or so battlegrounds. Mook felt like he had a limited budget to play with, so it made sense to him to spend on the programs he thought were most efficient and in the states where the campaign needed the most firepower. Hillary was in better shape in Colorado than she was in other states; Ruiz would have to do without.

But the decision was deeply unsettling to her. It felt like Brooklyn was taking Colorado for granted, and she believed the race was too volatile for that. Whatever the analytics showed, Ruiz's political tuner told her that Trump was gaining ground on Hillary. That fear had actually heightened through August, just as the campaign's leadership was paring its operation. Hillary had spent $52 million on general-election TV ads, supplemented by another $37 million from supportive outside groups by August 9, according to Advertising Analytics. Trump hadn't paid for a single spot at that point. And while Hillary's postconvention rise in the polls had peaked at 7.9 points on that same day, she hadn't been able to shake her rival.

Now, just as she had extended her lead, it felt like Hillary was easing back. She was working the fund-raising circuit hard, but for the public—and for her own staffers in the states—she had all but vanished from view. And she had done so at precisely the moment that Trump was starting to rev his engine.

IT WASN'T JUST the crew in the states that questioned Mook's methods. In Brooklyn, Podesta had complained with increasing irritation over the course of the campaign that Mook wasn't sharing information with him. Podesta gravitated toward the older set of a generational divide within the campaign that thought the young campaign manager was too driven by data and ignored the advice he got from more experienced hands.

For his part, Mook thought Podesta only wanted to deal with issues that interested him and couldn't be nailed down to sign off on strategic or tactical decisions. Podesta, whose temper had earned him the alter-ego nickname "Skippy" during Bill Clinton's presidency, would rant and call Mook names—and, to his credit, he did it to Mook's face. The campaign chairman, ostensibly the steady guiding hand, created the old-school drama that Mook had been instructed to eradicate from Hillary's operation. In short, Mook thought Podesta was a dick.

It was all terribly confusing for their lieutenants, who couldn't figure out which man's orders to follow—or, in some cases, picked the instructions they preferred. Hillary had heard the complaints, and she had added Minyon Moore to the mix in the spring in part to break up some of the silos. The Super Six construct had eased some of the tension—but not all of it. The decision-by-committee approach only worked if all the issues facing the campaign were aired and discussed openly by the group, and Mook, who had adroitly managed Hillary in sidelining rivals and putting on a show of hiring more field organizers during the primaries, continued to guard potentially negative information from colleagues who felt a responsibility to act as a check on his decisions.

"Robby's a person whose style was to try to work out a solution to the problem before he says there is a problem," said one highly placed official.

Back in June, at a senior staff retreat in upstate New York, Mook gave a presentation intended to make it clear to everyone who was responsible for what and how the campaign leadership could operate more smoothly. He asked for commitments that meetings would start on time, that everyone would show up promptly, and that there would be a clear purpose for each meeting. For those who knew the precisionist Mook well, these weren't unreasonable or surprising requests. On previous campaigns, he'd run meetings with a whiteboard at his fingertips and was "absolutely anal about every meeting ending with action items," as Michael Halle, who would go on to serve as Hillary's director of battleground analytics and strategy, put it in a 2014 profile of Mook.

When it was Podesta's turn to talk, he cut to the chase.

"Robby is passive-aggressive," he said in front of Mook and everyone on the campaign's leadership team. "I'm merely aggressive."

That Podesta felt that way was not a surprise, nor was he alone. Mook's tight control over information infuriated other senior campaign officials. That Podesta would voice those frustrations so boldly and unapologetically in a room full of top aides was stunning—even more so was the fact that the fight didn't leak to the press.

"It is a testament to how much people really sincerely loved and cared about Hillary that a lot of this was not made public," said one person who watched the exchange and thought Podesta was right about Mook. "There were a lot of issues and challenges and frustrations that weren't aired out of loyalty to her, and that benefited him."

The relationship between Hillary's baby-boomer chairman and her millennial-style manager would remain fraught throughout the campaign. It mattered because Podesta didn't always have a window into the strategy and tactics guiding Mook's decisions. The campaign chairman, who should have been in a position to raise red flags, didn't feel like he had enough information to do that.

The practical implications of the dysfunction at the top of the campaign were felt throughout the ranks. Because she couldn't risk alienating Bernie's voters, Hillary had waited as long as possible to start running her general-election campaign. For veterans of Obama's 2012 campaign, the calendar was condensed. "We had to put together a massive national organization, and we had to do it in three or four months between June and Labor Day," said one Brooklyn official who noted that the internal power tussle complicated those efforts. "It was a campaign in which no one ever had full authority on anything. So in order to implement something, it required getting the buy-in from multiple people." The delays compounded the challenge presented by building all of those state-level organizations at once, and Mook's strategy called for playing in every competitive state and trying to create opportunities where they hadn't existed before.

One aide described the way Brooklyn looked at acquiring the 270 electoral votes needed to win this way: "Put as many options as possible on the table. If something does go wrong, we want to be competitive in a lot of places."

As far back as December 2015, when he disagreed with Jen

O'Malley Dillon over the strategy for the general election, Mook had identified nine traditional battleground states and six "watch" states—Michigan, Wisconsin, Minnesota, Oregon, Maine, and New Mexico—that leaned Democratic but that the campaign should keep its eye on. By August, Mook, Marshall, and battleground states director Meg Ansara were starting to look at the map, and the allocation of resources, differently. The analytics suggested Hillary wasn't likely to win in Ohio or Iowa, but the imperative to avoid signaling this to the press and the public drove some of the decision making. That is, they kept real campaigns going in those states just to keep up the appearance that they were competitive.

"If we had pulled back in Ohio or Iowa in August," the official said, "we would have been killed on that. So, I think the decisions we were facing, maybe we should have. But, at the time, with the information we had, it was the right decision."

Ohio and Iowa would have been delicious cherries on top of a victory sundae, but in Kriegel's rank order of states necessary for Hillary to hit the magic number of 270, they were just that. Throughout the campaign, and in a variety of iterations and combinations, Mook identified three keystone states that would pave the path for Hillary's victory: Pennsylvania, Florida, and North Carolina. "What analytics did for us is give us the path of least resistance. It told us what the most likely scenarios were for winning and losing," said one Mook ally. "We knew path one was Florida, path two was Pennsylvania and the Midwest. Path three was North Carolina and New Hampshire and Nevada." All of those scenarios assumed Hillary would win the Big Ten states of Michigan and Wisconsin.

On the other side, Trump was focused intently on a Rust Belt strategy that would drive into Democratic-leaning territory. (While Florida and North Carolina are outside that region, he would also need them to win.) As Trump would later confide to a top Democratic official soon after the election, he targeted the upper Midwest in the general election because he saw "the hostility" there.

While Hillary was out raising money in the summer enclaves of the rich and powerful, Trump was serving up red meat to angry voters across the country. At the same time, Brooklyn was fighting over lines of authority and Hillary's state directors were begging for relief from the diktats of analytics.

AS SHE BEGAN speaking at a Labor Day rally in Cleveland on September 5, Hillary suffered through an epic coughing fit. She had been having such episodes for weeks, but she tried to laugh it off. "Every time I think about Trump, I get allergic," she joked to the crowd. But there was a more serious political dynamic at play. While she had been raising money in August, Trump had attacked her for not having the "mental and physical stamina" for the presidency. Some of her allies thought it was a sexist line of argument. As a woman, she wasn't tough enough to hack it, he seemed to be saying. And yet Obama had worried that she was pushing herself too hard when he'd seen her at the convention.

Either way, her struggle to get through the Cleveland speech played right into Trump's hands. The coughing fit happened at an inauspicious moment for Hillary. For most of the campaign, she had assiduously avoided direct encounters with the national media, going so far as to have aides move a rope to wall them off from her while she walked in a New Hampshire Fourth of July parade in 2015. Labor Day 2016 was the first time her traveling press corps was allowed to fly on her plane. When she went back to chat with them after the Cleveland rally, she was overcome with another coughing fit. Once she recovered, she was, of course, asked whether there was anything to Republican claims that her health had faltered. "I'm not concerned about the conspiracy theories," she said. "I pay no attention to them."

But this wasn't a conspiracy theory. Even some of her staff members wondered what was wrong with her. One aide who had traveled with her over the previous several weeks could tell that Hillary was fighting an illness. *This woman is coughing a lot,* the aide thought. *Clearly, she needs antibiotics.* But the aide didn't raise any concerns.

Not only was Hillary feeling run-down, but Trump had virtually eclipsed her for a month, combining the free media tools he'd used so well in the primaries—Twitter and big, nationally televised rallies—with a new advertising blitz. Over the course of less than four weeks, he slashed her 7.9-point postconvention advantage to 3.2 points nationally. She was sucking wind politically, and both her political standing and her physical standing were about to take much bigger hits.

The former came first, at an LGBT gala for the Hillary Victory Fund in New York on Friday, September 9. For a couple of weeks, Hillary had been sharpening her rhetoric against not just Trump but his supporters. Megan Rooney, a talented young speechwriter who had been with her at State and had penned speeches for Obama in the White House, provided the prose that sought to frame Trump as the leader of a movement far outside the mainstream of American politics. In late August, in one of her few notable public appearances, Hillary had gone off on the "alt-right," a group of largely white nationalist conservatives who gravitated to the Breitbart website long run by the new CEO of Trump's campaign, Steve Bannon.

It was an escalation from a similarly pugnacious speech, also written by Rooney, that Hillary had given toward the end of the primaries in which she had portrayed Trump as temperamentally unfit for the presidency. Back then, her policy and speechwriting team felt that they had solved a puzzle that had bedeviled the GOP field. They would use Trump's words—and those of his top allies—to show that he shouldn't be commander in chief. At the beginning of that speechwriting process, Rooney had started with a contrast about Hillary's values and working with allies. But Jim Steinberg, who had served as a deputy secretary of state under Hillary and who was advising her policy team, said Rooney was looking at it wrong. It was true that Trump said a lot of things that would upend traditional establishment foreign policy thinking—he wanted to abolish NATO, talked about keeping nuclear war on the table, and had a soft spot for Russian president Vladimir Putin, among other things—but Steinberg said the main focus should be on Trump being erratic. Everything else, he argued, was less important. The speech had been extremely well received by a Democratic Party establishment that was anxious to see Hillary prove that she could be tough on Trump at the end of a brutal primary with Bernie Sanders.

The alt-right speech pushed past Trump and into the guts of his movement. The plain aim was to convince the establishment Republicans who had opposed Trump in his primary that backing him now would put them on the side of the bigots at the fringe of their party. She read off a series of headlines from Breitbart News, including "Would You Rather Your Child Had Feminism or Cancer?" and "Hoist It High and Proud: The Confederate Flag Proclaims a Glorious Heritage."

"This is not conservatism as we have known it," said Hillary, who had been a conservative supporter of Barry Goldwater as a high school student in 1964. "This is not Republicanism as we have known it. These are race-baiting ideas, anti-Muslim and anti-immigrant ideas, anti-woman—all key tenets making up an emerging racist ideology known as the 'Alt-Right.'"

In private, she would go further, referring to Trump's most ardent backers as "deplorables." All the while, she maintained in public, as she did in the alt-right speech, that she wanted to be a president for all Americans. Her private thoughts collided with her public statements—and her rhetoric about being a president for everyone with her chatter about the deplorability of Trump activists—at the LGBT Victory Fund gala. Unaware that the media had been brought in to cover her remarks—she'd grown accustomed to fund-raising events that were closed to the press—she opened up on Trump's backers.

"You know, to just be grossly generalistic, you could put half of Trump's supporters into what I call the basket of deplorables," she said. "Right? The racist, sexist, homophobic, xenophobic, Islamophobic—you name it. And unfortunately there are people like that." She added that they were "irredeemable."

The reaction to her remarks, so starkly at odds with her "Stronger Together" slogan, was swift and severe. That night, conservatives began using #basketofdeplorables to rally critics of Hillary, and Republican vice presidential nominee Mike Pence said at a conference in Washington the next day that Americans "are not a 'basket' of anything."

Hillary's traveling spokesman, Nick Merrill, initially tried to play down the remarks as part of the larger argument she'd been making about Trump's giving voice to bigots. But as night turned to morning, Hillary's advisers decided they needed a better plan—and quick. On an early Saturday morning conference call, they discussed whether and how Hillary should walk it back. The group decided to put out a half-apology immediately.

"Last night I was 'grossly generalistic,' and that's never a good idea," Hillary said in a statement. "I regret saying 'half'—that was wrong."

For a campaign staff that sometimes deliberated over the content of tweets for hours on end, the speedy resolution was a moment of clarity and alacrity. One Clinton aide later said the snappy decision making was "one of our finest moments internally."

But others thought it didn't do enough to limit the damage Hillary had done to herself. They knew they were witnessing their first unforced error of the fall. And it was ugly. "It was like, 'Oh my God,'" one campaign staffer said of his reaction to her original comment. "She didn't have the feel, the empathy."

Hillary had become the 2016 cycle's Mitt Romney. Back in 2012, he'd been caught on tape saying that he didn't worry about the "47 percent" of Americans who depended on government and that he would "never convince them they should take personal responsibility and care for their lives." Romney's cavalier commentary on such a large portion of the American electorate had cast him as out of touch with regular folks, including many Republicans and independents who benefited from direct government assistance. For all the messaging she'd done on inclusiveness, she now sounded like not only an elite but an elitist. If nothing else, she'd energized an already active Trump base. And still, things were about to get worse.

▼

EARLIER THAT DAY, Hillary's doctor had diagnosed her with pneumonia, which explained her cough. But most of the leadership of her campaign was kept in the dark about it. Of the Super Six, only Abedin knew. As a result, the media wasn't informed about a significant change in the Democratic presidential nominee's health, an omission that would be costly. Hillary had been advised by her doctor to take it easy, but she participated, without incident, in a debate-prep session in Westchester the next day and insisted on attending a September 11 memorial service in Manhattan that Sunday. She had represented the state in the Senate during and after the terrorist assault that felled the Twin Towers and killed nearly three thousand of her fellow New Yorkers in 2001. She was particularly proud of the work she'd done to win federal funding to benefit first responders.

During the service, Hillary began to feel overheated and faint. She walked away from the event and toward a waiting van with the assistance of an aide. As she moved to get into the van, her body pitched and slumped. She was dragged the last couple of feet into the vehicle, with her feet scraping across the curb. Her campaign initially said nothing and didn't even alert her traveling press pool of reporters that she would be leaving early.

The media learned of Hillary's departure when video of her being hoisted into the van surfaced online. For the next couple of hours, in the absence of any clarifying information from the campaign, media outlets played the video over and over, and pundits both professional and amateur speculated on social media about whether she was suffering from a serious health problem. Kaine e-mailed to check on her soon after the video began playing on television and she responded that she was fine. He hadn't been told of the pneumonia diagnosis either.

Between Trump suggesting she didn't have the "stamina" to be president, Karl Rove saying she might have suffered brain damage in a 2012 fall at her home, and the coughing fits, the stage had been set for full-on media and public speculation about whether there was something physically wrong with her. Many of her aides were scrambling to find out what was going on.

Part of the reason it took so long for Hillary's team to put out a statement is that Abedin hadn't shared the pneumonia diagnosis with any of her colleagues in Brooklyn. Such behavior wasn't unusual. Not only did Huma keep a tight lid on Hillary's schedule, shielding certain meetings from even the most senior aides on the campaign, she also acted as a lockbox for personal information about Hillary. That left the campaign without credible information to pass on to the press about what had happened.

"Palmieri was pissed that they're misleading the press because Huma hadn't even told people Hillary was sick," one top campaign official recalled. "It's just a Huma disaster." Those were piling up quickly.

Podesta was just returning to New York when his phone started buzzing. From his cell, he jumped into the fray with the Brooklyn team to start making decisions. The first was trying to figure out what information the campaign could put out from her doctor to quell the gathering media firestorm. They also discussed whether Hillary would have to come off the campaign trail—and determined that she did.

While these discussions played out, Mook and others grew deeply frustrated with news outlets that let speculation run rampant and then essentially blamed the campaign for failing to put an end to it with a quick and believable statement. "It's a perfect example of the media always taking something to its absolute worst conclusion, and then it's incumbent on us to roll it back," said one Hillary aide. "Then, what was insult to injury on this one was blaming us, like 'Well, you didn't tell us.'"

As it turned out, Hillary was fine to continue campaigning—after a brief period of rest—but she'd created questions about her physical fitness for the office. More important, she'd reinforced the public perception that she was always hiding something. She was so secretive that even her own campaign team didn't know when she was sick.

Between the "deplorables" remark and the health scare, Hillary looked off her game just as she was starting the final sprint to the presidency. In the days after the pneumonia incident, the remainder of Hillary's lead over Trump would evaporate. On September 18, Trump climbed to within nine-tenths of a point of Hillary in the average of polls, which typically reflected the snapshot of the horse race from a few days earlier. Neither being ill nor covering it up would help her with the millennial voters who didn't trust her, didn't like Trump, and were increasingly looking to third-party candidates.

TO COURT THE younger set, Hillary turned to an old rival who had inflicted great damage on her campaign: Bernie Sanders.

In late September, Clinton consultants Jim Margolis and Mandy Grunwald reached out to their Sanders camp counterparts, Tad Devine and Mark Longabaugh, to ask for Bernie's time and to share the script of an ad they hoped he would cut for Hillary. Devine talked to Bernie—who was happy to keep his promise to do whatever he could to help Hillary—and hightailed it to Burlington, where he would meet up with the Vermont senator and Jeff Weaver. Devine was waiting when Bernie turned the corner in a little Chevy, a startling change from the days when he'd been carted around in SUVs surrounded by Secret Service. Everything had returned to normal.

Once inside, Bernie and Devine went through a routine that had become familiar over the years. Bernie, wearing a blue dress shirt, open at the collar, sat down in a chair in the living room, in front of a brown leather couch and a sun-filled window. As Devine filmed, Bernie stopped from time to time to rewrite the script in his own voice. He was OK with the main thrust of the spot. He would say Hillary was good on education, health care, and the minimum wage and that Trump was wrong on climate change and the economy. No big deal.

But the final words on the page—"I'm with her"—were too much. Bernie couldn't bring himself to say them.

"It's so phony!" he griped. "I don't want to say that."

So he didn't. But he did do a bunch of different takes, not just on the main spot but on more narrow topics that could be used for digital advertising. In one, Bernie made the case against a vote for Libertarian presidential nominee Gary Johnson, who was an attractive alternative for many voters who couldn't stomach Hillary or Trump. Devine sent the film to Hillary's consultants. They sat on it for a couple of weeks before coming back with a request to make a few changes—a minimum wage graph should only go up to $12 an hour, not $15 an hour, and the like—and Bernie's team executed.

Another couple of weeks passed before Margolis delivered some bad news to Devine. Hillary's campaign wasn't going to use the ad at all. Her consultants had asked voters what they thought of Bernie's ad. Voters liked it, Margolis explained, but some of them raised doubts about whether Bernie fully supported Hillary. That wasn't shocking, Devine thought, because undecided voters who make it into focus groups so late in a campaign are generally pretty skeptical of politicians. Why else would they be undecided in October of an election year? He understood that there were a lot of cooks in the kitchen of Hillary's campaign and that the data drove a lot of the decision making. But still, killing an ad with Bernie endorsing Hillary, at a time when she was struggling to energize his base, was a real head-scratcher.

"It could have been really helpful to her," said one person who saw it.

But Bernie had hammered Hillary so hard during the primary that validating her now strained his credibility more than it strengthened hers. "People felt that it was him delivering his message, not Hillary's," said one Hillary aide familiar with focus group responses. "People didn't feel that it was an authentic pitch for her and what she wanted to do. It even had some backlash in folks saying that he's not really supporting her."

He'd called her corrupt. He'd called her dishonest. He had played to voters' worst fears about her and laid the groundwork for Trump to cement them. Neither side had any incentive to admit it, but Bernie never would have gotten off the ground if there wasn't significant antipathy toward Hillary Clinton within the Democratic Party. He might be able to persuade supporters who simply preferred him to back Hillary, but good luck with the people who hated her more than they liked him. Brooklyn nixed the idea of putting the ad on broadcast television but did use some of the shorter takes Devine had filmed for digital ads targeted to particular voters.

With Trump having closed the gap in polling, and Hillary coming off her health scare, many Democrats were worried that she might fade at the end of the campaign. But not everyone in the party was so discomfited. On September 21, Obama sat down with Robert Wolf, his longtime friend and donor, at the Plaza Hotel in Manhattan. The president was about to give a speech to the U.S.-Africa Business Forum, but Wolf wanted to get his sense of domestic politics.

"What are you thinking about the secretary?" Wolf asked.

"You know, she's going to be OK," Obama replied with typical reserve. "Don't worry."

But the answer didn't satisfy. Wolf stared at Obama for a moment. "I want you to look me in the eye," the financier said. Obama locked onto Wolf.

"She's got this," the president said.

Chapter 17

"DEMEANOR IS THE DEBATE"

ILLARY FOLDED HER ARMS ACROSS THE FRONT OF HER olive suit jacket. Her jaw set, her lips pursed. The swaying of her body—*left ... right ... left ... right*—betrayed growing irritation. Behind thick-framed black glasses, she squinted in disbelief across the debate stage at her opponent.

"Donald's plan to round up sixteen million people with a deportation force is wrong," she declared. "We have limited resources. We should use them on the people who are really dangerous, who threaten our safety, not on families—law-abiding people contributing to their communities ..."

"Like the thousand people that should be deported that you just gave citizenship to?" her rival crowed.

The moderator bailed her out: "Let's stop there."

"He is so annoying," Hillary fumed. "Just unbelievably annoying. God, so annoying!"

It wasn't clear to the small audience watching this practice session in a conference room at the Doral Arrowwood in White Plains, New York, on Saturday, October 15, whether she meant Trump or the man who was playing him, Philippe Reines. At this point, days before the third and final presidential debate, the personality didn't matter as much as what was really unsettling her. Trump's arguments on issues at the heart of his candidacy—jobs, immigration, and trade—packed more punch than Hillary's. His words were tough, and his ideas were easy to grasp. Hers were neither. That's what truly annoyed her. She was highly vulnerable to a disciplined version of Trump—one who pounded her on substance without taking her bait—even after she'd demolished the Republican nominee in two previous battles.

Ever since 1960, when a calm but energetic John F. Kennedy was more appealing to voters than the wan, sweaty Richard Nixon, presidential debates had held a special appeal in American politics. They were the only chance for voters to see the candidates engage in one-on-one political combat, providing an important window into how their respective arguments stood up under direct criticism and how they handled themselves under pressure. One of the debates—or even just a single moment—had the power to make or break a candidate: Ronald Reagan questioning Jimmy Carter's hallmark honesty with the line "There you go again" in 1980 or George H. W. Bush absentmindedly looking at his watch during a debate with Bill Clinton in 1992, for example.

Hillary absolutely hated the very idea that voters' decisions could come down to a zinger or a gaffe rather than a candidate's record, platform, or character. But she accepted the conventional wisdom that she could win or lose the presidency based on her performances against Trump—a rival who thrived on getting under the skin of an opponent. And what Reines found, as he practiced against her, round after round, is that Hillary's heavily nuanced policy arguments were boring and easy to pick apart with a sharp retort. Her strength and her weakness were one and the same: she mastered so much material.

"As the guy who would kick her ass over and over again," it was obvious to Reines that Trump's messaging was better, said a source with singular knowledge of his thinking.

LIKE TRUMP, REINES had a well-earned reputation for crossing lines of civility—even with his own colleagues. He was even more aggressive with reporters, having famously e-mailed BuzzFeed's

Michael Hastings with the sign-off "Have a good day. And by good day, I mean Fuck Off." His shtick was a mismatch for this new, no-drama-mantra version of Hillaryland. But Rooney, the campaign speechwriter who had first suggested he play the Donald stand-in toward the end of the primary season, thought it might be perfectly suited to this task.

In a Clinton operation full of supplicating sycophants, Reines knew how to get in Hillary's face—metaphorically and literally. He'd survived in her orbit in part because he was willing to make her uncomfortable. If she'd thought about firing him once, she'd thought about it a thousand times, and still he maintained a direct line to her and influenced her thinking about public relations strategy as much as, if not more than, anyone else. Like so many of the friends and allies Hillary had assembled over the years, Reines had attributes that made him very useful at particular times and in certain situations. Mostly, it worked to Reines's advantage that no one else had a brilliant thought on who could portray the billionaire in a way that would actually prepare Hillary for him. Hillary had been looking for a place to put Benenson, and his name surfaced in the discussions. Jennifer Palmieri thought Anthony Weiner might be able to pull it off, but, for obvious reasons, no one else thought that was a very good idea. Sullivan championed Reines, and, over the course of June and July, he normalized the idea within the upper ranks of the campaign before taking it to Hillary. She signed off with minimal hesitation.

In an e-mail sent the first Monday in August, Sullivan told Hillary's longtime spokesman he'd gotten the role. But a follow-up message contained an unambiguous admonishment: You've got to take this seriously. You've got to get it right. Reines understood that it wasn't just important that he nail the part but that he convince those on the campaign who doubted his maturity that he was taking it seriously. That was no small feat. After all, Trump himself couldn't be trusted to act like an adult in a debate. The line between accurately portraying Trump and behaving like a buffoon was particularly fine. Karen Dunn and Ron Klain, who ran debate-prep sessions for

Hillary, made that point on a conference call with Reines the next day. Klain, who had reservations about the campaign's most important impersonator, stressed that Trump, contrary to popular opinion, had actually put forth a lot of policy ideas. To play him right, Reines would have to study not just Trump's mannerisms but his platform and his style of thinking. Got it, Reines assured Klain, "I understand this is not a *Saturday Night Live* character imitation." Then he went to work on becoming Trump.

First stop: the men's department at Nordstrom. "I need to look like Donald Trump," he told his suit guy. "But not like Halloween." A week later, he'd have a slightly baggy blue suit with high cuffs—just like the Donald's. He ordered dress shoes with three-and-a-quarter-inch lifts, a backboard for his posture, and knee braces to combat his tendency to sway. He concluded that acquiring Trump's carrot skin tone would be too much of a distraction—but only after covering half his face in self-tanner one day to try it out. He bought Trump cuff links on Amazon and a Trump watch on eBay—for about $175. Reines even shelled out money for four podiums—two apiece for his apartment and an office at Clinton campaign lawyer Marc Elias's firm so that he could do mock debate sessions with friends before he faced off with Hillary. And then there was the "shackle." Worried about leaving his supersecret prep materials in an Uber, Reines bought a heavy-duty tether so that he could lock his briefcase to his wrist. He actually acquired two different versions—one of which was originally designed for bondage enthusiasts.

On the final day of August, Dunn and Klain convened a special Trump unit in midtown Manhattan. The space, where Hillary had held her prelaunch campaign discussions, functioned like a shadow headquarters, often reserved for sensitive projects. Getting ready for Trump and bringing Reines into a major role on the campaign both qualified.

Inside the lone conference room of a white-walls-and-glass-doors office that featured dramatic views of Times Square, Dunn, Klain, Reines, and Bob Barnett went to work on getting inside Trump's thinking. They were joined by two special guests: Tony

Schwartz, who had written Trump's bestselling book *The Art of the Deal,* and financier Robert Wolf.

As far back as March, with Trump starting to pull away from the Republican field, Wolf had suggested to Hillary that she bring in a few folks from the business community to help prepare her for Trump. He thought she'd benefit from understanding how the approach of a deal maker would differ from that of a politician, and he was volunteering for duty. She responded quickly and in the affirmative.

Over the course of three hours, Schwartz took the lead on the ins and outs of Trump's personality while Wolf painted the picture of a businessman turned presidential debater. How would Trump turn his own negatives into her weaknesses? What would he say to shift the back-and-forth of policy contrasts into a negotiation? How would he frame his lines of attack on infrastructure, Brexit, China, government regulation, and wages?

Reines, Dunn, Klain, and Bob Barnett, the Washington superlawyer and Hillary's agent, peppered Wolf and Schwartz with questions about the biggest wild card in American political history. As Reines listened, his confidence grew. These specialists didn't know more about Trump's policies and tendencies than he did after having watched each of the Republican primary debates repeatedly; they knew less. *I've got this down,* he thought. As they walked out of the conference room, Reines turned to Klain and Dunn. "I want to do this right now," he said, brimming with brio. "Get HRC."

Hillary had been in training too.

Since the primaries, her debate-prep show had been run by Dunn and Klain. Hillary felt comfortable taking direction from the straight-talking Dunn, a petite brunette with shoulder-length curls. The younger woman, once described as a "mini Hillary," was "emotionally comforting" to the candidate, said one person who participated in the sessions. She was considered a top contender for the post of White House counsel if Hillary won the presidency; Klain got frequent mention for that job and chief of staff. Together, Klain and Dunn had developed a debate-prep method that was widely viewed as the gold standard in Democratic circles. They had served in the same roles for President Obama's 2012 reelection effort.

Shortly after the Democratic convention, Klain, Dunn, and Sullivan—who technically oversaw them and who could translate answers into Hillary-speak—had traveled to the candidate's home in Chappaqua. Sitting in the living room of Hillary's carriage house, they went over the early version of a briefing book containing all the policies and political issues she would have to know cold by the time of the first go-round with Trump. This was the easy part for Hillary. Studying a briefing book, boning up on the issues—that was in Hillary's comfort zone. Public performance was always harder for her. But matching up against Trump presented a challenge far different from anything she'd experienced before on a debate stage. After all, his whole campaign was predicated on the idea that he wasn't a typical politician. For better and worse, he didn't debate like an experienced candidate. That's where Reines would come in. Her team could be sure that he would say outlandish and salacious things, yell, and point his finger to try to rattle Hillary. Her job would be to deliver her punches and deflect his attacks without losing her composure.

Hillary was painfully aware of the tightropes she'd have to walk, the same ones women in politics and business always had to tread with extreme caution. She'd have to be confident without appearing arrogant, defensive without being accusatory, and assertive without looking like a bitch. But in prep sessions dating back to the primaries, her voice, her body language, and her facial expressions often betrayed the traits she wanted to avoid in prime time.

Dunn was so conscious of the damage that could be done with one bad look or one sarcastic remark that she devised a mantra for Hillary: "Demeanor is the debate." Not only did Dunn say it, but it was featured on special one-sheet "debate on a page" memos that she and Klain gave Hillary on the day of each of the primary and general-election debates.

"Happy to be there! Smiling! Never rattled! You look great!" they wrote in one of them under the "Don't forget" category. "Tone, tone, tone," they put at the top of another cheat sheet.

They also included coaching on which topics Hillary should hit her opponent with, how to frame particular arguments, and reminders of what she was fighting for—"Women, Children, Families, Middle-Class, People Knocked Down"—and what she was fighting against, including drug, insurance, and oil companies, "reckless CEOs," and a deck stacked against most Americans. Even when she'd squared off against Sanders, her script called for taking shots at Trump. "Bigotry, bluster, bullying," one talking point reminded. "I was the first to stand up to him in this race." Another called for her to say "I'm the ONLY candidate with more votes than Trump."

But style mattered most. Hillary knew she could easily turn off voters if she didn't get that right because, as one person who knows her well put it, she was accustomed to being "a woman who is scored according to how much she's smiling and what her tone is."

Against Trump, her temperament would be all the more important because it would serve as a metaphor for the contrast at the heart of her main argument against him: she was steady, and he was dangerous. If she could keep her cool and get under his skin, she would reinforce that narrative. On the other hand, she could undermine her most potent weapon if she appeared rattled by him, or even if he could match her calm and discipline.

Moreover, Hillary's team believed Trump would come in with such low expectations that his performance would be considered a success if he didn't drool on his shoes. On the other hand, Hillary was supposed to shine in a format that rewarded preparation, quick recall of facts, and the ability to focus on both the answers at hand and an overall strategy. In other words, the bar was low for him and high for her.

The number one rule for any debate-prep team is to make sure the candidate isn't hearing, seeing, or feeling anything for the first time when he or she steps into the ring with an opponent. Because Trump was liable to say or do just about anything, that was an even bigger focus for Hillary's aides. Klain and Dunn had curated a database of all the questions that had ever been asked in general-election debates. "I don't think she heard any questions for the first time," said one participant who noted that a question Klain asked behind closed doors about a possible no-fly zone over Syria was repeated almost verbatim by moderator Chris Wallace in the third debate.

The trickier piece—and this is where Reines's obsessiveness came in—was predicting the ways in which Trump's behavior could throw Hillary off her game.

During one session at Hillary's debate-prep nerve center inside the Doral Arrowwood, Reines casually put his fingers on the neck of his microphone while Hillary was practicing hitting Trump on failing to pay contractors. The habit, one he'd picked up by watching countless hours of Trump's primary debates, produced audio feedback. Hillary kept talking. But Reines broke in. "This mic's not working," he said. "If the mic's not working, I don't pay the guy." With one quick and odd interjection, he'd given a succinct explanation of why Trump might have good reason to stiff a contractor. Reines didn't pull it out of the sky. At a rally in January, Trump had digressed from a speech to complain about the person responsible for the sound system. "Don't pay the son of a bitch," he'd said.

No detail was too small for Reines. He spent an entire day simply ignoring Hillary—even when she encouraged him to eat during a lunch break—and, during sessions, he stared at an X he'd put on one wall so that he wouldn't make eye contact with her or Klain, who played the moderator. Two days before the September 26 opening debate, Reines raised a concern. He thought Hillary should practice the traditional predebate handshake with Trump because it could be a tense moment. Trump could use his physical size to get in her space and intimidate her, maybe not even out of malice, but just out of sheer awkwardness. Trump might even try to kiss her. So at nine o'clock that night—full mocks started at the same time as real debates—Klain introduced Hillary Rodham Clinton and Donald J. Trump. As they crossed the prep stage, Reines made a beeline for Hillary with both arms extended in front of him like Frankenstein's monster. He was going in for a hug. Hillary wasn't having it. She ducked under one of his arms, a quarterback evading an oncoming pass rusher. Reines pursued, wrapping her up as she laughed at him.

Through serious drills and the occasional moments of levity, Hillary's team had prepared her for everything she might encounter from Trump. But neither her mastery of the subject matter nor her attention to deportment addressed the fact that Trump's positions—and his manner of articulating them—were often easier to grasp than hers.

"Some of his arguments were good," observed one of her aides. "Some of hers were not good."

At one point, there was a belief among Hillary's advisers that it made sense to go after Trump hard on finding a way to avoid paying income taxes. It only took about ten minutes of listening to Reines deflect questions to come to the conclusion that Hillary wasn't going to get a lot of traction from it.

Even when Trump was out of line with a majority of Americans on specific policy—say, building a wall on the US-Mexican border and banning Muslims from entering the country—his thrust of prioritizing the needs of American citizens first was clear. And he was good at turning his weaknesses into strengths with entertaining asides. When Hillary attacked on Trump's hiring of foreign workers at his resort Mar-a-Lago, Reines channeled him perfectly by talking about how hard it is to get people to work in the summer heat in Florida, arguing the first step in closing immigration loopholes is knowing where they are. "If you had seen debate prep, you would see why he was the nominee," said one person who was in the room. "You would not have said this woman is going to kick his ass."

During the private sessions, Hillary readied herself to defend against Trump's main attack lines—her health, conflicts of interest arising from the Clinton Foundation's work, and his call for her to be jailed, without charges or trial, for her e-mail scandal—and to go on offense. The latter part of her strategy revolved around driving home three main points: Trump was the poster boy for corporate insiders screwing the little guy, his temperament was ill suited to the Oval Office, and he was, in the words of one of her advisers, "a small-minded bigot."

Outside the retreat site, Hillary's postconvention bounce in the polls had eroded, washed away by her "deplorables" remark and her health scare. Trump taunted her from the campaign trail, contrasting her intense preparations with his seat-of-the-pants approach to training for the debates. He even rejected his advisers' entreaties to use a lectern in practice sessions so that he could get used to standing in place for an hour and a half.

Trump was right that Hillary obsessed over getting ready for a debate. "She had to understand everything about everything," said one of her advisers. "If it was policy, she had to understand the theory behind the policy. She needed to theorize everything to the ground. Everyone thinks she's scripted. But she goes deep on every topic." Her absorption of the material made her a better debater, but could leave her sounding wooden. Another aide said she had to work hard on turning specific questions into answers on larger themes or opportunities to go on offense. "The questions are supposed to be giving people a sense of how you think," this aide explained. "Her instinct is to answer the question very narrowly."

Those problems—her stiffness and her inability to reply to specific questions with thematic answers—were painfully obvious in the debate-prep sessions. Reines had been able to exploit them and outperform her. Heading into the first debate, held at Hofstra University on Long Island, Hillary and her team were nervous that Trump might do the same thing.

As she had done before facing Bernie Sanders in the primaries, Hillary huddled with Klain, Dunn, Sullivan, and Podesta before the debate. This time, she seemed on edge. There was so much riding on a curious, nationally televised piece of performance art. It was such a poor test, she thought, of which candidate would make a better president. Normally so stoic, she betrayed the butterflies in her stomach by nervously joking with her aides about the outsize significance the debates took on. They tried to reassure her. Have fun, they advised. The winner of the debate was usually the candidate who appeared to be enjoying the moment more.

By that measure, Trump was more prepared. In the predebate spin room, his advisers had a little hop in their step. Their guy was ascendant. They were loose, and confident that he could exceed expectations. Hillary's surrogates looked like they were walking in to take the SATs. Sure, they'd prepared, but they weren't at all certain of the outcome. And their futures all depended on a high score.

The big, gripping fear inside Hillary's camp was that, with her sliding and Trump rising in the polls, she would falter and he would do the heretofore unthinkable—waltz onto the debate stage, cool as a Klondike bar, and give the Oscar-worthy performance of a serious presidential candidate. Hillary's pregame jitters, and her penchant for slow starts, intensified the clenching of jaws as the two combatants took up positions behind their respective podiums.

A few minutes after 9 p.m., the concern turned to shock as Trump opened up with a calm, disciplined articulation of his plan to boost jobs, sprinkled with a toxic dose of Hillary as the status quo. This wasn't the P. T. Barnum version of Donald Trump; it was the Ronald Reagan version. When Hillary interjected with a canned line, "I call it Trumped-up, trickle-down," a collective groan echoed through the Democratic universe. Trump was fresh and on point. Hillary was a day-old bagel. He went in for the kill on trade, the issue that he hoped would deliver key Rust Belt states. "She's been doing this for 30 years," he charged. "And why hasn't she made the agreements better?" And he called out NAFTA, the pact so singularly associated with her husband. Hillary was in quicksand. "I will bring back jobs; you can't bring back jobs," Trump said. Clean, simple, to the point. Hillary countered with the mother of all establishment talking points: "independent experts" agreed with her. This was a debacle, an Opposite Day of a debate in which a commanding Trump had Hillary on her heels and backpedaling fast. Democrats furiously sent each other worried text messages and e-mails. Hillary had been in free fall before the debate and she was doing nothing to arrest it. Trump looked almost presidential. Would they look back at these early exchanges as the moment Trump won the White House?

But the feeling was different in Hillary's staff holding area, a hastily converted athletic training room complete with a full skeleton behind a blue curtain. Watching one of the TVs set up at the front of the long, narrow room, Dunn and Reines were picking up a different vibe. This Hillary was holding her ground and her cool better than the one they'd prepped. More important, they could detect a shift in Trump's demeanor. He'd entered the debate subdued. But Hillary had riled him twice already: first by pointing out he'd inherited his wealth and then by citing a tweet in which he'd called climate change a Chinese hoax. He really didn't like being quoted back to himself. They'd watched enough tape to know that. He was getting angrier, and that made him less disciplined. In an exchange over ISIS, he went to the well again on the attack that she'd been in Washington too long. You've spent your entire adult life fighting ISIS, he charged. The unpolitician was so married to his talking point, and so furious at Hillary, that he wasn't making sense. After that, Trump never regained control and Hillary never lost it.

But it wasn't until very late that she landed a prepackaged punch that would stagger Trump on the stage and ring in his head for several days thereafter. In gathering research on Trump, Dunn had read a story about the billionaire real-estate mogul tormenting a Miss Universe over her weight. At the time, in 1997, Trump co-owned the beauty pageant, and he didn't like that the reigning champ, Alicia Machado, had gained a few pounds. So he teased her, publicly, even inviting news crews to record her at a workout.

He called her "Miss Piggy" and "Miss Housekeeping"—a jab based on her Venezuelan heritage—according to Machado's account. Dunn was well aware of Trump's vile remarks about other women: "fat pigs," "dogs," "slobs," and "disgusting animals," as Fox's Megyn Kelly had reminded Trump during a GOP primary debate. *That's terrible,* Dunn thought when she'd read about Machado during an early research session, *just terrible.* So bad it was good. For most Americans, the introduction of Machado would be a new exhibit in Hillary's case that Trump was misogynistic, anti-Hispanic, and a bully. As Hillary had practiced recounting Machado's tale during one debate-prep session, Dunn had offered a suggestion. Not only should Hillary repeat Trump's sleazy sobriquets, but she should add a line at the end of her attack: "By the way, she has a name."

Before the real debate, Dunn had encouraged Hillary to keep her Machado attack ready for the right moment. "You've got to do this," the younger woman said, thinking it could provide a powerful illustration of Trump's character flaws. They both understood that the rhythm, flow, and topics of a debate didn't always lend themselves easily to the lines a candidate planned to deliver, even if Hillary was determined to get to Machado, as one aide put it, "come hell or high water."

As the debate wound down toward its final fifteen minutes, there still hadn't been a chance to bring up Machado. And then Trump got personal with Hillary.

"She doesn't have the look. She doesn't have the stamina," Trump said. "I don't believe she does have the stamina. To be president of this country, you need tremendous stamina." Debate moderator Lester Holt had asked Trump about something he'd said on the campaign trail—that Hillary didn't have the "presidential look"—and clearly wanted to know whether the Republican nominee was suggesting that a woman couldn't look like a president. Trump's transition to stamina sounded like a deft pivot from gender to Hillary's health—a reminder of her fainting episode just a couple of weeks earlier.

But Hillary, giving a knowing look, exploited an opening on his flank. "You know, he tried to switch from looks to stamina. But this is a man who has called women pigs, slobs and dogs," she said to introduce her memorized paragraph on Trump's remarks about the pageant winner. "Donald, she has a name," Hillary charged.

Suddenly, Trump was in a box. If he said her name, he'd acknowledge he knew what Hillary was talking about. If he refused, Hillary could hit him on that.

"Where did you find this?" Trump shouted. "Where did you find this?"

"Her name is Alicia Machado," Hillary said, with Trump trying to interrupt her. "And she has become a U.S. citizen, and you can bet she's going to vote this November."

Watching live in the debate hall, on screens in a room outside it, and in the Brooklyn headquarters, Hillary's allies were pumped up by the exchange. Those on her debate team had hoped Hillary would get the chance to bring up the Machado episode, but they had no idea exactly how hard the punch would land.

When Hillary arrived backstage, she was greeted with a chorus of huzzahs from her debate team. But it wasn't until Sullivan, the resident pessimist, gave his reserved assessment—"I think you won"—that the victory really sank in. In Brooklyn, the mood was a little more anxious. Her data-focused aides thought she'd done well, but this was the election season in which the insiders were almost always wrong about public sentiment. Time and again, Trump had looked buffoonish in primary debates and won over GOP voters. So, in Brooklyn, Hillary's aides waited for numbers from dial tests—real-time measurements of voters' reactions to the candidates—to assess how she'd done.

"It wasn't immediate," said one aide, who described a more gradual shift in the recognition that Hillary had stabilized a floundering campaign. "The mood within two or three hours after it was really ebullient."

There was no such hesitation in Washington Republican circles, where Trump had been seen as gaining steam before Hillary introduced Machado to the country. "At that particular point, we had the momentum," said one GOP official. In an instant, it was gone.

Trump's poor debate performance and Hillary's mastery immediately convinced the Washington establishment that a fundamental shift in the race had taken place. Hillary had looked presidential, and Trump had shown himself to be less than that. The debate had gone so badly for Trump that, as Reines had so presciently predicted in a prep session, he resorted to complaining about his microphone in the postgame spin room. "It was fine," he said of the debate.

Inside, he was furious. And, as was his wont, he focused intently on an opponent he felt he could defeat: Machado. As he had with Khizr Khan, he went after her with a fury. "She gained a massive amount of weight, and it was a real problem," he said on Fox the next morning.

In the hours after the debate, he demanded that his campaign and other Republicans go after Machado personally to undermine her credibility. On conference calls that week, Trump campaign CEO Steve Bannon shouted into the phone that the party needed to do more to defend the nominee and hammer the beauty pageant contestant. But few others in the GOP wanted to be associated with fat- and slut-shaming Machado.

"The Machado stuff was just unbelievable," said one source who listened in shock. "People are screaming on conference calls to engage on this stuff." On the other end of the line, Republican communicators cringed. It wasn't just bad political strategy in the traditional, establishment thinking to trash Machado—a repeat of Trump's distracting personal feuds with Judge Gonzalo Curiel, Khizr Khan, and Megyn Kelly, among others—but it was just plain distasteful.

For three days, with the Machado moment dominating political panels on cable news channels, Trump was forced to stew in the juices of his own failure. He'd had a chance, with Hillary cratering in the polls, to prove himself presidential. Instead, he'd looked sullen, and voters had been reminded of his mistreatment of women and Hispanics. He'd choked—like one of the "losers" he'd dispatched in the Republican primary. Unable to sleep—incapable of controlling his id—he tapped out a message on his Android phone shortly before 3:30 a.m. and hit the tweet button. Then he did it again and again.

"Wow, Crooked Hillary was duped and used by my worst Miss U. Hillary floated her as an 'angel' without checking her past, which is terrible!" he tweeted. "Using Alicia M in the debate as a paragon of virtue just shows that Crooked Hillary suffers from BAD JUDGEMENT! Hillary was set up by a con," he wrote in a second 140-character character attack. And, he wrote, "Did Crooked Hillary help disgusting (check out sex tape and past) Alicia M become a U.S. citizen so she could use her in the debate?" There wasn't really a sex tape, just a poorly lit scene from a Spanish-language reality TV show.

Trump's targeting of Machado's character only deepened the fast-developing conventional wisdom that he had imploded just as he had gotten within striking distance of Hillary. "I never thought it was going to be a week of that. I don't think anyone did," said one Hillary aide who had watched her test out the line in debate prep. "No one knew he'd attack her on Twitter at three thirty in the morning."

Trump's trip into quicksand wasn't just a matter of which candidate was reacting worse to the debate. The Brooklyn brain trust tracked his poll numbers as they slid that week, just as they had after Trump had attacked Khizr Khan.

Toward the end of the debate, Trump had left a few bread crumbs to signal where he'd be heading the next time they met, on October 9. "You want to know the truth?" he asked rhetorically. "I was going to say something extremely rough to Hillary, to her family, and I said to myself, 'I can't do it. I just can't do it. It's inappropriate. It's not nice.' But she spent hundreds of millions of dollars on negative ads on me, many of which are absolutely untrue. . . . It's not nice. And I don't deserve that."

It didn't take a veteran tea-leaf reader to know Trump was talking about attacking Bill over a series of allegations of sexual impropriety over the years. Now, cornered and flailing, that's exactly where he planned to land a punch.

Chapter 18

RED OCTOBER

A FEW MINUTES AFTER 2:30 P.M. ON FRIDAY, OCTOBER 7, the US intelligence community dropped a political bomb: the Russians were behind cyberattacks on the Democratic National Committee. In July, Robby Mook had alleged just that—and that the Russians were doing it to help Trump. The Republican nominee's response had been to publicly plead with Moscow to hack e-mails from Hillary's private server. "Russia, if you're listening, I hope you're able to find the 30,000 emails that are missing," he'd said at a news conference in Doral, Florida. In the same setting, he also said he wanted to "have Russia friendly" and indicated that he might accept Russia's annexation of Crimea—a move that had prompted the Obama administration to sanction individuals and institutions with close ties to President Vladimir Putin. The intelligence community report was a godsend—a piece of hard evidence upon which Hillary could start to really build the case that Trump was actually in league with Moscow.

Putin might not be a Communist anymore, but he was a Russian autocrat who came to power after a distinguished career in the KGB. This was the kind of spy-thriller shit that would surely break through in the press. If the public saw Trump putting Russian interests above American sovereignty, Hillary's aides thought, the story had the potential to break his back. After all, in the Red Scare days,

Republicans had portrayed liberal Democrats as un-American in unflinching terms.

Shortly after the news broke, Mook summoned Jake Sullivan, press secretary Brian Fallon, and a new addition to the team, public relations specialist Glen Caplin, to his office at the Brooklyn HQ. From there, they jumped on a conference call with aides who were working at a debate prep with Hillary in Westchester so they could formulate a response from John Podesta.

A few minutes after 4 p.m., as they batted around ideas for Podesta's statement—it would ultimately charge Trump with making "apologies for the Russians"—a loud commotion erupted outside Mook's office. Shortly thereafter, Christina Reynolds, the campaign's research director, interrupted the call to inform her colleagues of another explosion. The *Washington Post* had posted a video clip of Trump bragging that he liked to grab women "by the pussy." Mook didn't have a television set in his office because he found the constant humdrum of cable news distracting. But he craned to look through the glass wall at a TV propped atop a filing cabinet. The video clip, an outtake from an *Access Hollywood* taping in 2005, was being played over and over.

Neither Mook nor the rest of the campaign's top brass thought much of the video, which they hadn't yet experienced with the all-important audio. The Russian hacking story seemed like a much bigger deal. "The *Access Hollywood* tape didn't divert our attention away from what we were doing at that moment," said one person who was on the call.

"At the time, nobody really appreciated it," another source said. "We were convinced that the statement about the Russians was going to be the big deal that day."

On any normal day, one of these two stories that had broken within thirty minutes of each other would have been the most important news in the political realm. But October 7, 2016, was no normal day. It was the most unusual, portentous day of an incomprehensibly wild presidential election.

At 4:32 p.m., WikiLeaks, the online purveyor of hacked and stolen government documents, published the first batch in a series of e-mails pilfered from Podesta's Gmail account. WikiLeaks announced the release in a tweet that was quickly and widely picked up by major media outlets.

Bang-bang-bang: Three blockbusters, any one of which could alter the course of the campaign, pushed out in two hours. The first two seemed like sure winners for Hillary, but the WikiLeaking of Podesta's e-mails threatened to offset or even overwhelm them.

The Clinton campaign wasn't entirely surprised by the dumping of Podesta's private e-mails. After the DNC e-mails were first leaked in July and posted on a website called DC Leaks, Democrats had done a forensic analysis of the documents to determine whether it was possible that any of them had come from a source other than the national committee. They had identified at least one that plausibly could have come from the personal e-mail accounts of either Podesta or longtime Hillary confidante Capricia Marshall. The day before the Podesta dump, DC Leaks published some of Marshall's e-mails, none of which were particularly damning.

And, in an opinion piece about the Marshall e-mails on the morning of the seventh, the *New York Observer,* the news outlet owned by Trump's son-in-law, Jared Kushner, carried a harbinger for Hillary: "It's one of several releases from DC Leaks in the past few weeks, in addition to the documents released by WikiLeaks and Guccifer 2.0, with more expected in the coming few weeks leading up to election day." Guccifer 2.0 was the screen name of a source claiming to be a Romanian hacker. After the election, US intelligence agencies would conclude in an unclassified report that it was actually a persona created by Russian military intelligence hackers.

And despite their awareness that more hacked documents were coming, Clinton's aides didn't know that batches of Podesta's e-mails would be released day after day from October 7 until November 7, the last day before the election. Nor could they have imagined that the intelligence finding of Russian interference in the election would so quickly get drowned out by the combination of the Trump *Access Hollywood* video and the Podesta e-mails.

"Could you imagine a day so fucking crazy that no one gives a shit about this?" one aide said of the October 7 intelligence report. Suddenly, the upside-down dynamics of the 2016 election came into sharp relief. A Russian attempt to subvert American elections got buried under an avalanche of more titillating news. "That is the single most illustrative moment of what this campaign was," said another aide. "Here's something Donald Trump did and said and was arguably disqualifying to a lot of voters—something that could put the race away—but within moments, a factor related to e-mails comes around and puts the thumb on the other side of the scale."

At the time, though, Republicans were scrambling to deal with the fallout from the *Access Hollywood* video, which pushed even the e-mail story almost entirely out of the news cycle for the time being. Utah representative Jason Chaffetz, one of Hillary's most vocal Republican critics, withdrew his support for Trump immediately and several other lawmakers and Republican luminaries would follow suit as the story continued to dominate the cable networks over the weekend. "Donald Trump should not be president," former secretary of state Condoleezza Rice wrote on Facebook. "He should withdraw."

At the offices of the Republican National Committee in Washington that Friday afternoon, the Podesta e-mails were a lifeline. The Trump videotape was so compelling, "the silver bullet you never find" as one GOP official put it, that there was little anyone in the party could do to counter it. That is, until WikiLeaks posted Podesta's e-mails, which included the elusive transcript of Hillary's paid remarks to Goldman Sachs. Unlike a targeted leak, the nature of the WikiLeaks dump—two thousand private e-mails made available to all news outlets at once—meant that editors had to divert reporters to comb through them and find anything newsworthy. Once those resources were committed, the demand to publish something—and quickly—was high inside newsrooms across the country.

Although the Goldman Sachs transcript wasn't as flashy as the Trump video, the Podesta e-mails tied into several of Hillary's major vulnerabilities: in particular, opposition research the campaign had done on Bernie Sanders and Hillary's "dream" of "open trade and open borders."

Sanders had hammered her in the primary for refusing to release the transcript publicly. If she had nothing to hide—if she wasn't conspiring with Wall Street types to rig the system against the little guy—he argued, she would let everyone know just what she'd said. The issue spoke both to the question of whose interests Hillary represented and to her lack of transparency. Trump had been echoing Bernie's attacks on Hillary. So, while the transcript was fairly mundane, its very existence showcased the flaws Bernie had identified and Trump had exploited. Beyond that, the posting of Podesta's messages reminded voters of Hillary's e-mail scandal. In this case, as when the DNC's e-mails were hacked, she and the Democratic Party were the victims, not the perpetrators. But for many voters, the term "e-mail" had become shorthand for her untrustworthiness. And, ever since the primary, her "trust numbers were horrifying," said one source who had seen internal campaign focus group data.

The conflation of Hillary's private e-mail server issue with the cyberattacks on the DNC and Podesta would turn out to be a much greater threat than anyone on her team understood at the time. And Podesta's e-mails, in particular, would become the kind of slow-bleed story line that plagued her longer than the *Access Hollywood* video hobbled Trump. "It wasn't one big medical episode," one of Hillary's senior aides said. "It was a chronic disease."

Republicans weren't sure how much mileage they would get out of it either. But it was something to throw into the political ether to cloud the Trump video. "We just jumped on that, trying to get it into every story," the GOP official said.

Two days before the second presidential debate, and barely a month before the election, all Republicans could do was scrape Hillary while Trump gushed blood. Over the weekend, even after

Trump issued a semiapology for the video, there was serious talk in Republican circles about whether he could be replaced on the ballot. By Sunday, more than two dozen prominent Republicans, including several members of the Senate, had called on Trump to step aside and let Mike Pence lead the party into November. Trump surrogates quipped privately that there weren't many of them left in an already small campaign to defend their candidate. And the headlines were brutal: "Can Donald Trump Recover from This?" CNN asked. "Is Trump's Campaign Over?" a Politico headline blared. Days later, piling onto the lingering questions, the *New York Times* ran a story about how the Republican nominee had groped and kissed women against their will.

Saturday Night Live imagined Hillary reacting to the tape by throwing a party at her headquarters and guzzling champagne from a bottle as Kool and the Gang's "Celebration" played. It was ironic to the real staffers who at that late hour on a Saturday night were sitting at their headquarters desks, focused on the DNC and Podesta hacks. "That was not like a joyful day," one of them recalled. "We weren't like 'Yeaaaaahhhh!' People did their work."

That's how RNC officials treated the situation too—they put their heads down and tried not to get too caught up in the morale-busting moment. "I don't know how many people were optimistic about winning," the official said. "There was not a day in 2012 that was that bad."

Through it all, Trump managed to ride out the story lines that had labeled him a womanizer. After he was pummeled for days, a *Washington Post–ABC News* poll revealed that only 13 percent of Republicans and 38 percent of independents said they were less likely to vote for Trump because of the *Access Hollywood* video. The Republican nominee's campaign was discovering one hard fact, as campaign manager Kellyanne Conway would later put it: "There's a difference for voters between what offends you and what affects you."

That's why the most jarring and memorable video clip in modern campaign history—a tape that should have rattled the "family values"–minded Republican establishment to its core—couldn't put

Trump away. Early in the campaign, Trump had said he could stand in the middle of Fifth Avenue shooting people and not lose a vote. Maybe he was right. "You would think, in any other election, that would be the end of a candidate," said one veteran Hillary aide.

It was a terrifying realization, but one that had taken hold in Brooklyn long before that moment. If the rest of his antics and insults hadn't suppressed his base, this tape wasn't going to do it. "People already knew he was a womanizing piece of shit," a senior Clinton aide said. "It doesn't change the narrative."

THE MOST SPIRIT-CRUSHING job in modern political history—managing the Podesta e-mail portfolio—fell on the shoulders of Glen Caplin. Every morning, for the full month before the election, the forty-four-year-old former spokesman for Senator Kirsten Gillibrand would put on his hipster-style black-framed glasses, roll out of bed, and come into the Brooklyn office knowing that he and his team of as many as a dozen staffers would spend the day reading hundreds or thousands of Podesta's e-mails looking for the needles in the haystack that would stick in Hillary's skin—and, more important, any hidden land mines that could blow up the campaign.

His team toiled in an office dubbed the "room of tears." On a massive whiteboard with wheels, Caplin dutifully recorded each scandal story line produced by the e-mails. It showed which staffer was working on which topic and whether the campaign had deployed talking points on the subject yet. Caplin would roll the whiteboard, like a ball and chain, from one dreary meeting to the next.

The vast majority of the e-mails, which dated back to 2008, contained little of interest—the time of an upcoming conference call or meeting and the like. But others held sensitive deliberations about campaign strategy and nasty comments about players in the Democratic Party. None of them, Caplin knew, would *help* Hillary. All the new revelations could do was hurt. And they did—day after day after day.

In one message, former Clinton Foundation executive Doug Band had called Chelsea Clinton a "spoiled brat." Neera Tanden, the president of the liberal think tank Center for American Progress and a former Clinton aide, wrote in another that Hillary's "instincts are suboptimal." A June 2015 note from Mook called New York mayor Bill de Blasio a "terrorist." And, in a message with the dismissive air of Hillary's "deplorables" remark, communications director Jennifer Palmieri had noted to Podesta in 2011—before they worked for Hillary—that she wasn't impressed with elite Catholic Republicans. "I imagine they think it is the most socially acceptable politically conservative religion. Their rich friends wouldn't understand if they became evangelicals," she wrote. Palmieri and Podesta are both Catholic, but the message read as a stab at Republicans who chose Catholicism and all evangelical Christians.

At a time when Hillary was struggling with working- and middle-class white voters in Rust Belt states, the e-mail was toxic. Philadelphia, Detroit, Cleveland, and Milwaukee are among the biggest dioceses in the United States. Even outside the major metropolitan areas, the industrial Midwest is full of white Catholic enclaves. For example, in Brown County, Wisconsin, where Obama and Clinton were supposed to have had their first joint appearance, more than 100,000 of the 250,000 people identify as Catholic.

In part because they had fought through the private-server scandal and the DNC hacks stories already, and in part because the Podesta e-mails didn't all hit at once, it took a while for Clinton and her team to appreciate just how much damage WikiLeaks would do over the final four weeks of the campaign. Sullivan didn't realize the extent to which the e-mails had bled into the public consciousness until a trip with Podesta to Hillary's midtown Manhattan personal office. They were in a subway station when a stranger recognized Podesta and walked up to chat. For months, the two aides had made the same trek from time to time without incident. Now Podesta had become a familiar face.

Fuck, Sullivan thought, *if people are recognizing John Podesta on the street, this is breaking through.*

▼

THERE WAS AN element of mordant humor in the way the campaign's leadership tried to manage the fallout from a set of e-mails that one staffer described as "the Rosetta Stone of Democratic politics." The e-mails, which included long chains that Podesta was just copied on, were a key to the encoded secrets of Hillary's strategy and the way she and her campaign dealt with fellow Democrats.

Mook posted a sign over urinals in the men's room advising staffers that they should treat passwords like toothbrushes and not share them—but the humor was a thin veil for the feelings rubbed raw when staffers read what their bosses and colleagues thought of them. And that's to say nothing of the reaction among Democratic officials outside the campaign who were targets of derision. After his e-mail about de Blasio was revealed, Mook called to try to smooth over hurt feelings. *I'm sorry I called you a terrorist* was not something he ever thought he'd be saying to the mayor of New York.

On the one hand, it was a challenge to keep everyone from tearing each other limb from limb. That was manageable, if uncomfortable. The harder part was finding a way to prevent the daily release of sensational—or more often sensationalized—e-mails to drown out the rest of the campaign's message. The main tactic deployed by the campaign was to refuse to acknowledge the accuracy of the e-mails. That way, surrogates speaking for Hillary on TV could address any new details by saying they couldn't confirm their veracity and quickly pivoting to whatever the campaign's message of the day was. Still, that was a partial salve. The surrogates still had to talk about the WikiLeaked e-mails, which meant less time for bashing Trump and promoting Hillary.

IT WASN'T JUST defense that occupied Caplin. He and others on the campaign believed that eventually the news media—and voters—would put more emphasis on a foreign government tampering with American democracy than on the details of each Podesta e-mail. They thought Russia's meddling would have better legs. As WikiLeaks published more and more messages, campaign aides came to believe that there was a big and telling difference between the disclosure of DNC e-mails earlier in the summer and the reveal of the Podesta rounds. Rather than a massive, untargeted one-time release, this time there seemed to be greater political sophistication in the slow-burn method of daily releases for the final month of the campaign—and the Podesta e-mails were presented in an easily searchable format. The biggest difference they detected was that WikiLeaks had seemed to acquire a close enough understanding of American domestic politics to time its releases and publish e-mails on days when they would have greater relevance in the news.

It's clear the Russians have now weaponized WikiLeaks to try to influence the election, Caplin thought. *What can or should we do to tell that part of the story?*

The initial response—Podesta calling Trump an apologist for Russia—would turn out to be cautious considering how long the story would stay in the news. But over the course of the final month, the campaign would try a variety of methods to force the media into giving more airtime and ink to the idea that Russia was trying to throw the election than to the contents of Podesta's e-mails. Hillary would raise the issue herself repeatedly in debates. "We have 17—17—intelligence agencies, civilian and military, who have all concluded that these espionage attacks, these cyberattacks, come from the highest levels of the Kremlin," she would say at one of the debates. "They are designed to influence our election." The charge actually drew more conclusions than the intelligence community had publicly, and Trump deflected by saying there was no proof Russia was behind the theft and leaking of the Podesta e-mails. In the debate before the intelligence community assessment was released, he said it could have been China or "somebody sitting on their bed that weighs 400 pounds." The subtle but effective dig: anyone could hack into one of Hillary's e-mail systems. Never mind that it was Podesta's personal Gmail account that was compromised or that there was no reason to think Hillary's private server—the subject of so much controversy in the campaign because of the perception that she hadn't protected top government secrets—had ever been compromised. Long after the *Access Hollywood* video had flashed in the political pan, the Podesta e-mails would continue to cook slowly on the back burner.

THE OTHER THING that kept Caplin up at night was the "sleeping whale." A friend who sailed the ocean had told him that a boat's systems wouldn't detect a whale resting just beneath the surface of the water. It didn't happen often, but a boat could be destroyed without warning if it struck a sleeping whale. Caplin lived with the fear that an unanticipated e-mail surfaced by WikiLeaks would be his version of a sleeping whale.

The steady drumbeat of Podesta e-mails took a psychic toll on the campaign and distracted from Hillary's ability to deliver her message. "We were the bull that was being stabbed repeatedly in the ring and that was dripping blood," said one aide who worked at the Brooklyn headquarters.

More important, as Hillary's team picked up in focus group interviews with voters, people conflated the WikiLeaks releases of DNC and Podesta e-mails with Hillary's State Department e-mail scandal. "It had the effect of just keeping e-mails in people's minds," said one person familiar with the responses. At the same time, Trump would read the contents of the Podesta e-mails from the stump to hit Hillary. "Hillary wrote that the governments of Qatar and Saudi Arabia are 'providing clandestine financial and logistical support to ISIL,'" he said at a Charlotte, North Carolina, rally in mid-October. "Yet in that same year Bill and Hillary accepted a check from Saudi Arabia. So Hillary thinks they are funding ISIS, and still takes their money! And you know their views on gays and you know their views on women."

It's hard to measure the exact effect that WikiLeaks had on the outcome of the election—Hillary led Trump by 4.7 points when the *Access Hollywood* video and first Podesta e-mails circulated and by

7 points ten days later—but she and her team would be convinced that they played a role in preventing her from running away with the presidency.

"It hurt us more than we realized," said one senior campaign official. "Another drip, drip, drip. A thing that turned good narrative days into mixed narrative days. A whole lot of people read those e-mails or stories about those e-mails or chyrons about those e-mails."

In that first week of October, DNC chairwoman Donna Brazile became even more worried about the absence of ground forces in major swing states. On a pad from the Ritz-Carlton in Naples, Florida, she scrawled out the top priorities: Michigan, Florida, Pennsylvania, and North Carolina. She tore off the top page and handed it to Adam Parkhomenko, who had moved over to the DNC during the summer, and Donnie Fowler, a veteran political operative turned Silicon Valley tech CEO who had been picked to run the committee's Get Out the Vote effort.

She instructed them to call every political hand they could find in those states, determine how bad the situation was, and report back on what they needed in terms of paid canvassers and other troops on the ground. "I fear it's too late," she said, "but see what we can do, if anything." The order was at odds with Mook's admonition that the DNC should stay out of Brooklyn's way in planning for the battleground states, and it ran counter to the general air of confidence that permeated the campaign's headquarters.

One volunteer who phone-banked from Brooklyn several times in October was assigned to make calls to registered Democrats in Florida. The main goal was to make sure these swing-state Democrats had received mail-in ballots. But the volunteer was also tasked with asking for whom the voter intended to cast his or her ballot—information that would be relayed to the analytics team. The majority of respondents either said outright that they weren't going to vote for Clinton or declined to say whom they would support, which surprised the volunteer. After all, these were registered Democrats. More alarming, some of them reported they would vote for Trump. After one session, the volunteer left the phone-banking area to mingle with the paid staff on another floor. "The energy in the room juxtaposed to the lack of enthusiasm I was hearing on the calls. Campaign staffers seemed so confident," the volunteer said. "They were acting like they had this in the bag."

TRUMP HAD A strategy for the second debate that was sure to refocus the press and the public. He would drag Bill into the discussion of sexual mores.

Held on October 9, just two days after the *Access Hollywood* video surfaced, it was clear the debate would become a forum for lurid allegations. Trump's strategy was to turn the campaign narrative away from his comments and toward Bill Clinton's misconduct. He'd been laying the groundwork for that line of attack for ten months, previewing his strategy in a December 2015 tweet during the Christmas to New Year's lull: "If Hillary thinks she can unleash her husband, with his terrible record of women abuse, while playing the women's card on me, she's wrong!" And in a Fox News appearance in May 2016, he had mused that Bill might "bring 'The Energizer' with him" if Hillary won the White House.

This code name had been bestowed by the Secret Service on Julie Tauber McMahon, a woman who had for years been rumored to be Bill's on-again, off-again mistress. Some Clinton aides had heard about "Julie"—a fifty-six-year-old blond, toned divorcee who also resided in Chappaqua—in his post–White House years. They would often ask reporters what—if anything—they knew about McMahon, shaking their heads that another Bill entanglement could rear its ugly head as the other Clinton entered the presidential race. And they discussed the possibility of a damaging new scandal internally over the course of the campaign.

"Who is the 'Energiser' who has been Clinton's secret lover? sic" the subject line of one e-mail from Cheryl Mills to John Podesta read. Podesta instructed his assistant to schedule a conference call for him with Mills and Bill's chief of staff, Tina Flournoy. "Julie" came up again in another e-mail from Podesta. "Saw her pic in this or last weeks Enquirer," he wrote. "Probably need to revisit our Whitehaven conversation."

Mills replied back "k," short for OK.

The infidelities would dog Bill and his wife's campaign, even if the Republican Party had already concluded that bringing them up wasn't a compelling attack. The Republican National Committee had surveyed voters in 2015 to find out how effective it would be to hit Hillary on her treatment of women who had accused her husband of misconduct. The answer: not very. GOP officials decided that television talking heads could safely portray Hillary as Bill's enabler to deflect attacks on Trump's womanizing. But, as one party operative put it, "as a persuasive argument, it really wasn't there." Trump proceeded to buck his party on the issue, finding it a necessary part of his narrative against the Clintons. At the very least, it could be used to distract from other campaign missteps or knock the Clintons off stride. The media couldn't resist a story about Bill Clinton and sex.

The battle lines were drawn as Trump and Hillary arrived at Washington University in St. Louis for the town hall–style debate. Reines knew it was his job to get Hillary ready for whatever might be thrown at her. Trump would dismiss his own behavior as "locker room" talk, as he'd done in the press, then move on to describe himself as the candidate who could protect women from predators. Hillary, he'd argue, couldn't be that candidate because she'd attacked Bill's accusers over the years.

As he played Trump, Reines made sure to drop in the word "rape" in reference to Bill. It wasn't pleasant, it wasn't couth, and, surprisingly, it wasn't jarring to Hillary. Practice exchanges on the topic were saved for the end of prep sessions because Hillary's aides naturally feared that they could blow up the entire process. If that was going to happen, better it be after they had gotten some work done on other issues. It wasn't like Hillary was hearing that her husband was a predator for the first time. He'd been impeached for his affair with an intern, he'd been sued, he'd lost his law license, and she'd defended him—or at least stood by him. Trump had even been pointing a finger at her for months. But still, reading a tweet was a lot different from being accused face-to-face in the middle of a presidential debate. "You're really getting her used to discomfort or just the sting of it, which is no different than the rest of the debate prep," said one person who was present for the sessions. Despite all that, no one could have predicted the way Trump would try to hijack the second presidential debate.

BILL CLINTON WAS getting ready to leave his hotel when he found out that Trump had set up a video event with four women who had accused the former president of a litany of sexual improprieties ranging up to rape.

He was livid, unsure how to react. This was beneath the dignity of the office that Trump sought, but it wasn't like Bill to back down from a fight. His team and Hillary's quickly conferred about whether he should stay away from the debate altogether. But that idea was swiftly scuttled because it would have added fuel to the story. Bill didn't want to do that. "I'm not going to play this game with them," he told one aide. "I'm not going to get bogged down in this."

At the same time, in a backstage greenroom at Washington University, Dunn, Klain, Podesta, Palmieri, and Sullivan began to focus on how Hillary should respond to either Trump or the moderators bringing up the four Bill accusers, who would be seated in the debate hall.

When Hillary arrived, with just a few minutes to spend with her advisers, she cut to the chase. "How do you expect this is going to play in the debate?" she asked. Dunn was the aide designated to give Hillary a final list of points to remember before the start of the debate. It's a stunt designed to rattle you, Dunn said. Don't let him get inside your head. A few minutes later, when the two candidates took the stage from opposite wings, Hillary nodded at Trump with a don't-fuck-with-me smile plastered on her face. She stopped abruptly before the midpoint of the stage, leaving him to shuffle awkwardly to his mark without a handshake. She had no intention of touching him.

A few minutes later, one of the moderators, Anderson Cooper, asked Trump about the video. It was "locker room talk," Trump replied, adding a rare apology—to his family and to the American people. "I am not proud of it," he said.

During a follow-up from a voter, though, he turned quickly to Bill and Hillary. "Bill Clinton was abusive to women," he charged. "Hillary Clinton attacked those same women and attacked them viciously. Four of them [are] here tonight."

Hillary brushed it off. "He gets to decide what he wants to talk about," she said, "instead of answering people's questions, talking about our agenda, laying out the plans that we have that we think can make a better life and a better country. That's his choice."

During the debate, Trump often lurked behind Hillary on the theater-in-the-round stage—something Reines had practiced in the Doral prep sessions on a town hall set that Obama lent to Hillary. His presence was a physical reminder that he loomed over Hillary's shoulder—just a few paces back in the rearview mirror—in the race for the presidency. By that point, it almost didn't matter what Hillary said.

Sure, she won the debate, but all anyone could talk about was Trump's audacious pregame gimmick. Afterward, her aides didn't know what to say. They were afraid to tell her that she'd won because they weren't certain that her victory on the debate stage would break through Trump's masterful manipulation of the media. They were trying to sort it all out when Hillary arrived backstage. "You did a really good job," one of them offered, "but we don't know how it will be perceived." Hillary's aides no longer fully trusted their own political tuners in a campaign season during which Trump had thrown all the traditional rules out the window. It's possible, they thought, that no one would pay attention to Hillary's debate performance. Hillary would go on to win the third and final debate too—Trump stoked a new controversy by calling her "such a nasty woman" during it—but she didn't get what she wanted out of what most political insiders thought were three near-flawless performances.

In a normal election, such a run of success would be expected to seal the presidency. Instead, Hillary stopped her fall, found her footing, and enjoyed a moderate polling bounce without putting the race away.

"These debates had no shelf life to them," one top Hillary aide lamented. "None. Zero."

There was another way to look at it: The debates served to re-inforce the public perceptions of Hillary and Trump. She was more presidential, totally establishment, and super-rehearsed. He embodied change—for good and for ill. He could be genuine while lying; she came off as inauthentic even when she was telling the truth.

Hillary had done what she was supposed to do to win, and Trump had blown chance after chance to impersonate a traditional commander in chief. In most minds, there was little question after the final debate on October 26 that Hillary was poised to become the next president. But Trump was still lurking, closer to striking distance than even the sharpest election analysts knew.

Chapter 19

COMEY

I N A PRIVATE MOMENT ON THE CAMPAIGN TRAIL, JUST A FEW days before the election, Hillary grew reflective about her relationship with the American public.

"I know I engender bad reactions from people, and I always have," she confided in an aide who was traveling with her on a swing through several battleground states. "There are some people in whom I bring out the worst. I know that about myself, and I don't know why that is. But it is."

"That's going to be one of the main problems you're going to face as president," the aide replied.

"Yep," she said. "It is."

After suffering eighteen months on the trail, vicious campaigns against Bernie Sanders and Donald Trump, the oppressive weight of the e-mail scandal, and the pain of being seen as dishonest and corrupt by a large portion of the electorate, Hillary was finally turning a corner with about a hundred hours left before the voting. She could now see the presidency in her hands. She was going to overcome the anger she'd sensed in America—the frustrations she'd had so much trouble putting her finger on. In her heart of hearts, she knew that some of it was less generic, less about the establishment, and more about her personally. But she'd survived it all, she thought, even an eleventh-hour intervention by an old nemesis, FBI director James Comey.

▼

AT LUNCHTIME on Friday, October 28—with early voting still going on in some states and just eleven days until the election—Utah representative Jason Chaffetz sent a nuclear warhead into the Twittersphere.

"FBI Dir just informed me, 'The FBI has learned of the existence of emails that appear to be pertinent to the investigation.' Case reopened," Chaffetz tweeted. More precisely, Comey had sent a letter to Congress with that cryptic message, which he would later say was designed to fulfill his pledge to update lawmakers on any new developments regarding Hillary's e-mail.

Hillary had just boarded her jet for a flight to Cedar Rapids, Iowa. Robby Mook was making a rare trip with her. With the debates in the rearview mirror, the Podesta e-mails were threatening a fifty-thousand-cuts end to the campaign. His mission was to push reporters to write about Hillary's stretch-run schedule by discussing why she was going to each place. Jennifer Palmieri and traveling press aide Nick Merrill, both of whom were also on the flight, had remarked to each other that week that things seemed too quiet in the campaign, aside from the soft, dark background music of WikiLeaks. One morsel Mook had to offer as a shiny object for reporters: Hillary was going to visit Arizona, a trip that suggested she was confidently looking to expand the electoral map beyond Democratic-held turf and traditional swing states. But soon reporters would have something much different—and much worse for Hillary—to write about.

Merrill was in the back of the plane with the press when Chris Megerian of the *Los Angeles Times* asked whether he had any response to the reopening of the FBI's investigation into Hillary's handling of sensitive e-mails.

"Very funny," Merrill replied, thinking it was a joke.

Megerian assured him that it was not. On a plane with spotty WiFi service, the reporter had seen Chaffetz's tweet. Merrill walked up toward the front of the plane and settled into a space in the back of the front cabin with no seating. He told Mook and Palmieri what was going on. Ever the optimist, Mook wasn't sure it was true. "I don't know, maybe somebody got confused in a game of telephone," he said. "I guess we'll just have to wait for the Internet." Merrill tried to get online to confirm the story and finally got hold of an MSNBC transcript with some of the details.

At the time, Hillary was in the front of the plane with childhood friend Betsy Ebeling and celebrity photographer Annie Leibovitz, who had come aboard to take candid pictures of Hillary working and, later, getting off the plane. She was blissfully unaware of the major breaking news that was consuming Washington and the cable news airwaves. Once her aides were sure the story was real—that Comey had, in fact, told Congress that there might be more to the e-mail investigation—they contacted the Brooklyn headquarters and made a plan to discuss strategy once the plane was on the ground.

A knot began to form in the pit of Mook's stomach as the plane touched down on the runway. *We've worked so hard and come so close, and of course this just happened to us,* he thought. *What the fuck?*

The same feeling had taken hold in Brooklyn, where John Podesta, Jake Sullivan, and Brian Fallon, the national press secretary and former Justice Department spokesman, gathered in Podesta's office for the conference call. *This is going to be a category 5 hurricane,* Fallon thought.

With the plane coming to a stop, Mook, Palmieri, and Merrill moved to the front to tell Hillary the bad news. Leibovitz was snapping pictures as they told the candidate to hang back for a moment. The task of telling Hillary fell to Palmieri, who had grown close to her during the course of the campaign. The former Obama White House communications director had developed a knack for apprising Hillary of setbacks without getting her worked up. It was one of the reasons Hillary liked having her around—reduced drama, even in a moment when the circumstances may have demanded a more urgent response.

"You're not going to believe this," Palmieri said, dispensing the few known details in an isn't-this-crazy tone of voice. Irritated but unsurprised, Hillary rolled her eyes.

"Well," she replied, "there's always something." Hillary thought Comey had been way out of line when he'd talked about her case publicly in July and that this was clearly another instance of him violating Justice Department protocols in the middle of an election. But she had a rally to go to. "When you're on the campaign trail, you've got to compartmentalize," one of her aides later explained. "There's not time to heat up and cool down."

On the conference call, aides in Brooklyn shared what they knew, but it was still hard to ascertain what Comey was talking about. In a letter to relevant congressional committees, he'd written that he had an update on his original testimony on the e-mail case, when he had said the investigation was closed.

"In connection with an unrelated case," he wrote, "the FBI has learned of the existence of emails that appear to be pertinent to the investigation." He added that the bureau would continue to look into the matter but noted that he could not yet "assess whether or not this material may be significant." He didn't clarify what the other case was or what he thought he had. Never mind that he already had concluded it would be inappropriate to prosecute her over the e-mail or that the Justice Department had a long-standing policy against taking action just before an election. Comey had done just that—again. Reporters would soon start circulating that Comey was talking about e-mails found when the FBI seized a computer in connection with investigating Anthony Weiner, who had apparently sent lewd text messages to an underage girl. Huma Abedin, who was traveling with Hillary that day, became increasingly nervous that she might be in the middle of another scandal that could hurt Hillary. She started to rack her brain to figure out whether she'd given her husband a laptop or if he had access to one that was hers. At the same time, Fallon grabbed his phone and started dialing reporters he'd known from his days at the Justice Department. He was hoping to shake loose any tidbits that hadn't yet been reported.

Working with little hard information, Hillary's aides in Brooklyn and Cedar Rapids came to one important conclusion: "It was next to impossible, if not impossible, for anything new to be in those e-mails," said one of the aides on the call. "No matter what device it was on or what it was, there was no way that it could have been anything new based on what we knew."

They believed that any more meat Comey put on the bone would likely be exonerating, but it was dangerous to attack an FBI director without knowing what he might have in his back pocket.

Sitting in Podesta's office, Sullivan listened to the rest of the group and then suggested that they publicly push Comey to reveal more. Short of a longer explanation, it would look like there was a serious chance of Hillary being prosecuted *after* the election. That would hurt her with voters. And, indeed, Trump would seize on the vague Comey letter to call Hillary "guilty" from the stump.

Instead of accusing Comey of misconduct or deception immediately, they coalesced around Sullivan's more cautious plan. "We held fire, because you don't want to say something that isn't the case or is off the mark," the aide said. "We all thought that if he's taking this extraordinary step, there must be something we're not understanding."

More than two hours after the news first broke, they pushed out a statement from Podesta: "The director owes it to the American people to immediately provide the full details of what he is now examining," he said. "We are confident this will not produce any conclusions different from the one the FBI reached in July." But once again, the words "Hillary" and "e-mail" dominated the news. Mook knew that every time one of the candidates had been featured in the news in 2016 that candidate's numbers went down, and he was certain this new revelation would follow the same pattern.

Hillary had been separated from the staffers who were planning the response while she went on stage for her rally at the NewBo City Market in Cedar Rapids. When Palmieri slid into Hillary's car for the ride back to the airport, Hillary found out the source of the "new" e-mail problem: Anthony.

▼

AT THE REPUBLICAN National Committee headquarters, the celebration was akin to the rebels' reaction to the destruction of the Death Star in the original *Star Wars*.

"Think of the command center when you hit the target and everyone cheers," said one person who was there. "Regardless of what actually comes of it, it plays to all of her weaknesses. She is constantly buffeted by these allegations based on her conduct and who she had around her." They recognized the news for what it was—another earth-shifting quake in a spectacularly unsettled campaign—even if Hillary's camp was slow to go into war mode against Comey.

But over the course of the next seventy-two hours, on a series of conference calls, her team would radically reshape their approach to the final days of the campaign. In an effort to close a nasty contest on a high note and set herself up to govern from a more aspirational place, she had planned to spend millions of dollars on positive television ads in battleground states. The reintroduction of her e-mail scandal—and its attachment to Weiner—meant that she wouldn't be able to concentrate on getting undecided voters to feel good about picking her. They already had deeply held concerns about her character, and this was going to add "Clinton fatigue" to the mix. Comey had raised the prospect of her facing criminal inquiry from the Oval Office and the country being plunged back into the nasty, queasy politics of Bill Clinton's final years in office.

Instead of just promoting herself on the airwaves, Hillary's aides decided, she would use more of her cash to throw mud on Trump, to try to prevent him from getting a free ride while she again slogged through the e-mail saga. Her end-of-the-race persuasion campaign would be more of a reiteration of the case against Trump. She had to convince voters that he was even worse. "When the Comey letter hit, we definitely amped up the negative," said one aide familiar with the change of direction.

It was a major shift in strategy, but one that Hillary's team felt she had no choice but to pursue. She had to try to push voters' focus back to Trump and his shortcomings, not the question of whether she might be in legal jeopardy if she won the White House. "We were able to get her into a place after the e-mail eruptions where people liked her—respected her—again. They got into a comfort zone that she was going to be president," said another aide involved in the decision for Hillary to lean more heavily on negative advertising and go after Trump. "The Comey thing brought it all back."

The resurrection of the e-mail scandal and the go-negative response highlighted the fundamental challenge that the campaign never solved, one that probably couldn't have been solved. "We had trouble moving numbers with a positive message," one of the aides said. There was a silver lining that allowed her to increase her spending across the board: Comey energized her supporters to donate. "We were bringing in more money than we had planned on and we were shoveling it out the door."

AS SOON AS the story broke, Mook had instructed Elan Kriegel, the data master, to increase the number of people the analytics team surveyed each night. He wanted to make sure that any changes in the mood of the electorate could be detected quickly and addressed. Sullivan, a self-confessed bed wetter, had the strongest visceral sense of doom. Suddenly, he believed there was a reasonable chance Hillary would lose the election, and he began pressing Mook and others to abandon efforts to expand the Electoral College map in favor of locking down states that added up to 270.

No one in Hillary's camp thought Comey really had new information that could lead to a prosecution, but they knew that perception mattered more than reality in a campaign—especially with so little time to make their case. The peril was compounded by the fact that the FBI had connected Hillary's server investigation to a probe into Weiner's sexting scandal. The tie-in: some of Abedin's State Department e-mails had been accessible from the laptop. Hillary was again connected to a politician charged with sexual misconduct. It wasn't her own husband this time, but it was hard to find someone closer to her than Abedin.

Huma was such a powerful force within Clintonworld that few of her colleagues dared to cross her. But some of them had always viewed her as a major vulnerability—even a "national security threat" because of her potential to prevent Hillary from winning the presidency, as one of them put it. She was at the center of the private-server controversy. She was being investigated by the Senate for her outside employment while at State. Her husband had repeatedly been drummed out of politics because of his addiction to sexting with strangers. Regardless of her level of culpability—and her defenders say she's unfairly targeted because she's so close to Hillary—Huma was a disaster waiting to happen. In any other political operation, she would have been cast aside publicly and brutally long before this moment. Now her detractors' fears were being realized, and the risk could no longer be ignored.

Hillary knew she needed Huma to vanish. But she didn't want to have that conversation with a woman for whom she felt a deep, almost maternal compassion. This was a gut-wrenching time for Hillary, pitting her abiding sense of loyalty—the value she held above all others—against her own self-interest and the fates of the Democratic Party and the nation. Beyond that, there was more than a little chutzpah in Hillary's punishing another woman for a husband's sexual misconduct. Neither banishing Huma nor keeping her at hand was a perfect solution. But one instinct—winning the presidency—clearly outweighed the other.

Huma chose to fall on her own sword. Through her lawyer, the same Karen Dunn who had prepared Hillary for the debates, Huma recused herself from further deliberation on the response to Comey and turned her own fate over to the campaign's leadership. If they wanted her off the trail—where she couldn't be photographed next to Hillary—she would accept that judgment. "I'll do whatever," she said, well aware of the maxim that staffers aren't supposed to become the story. "I'll put my situation in your hands." She was pulled off the campaign trail, replaced by longtime Hillary confidante

Capricia Marshall and other close allies in the final days of the campaign.

THE COMEY LETTER was just the biggest of a series of forces outside Hillary's control that were taking a toll on her in the polls.

At a rally in Flint, Michigan, in early October, Bill Clinton had given voice to the frustrations of working- and middle-class voters who saw their health insurance premiums rising in the Obamacare era. "You've got this crazy system where all of a sudden 25 million more people have health care and then the people who are out there busting it, sometimes 60 hours a week, wind up with their premiums doubled and their coverage cut in half," he'd said. "It's the craziest thing in the world."

Bill's words matched up nicely with Republican talking points on the president's signature domestic policy achievement. Of course, he didn't agree with the GOP's repeal-and-replace mantra; he was a big believer in Obamacare, which looked a lot like the Hillarycare plan from his administration. But he knew how to talk to working-class voters. He understood how to speak to their frustrations. Empathy was the trait that had carried him through a lifetime in politics, and his ability to persuade an audience with it was perhaps the most important distinction between his style and his wife's. Both Obama and Hillary had said the law needed fixing, so Bill wasn't exactly freelancing on the idea of change. His language might have been more coarse than theirs—"the craziest thing in the world"—but that's exactly the kind of non-Washington-speak that appealed to the Bernie and Trump voters who didn't feel a bond with Hillary. Bill sure seemed to know what he was doing.

To the campaign, though, his remarks sounded like nails on a chalkboard. Hillary's aides were trying to win the race by rallying the party's base. Taking a swing at Obamacare wasn't an approved method of doing that. When fellow Democrats raised objections, Bill backtracked quickly. He might have been a little sloppy, but he was talking about a more narrow issue within the health care system: some working- and middle-class earners who made too much money to qualify for subsidies would see massive premium spikes.

That would become much more evident over the course of October as states and the federal government announced that premiums would rise, often by double- and triple-digit percentages, for consumers. For example, in Pennsylvania, a state both campaigns saw as a critical stepping-stone on the path to 270 electoral votes, people using the popular silver plan were facing a 53 percent increase in premiums. Bill touched a hot stove by taking a swipe at Obamacare, but he grasped the frustration of many key voters. Trump understood the power of the issue too. "Repealing Obamacare and stopping Hillary's health care takeover is one of the single most important reasons that we must win on November 8th," he said at a Florida rally three days before the Comey bombshell.

Now, with less than two weeks left to go, Hillary found herself at the mercy of events—ongoing WikiLeaks releases, the Comey letter, and Obamacare premium increases—that she couldn't do much about. And many dissatisfied voters had not yet decided which candidate was the lesser evil. Trump's allies believed, or at least hoped, that voters' indecision would play to his advantage. "The one thing that's fascinating this cycle is the volatility in the electorate. They respond to ups and downs like I've never seen before," one senior Republican with ties to the Trump campaign said on October 26. "We have started to trend way back up in key states. If he keeps his fucking mouth shut for the next twelve days, there are a couple of states that are going to surprise you."

At the time, Republican officials were eager to share details of their own data-driven operations in advance of the election. Win or lose, they wanted to get credit for having modernized the party after an embarrassing data failure in 2012. Yet when the RNC conducted a briefing for reporters in early November, figures for Pennsylvania and Michigan were withheld because the upticks there were so rosy that party officials didn't believe their own data. They didn't want the projections held against them if, as was widely expected, Trump didn't win those states. The numbers were perceived internally as "overly optimistic" and that meant everyone associated with them would "look bad," one source said.

At the same time, Hillary's team could detect the earth shifting in the wake of the Comey letter. On the ground in swing states, said one campaign official who traveled in the final days of the campaign, "you could feel a chilling effect." Before the letter, this aide said, voters were energized. "The kind of thing where lines get longer for people waiting to get into events, crowds get bigger, people are more raucous," the aide said. "People feel like you might be the person." Comey sucked that energy right out of campaign events. "People on the ground felt more nervous about it. It just felt different."

In focus groups, consultants heard undecided voters express worry that Hillary would win the presidency and then be the subject of federal investigations throughout her administration. On the macro level, Kriegel and his team could see Trump gaining an edge with a certain kind of voter.

For most of the campaign, an unexpectedly high number of voters who should have been with Trump or Clinton based on their analytics scores were saying they were undecided or would cast their ballot for a third-party candidate. In mid- to late October, much later than normal, they started moving toward their own party's candidate— Republicans to Trump and Democrats to Clinton. "Over the last couple of weeks we saw the strong people were coming home," said one person who had access to the Clinton campaign's analytics.

At first, that meant Democratic-leaning voters were picking Clinton and Republican-leaning voters were going with Trump. But that pattern changed. "When that Comey letter came out," the source said, "Trump people actually sped up with coming home. The people who should have been with Trump but were saying they were going third party were coming home. Ours weren't." Republicans saw the same trend in their data. During the debates, and partially on the strength of the *Access Hollywood* video, Hillary had been gaining ground. The Comey letter "slowed the momentum back down," one GOP source said. In short, the Comey letter made it easier for reluctant Republicans to choose Trump and harder for wary Democrats to sign up with Hillary.

Specifically, the Clinton team could see Trump closing ground across the Rust Belt. It was the area that he had targeted, despite conventional wisdom that held the Democratic "blue wall" would come through for Hillary in the end. Suddenly, Trump's quixotic ride into the heartland looked a lot more strategically sound, and Hillary's attention to expanding the electoral map seemed misguided. Her aides knew the trend lines were bad, and they had no way of making sure their survey data was accurate.

The campaign adjusted by dumping millions of dollars into television ads in Michigan and Wisconsin and by repeatedly dispatching vice presidential nominee Tim Kaine to Wisconsin. "Michigan was trending hard against us," said one midlevel campaign official. "Ohio, in particular after the Comey letter, it was done. Ohio and Michigan aren't that different. Ohio and Pennsylvania aren't that different. Basically every state in the Midwest did trend toward Trump at the end," the aide said.

Kriegel had always looked at Michigan and Pennsylvania as the "tipping point" states. What that meant was that he could rank-order states in terms of their likelihood to go for Clinton or Trump, and those were the two states most likely to indicate which candidate could win 270 or more electoral votes on Election Day. Everyone in Hillary's campaign expected both of them to go in her direction, and that was a big part of the reason she had spent time trying to win states that were a bigger reach. There wasn't any warning at all that the Midwest states were truly in play until the FBI letter, said one campaign official: "Those states, the bottom didn't fall out until Comey."

Even in the face of declining numbers, Brooklyn felt comfortable that Hillary still had a pad in Michigan and Wisconsin. "We did not believe we were in danger of losing those two states," said one aide involved in strategy discussions. But because of Comey and the slipping margins, Hillary's aides chose to be what the aide called "more defensive" in the campaign's spending—meaning less money for states at the edge of the electoral map and more for those she absolutely needed to win to become president.

Still, the campaign's only measure of the head-to-head numbers between Clinton and Trump—the analytics surveys—showed Hillary with a lead in the battleground states. Mook had chosen not to spend money on polling, to the great frustration of some of the campaign's aides and advisers in key states. In Florida, Craig Smith, the former White House political director, and Scott Arceneaux, a veteran southern Democratic political operative, had begged Mook to poll the state in October to no avail. Mook believed it was a waste of money. He had learned from David Plouffe, Obama's campaign manager, that old-school polling should be used for testing messages and gauging the sentiments of the electorate and that analytics were just as good for tracking which candidate was ahead and by how much in each state. Plus, the analytics were quicker and much cheaper.

In Mook's mind, the two forms were indistinguishable in terms of testing the horse race, and he was worried about overspending, even after the Comey letter produced a windfall of contributions from concerned Democrats. So he declined to use pollsters to track voter preferences in the final three weeks of the campaign. Some Clinton aides and advisers thought that was an unwise decision because it robbed him of another data point against which to check the analytics. "They just cut it too tight to the edge and that was because of that absolute belief of Elan. And then it was Robby not wanting to spend money, and it was no checks and balances and transparency in the system," said one person who thought Mook could have done more to understand where Hillary stood in the stretch run. "That's how you end up with realizing it too late."

There's no guarantee that Hillary's pollsters would have come up with different numbers, but many officials on the campaign and in the larger Democratic Party believed at the time that Mook relied too much on analytics. Still, it was hard to fight with him because no one wanted to sound like a Luddite in the face of data, and the candidate herself had long since blessed his approach.

Even when the numbers tightened following the Comey letter, they showed she still had a substantial edge in enough states to win the presidency comfortably. As had been the case throughout the campaign, Mook based nearly every spending decision and deployment of resources on Kriegel's data.

So Hillary never went to Wisconsin—the state where she had been forced to cancel her first planned joint appearance with Obama earlier in the year. Despite a major field operation in the state, her organizers were frustrated that Mook wouldn't provide basic resources like campaign literature so they could try to persuade voters to back Hillary. "What is the point of having a hundred people on the ground if you're not giving them any of the tools to do the work?" said one veteran Democratic organizer familiar with the Wisconsin operation. "That should be part of the plan." The complaint echoed those of campaign leaders across the battleground states.

In Michigan, the campaign feared that sending Hillary would actually backfire. "We spent a lot more money in terms of field and digital and mail than President Obama ever did," said one person familiar with the decisions. "Our strategy was from all the data we saw. Every time there was a mention of the election there, we did worse. To make the election a bigger deal was not good for our prospects in Michigan." So they largely kept the candidate out of the state, rather than figuring out how to alter that dynamic. The strategy ran counter to Bill's core belief that a candidate had to show up to sway voters. Hillary did end up making a last-minute visit to Grand Rapids the day before the election—after a lot of pressure from political officials in the state—but more for insurance than out of fear that she would lose there.

As she lost ground in the Rust Belt, the discussion among Hillary's aides intensified. They weighed the risk of alerting the media and Trump to her vulnerability by changing her manifest. "We could have ripped up events from other places and then tried to throw together an event in [the Rust Belt], but then the press would have been like 'Oh, my god, panic' and that would have put bright lights around" the state for Trump.

None of the complaints were new. Mook and his *Moneyball* approach to politics rankled the old order of political operatives and consultants because it made some of their work obsolete. He had been fighting that battle from the earliest days of the campaign, and he didn't see any reason to change strategies and tactics that appeared to be working. Hillary was poised to win the presidency and to do it with a little bit of money left in the bank. The efficiencies had helped pull her through the darkest days, and the numbers showed that she was still in control of the race. The analysts felt like they could trust their data in part because early voting in swing states matched up well with their projections. They didn't think there was any reason to expect that Election Day turnout would vary significantly. The memo that one Hillary adviser had sent months earlier warning that they should add three or four points to Trump's poll position was a distant memory.

The early voting numbers in Florida were so good that even Bill Clinton, who had chafed at Brooklyn's tendency to ignore his feel for politics on the ground, excitedly told one campaign aide the Friday before the election that the Sunshine State was in the bag.

And Mook and Kriegel were not operating in a total information vacuum outside of the data analytics. Public polling showed Hillary with a clear lead nationally and in enough battleground states to carry the election with room to spare. The *New York Times'* Upshot, Nate Silver's FiveThirtyEight, and other election prognosticators rated Hillary as the overwhelming favorite—though Silver's projection wasn't quite as rosy. By the time Comey returned to the spotlight two days before the election to say he still wouldn't recommend charges against Hillary, it was hard to find serious election analysts who were predicting a Trump victory.

Hillary was on her plane when Comey announced there was nothing more to the investigation. Merrill walked to the front, where she was sitting with Cheryl Mills. The FBI just put out another letter, Merrill said, and it turns out there was nothing to the first one.

Hillary rolled her eyes again. "What a surprise," she said sarcastically. But she was in a good mood generally. "We were feeling good about Florida, North Carolina, and Pennsylvania," said an aide who was traveling with her. "We knew we had taken a hit from Comey, but we didn't think it would be an insurmountable one. It was fun. There was an energy."

Everything Hillary was hearing and seeing pointed to a victory. Even Sullivan, the incorrigible pessimist, thought she was going to win in the final days. Nearly a decade after she'd launched her first campaign for the presidency, the glass ceiling was within Hillary's reach and the hammer of the American electorate was in her grasp. She would finally get the chance to run the country that she loved.

"In those final days she believed she was going to win. And she was probably more bearish than most of us," said one senior campaign aide. "She was getting comfortable with the idea that it was going to happen. She was thinking a lot about government."

But while Hillary was measuring the drapes in the Oval Office, her team was mismeasuring the electorate.

Chapter 20

"I'M SORRY"

N O! NO! NO!" MINYON MOORE SCREAMED INTO HER PHONE.
"Yes," the voice on the other end of the line repeated. "She's getting ready to call Trump."

It was 2:30 a.m. Moore had stepped away from the election analysts in Hillary's midtown Manhattan boiler room for this call, and the other aide was inside the Peninsula Hotel, not far from a candidate who was about to concede the presidency to a reality-TV star.

"Well, why the hell are you telling me for if she's getting ready to call?" Moore snapped back. "She shouldn't do it."

If there was anyone who spoke for the heart of Hillaryland, it was Moore. During the darkest days of the primaries, she'd been brought into the campaign—her fourth for the Clintons—because she knew the candidate so well and because she could apply a steady veteran hand to a machine being run by outsiders.

Now, a bunch of outsiders had determined it was time for Hillary, the first woman ever nominated for the presidency, to give up. She was losing Pennsylvania, Michigan, and Wisconsin. The AP had called the race. President Obama had urged her to end it. And the data-wielding millennials on her own team saw no remaining path to victory. But for Moore and a handful of other true Hillary loyalists, many of whom had lived through Al Gore's too-quick concession in 2000, it wasn't time to concede. Not yet. The numbers might flip by morning. "It's too murky," Moore insisted.

But Hillary was already midsurrender. "Give me the phone, I'm calling him," she'd instructed her aides. It took a few minutes—giving Moore time to register her objections—but Huma Abedin finally connected with Trump campaign manager Kellyanne Conway. Huma handed the phone to Hillary, who put it to her cheek and uttered two words she'd never expected to hear in her own voice: "Congratulations, Donald."

HILLARY'S AIDES BEGAN arriving at a midtown Manhattan boiler room before sunup on Election Day. Addisu Demissie, a double-Yale grad who worked on Hillary's "states" team, had barely had time to shower on his way to the office. At 3 a.m., he'd been at the airport in White Plains, thirty miles north of the city, to greet Hillary's jet after her final rally of the campaign—a midnight affair in Raleigh, North Carolina, that featured Bon Jovi. Then he'd hightailed it back to the city. Demissie would spend the next twenty-two hours or so in the boiler room, kept company by fellow voter-turnout specialists and CNN playing on the lone TV screen in the office's conference room.

A team of number crunchers settled into one of several side offices early. By the time consultants Joel Benenson, Jim Margolis, Mandy Grunwald, and John Anzalone trickled in, Hillary was on her way to cast her vote at an elementary school in Chappaqua. Election-law specialist Marc Elias set up shop in the midtown office, as did Minyon Moore, Charlie Baker, and Michael Whouley—the Dewey Square Group consultants who had helped Hillary plot her run from the start. DNC chairwoman Donna Brazile and Robby Mook floated in and out during the day. Mook couldn't shake the feeling that something bad was about to happen—a common fear for campaign managers on Election Day, but an unsettling one all the same. *We're not allowed to have nice things on this campaign,* he thought. *So what's the nice thing that we're not going to be able to have today?*

When the first early exit polls came in and hinted that Trump was running a little stronger than expected in the Rust Belt, Mook believed the numbers were still in line with what Hillary would need to take key battleground states. As he made his way around Manhattan that Tuesday, though, his optimism was tempered by that nagging feeling that something—minor or cataclysmic—would go wrong.

Hillary's communications team decamped to the Javits Center in the Hell's Kitchen section of Manhattan, where preparations for her victory party were being made. The venue, which would fill with Hillary aides, donors, friends, and well-wishers over the course of the day, was chosen in large part because of its distinctive feature: a glass ceiling. If everything went as planned, it would be the glass ceiling of the presidency that lay shattered under Hillary by the end of the night.

A handful of key aides remained in the campaign's Brooklyn headquarters for election night, but the top brass, including Mook, John Podesta, and Cheryl Mills, joined Hillary and Bill Clinton on their floor at the top of the Peninsula Hotel, a five-star facility a block from Trump Tower. The Clintons had their own suite, and the rest of the floor had been rented out for staff workspace and for aides, including Podesta and Abedin, to have private bedrooms.

AT THE START of the night, the Javits Center was electric: it had the buzz of a debut performance on Broadway. Outside, a seemingly endless line formed down Fortieth Street, near artists who had sketched Hillary's portrait next to Obama's and vendors who sold buttons with the candidate's name. Supporters resplendent in their "I'm with Her" and "Madam President" T-shirts filed in and stood shoulder to shoulder as they watched the returns trickle in on the large television monitors overhead. Under the signature glass ceiling lit by an ocean-blue hue, they watched the network broadcasts and listened to a string of surrogates from pop star Katy Perry to Senator Chuck Schumer fire up the crowd.

Clinton's campaign anthem, "Fight Song," blared across the room, and an official block party formed outside for a spillover crowd who held American flags and prepared for victory. A block away, at the historic Hudson Mercantile building, Hillary fundraising chief Dennis Cheng threw a lavish party for longtime Clinton loyalists. They watched TV and scrolled through their smartphones to check on election results. The plan was for these Clintonites to make their way from the airy event space to the Javits Center as Hillary's victory drew closer.

Just before polls closed on the East Coast, Hillary summoned Jake Sullivan, Dan Schwerin, and Megan Rooney to her suite to go over her victory speech. She'd been sent drafts over the previous few days but hadn't really focused on it until now. When the writers arrived, Bill and Hillary were already in the suite's study. Hillary sat behind a desk, picking over a salad. She had donned a jewel-toned scarf and traded the gold jacket she'd had on earlier in the day for a more comfortable wool jacket. The writers pulled up chairs around the desk, while Hillary gave them instructions. She wanted to scrub the speech of anything that could be perceived as critical of Trump and his supporters. She added a mention of children with disabilities to a list of policy issues to which she would call attention. And she beefed up the "shout out" section to name-check more friends and supporters. Bill jumped in with a few names of his own. As the group tightened and rearranged her remarks, vote totals started trickling in. When Hillary was satisfied with the text, Bill walked into the living room and laid claim to the couch. He would remain parked there for the rest of the night, watching television and dialing friends across the country. The concession version of Hillary's speech, a grim assignment that had fallen to Rooney several days earlier, remained tucked away, undiscussed.

Mook and Jennifer Palmieri had been in a staff room on the same floor, watching CNN, when polls closed in Virginia and Florida at

7 p.m. As the first returns came in, Mook dashed into the room next door, where Elan Kriegel and a couple of his data analysts compared the results with the campaign's projections. Having guided Terry McAuliffe's gubernatorial campaign in 2013, with Kriegel at his side, Mook knew the nooks and crannies of Virginia precincts as well as anyone in the political universe. *It's OK,* he thought. *It isn't great, but it's OK.* Then a cluster of African American–majority precincts around Jacksonville, Florida, came in. Those numbers looked strong, robust enough for a few fist pumps around the room.

"Florida started coming in fine," one top Hillary aide said. "And then Florida started getting tight."

FUCK YOU, John Anzalone thought. *You're being too pessimistic.* From the boiler room, the veteran pollster and his fellow Clinton campaign consultant Jim Margolis were on the phone with Steve Schale, an old pal from their Obama days. It was 7:45 p.m., and Schale had called to say Hillary was in deep trouble in Florida. No one in the party had a better feel for the state than Schale, a Tallahassee-based operative who had worked on the Draft Biden campaign in 2015.

"It's in real bad shape," Schale warned his friends.

"What the fuck are you talking about?" Anzalone asked. Hillary was on her way to turning out more Sunshine State voters than any previous candidate of either party. Yeah, Trump was winning exurban and rural areas, but surely Democratic hot spots like Miami-Dade and Broward would erase the deficit.

No, Schale explained, Trump's numbers weren't just big, they were unreal. In rural Polk County, smack-dab in the center of the state, Hillary would collect 3,000 more votes than Obama did in 2012—but Trump would add more than 25,000 votes to Mitt Romney's total. In Pasco County, a swath of suburbs north of Tampa–St. Petersburg, Trump outran Romney by 30,000 votes. Pasco was one of the counties Schale was paying special attention to because the Tampa area tended to attract retirees from the Rust Belt—folks whose political leanings reflected those of hometowns in the industrial Midwest. In particular, Schale could tell, heavily white areas were coming in hard for Trump.

At the same time, in the suite at the Peninsula, Bill got on the phone with Craig Smith, his guy in Florida.

"What's going on?" Bill inquired.

"Numbers are tighter than they're supposed to be," Smith said.

"Where are we not hitting our numbers?" Bill asked. Smith gave him a readout similar to the one Schale was reporting to the consultants in the midtown boiler room. Pinellas, Polk, and Volusia Counties were the bellwethers he used. The campaign should have been overperforming Obama in those spots, and it was underperforming him.

All over the state, the returns looked the same. Schale and Smith knew there just weren't enough votes left in Democratic territory to offset the Trump surge.

"You're going to come up short," Schale told Margolis and Anzalone.

AT 8:03 P.M., on the campaign's hourly election-night conference call, veteran Clinton consultant and summoner of gray clouds Mandy Grunwald told Mook she didn't like the early returns in Virginia.

"These numbers are looking pretty soft," she said from the midtown boiler room.

"They're a little soft," Mook agreed from his perch at the Peninsula. "But our model is holding."

"It doesn't look like the model is holding," Grunwald shot back.

AFTER TALKING WITH Anzalone and Margolis, Schale started getting text messages from Clinton number crunchers in New York who didn't see what he did in Florida. He'd set off an alarm bell—unnecessarily, in the view of some of Hillary's senior aides. They demanded to know what data he was using to determine that the race in Florida was over so early.

But inside one of the rooms on the Clinton floor at the Peninsula, a frightening realization slowly took hold of Mook and Kriegel as they watched results pour in from must-win states. Their vaunted model was way off in Florida. Worse, they had missed the mark in North Carolina too. Schale, they saw, was right. They could win without Florida or North Carolina, but the way Trump was running up the score in areas full of non-college-educated whites sent shivers down their spines. If the models were so wrong, they could be off in the same way in other parts of the country. They were looking at the early warning signs of a wave; all they could do was hope that it didn't wash over the Rust Belt.

Not only were Florida and North Carolina, separately, the keystone states for two of Hillary's three paths to victory, but the campaign had poured money, time, and surrogates into both of them. Hillary had closed her campaign just hours earlier with a midnight rally in Raleigh, and her first joint appearance with Obama, back in June, had been in Charlotte. She had unveiled her running mate, Tim Kaine, in Florida. She could afford to lose one or both of the states, but the chances of her winning the presidency would shrink dramatically.

Mook walked down the hall and into the Clinton suite, where he found Bill and Hillary in the living room. He stood over them—Hillary sitting in a big chair and Bill on the couch—and did his best not to sugarcoat what he was seeing in the numbers. "We need North Carolina, Florida, or Pennsylvania, and then we need other states," he told them. "Florida and North Carolina don't look great."

He stopped short of telling them that Hillary would lose Florida, but he knew that he could be looking at the front edge of that terrifying wave. "We need to see if this is a Southeast problem," he said.

While there was a chance that exurban voters in Florida and North Carolina were a bellwether for their counterparts in the Rust Belt, he explained, it was also possible that the effect would be limited to the region.

Hillary sat stone-faced, trying to process the unexpected and abrupt reversal of her fortunes. "OK," she said over and over as she nodded. It was all she could muster.

Down in Florida, Craig Smith's phone rang. The former White House political director, and the very first person hired onto Bill Clinton's 1992 campaign, had been ignoring calls and texts. This one, he took. The raspy voice on the other end of the line asked him if Florida could be turned around.

"Sorry to be the one to tell you," Smith said in an Arkansas drawl echoing the former president's, "but we're not going to win Florida." Bill hung up and called Governor Terry McAuliffe, who was eager to depart Virginia for the victory party at the Javits Center. Don't bother coming, Bill told him.

ON THE CAMPAIGN'S regular conference call in the nine o'clock hour, Mook gave his assessment to the rest of the team. "We're confident," he said. "We underperformed our model in the Southeast, but it doesn't yet appear as a trend borne out nationally." Normally upbeat, Mook said this with a little extra gusto. He knew he had to sell it because the message was so different from what he would say if he were truly confident: *We're feeling really good about Florida!*

His optimism did the trick for most of the officials on the call joining the Peninsula with Brooklyn and the midtown boiler room, but not everyone. Already, recriminations were beginning to fly. Benenson pointed his finger at the analytics team, which had failed to predict Trump's turnout.

In a second conversation with Hillary and Bill, after more of the returns had come in, Mook pivoted. The moment of truth—the reporting of votes in key Rust Belt states—would soon be at hand.

"I don't see how we win Florida and North Carolina," Mook said. "So now it's all eyes on Pennsylvania, and then probably Michigan and Wisconsin as well."

Hillary was still surprisingly calm, unable or unwilling to delve into the details of how her dream was turning into a nightmare. Bill was less reticent. He'd had a sinking feeling that the British vote to leave the European Union had been a harbinger for a kind of screw-it vote in the United States. He'd seen the transatlantic phenomenon of populist rage at rallies across the country, and warned friends privately of his misgivings about its effect on Hillary's chances. Now his focus turned back to the international movement he'd seen gathering.

"It's like Brexit," he lamented. "I guess it's real."

AROUND 10 P.M., Mook jumped back on a conference call with top campaign officials and repeated, almost word for word, what he'd said the last time about being hopeful that the dynamics in Florida and North Carolina wouldn't be evident in the Rust Belt states. The first time, he'd only talked about Michigan and Wisconsin. This time, he said "three" Rust Belt states. Pennsylvania, long thought to be fairly safe Democratic territory, was now in play. Hillary had run up the numbers, as expected, in Philadelphia and its suburbs, but the turnout for Trump across the spacious state looked a lot like what they had seen in Florida. On this call, Mook sounded less confident about his bullish message. *I know Robby,* one aide on the call thought, *and that does not sound like he believes what he's saying.* He didn't.

Mook could only help others suspend their disbelief for so long. "We definitely saw it, but we believed what Robby was saying on the first call," one of his lieutenants said. "But when you start seeing real numbers coming in from the Pennsylvania T or upstate Michigan, you see actual data that confirms your fears."

Over the course of a few hours on election night, the Democratic universe had gone from the boisterous expectation of shattering that "highest, hardest glass ceiling" to the silence of nervously awaiting an uncertain outcome to the solitude of an impending defeat. The evolution attacked the Democratic body politic in waves of stomach-turning recognition, emanating from the four electronically connected nerve centers in New York: the Peninsula, the Brooklyn headquarters, the midtown boiler room at Hillary's personal office, and the Javits Center, where thousands of supporters had gathered.

AT THE HUDSON MERCANTILE party, they kept waiting for a change for the better. Instead, positive returns were few and far between. At the Javits Center, campaign aides had gathered backstage in a space that looked like a loading dock, complete with exposed pipes and drapes doubling as walls to separate rooms. Some had arrived at the crack of dawn, eagerly awaiting poll closings with the cautious optimism of front-runners. Early jitters about Virginia settled after word came through that Mook and Kriegel thought it would be fine. But everyone could see that Florida and North Carolina were going sideways. Like the senior officials at the Peninsula, the midtown boiler room, and the Brooklyn headquarters—but on a little bit of a time delay—these aides were slowly realizing that Hillary's chances of winning the presidency would boil down to her performance in the Rust Belt.

About 9:30 p.m., one of Hillary's consultants sidled up next to spokesman Jesse Ferguson at a urinal. The early numbers in Michigan looked so bad, the consultant said, that Hillary was probably finished. On the convention hall floor, grown men and women groaned with each burst of additional bad news. Some cried. Others left early. The block party, once so boisterous, cleared out quickly, and a spillover room just off the stage never filled as aides had anticipated.

The torture was excruciating in large part because, while it was clear Trump was outperforming expectations, the races in Pennsylvania, Michigan, and Wisconsin were too close to call definitively. They were all much worse for Hillary than her private modeling and public polling had projected. It would take some time to figure out just how bad. The campaign had a contract to hold the Javits

Center until 2:30 a.m. Eastern time, but the program was only long enough to last until 11 p.m.—the time at which Hillary had originally expected to know definitively that she'd won. As that program wound down and eleven o'clock approached, optimism was in short supply. In the midtown boiler room, Anzalone tapped out a message to a reporter who asked what was happening.

"Wish we knew," he wrote. "Our analytics models were just really off. Time to go back to traditional polling. This happened in the primaries as well. They just put too much faith in analytics. We did not do any tracking by pollsters for the last month. Just maddening."

In the conference room next door, Hillary's "states" team—keeping track of the operations and results in each of the states—flipped the TV to the reviled Fox News Channel. The other networks simply weren't calling races as aggressively. At 11:30 p.m., Fox's Megyn Kelly reported that Trump had won Wisconsin and, in the same breath, explained the real significance of the state's ten electoral votes: "There goes her blue wall."

Until that moment, most Democrats—including most of Hillary's team—believed that she would hold the states that Democrats had won in every election since 1992. Called the "blue wall," these states accounted for all but twenty-eight of the electoral votes she would need to capture the presidency. None of the states she'd lost to that point—not Florida or North Carolina or Ohio—was part of the blue wall. Wisconsin wasn't even the most vulnerable brick. Mathematically, she could still win, but it would take a miracle on a night when Hillary couldn't catch a break. A nation of Democrats sat in stunned silence. They hadn't been warned. Hillary hadn't been warned. Even her pollsters had been in the dark, sidelined in favor of an analytics team that insisted she was poised to win.

High above Times Square, disbelief stifled the once-boisterous boiler room. It fell quiet. A new reality took hold: Short of a divine reprieve, Hillary was going to lose. Donald Trump would be president. "No one saw this coming," Anzalone told the reporter.

▼

AT 11:11 P.M., White House political director David Simas was seated at a conference table in the West Wing looking at results with fellow Obama aides and perusing Twitter when the AP called North Carolina for Trump. At the time, Hillary was leading in Pennsylvania, but many of her strongholds had already reported vote counts. Twenty minutes later, Fox News called Wisconsin for Trump—a judgment that other news agencies declined to validate for hours. At the White House, the writing on the wall was clear. It was just a matter of time before Donald Trump would be declared successor to Obama.

When he was sure there was no path to victory, and after having conferred with the president, Simas placed a call to Mook, who was in Hillary's suite at the Peninsula.

"What's going on in your camp?" Obama's aide asked.

"I don't think we're going to win," Mook replied.

"I don't think you are either," Simas agreed. "POTUS doesn't think it's wise to drag this out."

Mook now stood between a president interested in ensuring the smooth, democratic transfer of power after Trump had complained for months that the election might be rigged and a candidate who hadn't yet given up on the idea that Rust Belt states might flip in her direction.

Mook stalled. "Look, we're waiting for a few things," he explained to Simas. "Pennsylvania needs to get called. That's the linchpin." Beyond that, Mook had made a deal with Trump campaign manager Kellyanne Conway that a concession call would come within fifteen minutes of the Associated Press declaring a winner in the overall race. That hadn't happened yet. And, he said, "I think we're getting awfully late for her to go out and give what's an important speech." After all, Hillary was the first woman ever nominated for president by a major political party, and she would want to recognize the achievement in a way that elevated rather than diminished it.

"Our plan," Mook said, "is for her to go out tomorrow."

Simas listened politely, but he didn't like what he was hearing. He reiterated the bottom line. "We can't drag this out," he said. "The president doesn't think it's wise."

Mook hung up and steeled himself. It was pretty clear the president had given him a writ, through Simas, to convince Hillary that it was over and that she should concede graciously and quickly. He walked over to Hillary.

The president wants you to concede, Mook told her, adding his own analysis: "I don't see how you win this."

"I understand," she said. But she used her place in history as a shield in the same way Mook just had with Simas. "I'm not ready to go give this speech." Though she focused her pushback on the nature of her remarks—How should she frame the election of Donald Trump? What would she say to little girls and elderly women who treated her as a champion? Could she hit the right notes?—the effect was the same. Hillary wasn't quite ready to put an end to the dream she'd pursued for at least the past decade.

"You're right," Mook assured her. "'I lost. Have a good night' isn't the way to go." It would take more firepower than Mook had—more than a call from a White House aide to one of her aides—to move Hillary.

During their call, Simas had asked Mook for Podesta's number so that the president could call his former aide and the chairman of Hillary's campaign. Podesta had just left the Peninsula for the Javits Center. He went over because the campaign's contract expired at 2:30 a.m., which was nearing, and there was still no decision from Hillary on what she wanted to do, other than avoid giving a public concession speech that night.

Within the campaign, there was a divide in the ranks. The young, up-and-comer aides thought the election was over and Hillary was just prolonging the inevitable. But some of the veteran Hillarylanders, both because they had seen strange things happen in elections and because this was their last hurrah, argued that the races in swing states were too close to give up on.

As aides shuffled between the suite and the staff room down the hall around 1 a.m., they began discussing whether someone should go over to the Javits Center and make a statement—and, if so, what it should say. As they were talking, the AP called Pennsylvania and its twenty electoral votes for Trump, removing one of Mook's stated barriers for a Hillary concession. Abedin came into the staff room to say that it was time for someone to make the trip to Javits.

"Fuck it," Podesta said. "I'll do it."

FORTY-FIVE MINUTES LATER, Podesta peered out from behind the podium at the Javits Center. Thousands of Hillary supporters had come to watch her make history, but Podesta was so jarringly in the bleak present. His brief remarks reflected the ambivalence of the campaign.

"Several states are too close to call," he announced, "so we're not going to have anything more to say tonight." The glum looks on the faces of exhausted loyalists told a different story. Most of them knew it was over and just a matter of how long the misery would extend. Podesta was saying it would be several more hours, at least. "Let's get those votes counted, and let's bring this home," he said to polite applause. That was it. No concession from Hillary. No concession from her campaign chairman. The White House had been worried that Hillary might leave it all up in the air, and that's just what Podesta did for her. The night, it appeared, would end without a fully legitimized president-elect.

Podesta made his way from the podium to the backstage area where Hillary's mid- and junior-level staffers had congregated for the previous twenty hours. Facing the bereaved aides, he searched for soothing words.

"Thank you," he managed. "Hang in there." It was hardly the kind of pep talk they'd have gotten from a senior official who expected to win.

"We all knew it was likely over," said one of the aides. "It wasn't like we were going to win this thing."

▼

HILLARY CRADLED the phone. The smooth, confident voice on the other end of the line was as familiar to every American as it was to her.

"You need to concede," President Obama told his former secretary of state. For the past eight years, their interests had aligned almost perfectly. She'd lent him credibility with her own supporters and in the Washington establishment. He'd given her the State Department springboard from which to relaunch her political career.

At one time, she'd thought about distancing herself from him to win the presidency, but their closeness helped her draw contrasts with Bernie Sanders and Donald Trump. Obama and his wife, Michelle, had campaigned for Hillary like his legacy depended on her victory—and it did. But now, with Trump the clear winner of the election, the interests of Barack Obama and Hillary Clinton diverged again. The shotgun marriage that had evolved into nearly as much of a friendship as an alliance was no longer Obama's priority. He needed to ensure that the end of his presidency didn't devolve into a postelection circus. He had vouched for the sanctity of the electoral process and he needed Hillary to follow along.

She wasn't ready yet. But she was getting there. One by one, the obstacles were being removed. Pennsylvania was gone. The AP had just declared Trump the winner of the election. Now the president—the one who had convinced her to take the State job by framing it as a patriotic call to duty—was asking her to do the right thing for the good of her country. He wanted her to make it abundantly clear to the public that she wasn't going to fight the result.

Hillary was torn.

While she was on the phone with the president, her team was still hashing out whether it was worth waiting until morning. "There was a lot of discussion about Michigan and Wisconsin and whether the numbers could flip it," said one person involved in those conversations. Moore was among the more ardent advocates for holding off on a concession. But she was in the boiler room, removed from the central discussion. As Hillary and Obama talked, Moore's friends at the Peninsula lit up her phone with requests for her to come and talk to Hillary. The pressure on Hillary—from the president and from aides who believed the race was over—had no effective counterbalance. Hillary was tipping toward a concession.

AFTER OBAMA HUNG UP with Hillary, he called Podesta, who was on his way back to the Peninsula to meet up with Hillary and the rest of the team there. Podesta had gone over to the Javits Center with the hope—but only the hope—that the campaign would find baskets of votes in late returns in the key Rust Belt states. But he also knew Hillary wasn't ready to make any public statement.

Obama was determined to make sure his friend understood that the election was over.

It's done, he said. Realize that. Deal with it with dignity and move on. After Trump had questioned the legitimacy of the election, the last thing Obama wanted was for Hillary to reinforce that message. As president, it was his job to safeguard the integrity of the political process.

Podesta explained Hillary's position that she wasn't ready to face the public and that the campaign was still hoping for a miracle. Obama reinforced what he'd said to Hillary. He didn't see any point in prolonging the inevitable. It wasn't a question of when she would give a concession speech but rather of making sure that she didn't try to turn the election into a recount mess. Turning around and playing Trump's game of questioning the institutions of American democracy wouldn't be good for the country, he said. With his message now delivered to Hillary, Mook, and Podesta, the president hung up.

AT THE PENINSULA, Hillary had made up her mind once she'd talked to Obama. She cut off the staff-level debate. It was time for her to talk to Trump. "Give me the phone," she said. "I'm calling him."

Mook had watched on TV as Trump arrived at the Hilton to greet his euphoric supporters. He was painfully aware of his agreement with Conway pegging the timing of a concession call. When he'd made the deal, he'd expected to be on the receiving end of the call. Now he scrambled to reach Conway. He couldn't get her to pick up.

Eager for Hillary to concede, and to make sure he kept his own word, Mook asked Huma Abedin to try Conway and, failing that, Trump's son-in-law, Jared Kushner. The delay bought a little bit of time for the camp that didn't want Hillary to concede. Several of them continued to reach out to Moore. Maggie Williams, Hillary's White House chief of staff and one of a small cluster of longtime loyalists at the Peninsula, said Hillary should wait. The margins were still so close that the AP hadn't called Michigan. Pennsylvania and Wisconsin were supertight too. Trump would end up winning all of them by less than one percentage point. "Had anybody known that night, no one would have conceded," said one of the aides who favored the cautious approach. Once a concession call was made, though, it would be much more politically difficult to demand careful counting—or recounting—of each vote.

Hillary was done, though. Conway picked up Huma's call and handed her phone to Trump. Hillary took Huma's phone and faked a smile with her voice. "Congratulations, Donald," she said, suppressing the anger that touched every nerve in her body. "I'll be supportive of the country's success, and that means your success as president." Trump credited her for being a smart opponent who ran a tough campaign. The denouement lasted all of about a minute.

The news spread fast because Mook was on a conference call with other top officials. Hillary's voice carried over his open line. "She's literally in the background," one campaign aide said. "You could hear her talking to Trump, conceding."

Original Hillarylander Capricia Marshall, the former White House social secretary and chief protocol officer of the United States, couldn't come to terms with the decision. She retreated to the living room, finding a spot on the couch that had been Bill

Clinton's home for most of the night. Now, as Trump made his way to the podium at the Hilton, Bill chomped on the back end of a cigar. Philippe Reines, a third refugee from the discussion around Hillary, came in to watch Trump's victory speech. Bill looked over at the man who'd played Trump in debate-prep sessions. "I wish it was you up there," he said wistfully.

IN THE FOG of a shocking defeat, there was one moment that crystallized everything for Hillary. Not long after the concession call, Huma Abedin approached her once again, phone in hand.

"It's the president," Huma said.

Hillary winced. She wasn't ready for this conversation. When she'd spoken with Obama just a little bit earlier, the outcome of the election wasn't final yet. Now, though, with the president placing a consolation call, the reality and dimensions of her defeat hit her all at once. She had let him down. She had let herself down. She had let her party down. And she had let her country down. Obama's legacy and her dreams of the presidency lay shattered at Donald Trump's feet. This was on her. Reluctantly, she rose from her seat and took the phone from Huma's hand.

"Mr. President," she said softly. "I'm sorry."

Chapter 21

THE AFTERMATH

ONCE SHE'D SPOKEN TO TRUMP AND OBAMA, HILLARY SAT down at the long table in her suite's narrow dining room to read the hastily written draft of her concession speech for the first time. Early in the evening, before the polls closed, chief speechwriter Dan Schwerin had chosen not to share a bare-bones version of the concession with her. He hadn't wanted the possibility of defeat clouding her mind, and he was confident she wouldn't be delivering it anyway.

But when losing became a likelihood that night, he and fellow speechwriter Megan Rooney had scrambled to meld parts of the victory speech she had planned to give with the concession. Over the course of a couple of hours, they hammered out remarks aimed at comforting Americans who feared a Trump presidency. They went heavy on themes of constitutional protections and mentioned Muslim Americans and women and others who might feel targeted by the new president. The thrust, one Hillary adviser said, was "We stand with them and we see them, and the fact that we lost this election doesn't mean that we're going to stop fighting for them."

As Hillary thumbed through the pages, the speech struck her as tone-deaf. *It's too charged,* she thought, *too political.* Reines, one of the more than half-dozen advisers assembled around the table, reacted similarly to what he believed would be taken as an unseemly contrast with Trump. When Hillary was done reading, she looked up and told her advisers it was too much.

"Look, I really just want to concede gracefully, wish him the best, thank everybody, and get off the stage," she said flatly. "This is not a moment for me to do more than that."

Jake Sullivan, her chief strategist, took the lead in defending the tone. "Everything you said, we're going to do in the speech," he said. "But you have been saying for many months that he's temperamentally unfit and that he would be dangerous, and if you meant it, you should say it. And you made a case that all these people's rights and safety are in danger—if you meant that, you should say it."

Reines countered. If Hillary did that, she would be portrayed in the media—and in the minds of many Americans—as a sore loser. Hillary had spoken so many times before about the sanctity of American democracy and the importance of a smooth transition of power. This was a time for statesmanship, not partisanship. He worried that it all sounded too much like a campaign stump speech. Hillary agreed.

I'm no longer a candidate or public official, she thought. *I'm not going to be the leader of a party in the future. I want to exit with grace—and do it quickly.*

"It's not my job anymore to do this," she said, her voice growing more forceful as Chelsea nodded in agreement. "Other people will criticize him. That's their job. I have done it. I just lost, and that is that," she continued. "That was my last race."

With clear marching orders, she instructed her speechwriting team to go back to the drawing board and strike a balance shorter on stating values and longer on graciousness.

The regal suit Hillary had planned to wear in her moment of triumph, gray with wide purple lapels and a matching satin blouse, sat untouched in her bedroom. The hard-earned lines in her face weren't masked by foundation. Her hair hadn't been touched up and recoiffed for the cameras, long after they'd captured her going to vote in Chappaqua that morning. "It's a humbling feeling," she'd said at her polling location.

But that couldn't compare to the crushing humiliation of the hours to follow. When she could focus on a task and block out the gravity of Trump's election, her defeat, and the end of her dreams of a return to the White House, Hillary was stoic. Her voice was quiet but firm, her face expressionless, and her hands, which she normally used to accentuate her points, were still. When aides apprised her of new information, she responded briefly and without emotion. "OK," she said over and over that night.

She asked Mook which decisions had been misguided, where they had erred in strategy and tactics.

"Our data was wrong," he said, defending the allocation of money and bodies on the basis that they were the right moves given the available internal analytics and public polling.

"OK," she replied.

Like the rest of the Democratic world, Hillary was in a state of shock. But, at a deeper level, she wasn't completely surprised. Over the course of her life, no matter how good things got for her, she was always waiting for the other shoe to drop. When two-thirds of Americans had approved of her during her tenure as secretary of state, she'd known those numbers would plummet back to Earth once she became a candidate again. This campaign had offered too many examples of that dynamic to count.

She'd cleared the Democratic field of boldfaced names and then run into a primary rival in Bernie Sanders who coupled antipathy toward her among some Democrats with his own ability to bring new voters into the process. Each time she thought she'd defeated him, he rose back up to give her fits again. She'd won back the support of African American voters who had opposed her in the 2008 primary, only to discover that her attention to their concerns pushed away some of the working-class whites who had been her base. When the FBI director announced that he would not recommend charges against her over her private e-mail server, he'd also taken the unprecedented step of condemning her behavior and enumerating the elements of the case against her. She had broken ground as the first female standard-bearer of a major party but had to listen to shouts of protest while she accepted the nomination. She'd drawn the general-election opponent she wanted and then found him to be a much tougher foe than she'd imagined. She'd won three debates hands-down—a long-accepted indicator of success in presidential elections—and they had not been dispositive this time. On the very day that the US intelligence communities pointed a finger at Russia—the most hated country in American politics in her lifetime—and a recording emerged of Trump saying that he liked to grab women "by the pussy," WikiLeaks had begun parceling out a month's worth of embarrassing and divisive internal campaign e-mails that had been housed in Podesta's Gmail account. She'd run a successful campaign to paint Trump as unqualified for the presidency and then watched voters who thought he was too dangerous for the job back him anyway. And then, riding high in the polls and coasting toward victory in late October, she'd been rocked by a letter the FBI director sent to Congress implying that a laptop seized in connection with an investigation into her closest aide's husband's sexting might yield new evidence in the probe into her server. Palmieri had coined the dark mantra of the campaign—*We're not allowed to have nice things*—but it perfectly described the way Hillary processed her loss as she sat in her suite at the Peninsula.

Her mind kept circling back to two factors: James Comey and Russia. For the first time that night, she lashed out. Her voice rose. Her eyes grew wider. Her hands began moving again. "These guys came in," she huffed. "We were doing better until this happened." Bill Clinton nodded in agreement and muttered something about Brexit.

As the night wore on, Reines, who had spent the early part of the evening in his room with friends, no longer wanted to be there. Capricia Marshall was furious. The mood couldn't have been more grim.

And then the door opened to Clinton's suite. A hotel server wheeled in a cart of sundaes, with sprinkles.

▼

HILLARY FINALLY WENT to bed with the bustle of Manhattan's morning rush hour beginning on the streets below. By 8 a.m., she had changed her mind about what she wanted to say to the public. Schwerin and Rooney had spent the wee hours on the floor of Reines's room, paring back passages aimed at assuaging the fears of her supporters and putting a heavier emphasis on her acceptance of Trump's victory. It was one of the toughest speeches they had ever written. At 5 a.m., Schwerin slipped the new version under Hillary's door.

Now the speechwriting duo had returned to her suite, along with Sullivan, to go over the concession one last time. They sat down at the dining room table again along with other advisers, and Hillary told them she wanted to strike a new balance. She had come to the conclusion that her supporters needed to hear a message of inclusiveness in the face of Trump's victory. *Not as aggressive as last night,* she thought, *but it needs something more.*

"We should go further than we have," Hillary said. She had written notes in the margins of her copy of the speech, and she began to dictate from them.

"I want you to put in the Constitution as a device," she said. She wanted to talk about the freedoms of speech and of the press and a third bullet that she described as being antidemagoguery.

"I think you're talking about rule of law," Cheryl Mills offered.

That's it, Hillary said.

The speech wouldn't be an enumeration of every subset of the country that Trump had offended or threatened during the course of the campaign. It would be more subtle than that. But, as one of her aides described it, the tone would be "graciously critical."

Hillary wanted another significant change. In one of the margins, she had drawn a circle with a cross beneath it—the symbol for women. She said she wanted to say something about the glass ceiling—that it would someday be shattered. Rooney added "sooner than we think" and "to all the little girls who are watching this, never doubt that you are valuable and powerful." She and her aides made tweaks right up until the time, around midday, that she stepped to a podium at the New Yorker Hotel.

Wearing the Ralph Lauren jacket with the purple lapels she'd expected to put on the night before, and flanked by Bill in a matching tie, Hillary advised those who opposed Trump to approach his presidency without prejudice. "We owe him an open mind and the chance to lead," she said.

But she also spoke to their fears, affirming American principles she worried Trump might not safeguard. "Our constitutional democracy enshrines the peaceful transfer of power and we don't just respect that, we cherish it," she said. "It also enshrines other things: the rule of law, the principle that we are all equal in rights and dignity, freedom of worship and expression. We respect and cherish these values too and we must defend them."

Before she exited the stage, a twice-defeated candidate for the presidency who had represented her country as first lady, senator, and secretary of state, Hillary touched on the Methodist roots at the heart of her approach to private and public life.

"Let us not grow weary in doing good," she said, paraphrasing Galatians 6:9, "for in due season, we shall reap if we do not lose heart."

ON A PHONE call with a longtime friend a couple of days after the election, Hillary was much less accepting of her defeat. She put a fine point on the factors she believed cost her the presidency: the FBI (Comey), the KGB (the old name for Russia's intelligence service), and the KKK (the support Trump got from white nationalists).

"I'm angry," Hillary told her friend. And exhausted. After two brutal campaigns against Sanders and Trump, Hillary now had to explain the failure to friends in a seemingly endless round of phone calls. That was taking a toll on her already weary and grief-stricken soul. But mostly, she was mad—mad that she'd lost and that the country would have to endure a Trump presidency.

In other calls with advisers and political surrogates in the days after the election, Hillary declined to take responsibility for her own loss. "She's not being particularly self-reflective," said one longtime ally who was on calls with her shortly after the election. Instead, Hillary kept pointing her finger at Comey and Russia. "She wants to make sure all these narratives get spun the right way," this person said.

That strategy had been set within twenty-four hours of her concession speech. Mook and Podesta assembled her communications team at the Brooklyn headquarters to engineer the case that the election wasn't entirely on the up-and-up. For a couple of hours, with Shake Shack containers littering the room, they went over the script they would pitch to the press and the public. Already, Russian hacking was the centerpiece of the argument.

In Brooklyn, her team coalesced around the idea that Russian hacking was the major unreported story of the campaign, overshadowed by the contents of stolen e-mails and Hillary's own private-server imbroglio. They also decided to hammer the media for focusing so intently on the investigation into her e-mail, which had created a cloud over her candidacy. "The press botched the e-mail story for eighteen months," said one person who was in the room. "Comey obviously screwed us, but the press created the story."

Hillary wasn't in the room that day. But, in private conversations with top aides in the immediate days following her loss, she struggled with the question of why Obama hadn't done more to apprise the public that the Russians had gone way beyond what had been reported. She wondered why the president hadn't leaned harder into making the case that Vladimir Putin was specifically targeting her and trying to throw the election to Trump. "The Russia stuff has really bothered her a lot," one of the aides said. "She's sort of learning what the administration knew and when they knew it, and she's just sort of quizzical about the whole thing. She can't quite sort out how this all played out the way that it did." On the long list of people, agencies, and international forces Hillary blamed for her loss, Obama had a spot.

In December, a partially declassified US intelligence community report commissioned by Obama would find that Russia interfered with the election in a bid to help Trump. The agencies involved wrote that Putin "ordered" the effort to tip the race to Trump. "Putin most likely wanted to discredit Secretary Clinton because he has publicly blamed her since 2011 for inciting mass protests against his regime in late 2011 and early 2012," the analysts found, "and because he holds a grudge for comments he almost certainly saw as disparaging him."

IN THE POSTMORTEM, Hillary and her aides identified dozens of reasons she had lost: low African American turnout in some key areas; a boost in the white vote for Trump in suburbs, small towns, and rural areas; misogyny; the Comey letters; and the Russians, among them. Most of them could be divided into the interrelated categories of narratives and turnout.

Exit polls in Pennsylvania showed that Clinton and Obama won women by thirteen-point margins in 2016 and 2012, respectively. But in a state that has never elected a woman governor or US senator, men favored Trump by seventeen points—a massive increase over Mitt Romney's three-point edge in 2012. From a geographical perspective, Hillary did better than Obama in Philadelphia and its surrounding suburban counties but lost working-class Democratic strongholds in Erie and Luzerne Counties that Obama had carried.

In Florida, Trump crushed Hillary in the suburban swing areas outside Tampa and St. Petersburg. As he did nationally, Trump did better with white Floridians than Romney had, doubling up Clinton at 64 percent to 32 percent. Romney had beaten Obama 61 percent to 37 percent among Florida whites.

Turnout in Milwaukee, the key vote center for Democrats in

Wisconsin, was off by sixty thousand or so votes from 2012, and nearly three dozen counties in the state saw the partisan margin from that year flip by 20 percentage points or more in 2016. Trump won 52 percent to 41 percent in Brown County, home of Green Bay, site of the visit that Hillary and Obama canceled after the Pulse nightclub shooting in Orlando. Obama had won the county by nine points in 2008 and lost it by two points in 2012. Hillary, who had been blown out by Bernie Sanders in the Wisconsin primary, never set foot in the state.

About a dozen counties in Michigan flipped from Obama to Trump, but one mattered most. Macomb County, flush with working- and middle-class whites, gave Trump more than his statewide margin of victory. Obama won the county by 16,103 votes in 2012; Trump took it by 48,348 votes, or about four times his statewide margin.

The closeness of the race brought into sharp relief the fundamental divide that ran deepest between Hillary's advisers throughout the campaign. After a quarter of a century on the national stage, and as one of the most polarizing figures in American public life for much of that time, Hillary had alienated a significant portion of the electorate before she even launched her bid. It would be difficult to reset preconceived notions. "The big challenge of this whole race was there were so many voters who were ungettable," said one high-level campaign aide.

Her approach, guided by Mook and informed by the demands of winning the primary, was to build a coalition focused on core strengths: African Americans, Latinos, college-educated whites, and women. But the more she catered to them, the more she pushed away other segments of the electorate.

The number crunchers on the campaign paid careful attention to turning out her supporters and chose not to throw money at trying to change minds with traditional door-knocking efforts. Persuasion, they had concluded, just wasn't feasible with face-to-face lobbying. "Imagine you're on the ground and you're sent to suburban white voters to persuade them to support Hillary Clinton," one top aide said derisively. "Imagine what that experience would have been like and how many households you could really change."

But another camp, which included Bill Clinton and many of the older generation of aides and advisers, believed it was a mistake to cordon her off from large swaths of the electorate. They understood the value of slicing and dicing voters to make efficient decisions, but they also felt that Hillary should be doing more to show that she wanted every vote. Some of them believed that instead of basing her campaign on Obama's core coalition, she should have begun with the working-class whites and Latinos who fueled her 2008 run and built out.

"We started from the wrong premise with her coalition," one leading adviser said.

Ultimately, it was a battle between those who believed that it was folly to think Hillary could show up in lower-population areas and change hearts and minds and those who believed, just as firmly, that politics and Hillary's path to victory were fundamentally about doing just that. That elemental split hung over nearly every internal skirmish over strategy and tactics—from the hard-and-fast reliance on data and the development of her message to where she held rallies and whether she bothered to distribute campaign literature in swing states.

Hillary—who had been the target of so much venom over the years and who had become a disciple of Obama's data-driven campaign style—sided with a younger generation that heavily favored science over the art of politics. At one point, plans had been laid to replace Mook as the person in charge of her general-election campaign. Hillary stuck with him. And after the election, she chose to blame factors other than the strategy she and her campaign manager had pursued.

From Hillary's perspective, external forces created a perfect storm that wiped her out. In this telling, laid out in scores of interviews with Clinton campaign aides and advisers for this book, the media bought into an absurd and partisan Republican-led investigation into her e-mail server that combined with Bernie Sanders's attack on her character and a conservative assault on the Clinton Foundation's practices to sow a public perception that she was fundamentally dishonest. From there, Comey's unprecedented public condemnation of her handling of the server, the Russian cyberattacks on the DNC and Podesta's e-mail account, and new voter ID laws suppressed support for her. In a twist, Clintonworld sources said, Comey's final exoneration of her enraged Trump backers and pushed them to the polls in droves. Along the way, they said, misogyny played a quiet role in turning men against her without an offsetting boost in support from women. Her most ardent defenders maintain that she nailed every major moment of the campaign. "Those debates were her. The Benghazi hearing. Her convention speech. Her getting off the mat in New Hampshire," said one senior campaign aide. "She just does not give up."

But another view, articulated by a much smaller number of her close friends and high-level advisers, holds that Hillary bears the blame for her defeat. This case rests on the theory that Hillary's actions before the campaign—setting up the private server, putting her name on the Clinton Foundation, and giving speeches to Wall Street banks in a time of rising populism—hamstrung her own chances so badly that she couldn't recover. She was unable to prove to many voters that she was running for the presidency because she had a vision for the country rather than visions of power. And she couldn't cast herself as anything but a lifelong insider when so much of the country had lost faith in its institutions and yearned for a fresh approach to governance. All of it fed a narrative of dynastic privilege that was woefully out of touch with the sentiment of the American electorate.

"We lost because of Clinton Inc.," one close friend and adviser lamented. "The reality is Clinton Inc. was great for her for years and she had all the institutional benefits. But it was an albatross around the campaign."

▼

ONE MONTH AFTER the election, Hillary returned to Capitol Hill, where she'd worked for eight years as a senator from New York, for retiring Democratic Senate minority leader Harry Reid's send-off party. In addition to Hillary, Vice President Joe Biden and incoming Senate majority leader Mitch McConnell gave tribute speeches. So did House minority leader Nancy Pelosi and New York senator Chuck Schumer. In her remarks, Hillary joked that "this is not exactly the speech at the Capitol I hoped to be giving after the election."

There was something different about her demeanor and the way she carried herself, said one powerful lawmaker who was with Hillary that day. She'd lost something since the last time they'd seen each other. The stateliness, the confidence, and the air of power were gone. *She's the unpresident,* the lawmaker thought.

Hillary's joke about having hoped to give an inaugural address from the Capitol understated the way she'd treated that possibility during the campaign. It wasn't just that she had hoped to look out over the National Mall and speak to a nation that had just elected her president; she had expected to do that. The defeat had left her at a loss. She didn't have a plan B. Right after Election Day, she'd returned to Chappaqua and begun returning to the seminormal life of a former public official. She walked in the woods by herself, and with Bill, had lunch with a neighbor, and went grocery shopping for Thanksgiving. When supporters came across her in public, they'd started taking selfies with her and posting them online—sparking a "Hillary in the wild" meme that Adam Parkhomenko, the Ready for Hillary cofounder, turned into a Twitter handle. The smiling photos belied the pain she was suffering. "I'd like to think that photo of her the next day is what it's like," one veteran adviser said of her looking unburdened.

"Inside, there's a person that's crushed," said a longtime friend. "There's a person that's got to rebuild her life." She started that process with small steps—planning a garden outside her house and spending time with her grandchildren. Behind the scenes, she tried to find jobs for some of her aides. In one case, she sent names to

Senator Dianne Feinstein, who was hiring for posts on the Senate Judiciary Committee. Worried about what her loss would mean for the big-ticket Obama policies, she instructed her aides to talk with White House officials about what could be done to protect the DREAMers, those undocumented immigrants who were brought to the United States as children, and key elements of Obamacare.

As for her own future, Hillary told friends that she was trying to figure out how she could best fight for her values. She wanted to wait on that, she said, because she was concerned that she could unintentionally incite supporters who despised Trump. "We will rise," she assured one confidante in a text message. It was a theme Hillary revisited a lot in the shadow of the election, as the thought of getting back off the mat helped her work through the jarring finality of the end of her presidential ambitions.

"She's really allowing herself the vulnerability and the openness that come with a broken heart," said one friend. "She's allowing herself to be mad. She's allowing herself to be grief-stricken." But Hillary, who had yet to settle on her path forward, told friends she would bounce back and rededicate herself to fixing problems. Before she could do that, there would be one final humiliation: as a former first lady, and someone who had emphasized the significance of a peaceful transition of power, she would attend Trump's inauguration. When the friend asked her about it in December, Hillary hadn't yet made up her mind about that. But she believed it would be a bruising experience if she did go. "They'll probably boo me," she said.

IN JANUARY 2017, shortly before Trump's inauguration, a friend casually mentioned to Hillary the recent reports that she might run for mayor of New York. "A lot of people are calling me," she replied, declining to shut the door completely. Before that, and just days after the election, the *New York Post* had reported that Chelsea Clinton was being "groomed" to run for Congress in a district long held by family ally Nita Lowey.

The Clintons and their allies weren't ready for the end of their era when it came. They had been planning on a triumphant return to the White House—not just during this last campaign but ever since they handed the keys over to George and Laura Bush in 2001. For their entire adult lives, Bill and Hillary Clinton had been plotting a political rise—first his, then hers. Suddenly, shockingly, they were without an office to seek or hold. The absurdities of the election—Russian cyberattacks, a rogue FBI director, and an orange-hued reality-TV star winning the Republican nomination—intensified the sense of grief for Hillary, Bill, and their inner circle. None of it seemed fair, and it had all happened so fast. No one in Clintonworld wanted to accept the end, but it had come. Hillary had acknowledged as much in her hotel suite on election night when she told her staff that the 2016 election was her "last race."

An even more symbolic affirmation followed eight days later, when she spoke at a Children's Defense Fund event honoring her. Her remarks that night, which included a powerful anecdote about her mother, were largely taken from the victory speech she'd never given on election night. At the CDF event, Hillary spoke of Dorothy Rodham, age eight, sitting on a train with her little sister on their way to live with family who didn't want them. "I dream of going up to her and sitting next to her and taking her in my arms," Hillary said, and telling her, "as hard as it might be to imagine, your daughter will grow up to be a United States Senator, represent our country as Secretary of State and win more than 62 million votes for president of the United States."

The original line from the undelivered victory speech ended differently: "as hard as it might be to imagine, your daughter will grow up and become president of the United States."

Notes

In reporting this book, we spoke to a wide variety of sources with insight into Hillary Clinton's campaign, as well as other aspects of the 2016 election. We spoke to them almost exclusively on "background" so that they would feel comfortable revealing sensitive information and observations during the height of the race and so that they would not have to fear reprisals. In many cases, we describe what someone *thought*. Obviously, we are not able to read minds. Instead, the *thinking* is derived from interviews in which a source said he or she thought something, those in which sources described what someone else said about his or her own thinking, or documents that suggest what a person was thinking. Much of the voting data came from uselectionatlas.org.

CHAPTER 1: "OR I WOULDN'T HAVE RUN"

2   **third-place finish:** Dan Balz, Anne E. Kornblut, and Shailagh Murray, "Obama Wins Iowa's Democratic Caucuses," *Washington Post,* January 4, 2008, accessed January 26, 2017, http://www.washingtonpost.com/wp-dyn/content/article/2008/01/03/AR2008010304441.html.

3   **When she conceded to Obama:** CQ Transcriptions, "Hillary Clinton Endorses Barack Obama," *New York Times,* June 7, 2008, accessed January 26, 2017, http://www.nytimes.com/2008/06/07/us/politics/07text-clinton.html.

4   **"I'm in it to win":** CNN, "Hillary Clinton Launches White House Bid: 'I'm In,'" CNN, January 22, 2007, accessed December 13, 2016, http://www.cnn.com/2007/POLITICS/01/20/clinton.announcement/index.html?eref=yahoo.

5   **Obama's February 2007 launch speech in Springfield:** Associated Press, "Illinois Sen. Barack Obama's Announcement Speech," *Washington Post,* February 10, 2007, accessed December 13, 2016, http://www

.washingtonpost.com/wp-dyn/content/article/2007/02/10/AR200702 1000879.html.

6   **Hillary adored the thirty-eight-year-old Sullivan:** Emily Heil, "Hillary Clinton Jokes About 'Future President,'" *Washington Post,* November 30, 2012, accessed December 13, 2016, https://www.washingtonpost.com /pb/blogs/in-the-loop/post/hillary-clinton-jokes-about-future-president /2012/11/30/962b7d94-3b08-11e2-a263-f0ebffed2f15_blog.html?out putType=accessibility&nid=menu_nav_accessibilityforscreenreader.

6   **the *New York Times* reported:** Michael S. Schmidt, "Hillary Clinton Used Personal Email Account at State Dept., Possibly Breaking Rules," *New York Times,* March 2, 2015, accessed December 13, 2016, http://nyti .ms/1AScOvH.

7   **"Did you have any idea of the depth of this story?":** Robby Mook, "Re: NYT," e-mail received by John Podesta, March 3, 2015, published by WikiLeaks, #47391, #38854.

8   **the marathon-running former top aide:** Caleb Daniloff, "A Running Conversation with John Podesta," *Runner's World,* May 1, 2014, accessed January 26, 2017, http://www.runnersworld.com/runners-stories/a-running -conversation-with-john-podesta.

8   **"This is creating trust problems on her end":** John Podesta, "Re: Fwd: Guidance Please," e-mail received by Jennifer Palmieri, March 9, 2015, published by WikiLeaks, #30406.

9   **He told another friend that Reines:** John Podesta, "Re: Phillippe going off the rails, FYI," e-mail received by Neera Tanden, March 5, 2015, published by WikiLeaks, #27329.

9   **On the night of March 8:** John Podesta, "Re: Leaks," e-mail received by Philippe Reines, March 9, 2015, published by WikiLeaks, #24803.

11   **He had helped navigate Obama:** NPR Staff, "Departing Obama Speechwriter: 'I Leave This Job Actually More Hopeful,'" NPR News, March 7, 2013, accessed January 26, 2017, http://www.npr.org/2013/03 /07/173751123/departing-obama-speechwriter-i-leave-this-job-actually -more-hopeful.

12   **Favreau once told the *New York Times*:** Ashley Parker, "What Would Obama Say?" *New York Times,* January 20, 2008, accessed December 13, 2016, http://www.nytimes.com/2008/01/20/fashion/20speechwriter.html.

12   **It was Muscatine:** Roxanne Roberts, "Hillary Clinton and Lissa Muscatine: From First Lady and Speechwriter to Author and Bookseller," *Washington Post,* June 15, 2014, accessed January 27, 2017, https://www .washingtonpost.com/lifestyle/style/hillary-clinton-and-lissa-muscatine -from-first-lady-and-speechwriter-to-author-and-bookseller/2014/06/15 /c820ec18-f3ed-11e3-bf76-447a5df6411f_story.html?utm_term=.cdd 0566c37f2.

12 **"human rights are women's rights":** Amy Chozick, "Hillary Clinton's Beijing Speech on Women Resonates 20 Years Later," *New York Times,* September 5, 2015, accessed January 27, 2017, https://www.nytimes.com /politics/first-draft/2015/09/05/20-years-later-hillary-clintons-beijing -speech-on-women-resonates/.

14 **"I think running on her gender":** Cheryl Mills, "Re: From The Washington Post: The Fix: How Hillary Clinton can correct the biggest mistake she made in 2008," e-mail received by Robby Mook and John Podesta, March 23, 2014, published by WikiLeaks, #32132.

14 **"to better illuminate Hillary's motivation":** John Podesta, "Re: Launch Draft 6.4.15," e-mail received by Lissa Muscatine et al., June 5, 2015, published by WikiLeaks, #50285.

15 **In early June, Palmieri told Podesta and Margolis:** Jennifer Palmieri, "guidance for Dan," e-mail received by Jim Margolis and John Podesta, June 6, 2016, published by WikiLeaks, #2063.

16 **Reporters immediately noticed:** David Martosko, "Millionaire Hillary Launches Campaign Do-Over with 'Slightly More Arrogant Woodstock' Rally on New York City Island as She Promises to Look Out for Ordinary Americans' Pocketbooks—but the 'Overflow' Crowd Zone Is Left EMPTY," *Daily Mail,* June 13, 2015, accessed January 27, 2017, http:// www.dailymail.co.uk/news/article-3122756/Millionaire-Hillary-launch -campaign-slightly-arrogant-Woodstock-rally-New-York-City-island -promises-look-ordinary-Americans-pocketbooks.html.

17 **The speech started as an acknowledgment of political icons:** Sam Frizell, "Transcript: Read the Full Text of Hillary Clinton's Campaign Launch Speech," *Time,* June 13, 2015, accessed January 27, 2017, http://time .com/3920332/transcript-full-text-hillary-clinton-campaign-launch/.

CHAPTER 2: THE MERCENARIES AND THE MISSIONARIES

20 **including Guy Cecil:** Jonathan Weisman, "Democrats' Man for Battles Will Lead New Senate Charge," *New York Times,* February 18, 2013, accessed January 27, 2017, http://www.nytimes.com/2013/02/19/us/politics /strategist-returns-for-democrats-2014-senate-battles.html.

20 **On the first day of April in 2014:** Robby Mook, "Re: Launch assessment," e-mail received by Cheryl Mills, John Podesta, and David Plouffe, April 5, 2014, published by WikiLeaks, #9408.

20 **a framework first developed:** Cheryl Mills, "Fwd: Thank you," e-mail received by John Podesta, December 13, 2014, published by WikiLeaks, #5637.

21 **In a private exchange:** John Podesta, "Re: Following Up," e-mail received by Cheryl Mills, December 18, 2014, published by WikiLeaks, #10664.

22   **he dashed off an e-mail:** Robby Mook, "Re: We are on for Nov 13," e-mail received by Cheryl Mills and John Podesta, November 5, 2014, published by WikiLeaks, #53138.

24   **She'd worked to turn out voters:** "Jen O'Malley Dillon," accessed January 27, 2017, Precision Strategies, http://www.precisionstrategies.com /team/.

27   **Parkhomenko had worked for Clinton's:** Ben Terris, "Meet the Clinton Staffer Who Has Devoted His Life to Her Cause. Will It Be Worth It?," *Washington Post,* January 28, 2016, accessed January 27, 2017, https://www .washingtonpost.com/lifestyle/style/meet-the-clinton-staffer-who-has -devoted-his-life-to-her-cause-will-it-be-worth-it/2016/01/28/466d39fa -c12e-11e5-bcda-62a36b394160_story.html?utm_term=.4b4d3968c418.

29   **he fumed to Podesta:** Robby Mook, "Fwd: RFH," e-mail received by John Podesta, January 20, 2015, published by WikiLeaks, #42102.

30   **Then, on April 1, 2015:** Anne Gearan, "Clinton Campaign Finally Ready for Ready for Hillary," *Washington Post,* April 1, 2015, accessed January 27, 2017, https://www.washingtonpost.com/news/post-politics/wp/2015/04 /01/clinton-campaign-finally-ready-for-ready-for-hillary/.

31   **Smith e-mailed Podesta:** John Podesta, "Re: RFH," e-mail received by Craig Smith, April 10, 2015, published by WikiLeaks, #22124.

33   **Abedin was a subject of interest:** Massimo Calabresi, "State Department Nomination Blocked over Clinton Email Inquiry," *Time,* August 5, 2015, accessed January 27, 2017, http://time.com/3985795/hillary-clinton -huma-abedin-chuck-grassley-teneo-emails/.

34   **"how much we'd want her":** John Podesta, "Re: Huma memo," e-mail received by Robby Mook, January 12, 2015, published by WikiLeaks, #13446.

CHAPTER 3: FEELING THE BERN

44   **on January 26, 2015, Guy Cecil:** Robby Mook, "Re: Sanders," e-mail received by Guy Cecil, Huma Abedin, and John Podesta, January 27, 2015, published by WikiLeaks, #6375.

45   **Hillary had just jumped into the race:** Hillary Clinton, "Getting Started | Hillary Clinton," YouTube, April 12, 2015, accessed January 28, 2017, https://www.youtube.com/watch?v=0uY7gLZDmn4.

47   **Bernie seemed surprised:** Brian Pearson, "Bernie Sanders." C-SPAN, April 30, 2015, accessed January 27, 2017, https://www.c-span.org/video /?c4536294/bernie-sanders.

48   **Lynn Sweet of the *Chicago Sun-Times*:** Lynn Sweet, "Sen. Bernie Sanders Challenges Clinton for Dem Nomination," *Chicago Sun-Times,* April 30, 2015, accessed January 6, 2017, http://chicago.suntimes.com/news /sen-bernie-sanders-challenges-clinton-for-dem-nomination/.

48   **he was born on third base and thought he hit a triple:** Christopher Nicholson, "1988 Convention Speech by TX's Jim Hightower," C-SPAN, August 13, 2015, accessed January 28, 2017, https://www.c-span.org /video/?c4548039/jim-hightower.

49   **Trump delivered a broadside against immigrants:** Time Staff, "Here's Donald Trump's Presidential Announcement Speech," *Time,* June 16, 2015, accessed January 28, 2017, http://time.com/3923128/donald-trump -announcement-speech/.

50   **Trump surpassed Bush:** "2016 Republican Presidential Nomination," RealClearPolitics, accessed January 27, 2017, http://www.realclearpolitics .com/epolls/2016/president/us/2016_republican_presidential_nomina tion-3823.html?utm_source=hootsuite.

51   **he drew a reported 27,500 supporters:** Kurtis Lee, Sarah Parvini, and Kate Linthicum, "Why a Huge Los Angeles Crowd Turned Out for Bernie Sanders," *Los Angeles Times*, August 11, 2015, accessed January 28, 2017, http://www.latimes.com/nation/la-na-sanders-california-20150811-story .html.

51   **comedian Sarah Silverman elicited cheers:** Ed O'Keefe and John Wagner, "100,000 People Have Come to Recent Bernie Sanders Rallies. How Does He Do It?," *Washington Post,* August 11, 2015, accessed January 28, 2017, https://www.washingtonpost.com/politics/how-does-bernie -sanders-draw-huge-crowds-to-see-him/2015/08/11/4ae018f8-3fde-11e5 -8d45-d815146f81fa_story.html?utm_term=.fd8ab621e3c4.

CHAPTER 4: THE SUMMER OF THE SERVER

53   **When news of her private e-mail server:** Michael S. Schmidt, "Hillary Clinton Used Personal Email Account at State Dept., Possibly Breaking Rules," *New York Times,* March 2, 2015, accessed January 28, 2017, https:// www.nytimes.com/2015/03/03/us/politics/hillary-clintons-use-of -private-email-at-state-department-raises-flags.html?action=click&con tentCollection=U.S.&module=RelatedCoverage&region=EndOfArticle &pgtype=article&_r=1.

53   **"choppy waters":** John Podesta, "Re: Thanks for helping steer the ship thru our first choppy waters," e-mail received by Hillary Clinton, March 11, 2015, published by WikiLeaks, #45026.

54   **Vice News' Jason Leopold sued:** Jason Leopold, "How I Got Clinton's Emails," Vice News, November 4, 2016, accessed January 28, 2017, https://news.vice.com/story/clinton-email-scandal-foia.

54   **Judicial Watch filed a lawsuit in federal court:** "JW Pushes in Court on Clinton Emails," Judicial Watch, March 20, 2015, accessed January 28, 2017, http://www.judicialwatch.org/press-room/weekly-updates/jw-pushes -in-court-on-clinton-emails/.

54   **The Associated Press also filed suit:** Steve Peoples, "AP Sues State Department, Seeking Access to Clinton Records," Associated Press, March 11, 2015, accessed January 28, 2017, https://www.ap.org/ap-in-the -news/2015/ap-sues-state-department-seeking-access-to-clinton-records.

54   **Palmieri and Schwerin floated the idea:** Dan Schwerin, "Re: HRC joke on emails at Emily's List," e-mail received by Joel Benenson et al., March 3, 2015, published by WikiLeaks, #3154.

55   **Several lines of tension were evident:** Jennifer Palmieri, "Re: Draft Statement for HRC for tomorrow," e-mail received by John Podesta et al., March 9, 2015, published by WikiLeaks, #31602.

55   **Podesta had initially wanted to release:** John Podesta, "Re: Fwd: Shelly," e-mail received by Cheryl Mills, March 3, 2015, published by WikiLeaks, #57309.

56   **President Obama demonstrated the perils of flying blind:** Reena Flores, "Obama Weighs In on Hillary Clinton's Private Emails," CBS News, March 7, 2015, accessed January 28, 2017, http://www.cbsnews .com/news/obama-weighs-in-hillary-clinton-private-emails/.

56   **Mills dashed off an urgent missive:** Cheryl Mills, "Fwd: POTUS on HRC emails," e-mail received by John Podesta, March 7, 2015, published by WikiLeaks, #31077.

56   **to start talking publicly:** Huma Abedin, "DiFi Call," e-mail received by John Podesta et al., March 9, 2015, published by WikiLeaks, #44886.

56   **"You do not need a law degree":** Karen Tumulty and Anne Gearan, "White House Says Clinton Did Not Heed E-mail Policy," *Washington Post,* March 4, 2015, accessed January 28, 2017, https://www.washington post.com/politics/clintons-use-of-personal-e-mail-at-state-dept-violated -obama-directive/2015/03/03/454d7938-c1b9-11e4-9271-6102738462 39_story.html?utm_term=.d34e02fea390.

57   **she said things that turned out to be patently false:** Zeke J. Miller, "Transcript: Everything Hillary Clinton Said on the Email Contro- versy," *Time,* March 10, 2015, accessed January 28. 2017, http://time.com /3739541/transcript-hillary-clinton-email-press-conference/.

57   **"They will go after the server":** Neera Tanden, "Re: Seemed to go well today," e-mail received by John Podesta, March 10, 2015, published by WikiLeaks, #12393.

58   **"I don't know how the story advances":** Ibid.

58   **Podesta joked with Hillary:** John Podesta, "Re: Thanks for helping steer the ship thru our first choppy waters," e-mail received by Hillary Clinton, March 11, 2015, published by WikiLeaks, #45026.

58   **He'd asked folks to volunteer:** Philippe Reines, "Re: email story," e-mail received by John Anzalone, March 10, 2015, published by WikiLeaks, #2294.

58   **A couple of days later, he added a little meat to the bone:** John Anzalone, "Re: Clinton email toplines," e-mail received by Teddy Goff et al., March 12, 2015, published by WikiLeaks, #41975.

59   **Hillary went through with the interview:** Eric Bradner, "Hillary Clinton: 'People Should and Do Trust Me,'" CNN, July 7, 2015, accessed January 28, 2017, http://www.cnn.com/2015/07/07/politics/hillary-clinton-iowa-first-interview/.

60   **State Department's inspector general reported:** Elise Labott, "Official: Clinton Emails Included Classified Information," CNN, July 24, 2015, accessed January 28, 2017, http://www.cnn.com/2015/07/24/politics/hillary-clinton-email-justice-department/.

60   **she turned flippant:** Ryan Struyk and Liz Kreutz, "Hillary Clinton Jokes About Wiping Email Server 'with a Cloth or Something,'" ABC News, August 18, 2015, accessed January 28, 2017, http://abcnews.go.com/Politics/hillary-clinton-jokes-wiping-email-server-cloth/story?id=33165517.

63   **relatively well-received speech:** Rachel Bade, "Clinton Sways the Doubters at Wing Ding," Politico, August 15, 2015, accessed January 28, 2017, http://www.politico.com/story/2015/08/clinton-wins-over-iowa-crowds-at-wing-ding-121391.

63   **right after the story broke, 50 percent of Americans:** "Clinton—Conducted March 13–15, 2015," CNN and ORC International, March 16, 2015, http://www.documentcloud.org/documents/1694667-rel3a.html.

63   **By May, a clear majority:** "2016—Conducted May 29–31, 2015," CNN and ORC International, June 2, 2015, http://www.documentcloud.org/documents/2091322-2016-conducted-may-29-31-2015.html.

64   **Tanden reached out to Podesta with some advice:** Neera Tanden, "Re: Emails—my thoughts," e-mail received by John Podesta, August 22, 2015, published by WikiLeaks, #22039.

66   **a CNN/ORC poll showed her:** "2016—Conducted April 16–19, 2015," CNN and ORC International, April 20, 2015, http://www.documentcloud.org/documents/1995850-rel4a-2016.html.

66   **In a survey taken from September 4 to September 8:** "Democrats 2016—Conducted September 4–8, 2015," CNN and ORC International, September 10, 2015, http://www.documentcloud.org/documents/2395821-democrats-2016-conducted-september-4-8-2015.html.

66   **Other pollsters pegged her lead:** "2016 National Democratic Primary," Huffington Post, accessed January 28, 2017, https://elections.huffingtonpost.com/pollster/2016-national-democratic-primary.

66   **Sanders took his first lead in Iowa:** "Iowa Democratic Presidential Caucus," RealClearPolitics, accessed January 28, 2017, http://www.realclearpolitics.com/epolls/2016/president/ia/iowa_democratic_presidential_caucus-3195.html#polls.

66   **at which time he'd already vaulted:** "New Hampshire 2016 Democratic
       Primary," RealClearPolitics, accessed January 28, 2017, http://www.real
       clearpolitics.com/epolls/2016/president/nh/new_hampshire_democratic
       _presidential_primary-3351.html#polls.

66   **When voters were asked to describe her:** "August 27, 2015—Biden
       Runs Better Than Clinton Against Top Republicans, Quinnipiac Univer-
       sity National Poll Finds; Trump GOP Lead Grows as Clinton Dem Lead
       Shrinks," Quinnipiac University, August 27, 2015, https://poll.qu.edu
       /national/release-detail?ReleaseID=2274.

67   **she started getting pressure from her friends:** Maggie Haberman and
       Amy Chozick, "Hillary Clinton's Long Road to 'Sorry' over Email Use,"
       New York Times, September 11, 2015, accessed January 8, 2017, http://
       nyti.ms/1UHUNLZ.

67   **Hillary went further than she had:** Maggie Haberman, "Hillary Clinton
       Takes 'Responsibility' for Email Use, Saying It 'Wasn't the Best Choice,'"
       New York Times, August 26, 2015, accessed January 28, 2017, https://
       www.nytimes.com/politics/first-draft/2015/08/26/hillary-clinton-takes
       -responsibility-for-email-use-saying-it-wasnt-the-best-choice/.

68   **Hillary said she was "sorry" for the confusion:** Alex Seitz-Wald, "Hillary
       Clinton Tells NBC News She Is 'Sorry' for Email Confusion," NBC News,
       September 4, 2015, accessed January 28, 2017, http://www.nbcnews.com
       /politics/2016-election/hillary-clinton-sorry-email-controversy-n421851.

68   **Tanden observed that it was a good performance:** Neera Tanden, "Re:
       She rocked it!!," e-mail received by John Podesta, September 4, 2016, pub-
       lished by WikiLeaks, #8961.

68   **Four days later, in an interview with ABC's David Muir:** ABC News,
       "Full Transcript: ABC's David Muir Interviews Hillary Clinton," ABC
       News, September 9, 2015, accessed January 28, 2017, http://abcnews.go
       .com/Politics/full-transcript-abcs-david-muir-interviews-hillary-clinton
       /story?id=33607656.

CHAPTER 5: THE BIDEN THREAT

70   **his voice:** Draft Joe Biden, "Joe Biden—'My Redemption,'" YouTube,
       October 7, 2015, accessed January 28, 2017, https://www.youtube.com
       /watch?v=7e6mzH0Y4G8.

72   **Politico published a story:** Edward-Isaac Devore, Gabriel Debenedetti,
       and Kenneth P. Vogel, "Biden Strategy for White House Run Taking
       Shape," Politico, August 14, 2015, accessed January 8, 2017, http://politi
       .co/1Pqrl6R.

72   **He shot Klain an e-mail:** John Podesta, "Re: We need to talk tomorrow,"
       e-mail received by Ron Klain, August 15, 2015, published by WikiLeaks,
       #20492.

72   **Podesta forwarded the chain to Palmieri:** Jennifer Palmieri, "Re: We need to talk tomorrow," e-mail received by John Podesta, August 15, 2015, published by WikiLeaks, #35979.

73   **Klain would later tell Podesta:** Ron Klain, "A great night," e-mail received by John Podesta, October 14, 2015, published by WikiLeaks, #5690.

74   **Beau wanted his father to run:** Maureen Dowd, "Joe Biden in 2016: What Would Beau Do?," *New York Times,* August 1, 2015, accessed January 28, 2017, https://www.nytimes.com/2015/08/02/opinion/sunday/maureen-dowd-joe-biden-in-2016-what-would-beau-do.html?_r=0.

74   **Biden asked him to reconsider:** John Podesta, "Re: Robert Wolf," e-mail received by Hillary Clinton, September 26, 2015, published by WikiLeaks, #28099.

74   **Podesta had heard Wolf was "cranky":** Ibid.

76   **she would repeat some version of the mantra:** Sam Frizell, "Hillary Clinton Wants Joe Biden to Do 'What's Right for Him,'" *Time,* August 26, 2015, accessed January 28, 2017, http://time.com/4012539/hillary-clinton-joe-biden/.

76   **speaking to a private group in Atlanta:** Peter Hamby, "Did Hillary Take a Swipe at Biden?," CNN, October 16, 2013, accessed January 28, 2017, http://politicalticker.blogs.cnn.com/2013/10/16/did-hillary-take-a-swipe-at-biden/.

77   **Confronted about that vote on the campaign trail:** Amanda Terkel, "Watch Elizabeth Warren's Candid Interview About Hillary Clinton from 2004," Huffington Post, October 25, 2015, accessed January 28, 2017, http://www.huffingtonpost.com/entry/elizabeth-warren-hillary-clinton_us_562e4eefe4b0ec0a389519e3.

78   **In August he wasn't convinced:** John Podesta, "Re:," e-mail received by John Harwood, August 1, 2015, published by WikiLeaks, #27401; John Podesta, "Re: do you believe Biden is 'leaning toward running'?," e-mail received by John Harwood, August 24, 2015, published by WikiLeaks, #25806.

78   **By September 1:** John Podesta, "Re: My prediction," e-mail received by Jennifer Palmieri et al., September 1, 2015, published by WikiLeaks, #30504.

78   **were having meetings:** Kate Offerdahl, "Agenda and Document for 10am," e-mail received by John Podesta et al., September 15, 2015, published by WikiLeaks, #49029.

CHAPTER 6: MRS. OCTOBER

80   **the *New York Times* had just published:** Amy Chozick, "Hillary Clinton to Show More Humor and Heart, Aides Say," *New York Times,* September 7, 2015, accessed January 9, 2017, http://nyti.ms/1UDaDSY.

80   **Clinton's appearances on *The Ellen DeGeneres Show*:** Amy Chozick, "Hillary Clinton Dances with the Stars (Ellen DeGeneres, Amy Schumer, Pink)," *New York Times,* September 8, 2015, accessed January 28, 2017, https://www.nytimes.com/politics/first-draft/2015/09/08/hillary-clinton-dances-with-the-stars-ellen-degeneres-amy-schumer-pink/.

80   ***The Tonight Show Starring Jimmy Fallon*:** Marianne Zumberge, "Watch: Hillary Clinton Debates Jimmy Fallon's Donald Trump on 'The Tonight Show,'" *Variety,* September 16, 2015, accessed January 28, 2017, http://variety.com/2015/tv/news/watch-hillary-clinton-debates-jimmy-fallons-donald-trump-on-the-tonight-show-1201595601/.

80   **Clinton would dance the Nae Nae:** Tessa Berenson, "Watch Hillary Clinton Do the Whip/Nae Nae on *Ellen,*" *Time,* September 10, 2015, accessed January 28, 2017, http://time.com/4029808/hillary-clinton-whip-nae-nae-ellen/.

82   **"An inauthentic strategy to make her look authentic is absurd":** Brent Budowsky, "Re: Where's Bill?," e-mail received by John Podesta, September 8, 2015, published by WikiLeaks, #36689.

83   **she campaigned in South Florida:** Amy Sherman, "In Broward, Hillary Clinton Takes Aim at Florida Republicans over Climate Change, Medicaid Expansion," *Miami Herald,* October 2, 2015, accessed January 28, 2017, http://www.miamiherald.com/news/politics-government/election/article37388307.html.

83   **Clinton showed up at a Marc Anthony concert:** Leila Cobo, "Hillary Clinton Joined Marc Anthony on Stage in Miami," *Billboard,* October 2, 2015, accessed January 28, 2017, http://www.billboard.com/articles/columns/latin/6715411/marc-anthony-hillary-clinton.

84   **Human Rights Campaign breakfast:** Monica Alba, "Hillary Clinton at HRC Event Pledges to Make LGBT Rights a Top Priority," NBC News, October 3, 2015, accessed January 28, 2017, http://www.nbcnews.com/politics/hillary-clinton/hillary-clinton-hrc-event-pledges-make-lgbt-rights-top-priority-n438066.

84   **The Human Rights Campaign had wanted her to be the featured speaker:** Kristina Schake, "Re: Action Items from Strategy Mtg," e-mail received by Robby Mook, John Podesta, and Jake Sullivan, August 6, 2015, published by WikiLeaks, #45783.

84   **None other than Joe Biden:** Alba, "Hillary Clinton at HRC Event."

85   **McKinnon as Hillary:** *Saturday Night Live,* "Hillary Clinton Bar Talk—SNL," YouTube, October 4, 2015, https://www.youtube.com/watch?v=6Jh2n5ki0KE.

85   **Biden was for the Iraq War before he was against it:** Zachary Roth, "Joe Biden Is No Savior for Progressives," MSNBC, August 25, 2015, accessed January 29, 2017, http://www.msnbc.com/msnbc/joe-biden-no-savior-progressives.

87   **she announced that she opposed the deal:** "Full Interview: Hillary Clinton on Trade Pact Doubts, Dealing with Putin," PBS, October 7, 2015, accessed January 29, 2017, http://www.pbs.org/newshour/bb/full-interview-hillary-clinton-trade-pact-doubts/.

89   **he had cut a fifty-point Clinton lead:** "2016 Democratic Presidential Nomination," RealClearPolitics, accessed January 29, 2017, http://www.realclearpolitics.com/epolls/2016/president/us/2016_democratic_presidential_nomination-3824.html.

89   **he actually passed her:** "Iowa Democratic Presidential Caucus," RealClearPolitics, accessed January 29, 2017, http://www.realclearpolitics.com/epolls/2016/president/ia/iowa_democratic_presidential_caucus-3195.html.

89   **Sanders handed Hillary a gift:** "Meet the Press Transcript—October 11, 2015," NBC News, October 11, 2015, accessed January 29, 2017, http://www.nbcnews.com/meet-the-press/meet-press-transcript-october-11-2015-n442476.

92   **her level of commitment to progressive values:** "CNN Democratic Debate—Full Transcript," CNN, October 13, 2015, accessed January 29, 2017, http://cnnpressroom.blogs.cnn.com/2015/10/13/cnn-democratic-debate-full-transcript/.

93   **Henderson, Nevada:** @maryaliceparks, "@BernieSanders campaign manager tells me they all stayed way out in Henderson, NV (15 miles away) and focused on responding to attacks," Twitter, October 13, 2015. https://twitter.com/maryaliceparks/status/654036614100873216.

94   **House majority leader Kevin McCarthy:** David Weigel, "Boehner's Likely Successor Credits Benghazi Committee for Lowering Hillary Clinton's Poll Numbers," *Washington Post,* September 30, 2015, accessed January 29, 2017, https://www.washingtonpost.com/news/post-politics/wp/2015/09/30/boehners-likely-successor-credits-benghazi-committee-for-lowering-hillary-clintons-poll-numbers/?tid=a_inl&utm_term=.4f31c05c0244.

95   **Biden went to the Rose Garden:** *Washington Post* Staff, "Full Text: Biden's Announcement That He Won't Run for President," *Washington Post,* October 21, 2015, accessed January 29, 2017, https://www.washingtonpost.com/news/post-politics/wp/2015/10/21/full-text-bidens-announcement-that-he-wont-run-for-president/?utm_term=.6e95dba8b650.

98   **In his opening statement:** "Hillary Clinton Testimony at House Select Committee on Benghazi, Part 1," C-SPAN, October 22, 2015, accessed January 29, 2017, https://www.c-span.org/video/?328699-1/hillary-clinton-testimony-house-select-committee-benghazi-part-1.

99   **Hillary broke into a coughing fit:** "Hillary Clinton Testimony at House Select Committee on Benghazi, Part 4," C-SPAN, October 22, 2015, accessed January 29, 2017, https://www.c-span.org/video/?328699-4/hillary-clinton-testimony-house-select-committee-benghazi-part-4.

99   **John Podhoretz tweeted:** @jpodhoretz, "Why doesn't Pompeo just go over and swear her in for president now—if he goes on like this he'll practically get her elected," Twitter, October 22, 2015, https://twitter.com /jpodhoretz/status/657275010797670400.

CHAPTER 7: "I WAS CERTAIN WE WERE GOING TO LOSE"

101   **"OH-EM-GEE!":** CNN, "'O-M-G,' as Wolf Blitzer says," *Facebook,* February 1, 2016, https://www.facebook.com/cnn/videos/1015443142894 1509/.

101   **journalists saw an upstart challenger:** "Coverage of the First Primary Caucus in Iowa; 11–12mn ET," CNN, February 1, 2016, accessed January 29, 2017, http://transcripts.cnn.com/TRANSCRIPTS/1602/01/se.05 .html.

101   **Hillary had increased her share:** "Iowa Caucus Results," *New York Times,* January 3, 2008, accessed January 29, 2017, http://politics.nytimes .com/election-guide/2008/results/states/IA.html.

104   **a black Chevrolet Express 1500:** Ali Elkin, "Everything You Need to Know About Hillary Clinton's 'Scooby Van,'" Bloomberg, April 14, 2015, accessed January 29, 2017, https://www.bloomberg.com/politics /articles/2015-04-14/everything-you-need-to-know-about-hillary-clinton -s-scooby-van-.

104   **her Iowa bronze medal had netted her fourteen delegates:** "Iowa Caucus Results," *New York Times,* January 3, 2008.

109   **surpassed her in New Hampshire:** "New Hampshire 2016 Democratic Primary," RealClearPolitics, accessed January 29, 2017, http://www.real clearpolitics.com/epolls/2016/president/nh/new_hampshire_democratic _presidential_primary-3351.html.

109   **Hillary's advantage in Iowa:** "Iowa Democratic Presidential Caucus," RealClearPolitics, accessed January 29, 2017, http://www.realclearpoli tics.com/epolls/2016/president/ia/iowa_democratic_presidential_caucus -3195.html.

112   **Joe Biden had praised Sanders's "authenticity":** Kevin Liptak, "Biden Praises Sanders on Income Inequality, Calls Clinton 'Relatively New' to the Fight," CNN, January 11, 2016, accessed January 29, 2017, http:// www.cnn.com/2016/01/11/politics/joe-biden-bernie-sanders-hillary -clinton-income-inequality/.

112   **Chelsea Clinton lit into Sanders:** Lauren Carroll, "Chelsea Clinton Mischaracterizes Bernie Sanders' Health Care Plan," PolitiFact, January 14, 2016, accessed January 13, 2017, http://www.politifact.com /truth-o-meter/statements/2016/jan/14/chelsea-clinton/chelsea-clinton -mischaracterizes-bernie-sanders-he/.

112 **"I was surprised and thought it was out of character":** Jonathan Easley and Amie Parnes, "Chelsea Clinton Goes on the Attack; Democrats Ask Why," *The Hill,* January 14, 2016, accessed January 13, 2017, http://thehill.com/homenews/campaign/265839-chelsea-goes-on-the-attack-dems-ask-why.

112 **The fact-checking website PolitiFact instantly rated Chelsea's claim:** Carroll, "Chelsea Clinton Mischaracterizes Bernie Sanders' Health Care Plan."

113 **When he was asked about it:** Easley and Parnes, "Chelsea Clinton Goes on the Attack."

113 **Bill Clinton did the same thing a week later:** Matthew Claiborne, "Bill Clinton Attacks Bernie Sanders on Planned Parenthood and Health Care," ABC News, January 20, 2016, accessed January 29, 2017, http://abcnews.go.com/Politics/bill-clinton-attacks-bernie-sanders-planned-parenthood-health/story?id=36407492.

113 **She delivered rebukes to Sanders over health care:** Team Fix, "The 4th Democratic Debate Transcript, Annotated: Who Said What and What It Meant," *Washington Post,* January 17, 2016, accessed January 29, 2017, https://www.washingtonpost.com/news/the-fix/wp/2016/01/17/the-4th-democratic-debate-transcript-annotated-who-said-what-and-what-it-meant/?utm_term=.d9a6eab9d5d9.

113 **No fewer than five public polls:** "Iowa Democratic Presidential Caucus," RealClearPolitics.

114 **The first was the paper's endorsement:** The *Register*'s Editorial Board, "Endorsement: Hillary Clinton Has Needed Knowledge, Experience," *Des Moines Register,* January 23, 2016, accessed January 13, 2017, http://dmreg.co/1Vh3oBb.

114 **the final in a series of *Register* polls:** Donnelle Eller and Jennifer Jacobs, "Clinton Keeps Slim Edge over Sanders in Latest Iowa Poll," *Des Moines Register,* January 30, 2016, accessed January 16, 2017, http://dmreg.co/1SQR1ye.

115 **the campaign's analytics-driven expectations:** Elan Kriegel, "Re: Short Iowa data update," e-mail received by Mandy Grunwald et al., January 31, 2016, published by WikiLeaks, #22259.

118 **flights out of Des Moines:** Catherine E. Schoichet and Holly Yan, "Iowa Braces for Blizzard, Winter Storm Right After Caucuses," CNN, February 1, 2016, accessed January 29, 2017, http://www.cnn.com/2016/02/01/politics/iowa-caucus-blizzard-winter-storm.

119 **On stage that night:** "Presidential Candidate Hillary Clinton Caucus Night Speech," C-SPAN, February 1, 2016, accessed January 29, 2017, https://www.c-span.org/video/?404037-1/hillary-clinton-caucus-night-speech.

CHAPTER 8: THE PRIZE AND THE PAIN

123 **an early excerpt of her book *Hard Choices* appeared in *Vogue*:** Hillary Clinton, "An Exclusive Excerpt from Hillary Clinton's Upcoming Book, *Hard Choices*," *Vogue*, May 11, 2014, accessed January 14, 2017, http://www.vogue.com/865125/hillary-clinton-book-hard-choices/.

123 **Hillary's first two ads:** Sam Frizell, "Hillary Clinton Praises Mother in First TV Ads of 2016," *Time*, August 2, 2015, accessed January 29, 2017, http://time.com/3981638/hillary-clinton-ads-mother-dorothy/.

124 **In successive polls released before the Iowa caucuses:** "New Hampshire 2016 Democratic Primary," RealClearPolitics, accessed January 29, 2017, http://www.realclearpolitics.com/epolls/2016/president/nh/new_hampshire_democratic_presidential_primary-3351.html.

129 **"He should have been a visible presence all along":** Brent Budowsky, "Re: Where's Bill?," e-mail received by John Podesta, September 8, 2015, published by WikiLeaks, #36689.

130 **Donald Trump tweeted:** @realDonaldTrump, "Hillary Clinton has announced that she is letting her husband out to campaign but HE'S DEMONSTRATED A PENCHANT FOR SEXISM, so inappropriate!," Twitter, December 26, 2015, https://twitter.com/realdonaldtrump/status/680908733455708160?lang=en.

134 **Internal campaign data culled just before the New Hampshire primary:** Navin Nayak, "Re: FOR OUR 4PM CALL," e-mail received by Robby Mook, John Podesta, and Jake Sullivan, February 8, 2016, published by WikiLeaks, #10526.

134 **In the early days of the campaign:** Sam Frizell, "Hillary Clinton Calls for an End to 'Mass Incarceration,'" *Time*, April 29, 2015, accessed January 29, 2017, http://time.com/3839892/hillary-clinton-calls-for-an-end-to-mass-incarceration/.

134 **The best-scoring attack lines against Bernie:** Nayak, "Re: FOR OUR 4PM CALL," February 8, 2016, WikiLeaks, #10526.

134 **Hillary flew to Flint, Michigan:** Logan Anderson, "Everything You Need to Know About Hillary Clinton's Trip to Flint in 2 Sentences,*" Hillary for America, February 8, 2016, accessed January 29, 2017, https://www.hillaryclinton.com/feed/everything-you-need-know-about-hillary-clintons-trip-flint-2-sentences/.

135 **a bruising Politico story surfaced:** Glenn Thrush and Annie Karni, "Clinton Weighs Staff Shake-up After New Hampshire," Politico, February 8, 2016, accessed January 14, 2017, http://politi.co/1SbP4MJ.

137 **"We weren't expecting a long formal speech":** Huma Abedin, "Re: Should I come over there?," e-mail received by John Podesta and Jennifer Palmieri, February 2, 2016, published by WikiLeaks, #5433.

137 **Hillary's campaign began to think about "evolving the core message":** Dan Schwerin, "Re: Evolving the core message," e-mail received by Ron Klain et al., January 27, 2016, published by WikiLeaks, #19461.

138 **She'd been asked about it on Rachel Maddow's show:** Steve Benen, "Clinton Responds to Rumors About a Staff Shake-up," MSNBC, February 8, 2016, accessed January 29, 2017, http://www.msnbc.com/rachel-maddow-show/clinton-responds-rumors-about-staff-shake.

139 **Sanders's heart-stopping twenty-two-point win:** "New Hampshire 2016 Democratic Primary," RealClearPolitics.

139 **She struck upbeat notes:** Jeff Stein, "Read: Hillary Clinton's New Hampshire Concession Speech," Vox, February 9, 2016, accessed January 29, 2017, http://www.vox.com/2016/2/9/10956458/hillary-clinton-new-hampshire.

140 **hugged their aides:** Glenn Thrush and Annie Karni, "How Clinton Hit the Reset Button on 2016," Politico, March 3, 2016, accessed February 7, 2017, http://www.politico.com/story/2016/03/how-clinton-saved-her-campaign-220165.

CHAPTER 9: BASE POLITICS

141 **Sanders snapped back:** Team Fix, "Transcript: The Democratic Debate in Milwaukee, Annotated," *Washington Post,* February 11, 2016, accessed February 2, 2017, https://www.washingtonpost.com/news/the-fix/wp/2016/02/11/transcript-the-democratic-debate-in-milwaukee-annotated/?utm_term=.f782bf4eb6a5. Subsequent quotations from this debate come from the *Post*'s transcript.

150 **One young girl, fighting back tears:** Hillary Clinton, "Brave—Hillary Clinton." YouTube, February 18, 2016, accessed February 3, 2017, https://www.youtube.com/watch?v=axN-hs4slpY.

151 **Bernie had released a spot:** Bernie 2016, "America—Bernie Sanders," YouTube, January 21, 2016, accessed February 3, 2017, https://www.youtube.com/watch?v=2nwRiuh1Cug.

153 **she really hammered it home in Harlem:** German Lopez, "Hillary Clinton's Emotional Call on Democrats to Take Systemic Racism Seriously," Vox, February 16, 2016, accessed February 3, 2017, http://www.vox.com/2016/2/16/11026408/hillary-clinton-race-speech.

156 **Former New Mexico governor Bill Richardson:** Bill Richardson, "Re: Phone conversation," e-mail received by John Podesta, February 11, 2016, published by WikiLeaks, #56763.

158 **On Valentine's Day, his horse-race analytics surveys:** Elan Kriegel, "NV and SC update," e-mail received by John Podesta et al., February 14, 2016, published by WikiLeaks, #33405.

158   **Three days later:** Elan Kriegel, "NV and SC tracker updates," e-mail received by John Podesta et al., February 17, 2016, published by WikiLeaks, #26377.

158   **Kriegel sounded optimistic:** Elan Kreigel, "NV and SC update," e-mail received by John Podesta, Mandy Grunwald, Joel Benenson, et al., February 14, 2016, published by WikiLeaks, #33405.

159   **the analytics team's surveys showed a four-point Hillary margin:** Elan Kriegel, "Data update," e-mail received by John Podesta et al., February 19, 2016, published by WikiLeaks, #31976.

161   **Hillary posted a respectable margin:** "Nevada Democratic Caucus," CBS News, accessed February 3, 2017, http://www.cbsnews.com/elections/2016/primaries/democrat/nevada/.

162   **Mook gathered Hillary's organizers into a circle:** Hillary Clinton, "Celebrating the Nevada Caucus Victory—Hillary Clinton." YouTube, February 21, 2016, https://www.youtube.com/watch?v=TqrwDMTByNM.

162   **he and Podesta began casting their eyes toward a shake-up:** Robby Mook, "Re: Call post-mortem," e-mail received by John Podesta, February 22, 2016, published by WikiLeaks, #29366.

162   **"We have to blow up the consultant team":** Robby Mook, "Re: Call post-mortem," e-mail received by John Podesta, February 22, 2016, published by WikiLeaks, #29366.

CHAPTER 10: TURNING THE CORNER

163   **didn't like what he saw:** Robby Mook, "Re: South Carolina," e-mail received by Tina Flournoy et al., February 14, 2016, published by Wikileaks, #1363, https://wikileaks.org/podesta-emails/emailid/13631.

163   **"He wants to know what he can do":** Robby Mook, "Re: South Carolina," e-mail received by Tina Flournoy, John Podesta, and Huma Abedin, February 14, 2016, published by WikiLeaks, #13631.

165   **Before Barack Obama won:** Real Clear Politics, average of Democratic primary polls in South Carolina in 2007–08, accessed February 6, 2017, http://www.realclearpolitics.com/epolls/2008/president/sc/south_carolina_democratic_primary-234.html.

165   **In a fit of pique:** Kevin Cirilli, "Bill Clinton's 8 Digs at Obama." Politico, September 5, 2012, accessed February 3, 2017, http://www.politico.com/story/2012/09/bill-clintons-8-digs-at-obama-080728.

165   **first visit to South Carolina:** Jamie Self, "Hillary Clinton Plans Return to SC, First Visit Since 2008," *The State,* May 13, 2015, accessed via *Charlotte Observer* website on February 7, 2017, http://www.charlotteobserver.com/news/politics-government/article20810877.html.

166   **"How many innocent":** Reena Flores, "Hillary Clinton: We Will Not Forsake Victims of Gun Violence," CBSNews.com, June 18, 2015, ac-

cessed February 6, 2017, http://www.cbsnews.com/news/hillary-clinton
-we-will-not-forsake-victims-of-gun-violence/.

166 **She subsequently released a plan:** Maggie Haberman, "To Curb Gun
Violence, Hillary Clinton Has a Plan for Possible Executive Action," *New
York Times,* October 5, 2015, accessed February 3, 2017, https://www.ny
times.com/2015/10/05/us/to-curb-gun-violence-hillary-clinton-has-a
-plan-for-possible-executive-action.html?_r=1.

168 **She'd cleaned Sanders's clock:** "South Carolina Primary Results," *New
York Times,* September 29, 2016, accessed February 3, 2017, http://www
.nytimes.com/elections/2016/results/primaries/south-carolina.

168 **black-majority Sixth District:** U.S. Department of Commerce; Economics and Statistics Administration; U.S. Census Bureau, "My Congressional
District," accessed February 3, 2017, https://www.census.gov/mycd/.

168 **seven delegates:** The Green Papers, "South Carolina Democrat," accessed February 6, 2017, http://www.thegreenpapers.com/P16/SC-D.

168 **He was campaigning for Hillary in Oklahoma:** "President Bill Clinton Campaigns for Hillary at Tulsa 'Get Out the Vote' Rally," News on 6,
February 27, 2017, accessed February 3, 2017, http://www.newson6.com
/story/31331909/president-bill-clinton-to-speak-at-tulsa-get-out-the-vote
-rally.

168 **getting into a verbal fight:** Sophie Tatum, "Bill Clinton Gets into Heated
Exchange with Benghazi Protesters," CNN, February 27, 2017, accessed
February 3, 2017, http://www.cnn.com/2016/02/27/politics/bill-clinton
-argument-over-benghazi/.

171 **Renteria was quoted:** Jamie Lovegrove, "Clinton Campaign Official
Admits Texas Effort Lagging," *Texas Tribune,* January 24, 2016, accessed
February 26, 2017, https://www.texastribune.org/2016/01/24/texas-dem
ocratic-presidential-primary-steps-gear/.

174 **rally in Worcester:** James A. Kimble, "Bill Clinton Makes Late-Night
Pitch for Hillary in Worcester," *Boston Globe,* March 1, 2016, accessed
February 6, 2017, https://www.bostonglobe.com/metro/2016/03/01/bill
-clinton-makes-late-night-pitch-for-hillary-worcester/xYoqpIhyYmLyRO
pqYjvGgN/story.html.

174 **She ended up winning the state by about 17,000 votes:** "Massachusetts
Democratic Primary," *Boston Globe,* accessed February 4, 2017, https://
apps.bostonglobe.com/election-results/2016/primary/democratic/massa
chusetts/.

174 **her victory speech that night in Miami:** Ryan Teague Beckwith, "Read
Hillary Clinton's Super Tuesday Victory Speech," *Time,* May 1, 2016, accessed February 4, 2017, http://time.com/4244178/super-tuesday-hillary
-clinton-victory-speech-transcript-full-text/.

174 **"We know we've got work":** Ryan Teague Beckwith, "Read Hillary
Clinton's Super Tuesday Victory Speech," Time.com, March 1, 2016,

http://time.com/4244178/super-tuesday-hillary-clinton-victory-speech
-transcript-full-text/.

CHAPTER 11: CANARY IN THE AUTO PLANT

180 **With African Americans constituting nearly 15 percent:** U.S. Department of Commerce; Economics and Statistics Administration; U.S. Census Bureau, "QuickFacts Michigan," accessed February 4, 2017, http://
www.census.gov/quickfacts/table/PST045215/26.

180 **While her internal numbers showed:** John Podesta, "Re: Michigan?,"
e-mail received by Neera Tanden, March 6, 2016, published by WikiLeaks,
#23666.

181 **Bernie sprinkled in an unvarnished attack:** Laura Koran, Dan Mer-
ica, and Tom LoBianco, "WikiLeaks Posts Apparent Excerpts of Clinton
Wall Street Speeches," CNN, October 7, 2016, accessed February 4, 2017,
http://www.cnn.com/2016/10/07/politics/john-podesta-emails-hacked/.

183 **In one ad that began running in Michigan on March 1:** Hillary Clinton, "Predatory—Hillary Clinton." YouTube, February 29, 2016, https://
www.youtube.com/watch?v=_glCj3DcPJs.

184 **She had personally signed off:** Hillary Clinton, "Re: New ad—'Valeant,'"
e-mail received by Oren Shur et al., February 28, 2016, published by
WikiLeaks, #36638.

184 **"What else besides Flint are we running":** Oren Shur, "Re: Ads,"
e-mail received by Hillary Clinton et al., March 2, 2016, published by
WikiLeaks, #45375.

184 **she'd nixed the particulars:** Hillary Clinton, "Re: College Ad," e-mail
received by Teddy Goff et al., February 25, 2016, published by WikiLeaks,
#38997.

184 **On March 3, analytics chief Elan Kriegel:** Joel Benenson, "Re: Data update," e-mail received by Elan Kriegel et al., March 4, 2016, published by
WikiLeaks, #37401.

184 **He would continue to find a similar gap:** Elan Kriegel, "Data update,"
e-mail received by John Anzalone, Robby Mook, John Podesta, et al.,
March 8, 2016, published by WikiLeaks, #20011.

184 **Kriegel thought he was taking a very conservative approach:** Elan
Kriegel, "Data update," e-mail received by John Anzalone et al., March 8,
2016, published by WikiLeaks, #20011.

185 **she arrived at the manufacturing plant that Friday:** Jennifer Epstein,
"Clinton Backs Rescinding Tax Breaks for Moving Jobs Overseas," Bloomberg, March 4, 2016, accessed February 4, 2017, https://www.bloomberg
.com/politics/articles/2016-03-04/clinton-backs-repealing-tax-cuts-for
-moving-u-s-jobs-overseas.

185 **On TPP, the issue that mattered most politically:** "Remarks at Detroit Manufacturing Systems on Creating More Good-Paying American Jobs," Hillary for America, March 5, 2016, accessed February 4, 2017, https:// web.archive.org/web/20161109012401/https://www.hillaryclinton.com /post/remarks-jobs/.

187 **Neera Tanden e-mailed Podesta:** Podesta, "Re: Michigan," March 6, 2016, WikiLeaks, #23666.

187 **Standing on a debate stage in Flint:** Amber Phillips, "The Hillary Clinton–Bernie Sanders Clash Over the Auto Bailout, Explained," *Washington Post,* March 7, 2016, accessed February 28, 2017, https://www.wash ingtonpost.com/news/the-fix/wp/2016/03/07/the-hillary-clinton-bernie -sanders-debate-over-the-auto-bailout-explained/?utm_term=.09ccb21 c5c05.

188 **Fact-checkers called Clinton out:** Ibid.

188 **Kriegel sent word:** Elan Kriegel, "Re: Data update," e-mail received by John Anzalone et al., March 8, 2016, published by WikiLeaks, #20696.

188 **Podesta wasn't sold on the numbers:** Tom Donilon, "Re: You around in DC on Saturday?," e-mail received by John Podesta, March 8, 2016, published by WikiLeaks, #8587.

189 **It accounted for a hair more:** "Michigan Exit Polls," CNN, accessed February 4, 2017, http://www.cnn.com/election/primaries/polls/mi/dem.

189 **Overall, Hillary lost the state narrowly:** "Michigan," CNN, accessed February 4, 2017, http://www.cnn.com/election/primaries/states/mi/dem.

189 **far smaller than the twenty-six-delegate victory:** "Mississippi," CNN, accessed February 4, 2017, http://www.cnn.com/election/primaries/states /ms/dem.

189 **"For Sanders—the 'democratic socialist' from Vermont":** David A. Fahrenthold, "Sanders Edges Out Clinton in Michigan in Surprisingly Tight Race," *Washington Post,* March 8, 2016, accessed February 4, 2017, https://www.washingtonpost.com/politics/michigan-primary-races -march-8-election-updates/2016/03/08/4222f230-e4e8–11e5-b0fd-073 d5930a7b7_story.html?utm_term=.598de154179c.

192 **In the high-value 2nd congressional district:** Richard E. Berg-Andersson, "Mississippi Democrat," Green Papers, accessed February 4, 2017, http://www.thegreenpapers.com/P16/MS-D.

CHAPTER 12: DAMAGE

201 **Her lead in the national polls was widening:** "2016 Democratic Presidential Nomination," Real Clear Politics, accessed February 7, 2017, http://www.realclearpolitics.com/epolls/2016/president/us/2016_demo cratic_presidential_nomination-3824.html.

201 **she had big leads in Florida and North Carolina:** "Florida Democratic Presidential Primary," Real Clear Politics, accessed February 7, 2017, http:// www.realclearpolitics.com/epolls/2016/president/fl/florida_democratic _presidential_primary-3556.html; "North Carolina Democratic Presidential Primary," Real Clear Politics, accessed February 7, 2017, http://www .realclearpolitics.com/epolls/2016/president/nc/north_carolina_democratic _presidential_primary-5175.html.

201 **minority voters would constitute a major share:** "Florida Exit Polls" and "North Carolina Exit Polls," CNN, accessed February 7, 2017, http:// www.cnn.com/election/primaries/polls/FL/Dem   and   http://www.cnn .com/election/primaries/polls/nc/Dem.

201 **Bernie was gaining on her in Ohio, Illinois, and Missouri:** "Ohio Democratic Presidential Primary," Real Clear Politics, accessed February 7, 2017, http://www.realclearpolitics.com/epolls/2016/president/oh /ohio_democratic_presidential_primary-5313.html#polls; "Illinois Democratic Presidential Primary," Real Clear Politics, accessed February 7, 2017, http://www.realclearpolitics.com/epolls/2016/president/il/illinois _democratic_presidential_primary-5567.html; "Missouri Democratic Presidential Primary," Real Clear Politics, accessed February 7, 2017, http://www.realclearpolitics.com/epolls/2016/president/mo/missouri _democratic_presidential_primary-5606.html.

203 **When she arrived at the Nelson-Mulligan:** Kevin McDermott, "Hillary Clinton, in St. Louis Speech, Accuses Trump of 'Political Arson,'" *St. Louis Post-Dispatch,* March 12, 2016, accessed February 7, 2017, http:// www.stltoday.com/news/local/hillary-clinton-in-st-louis-speech-accuses -trump-of-political/article_3c48e6c0-5766-50bf-87b6-c99c66443e7c.html.

203 **"You have every right":** Kevin McDermott, "Hillary Clinton, in St. Louis speech, accuses Trump of 'political arson,'" *St. Louis Post-Dispatch,* March 12, 2016, accessed Feb. 7, 2017, http://www.stltoday.com/news /local/hillary-clinton-in-st-louis-speech-accuses-trump-of-political /article_3c48e6c0-5766-50bf-87b6-c99c66443e7c.html.

203 **Elan Kriegel sent the candidate:** Elan Kriegel, "3/12 Data update," e-mail received by Robby Mook et al., March 12, 2016, published by WikiLeaks, #31249.

204 **she won comfortably—by fourteen points:** "Ohio Primary Results," *New York Times,* accessed February 7, 2017, http://www.nytimes.com /elections/2016/results/primaries/ohio.

204 **running up the score with African Americans:** "Ohio Exit Polls," *New York Times,* accessed February 7, 2017, https://www.nytimes.com/interac tive/2016/03/15/us/elections/ohio-democrat-poll.html?_r=0.

204 **Hillary took the stage:** "Hillary Clinton Primary Night Speech," C-SPAN, March 15, 2016, accessed February 7, 2017, https://www.c-span .org/video/?406676–1/hillary-clinton-primary-night-speech.

204 **as Podesta and Sullivan had wanted:** Joel Benenson, "RE: DRAFT: Remarks for Primary Night in Florida," e-mail received by Dan Schwerin, speechdrafts@hillaryclinton.com, and Nikki Budzinski, March 14, 2016, published by WikiLeaks, #38549.

205 **"Our next president has to be ready":** Ibid.

205 **"When we hear a candidate for president":** Ibid.

205 **Florida, Ohio, and North Carolina would end up netting her:** Wilson Andrews, Kitty Bennett, and Alicia Parlapiano, "2016 Delegate Count and Primary Results," *New York Times,* accessed February 7, 2017, https://www.nytimes.com/interactive/2016/us/elections/primary-calendar-and-results.html.

206 **The night before the primaries:** John Podesta, "Re: Missouri," e-mail received by Tina Flournoy, March 15, 2016, published by WikiLeaks, #16356.

211 **Podesta told Bill's chief of staff:** Ibid.

214 **he put together a list:** Cheryl Mills, "Re: People worth looking at," e-mail received by John Podesta, March 12, 2016, published by WikiLeaks, #16717.

214 **Podesta's first list included three dozen names:** Ibid.

215 **Podesta and Mills made edits:** John Podesta, "No Subject," e-mail received by Hillary Clinton, March 17, 2016, published by WikiLeaks, #15616.

215 **The final version added:** Ibid.

217 **He won seven of eight states:** Wilson Andrews, Kitty Bennett, and Alicia Parlapiano, "2016 Delegate Count and Primary Results," *New York Times,* accessed February 7, 2017, https://www.nytimes.com/interactive/2016/us/elections/primary-calendar-and-results.html.

218 **Her overall national favorability rating:** HuffPost Pollster, "Hillary Clinton Favorable Rating," Huffington Post, accessed February 8, 2017, https://elections.huffingtonpost.com/pollster/hillary-clinton-favorable-rating.

218 **it had slowly moved downward:** Ibid.

218 **a double-digit blowout:** "Wisconsin Primary Results," *New York Times,* accessed February 8, 2017, http://www.nytimes.com/elections/2016/results/primaries/wisconsin.

218 **Bernie had beaten her:** "Wisconsin Exit Polls," *New York Times,* accessed February 8, 2017, https://www.nytimes.com/interactive/2016/04/05/us/elections/wisconsin-democratic-primary-exit-polls.html.

218 **The numbers were a little bit more stark:** Ibid.

218 **Despite getting thrashed in the state:** "Wisconsin Primary Results," *New York Times,* accessed February 8, 2017, http://www.nytimes.com/elections/2016/results/primaries/wisconsin.

219 **Hillary had edged Bernie:** "Wisconsin Exit Polls," *New York Times,* accessed February 8, 2017, https://www.nytimes.com/interactive/2016/04/05/us/elections/wisconsin-democratic-primary-exit-polls.html.

219 **That attitude was evident in a memo:** Robby Mook, "To Hillary Clinton Supporters: The Facts on Where the Race Stands," *Medium,* April 4, 2016, accessed February 8, 2017, https://medium.com/hillary -for-america/to-hillary-clinton-supporters-the-facts-on-where-the-race -stands-87bf70654fbc#.bcy4j0b2t.

220 **He only picked up ten net delegates:** "Wisconsin Primary Results," *New York Times,* accessed February 8, 2017, http://www.nytimes.com /elections/2016/results/primaries/wisconsin.

220 **nine of the ten superdelegates:** Richard E. Berg-Andersson, "Wisconsin Democrat," Green Papers, accessed February 8, 2017, http://www .thegreenpapers.com/P16/WI-D.

220 **he got into a protracted battle:** Eric Bradner, "Bill Clinton Spars with Black Lives Matter Protesters," CNN, April 7, 2016, accessed February 8, 2017, http://www.cnn.com/2016/04/07/politics/bill-clinton-black-lives -matter-protesters/.

221 **a private South Carolina event:** Tyler Tynes, "Black Lives Matter Activists Interrupt Hillary Clinton at Private Event in South Carolina," Huffington Post, February 24, 2016, accessed February 8, 2017, http://www .huffingtonpost.com/entry/clinton-black-lives-matter-south-carolina _us_56ce53b1e4b03260bf7580ca.

221 **Hillary had already apologized:** Jonathan Capehart, "Hillary Clinton on 'Superpredator' Remarks: 'I Shouldn't Have Used Those Words,'" *Washington Post,* February 25, 2016, accessed February 8, 2017, https:// www.washingtonpost.com/blogs/post-partisan/wp/2016/02/25/hillary -clinton-responds-to-activist-who-demanded-apology-for-superpredator -remarks/?utm_term=.e96c2acad716.

221 **the campaign essentially sided with the protesters:** Amy Cozick, "Bill Clinton Says He Regrets Showdown with Black Lives Matter Protesters," *New York Times,* April 8, 2016, accessed February 8, 2017, https://www .nytimes.com/2016/04/09/us/politics/bill-clinton-apology-black-lives -matter-philadelphia.html.

223 **"Not a bad day's work":** Alex Seitz-Wald and Shaquille Brewster, "Bernie Sanders Eases Off, Then Tees Off on Clinton," NBC News, April 22, 2016, accessed February 8, 2017, http://www.nbcnews.com/politics/2016 -election/bernie-sanders-eases-then-tees-clinton-n560276.

223 **And Trump did his part:** Caitlyn Tyler, "Trump Reveals New Nickname for Clinton," *The Hill,* April 16, 2016, accessed February 8, 2017, http:// thehill.com/blogs/ballot-box/presidential-races/276583-trump-reveals -new-nickname-for-clinton.

224 **Sanders acknowledged two important substantive matters:** Daily News Editorial Board, "TRANSCRIPT: Bernie Sanders Meets with the Daily News Editorial Board, April 1, 2016," *New York Daily News,* April 4,

2016, accessed February 8, 2017, http://www.nydailynews.com/opinion/ transcript-bernie-sanders-meets-news-editorial-board-article-1.2588306.

224 **"That is their decision":** Ibid.

224 **Hillary seized the opening immediately:** Ken Thomas and Errin Whack, "Clinton and Sanders Clash Over Presidential Qualifications," Associated Press, April 7, 2016, accessed February 8, 2017, http://bigstory .ap.org/article/462891cbf31b4942ad8169f2e1aa9ef6/sanders-questions -if-clinton-qualified-be-president.

224 **Clinton said "I am quote-unquote not qualified":** Ibid.

225 **It showed clips of Trump's most outlandish statements:** Hillary Clinton, "Stronger Together—Hillary Clinton." YouTube, April 11, 2016, https://www.youtube.com/watch?v=CA5ZhyoaJec.

225 **Hillary ended up whipping Bernie:** "New York Primary Results," *New York Times,* accessed February 8, 2017, http://www.nytimes.com/elections /2016/results/primaries/new-york.

227 **Hillary cruised to victory anyway in Maryland:** Wilson Andrews, Kitty Bennett, and Alicia Parlapiano, "2016 Delegate Count and Primary Results," *New York Times,* accessed February 7, 2017, https://www.nytimes .com/interactive/2016/us/elections/primary-calendar-and-results.html.

CHAPTER 13: "TOO EASY"

232 **"He's tapped into the real and understandable frustration":** Heidi M. Przybyla, "AFL-CIO, Unions Target Potential Trump Voters," *USA Today,* May 25, 2016, accessed February 8, 2017, http://www.usatoday.com/story /news/politics/elections/2016/05/25/unions-hillary-clinton-donald -trump/84902368/.

236 **Democratic pollster Stan Greenberg:** Stan Greenberg, "Clinton and reforming politics and government," e-mail received by John Podesta, January 26, 2016, published by WikiLeaks, #32692.

236 **"With Trump and Cruz attacking crony capitalism":** Stan Greenberg, "Clinton and reforming politics and government," e-mail received by John Podesta, January 26, 2015, published by WikiLeaks, #32692.

237 **Hillary confided in aides:** John Podesta, "Fwd: British election," e-mail received by John Podesta, May 11, 2015, published by WikiLeaks, #39160.

239 **Cruz, the conservative Texas Republican:** Matt Flegenheimer and Maggie Haberman, "Donald Trump, Abortion Foe, Eyes 'Punishment' for Women, Then Recants," *New York Times,* March 30, 2016, accessed February 8, 2017, https://www.nytimes.com/2016/03/31/us/politics/donald -trump-abortion.html.

239 **The billionaire businessman had only raised:** Donald J. Trump for President, "FILING FEC-1079423," Federal Election Commission,

June 20, 2016, accessed February 8, 2017, http://docquery.fec.gov/cgi-bin/forms/C00580100/1079423/.

239 **by May 23 he led Hillary:** "General Election: Trump vs. Clinton," Real Clear Politics, accessed February 8, 2017, http://www.realclearpolitics.com/epolls/2016/president/us/general_election_trump_vs_clinton-5491.html.

241 **the same room in which Bill Clinton:** Peter Baker and John F. Harris, "Clinton Admits to Lewinsky Relationship, Challenges Starr to End Personal 'Prying,'" *Washington Post,* August 18, 1998, accessed February 8, 2017, http://www.washingtonpost.com/wp-srv/politics/special/clinton/stories/clinton081898.htm.

241 **Obama testified to Hillary's judgment:** Staff, "Transcript: President Obama's Full Remarks on Clinton Endorsement," *Philly Voice,* June 9, 2016, accessed February 8, 2017, http://www.phillyvoice.com/transcript-president-obamas-full-remarks-clinton-endorsement/.

242 **she won California on the night of Obama's video:** Wilson Andrews, Kitty Bennett, and Alicia Parlapiano, "2016 Delegate Count and Primary Results," *New York Times,* accessed February 7, 2017, https://www.nytimes.com/interactive/2016/us/elections/primary-calendar-and-results.html.

242 **she said the victory belonged:** Katie Reilly, "Read Hillary Clinton's Historic Victory Speech as Presumptive Democratic Nominee," *Time,* June 8, 2016, accessed February 8, 2017, http://time.com/4361099/hillary-clinton-nominee-speech-transcript/.

242 **But Bernie, speaking that same night:** Katie Reilly, "Read Bernie Sanders' Speech Vowing to Continue His Nomination Fight," *Time,* June 8, 2016, accessed February 8, 2017, http://time.com/4361146/bernie-sanders-democratic-primary-speech-transcript/.

245 **"I look forward to meeting with her":** Ryan Teague Beckwith, "Read Bernie Sanders' Comments After Meeting with President Obama," *Time,* June 9, 2016, accessed February 8, 2017, http://time.com/4363007/bernie-sanders-barack-obama-white-house-transcript/.

246 **Obama had won with 54 percent:** Brown County Clerk, "Brown County, Wisconsin Election Tabulation Report," November 18, 2008, accessed February 8, 2017, http://www.co.brown.wi.us/i_brown/d/county_clerk/2008novel45.htm?t=1235495676.

246 **then lost with 48 percent:** Brown County Clerk, "Official Canvass Summary," March 28, 2013, accessed February 8, 2017, http://www.co.brown.wi.us/i_brown/d/county_clerk/2012novel45.htm?t=1364503839.

246 **Three days before they were set to visit:** Ariel Zambelich and Alyson Hurt, "3 Hours in Orlando: Piecing Together an Attack and Its Aftermath," NPR, June 16, 2016, accessed February 8, 2017, http://www.npr.org/2016/06/16/482322488/orlando-shooting-what-happened-update.

246 Trump charged in a statement: Donald J. Trump, "Donald J. Trump Statement Regarding Tragic Terrorist Attack in Orlando, Florida," Donald J. Trump for President, June 12, 2016, accessed February 8, 2017, https://www.donaldjtrump.com/press-releases/donald-j-trump-statement-regarding-tragic-terrorist-attacks.

247 the administration and the Clinton campaign collided: Eli Watkins, "Bill Clinton Meeting Causes Headaches for Hillary." CNN, June 29, 2016, accessed February 8, 2017, http://www.cnn.com/2016/06/29/politics/bill-clinton-loretta-lynch/.

247 It went on for thirty minutes: Christopher Sign, "US Attorney General Loretta Lynch, Bill Clinton Meet Privately in Phoenix Before Benghazi Report," June 29, 2016, accessed February 8, 2017, http://www.abc15.com/news/region-phoenix-metro/central-phoenix/loretta-lynch-bill-clinton-meet-privately-in-phoenix.

247 Lynch backed off as if scalded: Mark Landler, Matt Apuzzo, and Amy Chozick, "Loretta Lynch to Accept F.B.I. Recommendations in Clinton Email Inquiry," *New York Times,* July 1, 2016, accessed February 8, 2017, https://www.nytimes.com/2016/07/02/us/politics/loretta-lynch-hillary-clinton-email-server.html.

249 the FBI director began reading: Federal Bureau of Investigation, "Statement by FBI Director James B. Comey on the Investigation of Secretary Hillary Clinton's Use of a Personal E-mail System," July 5, 2016, accessed February 8, 2017, https://www.fbi.gov/news/pressrel/press-releases/statement-by-fbi-director-james-b-comey-on-the-investigation-of-secretary-hillary-clinton2019s-use-of-a-personal-e-mail-system.

250 Brian Fallon, a former Justice Department official: Mark Landler and Eric Lichtblau, "F.B.I. Director James Comey Recommends No Charges for Hillary Clinton on Email," *New York Times,* July 5, 2016, accessed February 8, 2017, https://www.nytimes.com/2016/07/06/us/politics/hillary-clinton-fbi-email-comey.html.

254 Obama told the crowd in Charlotte: Katie Reilly, "Read President Obama and Hillary Clinton's Remarks from Their First Joint Rally," *Time,* July 5, 2016, accessed February 8, 2017, http://time.com/4394191/barack-obama-hillary-clinton-rally-transcript/.

254 "Everybody can tweet": Ibid.

CHAPTER 14: "HILLARY JUST CAN'T MAKE UP HER MIND"

257 Hillary invited Warren to a meeting: Nolan D. McCaskill and Daniel Lippman, "Clinton Hosts Warren Amid VP Buzz," Politico, June 10, 2016, accessed February 10, 2017, http://www.politico.com/story/2016/06/elizabeth-warren-meets-with-clinton-224177.

261 **Inside the event, Kaine's phone rang:** Karen Tumulty and Dan Balz, "How Hillary Clinton Proposed to Tim Kaine," *Washington Post,* July 23, 2016, accessed December 14, 2016, http://wpo.st/ObPM2.

261 **With dockworkers trying:** Michael A. Memoli, "A Locked Office, Getaway Car and Secret Flight: The Final Steps in Picking Clinton's Vice President," *Los Angeles Times,* July 23, 2016, accessed December 13, 2016, http://fw.to/Eag2Yna.

263 **WikiLeaks had released a trove:** "Search the DNC email database," WikiLeaks, accessed February 10, 2017, https://wikileaks.org/dnc-emails/.

263 **A cyberattacker going by the alias Guccifer 2.0:** Joe Uchill, "Guccifer 2.0 Releases New DNC Docs," *The Hill,* July 13, 2016, accessed February 10, 2017, http://thehill.com/policy/cybersecurity/287558-guccifer-20 -drops-new-dnc-docs.

264 **when she hired the party convention CEO:** Robby Mook, "Re: Convention CEO," e-mail received by Hillary Clinton and John Podesta, March 27, 2015, published by WikiLeaks, #3225.

264 **Mook characterized himself:** Ibid.

265 **Mook presented Hillary with options:** Heather Stone, "Documents," e-mail received by John Podesta, Sara Latham, and Robby Mook, December 27, 2015, published by WikiLeaks, #45735.

268 **61 percent of the student body is Hispanic:** Florida International University, "About Us," accessed February 10, 2017, http://www.fiu.edu /about-us/.

269 **Hillary thanked Wasserman Schultz:** "Vice Presidential Announcement." C-SPAN, July 23, 2016, accessed February 10, 2017, https:// www.c-span.org/video/?413100–1/hillary-clinton-campaigns-miami -running-mate-senator-tim-kaine.

CHAPTER 15: *BUT IT LOOKED GREAT*

271 **publicly called for her to resign:** Hayley Walker, "Bernie Sanders Calls for Debbie Wasserman Schultz to Resign in Wake of Email Leaks," ABC News, July 24, 2016, accessed January 22, 2017, http://abcnews.go.com /ThisWeek/bernie-sanders-calls-wasserman-schultz-resign-wake-dnc /story?id=40824983.

274 **arrived for the June 14 meeting:** John Wagner, David Weigel, and Abby Phillip, "Clinton, Sanders Talk After the Former Wins D.C. Primary," *Washington Post,* June 14, 2016, accessed January 22, 2017, https://www .washingtonpost.com/politics/sanders-prepared-to-meet-with-clinton-as -district-holds-final-democratic-primary/2016/06/14/0f43d200-3239 -11e6-8ff7-7b6c1998b7a0_story.html?utm_term=.4c8d1b86882a.

275 **the Clinton team negotiated:** "In Platform Draft, Democrats Weigh In on Marijuana, Climate, and Trade," CBS News, July 10, 2016, accessed

January 22, 2017, http://www.cbsnews.com/news/in-platform-draft-dem ocrats-weigh-in-on-marijuana-climate-and-trade/; Eric Bradner, "In Plat-form Fight, Sanders Loses on Trade but Wins on Minimum Wage," CNN, July 10, 2016, accessed January 22, 2017, http://www.cnn.com/2016 /07/09/politics/democrats-15-an-hour-minimum-wage-bernie-sanders -hillary-clinton/.

278 **Bernie's supporters booed:** Robert Schroeder, "Pelosi, Wasserman Schultz Booed as Email Leaks Upend Convention," MarketWatch, July 25, 2016, accessed January 22, 2017, http://www.marketwatch.com/story /boos-greet-pelosi-wasserman-schultz-as-democrats-convention-opens -2016-07-25.

279 **Bernie's delegates booed her:** Jonathan Easley, "'Bernie' Chants Erupt During DNC Invocation," *The Hill*, July 25, 2016, accessed January 22, 2017, http://thehill.com/blogs/ballot-box/presidential-races/289145-bernie -chants-erupt-during-dnc-invocation.

279 **Sanders sent a text:** Meghan Keneally, "Democratic Convention Hits Rocky Start, with Boos from Sanders Supporters," ABC News, July 25, 2016, accessed January 22, 2017, http://abcnews.go.com/Politics/dnc -kicks-off-chair-debbie-wasserman-schultz-gavel/story?id=40851427.

284 **"How we urge them":** Michelle Obama, "Remarks by the First Lady at the Democratic National Convention," whitehouse.gov, July 25, 2016, ac-cessed January 22, 2017, https://obamawhitehouse.archives.gov/the-press -office/2016/07/25/remarks-first-lady-democratic-national-convention.

288 **"In the spring of 1971":** Bill Clinton, "Full Text: Bill Clinton's DNC Speech," Politico, July 26, 2016, accessed January 22, 2017, http://www .politico.com/story/2016/07/full-text-bill-clinton-dnc-speech-226269.

288 **"Now, how does this square?":** Ibid.

290 **"You know, nothing":** Barack Obama, "Remarks by the President at the Democratic National Convention," whitehouse.gov, July 27, 2016, ac-cessed January 22, 2017, https://obamawhitehouse.archives.gov/the-press -office/2016/07/28/remarks-president-democratic-national-convention.

294 **Khan had bashed:** James King, "The Father of a Muslim War Hero Has This to Say to Donald Trump," Vocativ, December 8, 2015, accessed January 22, 2017, http://www.vocativ.com/259159/the-father-of-a-muslim -war-hero-has-this-to-say-to-donald-trump/.

294 **"best of America":** A. J. Willingham, "Six Facts to Catch You Up on the Khan Story," CNN, August 2, 2016, accessed January 22, 2017, http:// www.cnn.com/2016/08/02/politics/who-is-khizr-khan-trnd/.

295 **"Let me ask you":** Khizr Khan, "Khizr M. Khan's Remarks at the 2016 Democratic National Convention," Medium, July 28, 2016, accessed Janu-ary 22, 2017, https://medium.com/democratic-national-convention/let -me-ask-you-have-you-even-read-the-united-states-constitution-297c3f3b 9a03#.jpbnbir5y.

295 **Pakistani-born:** Willingham, "Six Facts to Catch You Up on the Khan Story."

298 **"I've been your First Lady":** Hillary Clinton, "Transcript: Hillary Clinton's Speech at the Democratic Convention," *New York Times,* July 28, 2016, accessed January 22, 2017, https://www.nytimes.com/2016/07/29 /us/politics/hillary-clinton-dnc-transcript.html?_r=0. Subsequent quotations from this speech come from the *Times'* transcript of Clinton's remarks.

CHAPTER 16: "IT'S SO PHONY"

301 **Calvin Klein, Harvey Weinstein:** Amy Chozick and Jonathan Martin, "Where Has Hillary Clinton Been? Ask the Ultra-Rich," *New York Times,* September 3, 2016, accessed January 22, 2017, https://www.nytimes.com /2016/09/04/us/politics/hillary-clinton-fundraising.html.

301 **For a minimum:** Cindy Adams, "Fundraising Is in Hillary Clinton's DNA," *New York Post,* August 16, 2016, accessed January 22, 2017, http:// pagesix.com/2016/08/16/hillary-clinton-set-for-nine-fundraisers-in -three-days/.

301 **"Hey Jude":** Chozick and Martin, "Where Has Hillary Clinton Been?"

301 **reported that Abedin's husband:** Rebecca Rosenberg and Bruce Golding, "Anthony Weiner Sexted Busty Brunette While His Son Was in Bed with Him," *New York Post,* August 28, 2016, accessed January 22, 2017, http://nypost.com/2016/08/28/anthony-weiner-sexted-busty-brunette -while-his-son-was-in-bed-with-him/.

302 **the day after the news broke:** Monica Alba and Elisha Fieldstadt, "Huma Abedin Announces Separation from Husband Anthony Weiner," NBC News, August 29, 2016, accessed January 22, 2017, http://www.nbc news.com/news/us-news/huma-abedin-announces-separation-husband -anthony-weiner-n639421.

303 **7.9 points:** RealClearPolitics average of polls, accessed January 22, 2017, http://www.realclearpolitics.com/epolls/2016/president/us/general_elec tion_trump_vs_clinton-5491.html.

304 **spent $37 million:** Bill Allison, Mira Rojanasakul, and Brittany Harris, "Tracking the 2016 Presidential Money Race," Bloomberg Politics, August 21, 2016, accessed January 22, 2017, https://www.bloomberg.com/poli tics/graphics/2016-presidential-campaign-fundraising/august.html.

304 **800 paid staff:** Alex Seitz-Wald, Didi Martinez, and Carrie Dann, "Ground Game: Democrats Started Fall with 5-to-1 Paid Staff Advantage," NBC News, October 7, 2016, accessed January 22, 2017, http:// www.nbcnews.com/politics/2016-election/ground-game-democrats -started-fall-5-1-paid-staff-advantage-n661656?cid=sm_tw.

304 grabbed the Clinton campaign's attention: Gabriel Debenedetti, "Trump fundraising sets off Clinton alarm bells," Politico, August 8, 2016, accessed February 7, 2017, http://www.politico.com/story/2016/08 /trump-fundraising-sets-off-clinton-camp-alarms-226779.

306 voted twice for Obama: Dave Leip's Atlas of U.S. Presidential Elections, accessed January 22, 2017, http://uselectionatlas.org/.

309 $52 million: Mark Murray, "Clinton Campaign Now Outspending Trump on Ads—$52 Million to 0," NBC News, August 9, 2016, accessed January 22, 2017, http://www.nbcnews.com/politics/2016-election/team -clinton-now-outspending-trump-ads-52-million-0-n626236.

313 "Every time I think": Daniella Diaz, "Clinton During Coughing Fit: 'Every Time I Think About Trump, I Get Allergic,'" CNN, September 6, 2016, accessed January 22, 2017, http://www.cnn.com/2016/09/05/poli tics/hillary-clinton-coughing-donald-trump-allergic/.

313 "mental and physical stamina": Glenn Kessler, "Trump's Claim That Clinton Lacks the 'Physical Stamina' to Be President," *Washington Post,* August 18, 2016, accessed January 22, 2017, https://www.washington post.com/news/fact-checker/wp/2016/08/18/trumps-claim-that-clinton -lacks-the-physical-stamina-to-be-president/?utm_term=.dbfb91b4465a.

313 "I'm not concerned": Tim Hains, "Clinton Addresses Question About Her Health: 'I'm Not Concerned About Conspiracy Theories,'" Real-ClearPolitics, September 6, 2016, accessed January 22, 2017, http://www .realclearpolitics.com/video/2016/09/06/clinton_addresses_question _about_her_health_im_not_concerned_about_conspiracy_theories.html.

314 3.2 points: RealClearPolitics average of polls.

315 The alt-right speech: Abby Ohlheiser and Caitlin Dewey, "Hillary Clinton's Alt-Right Speech, Annotated," *Washington Post,* August 25, 2016, accessed January 22, 2017, https://www.washingtonpost.com/news/the -fix/wp/2016/08/25/hillary-clintons-alt-right-speech-annotated/?utm _term=.d7d81aa7a872.

316 "not a 'basket'": Harper Neidig, "Pence: Trump Supporters Aren't a 'Basket of Anything,'" The Hill, September 10, 2016, accessed January 22, 2017, http://thehill.com/blogs/ballot-box/presidential-races/295286 -pence-trump-supporters-arent-a-basket-of-anything.

316 "'grossly generalistic'": Angie Drobnic Holan, "In Context: Hillary Clinton and the 'Basket of Deplorables,'" Politifact, September 11, 2016, accessed January 22, 2017, http://www.politifact.com/truth-o-meter/article /2016/sep/11/context-hillary-clinton-basket-deplorables/.

316 "47 percent": David Corn, "SECRET VIDEO: Romney Tells Millionaire Donors What He REALLY Thinks of Obama Voters," *Mother Jones,* September 17, 2012, accessed January 22, 2017, http://www.motherjones .com/politics/2012/09/secret-video-romney-private-fundraiser.

317 **suffered brain damage:** Emily Smith, "Karl Rove: Hillary May Have Brain Damage," *New York Post,* May 12, 2014, accessed January 22, 2017, http://pagesix.com/2014/05/12/karl-rove-hillary-clinton-may-have-brain -damage/.

CHAPTER 17: "DEMEANOR IS THE DEBATE"

323 **He was even more aggressive with reporters:** BuzzFeed Staff, "Hillary Clinton Aide Tells Reporter to 'Fuck Off' and 'Have a Good Life,'" BuzzFeed, September 24, 2012, accessed January 22, 2017, www.buzzfeed .com/buzzfeedpolitics/hillary-clinton-aide-tells-reporter-to-fuck-off.

326 **once described as a "mini Hillary":** Annie Karni, "Portrait of a Clinton West Wing," Politico, November 3, 2016, accessed January 22, 2017, http://politi.co/2feletx.

326 **She was considered a top contender:** Ibid.

328 **"Happy to be there! Smiling!":** Ron Klain, "Updated One Pager," e-mail received by Karen Dunn et al., November 13, 2015, published by WikiLeaks, #59053.

328 **"Tone, tone, tone":** Ron Klain, "One Page Debate Advice," e-mail received by John Podesta et al., March 6, 2016, published by WikiLeaks, #19948.

328 **reminders of what she was fighting for:** Klain, "Updated One Pager," November 13, 2015, WikiLeaks, #59053.

328 **"Bigotry, bluster, bullying":** Klain, "One Page Debate Advice," March 6, 2016, WikiLeaks, #19948.

329 **At a rally in January:** Elliot Smilowitz, "Angry Trump Rants About 'Bastard' Who Set Up Faulty Microphone," *The Hill,* January 13, 2016, accessed January 22, 2017, http://thehill.com/blogs/blog-briefing-room /news/265843-angry-trump-rants-about-bastard-who-set-up-faulty -microphone.

331 **Trump taunted her from the campaign trail:** Jim Acosta, "CNN Newsroom," CNN, September 21, 2016, accessed January 22, 2017, http:// www.cnn.com/TRANSCRIPTS/1609/21/cnr.20.html.

331 **He even rejected his advisers' entreaties:** Patrick Healy, Amy Chozick, and Maggie Haberman, "Debate Prep? Hillary Clinton and Donald Trump Differ on That, Too," *New York Times,* September 23, 2016, accessed January 22, 2017, https://www.nytimes.com/2016/09/24/us/poli tics/presidential-debate-hillary-clinton-donald-trump.html.

332 **Hillary interjected with a canned line:** Aaron Blake, "The First Trump-Clinton Presidential Debate Transcript, Annotated," *Washington Post,* September 26, 2016, accessed January 22, 2017, https://www.wash ingtonpost.com/news/the-fix/wp/2016/09/26/the-first-trump-clinton

-presidential-debate-transcript-annotated/?utm_term=.2b3e9d2a3873. Subsequent quotations from this debate come from the *Post*'s transcript.

333   **he didn't like that the reigning champ:** "Former Miss Universe Accuses Donald Trump of Fat Shaming: 'He Called Me Miss Piggy,'" *Inside Edition,* May 19, 2016, accessed January 22, 2017, http://www.insideedition .com/headlines/16497-former-miss-universe-accuses-donald-trump-of -fat-shaming-he-called-me-miss-piggy.

333   **Trump's vile remarks about other women:** YouTube, uploaded by The-Blaze, August 6, 2015, https://www.youtube.com/watch?v=xpRkPFu63to.

334   **And then Trump got personal with Hillary:** Blake, "The First Trump-Clinton Presidential Debate Transcript, Annotated."

336   **he resorted to complaining about his microphone:** Geoff Earle, "'Was That on Purpose?' Trump Questions Whether the Commission on Presidential Debates Deliberately Gave Him a Faulty Microphone," *Daily Mail,* September 27, 2016, accessed January 22, 2017, http://www.daily mail.co.uk/news/article-3809120/Did-commission-presidential-debates -deliberately-Donald-Trump-faulty-microphone.html.

336   **"She gained a massive amount of weight":** "Donald Trump: Miss Universe Alicia Machado Was 'the Absolute Worst,'" Fox News, September 27, 2016, accessed January 22, 2017, http://www.foxnews.com/entertain ment/2016/09/27/donald-trump-miss-universe-alicia-machado-was -absolute-worst.html.

336   **he tapped out a message on his Android phone:** @realDonaldTrump, "Anytime you see a story about me or my campaign saying 'sources said,' DO NOT believe it. There are no sources, they are just made up lies!," Twitter, September 30, 2016, 3:20 a.m., https://twitter.com/realDonald Trump/status/781755469488615424?ref_src=twsrc%5Etfw.

336   **"Wow, Crooked Hillary was duped and used":** @realDonaldTrump, "Wow, Crooked Hillary was duped and used by my worst Miss U. Hillary floated her as an 'angel' without checking her past, which is terrible!," Twitter, September 30, 2016, https://twitter.com/realDonaldTrump/sta tus/781784161044553728.

336   **"Using Alicia M in the debate":** @realDonaldTrump, "Using Alicia M in the debate as a paragon of virtue just shows that Crooked Hillary suffers from BAD JUDGEMENT! Hillary was set up by a con," Twitter, September 30, 2016, 5:19 a.m., https://twitter.com/realDonaldTrump/ status/781785509639118848?ref_src=twsrc%5Etfw.

337   **"Did Crooked Hillary help disgusting":** @realDonaldTrump, "Did Crooked Hillary help disgusting (check out sex tape and past) Alicia M become a U.S. citizen so she could use her in the debate?," Twitter, September 30, 2016, 5:30 a.m., https://twitter.com/realDonaldTrump/status /781788223055994880?ref_src=twsrc%5Etfw.

337 **There wasn't really a sex tape:** Dan Evon, "Doppelbangher," Snopes
     .com, September 29, 2016, accessed January 22, 2017, http://www.snopes
     .com/alicia-machado-adult-star/.

337 **Trump had left a few bread crumbs:** Blake, "The First Trump-Clinton
     Presidential Debate Transcript, Annotated."

CHAPTER 18: RED OCTOBER

338 **A few minutes after 2:30 p.m. on Friday, October 7:** @ODNIgov,
     "Joint DHS and ODNI Election Security Statement: https://www.dni
     .gov/index.php/newsroom/press-releases/215-press-releases-2016/1423
     -joint-dhs-odni-election-security-statement," Twitter, October 7, 2016,
     2:40 p.m., https://twitter.com/ODNIgov/status/784478639891120128.

338 **In July, Robby Mook had alleged just that:** Eric Bradner, "Clinton's
     Campaign Manager: Russia Helping Trump," CNN, July 25, 2016, ac-
     cessed January 23, 2017, http://www.cnn.com/2016/07/24/politics/robby
     -mook-russia-dnc-emails-trump/.

338 **The Republican nominee's response had been:** Ashley Parker and
     David E. Sanger, "Donald Trump Calls on Russia to Find Hillary Clin-
     ton's Missing Emails," *New York Times,* July 27, 2016, accessed January 23,
     2017, https://www.nytimes.com/2016/07/28/us/politics/donald-trump
     -russia-clinton-emails.html.

339 **ultimately charge Trump with making:** John Podesta, "Hillary for
     America Statement on U.S. Government Formally Naming Russia Re-
     sponsible for Election-Related Hacks," Hillary for America, October
     7, 2016, accessed January 23, 2017, https://www.hillaryclinton.com
     /briefing/statements/2016/10/07/hillary-for-america-statement-on-u-s
     -government-formally-naming-russia-responsible-for-election-related
     -hacks/.

339 **The *Washington Post* had posted a video clip:** David A. Fahrenthold,
     "Trump Recorded Having Extremely Lewd Conversation About Women
     in 2005," *Washington Post,* October 7, 2016, accessed January 23, 2017,
     https://www.washingtonpost.com/politics/trump-recorded-having
     -extremely-lewd-conversation-about-women-in-2005/2016/10/07/3b9ce776
     -8cb4-11e6-bf8a-3d26847eeed4_story.html?utm_term=.b0371e4a14ae.

340 **At 4:32 p.m., WikiLeaks:** @wikileaks, "RELEASE: The Podesta Emails
     #HillaryClinton #Podesta #imWithHer https://wikileaks.org/podesta
     -emails/," Twitter, October 7, 2016, 4:32 p.m., https://twitter.com/wikileaks
     /status/784491543868665856?lang=en.

340 **The day before the Podesta dump:** @DCLeaks, "Check @Hillary
     Clinton fundraisers' list in Capricia Marshall's correspondence http://
     dcleaks.com/emails/cApR/eml_download/Conversations_with_Clintons

Team/00000385.EML #DCLeaks," Twitter, October 6, 2016, 3:51 p.m., https://twitter.com/DCleaks/status/784134109572497409.

340 **on the morning of the seventh:** Michael Sainato, "DC Leaks Exposes Clinton Insider's Elitist and Embarrassing Emails," *New York Observer,* October 7, 2016, accessed January 23, 2017, http://observer.com/2016/10 /dc-leaks-exposes-clinton-insiders-elitist-and-embarrassing-emails/.

340 **US intelligence agencies would conclude in an unclassified report:** Office of National Intelligence, "Background to 'Assessing Russian Activities and Intentions in Recent US Elections': The Analytic Process and Cyber Incident Attribution," January 6, 2016, https://assets.document cloud.org/documents/3254237/Russia-Hack-Report.pdf.

341 **Utah representative Jason Chaffetz:** Mark Green, "Congressman Jason Chaffetz Withdraws His Endorsement of Donald Trump," Fox 13, October 7, 2016, accessed January 23, 2017, http://fox13now.com/2016/10/07 /congressman-jason-chaffetz-withdraws-his-endorsement-of-donald -trump/.

341 **"Donald Trump should not be president":** Condoleezza Rice, Facebook, October 8, 2016, https://www.facebook.com/condoleezzarice/posts /1293199674025554.

342 **Hillary's "dream" of "open trade and open borders":** Tony Carrk, "HRC Paid Speeches," e-mail received by John Podesta et al., January 25, 2016, published by WikiLeaks, #927.

343 **By Sunday, more than two dozen prominent Republicans:** Reena Flores, "Republicans Who Have Called on Donald Trump to Quit 2016 Race," CBS News, October 8, 2016, accessed January 23, 2017, http:// www.cbsnews.com/news/republicans-who-have-called-on-donald-trump -to-quit-2016-race/.

343 **"Can Donald Trump Recover from This?":** Stephen Collinson, "Can Donald Trump Recover from This?," CNN, October 8, 2016, accessed January 23, 2017, http://www.cnn.com/2016/10/07/politics/donald-trump -campaign-crisis/.

343 **"Is Trump's Campaign Over?":** Glenn Thrush and Katie Glueck, "Is Trump's Campaign Over?," Politico, October 8, 2016, accessed January 23, 2017, http://www.politico.com/story/2016/10/is-trumps-campaign -over-229341.

343 **the *New York Times* ran a story:** Megan Twohey and Michael Barbaro, "Two Women Say Donald Trump Touched Them Inappropriately," *New York Times,* October 12, 2016, accessed January 23, 2017, https://www .nytimes.com/2016/10/13/us/politics/donald-trump-women.html.

343 ***Saturday Night Live* imagined Hillary reacting:** *Saturday Night Live,* "VP Debate Cold Open—SNL," YouTube, October 9, 2016, https://www. youtube.com/watch?v=5sYGjoUcusM.

343 **only 13 percent of Republicans:** Scott Clement and Dan Balz, "Washington Post–ABC News Poll: Clinton Holds Four-Point Lead in Aftermath of Trump Tape," *Washington Post,* October 16, 2017, accessed January 23, 2017, https://www.washingtonpost.com/politics/washington-post-abc-news-poll-clinton-holds-four-point-lead-in-aftermath-of-trump-tape/2016/10/15/c31969a4-9231-11e6-9c52-0b10449e33c4_story.html?utm_term=.de0c0d7adc97.

343 **campaign manager Kellyanne Conway would later put it:** Karen Tumulty and Philip Rucker, "Shouting Match Erupts Between Clinton and Trump Aides," *Washington Post,* December 1, 2016, accessed January 23, 2017, https://www.washingtonpost.com/politics/shouting-match-erupts-between-clinton-and-trump-aides/2016/12/01/7ac4398e-b7ea-11e6-b8df-600bd9d38a02_story.html?utm_term=.75f489010a95.

344 **Trump had said he could stand:** Jeremy Diamond, "Trump: I Could 'Shoot Somebody and I Wouldn't Lose Voters,'" CNN, January 24, 2016, accessed January 23, 2017, http://edition.cnn.com/2016/01/23/politics/donald-trump-shoot-somebody-support/.

345 **Doug Band had called Chelsea Clinton a "spoiled brat":** John Podesta, "Re: Draft of Doug's Teneo et al. memo," e-mail received by Doug Band and Cheryl Mills, November 13, 2011, published by WikiLeaks, #2874.

345 **Neera Tanden, the president of the liberal think tank:** Neera Tanden, "Re:," e-mail received by John Podesta, January 17, 2016, published by WikiLeaks, #9572.

345 **A June 2015 note from Mook:** Robby Mook, "Re: TWEETS: Bill de Blasio on HRC speech / Bernie," e-mail received by Huma Abedin et al., June 10, 2015, published by WikiLeaks, #31857.

345 **communications director Jennifer Palmieri:** Jennifer Palmieri, "Re: Conservative Catholicism," e-mail received by John Podesta, April 11, 2011, published by WikiLeaks, #39051.

345 **in Brown County, Wisconsin:** Association of Statisticians of American Religious Bodies, "U.S. Religion Census 2010," http://www.rcms2010.org/compare.php.

346 **Mook posted a sign over urinals:** Annie Karni and Glenn Thursh, "22 Toxic Days for Hillary Clinton," Politico, October 16, 2016, accessed January 23, 2017, http://www.politico.com/story/2016/10/hillary-clinton-trump-wikileaks-229864.

347 **Hillary would raise the issue herself:** CQ Transcriptswire, "Transcript of the Third Debate," *New York Times,* October 20, 2016, accessed January 23, 2017, https://www.nytimes.com/2016/10/20/us/politics/third-debate-transcript.html.

347 **he said it could have been China:** Aaron Blake, "The First Trump-Clinton Presidential Debate Transcript, Annotated," *Washington Post,* September 26, 2016, accessed January 23, 2017, https://www.washing

tonpost.com/news/the-fix/wp/2016/09/26/the-first-trump-clinton
-presidential-debate-transcript-annotated/?utm_term=.2b3e9d2a3873.

348 **Trump would read the contents of the Podesta e-mails:** David Martosko, "Trump Attacks His Own Failing Teleprompters and Reads Wiki-
Leaks Email Showing Hillary KNEW the Saudis Were Funding ISIS
When the Clinton Foundation Took Their Money," *Daily Mail,* October 14,
2016, accessed January 23, 2017, http://www.dailymail.co.uk/news/article
-3839247/Trump-attacks-failing-teleprompters-reads-Wikileaks-email
-showing-Hillary-KNEW-Saudis-funding-ISIS-Clinton-Foundation-took
-money.html.

350 **previewing his strategy in a December 2015 tweet:** @realDonald
Trump, "If Hillary thinks she can unleash her husband, with his terrible
record of women abuse, while playing the women's card on me, she's
wrong!," Twitter, December 28, 2015, 7:12 a.m., https://twitter.com/real
donaldtrump/status/681447548133965824?lang=en.

350 **in a Fox News appearance in May:** Fox News, "Trump: The World Is a
Total Mess, I Can Fix It Hillary Can't," YouTube, May 20, 2016, https://
www.youtube.com/watch?v=Vyrg4XQSZS8.

350 **"Who is the 'Energiser'":** John Podesta, "Re: Who is the 'Energiser'
who has been Clinton's secret lover?sic," e-mail received by Tina Flournoy
and Cheryl Mills, July 26, 2014, published by WikiLeaks, #49306.

350 **"Julie" came up again in another e-mail from Podesta:** Cheryl Mills,
"Re: Julie," e-mail received by John Podesta, December 28, 2014, published by WikiLeaks, #7176.

353 **It was "locker room talk":** CQ Transcriptswire, "Transcript of the
Second Debate," *New York Times,* October 10, 2016, accessed January
24, 2017, https://www.nytimes.com/2016/10/10/us/politics/transcript
-second-debate.html.

353 **Trump stoked a new controversy:** Ibid.

CHAPTER 19: COMEY

356 **At lunchtime on Friday, October 28:** @jasoninthehouse, "FBI Dir just
informed me, 'The FBI has learned of the existence of emails that appear
to be pertinent to the investigation.' Case reopened," Twitter, October 28,
2016, 12:57 p.m., https://twitter.com/jasoninthehouse/status/792047597
040971776.

358 **In a letter to relevant congressional committees:** James Comey, e-mail
received by Richard Burr et al., October 28, 2016, CNBC.com, https://
www.scribd.com/document/329253226/FBI-investigation-letter-Hillary
-Clinton-s-email-server#from_embed.

358 **Reporters would soon start circulating:** Pete Williams, Kasie Hunt,
and Corky Siemasko, "Emails Related to Clinton Case Found in Anthony

Weiner Investigation," NBC News, October 28, 2016, accessed January 24, 2017, http://www.nbcnews.com/news/us-news/fbi-re-open-investigation -clinton-email-server-n674631.

359   **they pushed out a statement from Podesta:** John Podesta, "Statement from John Podesta in Response to FBI Letter to GOP Congressional Chairmen," Hillary for America, October 28, 2016, accessed January 24, 2016, https://www.hillaryclinton.com/briefing/statements/2016/10/28 /%25e2%2580%258bstatement-from-john-podesta-in-response-to-fbi -letter-to-gop-congressional-chairmen/.

363   **At a rally in Flint, Michigan:** Naomi Lim, "Bill Clinton Calls Obamacare 'the Craziest Thing in the World,' Later Tries to Walk It Back," CNN, October 5, 2016, accessed January 24, 2017, http://www.cnn.com/2016 /10/04/politics/bill-clinton-obamacare-craziest-thing/.

364   **people using the popular silver plan:** Department of Health and Human Services; Office of the Assistant Secretary for Planning and Evaluation, "Health Plan Choice and Premiums in the 2017 Health Insurance Marketplace," October 24, 2016, https://aspe.hhs.gov/sites/default/files/pdf /212721/2017MarketplaceLandscapeBrief.pdf.

364   **"Repealing Obamacare and stopping":** Patrick Healy and Abby Goodnough, "Seizing on Rising Costs, Trump Says Health Law Is 'Over,'" *New York Times,* October 25, 2016, accessed January 24, 2017, https:// www.nytimes.com/2016/10/26/us/politics/hillary-clinton-donald-trump -affordable-care-act.html?_r=0.

369   **The *New York Times*' Upshot:** Josh Katz, "Who Will Be President?," *New York Times,* November 8, 2016, accessed January 24, 2017, https:// www.nytimes.com/interactive/2016/upshot/presidential-polls-forecast .html.

369   **Nate Silver's FiveThirtyEight:** Nate Silver, "Who Will Win the Presidency?," FiveThirtyEight, November 8, 2016, accessed January 24, 2017, https://projects.fivethirtyeight.com/2016-election-forecast/.

CHAPTER 20: "I'M SORRY"

371   **The AP had called the race:** Lauren Easton, "Calling the Presidential Race State by State," Associated Press, November 9, 2016, accessed January 24, 2017, https://blog.ap.org/behind-the-news/calling-the-presidential -race-state-by-state.

381   **At 11:30 p.m., Fox's Megyn Kelly reported:** Fox News, November 8, 2016, https://grabien.com/file.php?id=127705.

382   **White House political director David Simas was seated at:** Pat Cunnane, "Watching Trump Win from the White House," *New Yorker,* January 19, 2017, accessed January 24, 2017, http://www.newyorker.com/culture /culture-desk/election-night-at-the-white-house-with-waffle-fries.

382 **AP called North Carolina for Trump:** Easton, "Calling the Presidential Race State by State."

384 **AP called Pennsylvania:** Ibid.

384 **"Several states are too close to call":** Tim Hains, "Podesta at Clinton HQ: We Will Have More to Say Tomorrow. She Is Not Done Yet," Real-ClearPolitics, November 9, 2016, accessed January 24, 2017, http://www.realclearpolitics.com/video/2016/11/09/podesta_at_clinton_hq_we_will_have_more_to_say_tomorrow_she_is_not_done_yet.html.

CHAPTER 21: THE AFTERMATH

390 **"It's a humbling feeling," she'd said:** Amy Chozick, "Hillary Clinton Votes in Chappaqua: 'It's a Humbling Feeling,'" *New York Times,* November 8, 2016, accessed January 25, 2017, https://www.nytimes.com/2016/11/09/us/politics/hillary-clinton-voting.html?_r=0.

391 **two-thirds of Americans had approved:** Patrick O'Connor, "Hillary Clinton Exits with 69% Approval Rating," *Wall Street Journal,* January 17, 2013, accessed January 25, 2017, http://blogs.wsj.com/washwire/2013/01/17/wsjnbc-poll-hillary-clinton-exits-with-69-approval-rating/.

394 **Hillary advised those who opposed Trump:** CNN Politics, "Hillary Clinton's Concession Speech (Full Text)," CNN, November 9, 2016, accessed January 25, 2017, http://www.cnn.com/2016/11/09/politics/hillary-clinton-concession-speech/.

396 **In December, a partially declassified:** Office of National Intelligence, "Background to 'Assessing Russian Activities and Intentions in Recent US Elections': The Analytic Process and Cyber Incident Attribution," January 6, 2016, https://assets.documentcloud.org/documents/3254237/Russia-Hack-Report.pdf.

396 **Exit polls in Pennsylvania showed that Clinton:** "Exit Polls," CNN, November 9, 2016, accessed January 25, 2017, http://www.cnn.com/election/results/exit-polls/pennsylvania/president.

396 **Obama won women:** "Exit Polls," CNN, December 12, 2012, accessed January 25, 2017, http://www.cnn.com/election/2012/results/state/PA/president/.

396 **Trump did better with white Floridians:** "Exit Polls," CNN, November 9, 2016, accessed January 25, 2017, http://www.cnn.com/election/results/exit-polls/florida/president.

396 **than Romney had:** "Exit Polls," CNN, December 10, 2012, accessed January 25, 2017, http://www.cnn.com/election/2012/results/state/FL/president/.

396 **Turnout in Milwaukee:** "Wisconsin Results," CNN, November 28, 2016, accessed January 25, 2017, http://www.cnn.com/election/results/states/wisconsin.

397 **votes from 2012:** "President: Wisconsin," CNN, December 10, 2012, accessed January 25, 2017, http://www.cnn.com/election/2012/results /state/WI/president/.

397 **nearly three dozen:** Jackie Borchardt and Rich Exner, "Donald Trump flipped Rust Belt states by boosting rural vote; Hillary Clinton couldn't make up the difference," Cleveland.com, November 11, 2016, accessed February, 7, 2017, http://www.cleveland.com/politics/index.ssf/2016/11 /donald_trump_flipped_rust_belt.html.

397 **and lost it by two points in 2012:** "President Map," *New York Times,* November 29, 2012, accessed January 25, 2017, http://www.nytimes.com /elections/2012/results/president.html.

397 **About a dozen counties in Michigan:** "Presidential Election Results: Donald J. Trump Wins," *New York Times,* January 4, 2017, accessed January 25, 2017, http://www.nytimes.com/elections/results/president.

397 **Obama won the county:** "Macomb County, Michigan, November 6, 2012, Election," Macomb County Clerk, November 26, 2012, accessed January 25, 2017, http://m.clerk.macombgov.org/sites/default/files/con tent/government/clerk/pdfs/electionresults/macomb_county_election _results_november_6_2012.pdf.

397 **Trump took it:** "Electors of President and Vice President of the United States," Macomb County Clerk, November 22, 2016, accessed January 25, 2017, http://www.newsroomsolutions.com/m18/105.html.

400 **Hillary returned to Capitol Hill:** Chelsea Bailey and Monica Alba, "Hillary Clinton Returns to D.C., Praises Reid's Legacy, Condemns Fake News," NBC News, December 8, 2016, accessed January 25, 2017, http:// www.nbcnews.com/news/us-news/hillary-clinton-returns-d-c-praises -reid-s-legacy-condemns-n693821.

401 **the *New York Post* had reported:** Emily Smith, "Chelsea Clinton Being Groomed to Run for Congress," *New York Post,* November 10, 2016, accessed January 25, 2017, http://nypost.com/2016/11/10/chelsea-clinton -being-groomed-to-run-for-congress/.

402 **At the CDF event, Hillary spoke of Dorothy Rodham:** Katie Reilly, "Read Hillary Clinton's First Speech Since Conceding: 'Believe in Our Country, Fight for Our Values,'" *Time,* November 17, 2016, accessed January 25, 2017, http://time.com/4575126/hillary-clinton-childrens-defense -fund-transcript/.

Acknowledgments

FIVE YEARS AGO our literary agent, Bridget Wagner Matzie, could see Hillary Clinton engaged in another battle for the presidency, and she could see us telling that story. For your vision, your persistence, your patience, your wisdom, and your friendship, we are forever grateful.

Our editor, Kevin Doughten, is almost as demanding as he is talented. It shows. This book was harder than the last one—as much for him as for anyone in this process. And he played the roles of editor, slave driver, and psychologist with equal flair. Thank you, Kevin, for your skill and perseverance.

Ethan Cohen, the lead researcher on this book, gracefully handled a barrage of assignments on tight deadlines. He took on tasks large and minute and operated with minimal guidance. We can't thank him enough for all of his hard work. Researcher Rachel Bluth transcribed hours upon hours of audio, kept detailed records for us, and contributed valuable insights. We appreciate her hard work.

At Crown, we'd also like to thank our publisher, Molly Stern, for her continued support, as well as Maya Mavjee, Annsley Rosner, Rachel Rokicki, Liz Wetzel, Linnea Knollmueller, Christine Tanigawa, Lauren Dong, Christopher Brand, Lance Fitzgerald, Christine Edwards, Candice Chaplin, and Jesse Aylen.

Finally, we are thankful that so many sources decided that

this was a story too important to leave untold—even if it left them shattered.

—JA and AP

HILLARY CLINTON will forever be connected to the phrase "It takes a village." I never fully understood the significance of the African proverb until a few years ago, when my own village stepped in to pick up the slack in ways I'd once found unimaginable. This village celebrated with me on the best days and, time and again, helped me catapult the hurdles. Its members listened to me vent, put their arms around me when I felt helpless, offered to connect me to others who might help. I am so lucky to be surrounded by all of you because I could never, ever do it alone.

First, to you, Jon. Thank you for making this all happen a second time. While we have had our fair share of differences (always have, always will), we've been in the foxhole together twice now and somehow it all comes together in the end. Thank you, partner-in-crime, for your hard work on this book, for putting up with my constant changes of heart, and for bearing with me in a different locale.

I send unending gratitude to my wonderful bosses at *The Hill*, Bob Cusack and Ian Swanson, who have been beyond supportive and encouraging throughout this entire project.

I cannot overstate what my mom, Esther Parnes, has done to make this process hum smoothly for the last two years. She uprooted her life and made sure I was well-fed, well-caffeinated, well-loved, and supported 1,000 percent. And if that wasn't enough, she logged hundreds of hours babysitting for me while I locked myself in a room and didn't come out. The funniest part of it all is she tells me all the time that she hasn't done a thing. That couldn't be further from the truth. This book wouldn't have happened without you, Mom. Thank you for your love, guidance, and strength.

Sherry Parnes, my sister, best friend and loving aunt, thank you for being my confidante and gut-check and mostly for keeping my spirits up when this process seemed so far from over.

Sending love and gratitude to Henry Parnes; Abraham Zadi; Phillip and Magny Zadi; Tiffany, Jaron, and Alli Zadi; and Garri and Debbie Hendell. And special love and hugs and kisses to John and Cal.

I would be nowhere without my best friends in the world: Jarah Greenfield—who would repeatedly tell me to "just keep swimming," in the bleakest hours—is one of those friends who takes time off from work and moves in to make life easier (and more organized!). Craig Bode who always keeps the laughter and encouragement coming when I need it most, always knows how I'm feeling even before I'm feeling it. Thank you for always knowing just what I need. Lesley Clark, one of the most steady and solid people I've ever come to know, offered her wise counsel during this book's most dramatic turns.

Thank you also to my friends Michael Collins, Niall Stanage, M. E. Sprengelmeyer, Bridget Petruczok, Jennifer Martinez, Karin Tanabe, Megan Chan, Sarah Courtney, Kendra Marr Chaikind, Lale Mamaux, Rebecca Samuels, Judy Kurtz, Jen Goldschmidt, Maria Underwood Davis, Jessica Reimelt, Melissa Gross, Jenn Grage, Bethany Lesser, Sarah Mamula, Jamie Radice, Dolly Hernandez, Becca Polisuk, Erin Scheithe, Philly Bubaris, and Sue Alexander for always being there.

Finally, here's to you, Remy Maddox, the greatest addition to my village in the last two years. What did I ever do without you?

—AP

IT'S IMPOSSIBLE to overstate the sacrifices Stephanie Allen has made in support of my dreams or the unwavering nature of the love she has shown me. I couldn't have written this book without her counsel, her humor, her dedication, and her constant encouragement—all while balancing a demanding career and doing more than her share of caring for our two wonderful children. She is a model partner, and I am better for each day I spend with her. I love you, Stephanie.

My son, Asher, now five, has been through two books already. He doesn't want me to write another one for a while, and I get it. I miss him when I'm sequestered with a laptop. That's why I'm looking forward to another summer at the ballpark, watching our beloved Nationals, and visits to Washington's many monuments and museums in the coming months and years. He's thoughtful, inquisitive, and so sweet that he is a walking reminder of the human capacity for kindness. He's got a gift for picking up the English language, and, unlike his dad, he's great at math. I also look forward to the day, in the not-to-distant future, when he can read this book, though I know he can already make out these words: I love you, Ace.

Emma, now three, has developed a strong personality in her short time in the world, which began while I was working on HRC. She's smart and tough, and she always seems to be unperturbed by life's little setbacks. I am hopeful that she won't run into any glass ceilings in her lifetime, but I'm confident she'll bust through them if she does. It will take her a little longer, but I also look forward to the day she can read this: I love you, Emma.

My parents, Ira and Marin Allen, continue to be a constant source of support. They shared with me their love of politics, public policy, and writing, and I am forever grateful for everything they've given me and my own family. My sister, Amanda Allen, continues to love me despite me, and I'm inspired by her compassion, her intellectual rigor, and her unstinting loyalty to her family and friends. I'd want to be her friend, even if we weren't related. Mom, Dad, and Amanda: I love you.

I want to thank Andy Bromberg, Tucker Bounds, Meredith Carden, Caroline Chalmers, and the rest of the crew at Sidewire for bringing me into a fascinating and fun company dedicated to creating an environment for a more sophisticated and civil discussion of politics, policy, and tech on the Internet. And I want to thank our Newsmakers and readers for forming a vibrant community that proves why expertise still matters. All signal, no noise! I also want to thank Kris Viesselman, Ed Timms, Adriel Bettelheim, Robert Tomkin, and my other colleagues at CQ/Roll Call, where quality journalism is still practiced every day, as well as Ellen Shearer and all of my students at Northwestern University, who give me faith that the next generation of journalists will be better than the last. I'm greatly appreciative of the work my agents Tom Neilssen of the Bright Sight Group and Keith Urbahn of Javelin Group have done on my behalf. And, for the courtesy of letting me use their shops as writing spaces, I want to thank Tegest and the crew at TG Cigars, as well as the staffs of Drapers and Shelly's Backroom.

I am deeply appreciative of a whole slew of friends and family who have offered everything from insights to moral support during the writing of this book: Bill, Ronnie, Adam, Tory, and Ellis Weintraub; the Pearsons, Bergmans, and Cohens; and David Mortlock, Del Wilber, Greg Giroux, Hank Thomas, David Fishback, Dahlia Schweitzer, Craig Gordon, Laurie Hays, Nick Johnston, Hugh Hewitt, Jed Weiss, Dan McBride, Janet Crowder, and Hayley Alexander.

And last, but certainly not least, to my friend, collaborator, and co-conspirator Amie Parnes: you're a woman of tremendous talent and drive who has taught me a ton about reporting and storytelling. It's been a roller coaster these last four-plus years, but I couldn't ask for a better seatmate.

—JA

Index